Intelligent Data Analytics, IoT, and Blockchain

This book focuses on data analytics with machine learning using IoT and block-chain technology. Integrating these three fields by examining their interconnections, *Intelligent Data Analytics, IoT, and Blockchain* examines the opportunities and challenges of developing systems and applications exploiting these technologies. Written primarily for researchers who are working in this multi-disciplinary field, the book also benefits industry experts and technology executives who want to develop their organizations' decision-making capabilities. Highlights of the book include:

- Using image processing with machine learning techniques
- A deep learning approach for facial recognition
- A scalable system architecture for smart cities based on cognitive IoT
- Source authentication of videos shared on social media
- Survey of blockchain in healthcare
- Accident prediction by vehicle tracking
- Big data analytics in disaster management
- Applicability, limitations, and opportunities of blockchain technology

The book presents novel ideas and insights on different aspects of data analytics, blockchain technology, and IoT. It views these technologies as interdisciplinary fields concerning processes and systems that extract knowledge and insights from data. Focusing on recent advances, the book offers a variety of solutions to real-life challenges with an emphasis on security.

Intelligent Data Analytics, IoT, and Blockchain

Edited by
Bashir Alam
Mansaf Alam

CRC Press
Taylor & Francis Group
Boca Raton London New York

CRC Press is an imprint of the
Taylor & Francis Group, an **informa** business

AN AUERBACH BOOK

First edition published 2024
by CRC Press
2385 Executive Center Drive, Suite 320, Boca Raton, FL 33431

and by CRC Press
4 Park Square, Milton Park, Abingdon, Oxon, OX14 4RN

CRC Press is an imprint of Taylor & Francis Group, LLC

© 2024 Taylor & Francis Group, LLC

ISBN: 978-1-032-44278-5 (hbk)
ISBN: 978-1-032-44279-2 (pbk)
ISBN: 978-1-003-37138-0 (ebk)

DOI: 10.1201/9781003371380

Typeset in Garamond
by SPi Technologies India Pvt Ltd (Straive)

Contents

24 A Survey of Security Challenges and Existing Prevention Methods in FANET

JATIN SHARMA AND PAWAN SINGH MEHRA

25 MENA Sukuk Price Prediction Modeling Using Prophet Algorithm

TAUFEEQUE AHMAD SIDDIQUI, MOHD RAAGIB SHAKEEL, AND
SHAHZAD ALAM

About the Editors

Bashir Alam, PhD, is a professor at Jamia Millia Islamia, New Delhi, India, where he heads the Department of Computer Engineering. He has 22 years of teaching and research experience. His areas of research include big-data analytics, artificial intelligence, parallel and distributed systems, cloud computing, machine learning, GPU computing, blockchain, and information security.

Mansaf Alam, PhD, is a professor in the Department of Computer Science, Faculty of Natural Sciences, Jamia Millia Islamia. A Young Faculty Research Fellow and the editor-in-chief of the *Journal of Applied Information Science*, he pursues research in artificial intelligence, big-data analytics, machine learning, deep learning, cloud computing, and data mining.

Contributors

Farhan Jalees Ahmad
School of Interdisciplinary Sciences and
Technology, Jamia Hamdard
New Delhi, India

Bashir Alam
Department of Computer
Engineering, Jamia Millia Islamia
University
New Delhi, India

Irfan Alam
Department of Computer Science and
Engineering, Delhi Technological
University
New Delhi, India

Mansaf Alam
Department of Computer
Sciences, Jamia Millia Islamia
University
New Delhi, India

Shahzad Alam
Department of Computer Engineering,
Faculty of Engineering and
Technology, Jamia Millia Islamia
University
New Delhi, India

Bhavya Alankar
Department of Computer Science and
Engineering, School of Engineering
Sciences and Technology,
Jamia Hamdard
New Delhi, India

Mohammad Amjad
Jamia Millia Islamia University
New Delhi, India

Aayesha Ashraf
Department of Computer Science
and Engineering, Jamia Hamdard
(Deemed to be University)
New Delhi, India

Varun Barthwal
H.N.B. Garhwal University
Srinagar, India

Siva Prasad Behera
Department of Mathematics,
C.V. Raman Global University
Bhubaneswar, India

Anupam Bhatia
CRSU
Jind, India

M. Bhargav Chowdary
Jawaharlal Nehru Technological
  University
Kakinada, India

Mohd Danish
Jamia Millia Islamia University
New Delhi, India

Heta S. Desai
Saurashtra University
Rajkot, India

Shaikh Mohammed Faizan
Department of Computer Engineering,
  Jamia Millia Islamia University
New Delhi, India

Atul M. Gonsai
Saurashtra University
Rajkot, India

M. Govindarajan
Department of Computer Science
  and Engineering, Annamalai
  University
Annamalai Nagar, India

Muhammad Hamid
Department of Computer
  Engineering, Jamia Millia Islamia
  University
New Delhi, India

Nabeela Hasan
Jamia Millia Islamia University
New Delhi, India

Aderonke J. Ikuomola
Department of Computer Science,
  Olusegun Agagu University of
  Science and Technology
Okitipupa, Nigeria

S. Indu
Delhi Technological
  University (AICTE)
Delhi, India

Stephen O. Johnson-Rokosu
Olusegun Agagu University of Science
  and Technology
Okitipupa, Nigeria

Dr. Sandeep Joshi
Department of Computer Science
  and Engineering, Manipal
  University Jaipur
Jaipur, India

Joseph Abraham Sundar K.
School of Computing, SASTRA
  Deemed University
Thanjavur, India

Harleen Kaur
Department of Computer Science and
  Engineering, School of Engineering
  Sciences and Technology,
  Jamia Hamdard
New Delhi, India

Sakshi Kaushal
Department of Computer Science
  and Engineering, UIET, Panjab
  University Chandigarh
Chandigarh, India

Sudipta Majumdar
Delhi Technological University
  (AICTE) India
Delhi, India

Ela Kumar
Indira Gandhi Delhi Technical
  University for Women
New Delhi, India

Harish Kumar
Department of Computer Science
and Engineering, UIET, Panjab
University Chandigarh
Chandigarh, India

Kamal Kumar
Department of Mathematics, Baba
Mastnath University
Rohtak, India

Sushil Kumar
School of Computer & Systems
Sciences, Jawaharlal Nehru University
New Delhi, India

Vinod Kumar
Department of Mathematics, PGDAV
Collage, University of Delhi
New Delhi, India

Manoj M. M.
School of Computing, SASTRA
Deemed to be University
India

Manoj Kumar
Department of Computer Science and
Engineering, Delhi Technological
University
New Delhi, India
School of Computing, SASTRA
Deemed to be University
Thanjavur, India

Kamal Lochan Mahanta
Department of Mathematics,
C.V. Raman Global University
Bhubaneswar, India

Pawan Singh Mehra
Department of Computer Science and
Engineering, Delhi Technological
University
New Delhi, India

Debdas Mishra
Department of Mathematics,
C.V. Raman Global University
Bhubaneswar, India

Barkha Singh
ECE Dept (Of AICTE), Delhi
Technological University (AICTE
Delhi, India

Khurram Mustafa
Department of Computer Science,
Jamia Millia Islamia University
New Delhi, India

Naveen Naveen
CRSU
Jind, India

Kehinde S. Owoputi
Department of Computer Science,
Olusegun Agagu University of
Science and Technology
Okitipupa, Nigeria

Om Pal
MeitY, Government of India
New Delhi, India

Pallavi
Department of Computer Science
and Engineering, Manipal
University Jaipur
Jaipur, India

Premaladha J.
School of Computing, SASTRA
Deemed to be University
Thanjavur, India

Shamimul Qamar
Department of Computer Science &
Engineering, King Khalid University
Abha, Kingdom of Saudi Arabia

S. M. K. Quadri
Jamia Millia Islamia University
New Delhi, India

Prasanta Kumar Raut
Department of Mathematics,
C.V. Raman Global University
Bhubaneswar, India

Manmohan Singh Rauthan
H.N.B. Garhwal University
Srinagar, India

Rubi
School of Interdisciplinary Sciences and
Technology, Jamia Hamdard
New Delhi, India

Seema
Department of Mathematics, Baba
Mastnath University
Rohtak, India

Amardeep Saha
Computer Science and Engineering,
Indian Institute of Information
Technology Ranchi
Ranchi, India
Department of Mathematics, Baba
Mastnath University
Rohtak, India

Shashank H. S.
School of Computing, SASTRA
Deemed to be University
Thanjavur, India

Satish Royal G.
School of Computing, SASTRA
Deemed to be University
Thanjavur, India

Giddaluri Bhanu Sekhar
Jawaharlal Nehru Technological
University Kakinada
Kakinada, India

Prabu Selvam
School of Computing, SASTRA
Deemed University
Thanjavur, India

Bhavna Sethi
UIET, Punjab University Chandigarh
Chandigarh, India

Mohd Raagib Shakeel
Department of Management Studies,
Jamia Millia Islamia University
New Delhi, India

Mohd Shaliyar
Department of Computer Science,
Jamia Millia Islamia University
Department of Computer Science and
Engineering, Delhi Technological
University
New Delhi, India

Jatin Sharma
Department of Computer Science and
Engineering, Delhi Technological
University
New Delhi, India

Pranav Shrivastava
Department of Computer
Engineering, JMI
New Delhi, India

Farheen Siddiqui
Department of Computer Science and
Engineering
Jamia Hamdard (Deemed to be
University)
New Delhi, India

Taufeeque Ahmad Siddiqui
Department of Management Studies,
    Jamia Millia Islamia University
New Delhi, India

Bam Bahadur Sinha
Computer Science and Engineering,
Indian Institute of Information
    Technology Ranchi
Ranchi, India

Rajeshwari Sissodia
H.N.B. Garhwal University
Srinagar, India

Smita
CSE, Indira Gandhi Delhi Technical
    University for Women
New Delhi, India

M. Srilatha
Jawaharlal Nehru Technological
    University Kakinada
Kakinada, India

Javvaji Srinivasulu
Jawaharlal Nehru Technological
    University Kakinada
Kakinada, India

Bhuvaneswari Swaminathan
School of Computing, SASTRA
    Deemed University
Thanjavur, India

Usman
Jamia Millia Islamia University
New Delhi, India

Nirmala V.
School of Computing, SASTRA
    Deemed to be University
Thanjavur, India

Subramaniyaswamy Vairavasundaram
School of Computing, SASTRA
    Deemed University
Thanjavur, India

Ritesh Yaduwanshi
School of Computer & Systems
    Sciences, Jawaharlal Nehru
    University
New Delhi, India

Chapter 1

Skin Cancer Classification Using Image Processing with Machine Learning Techniques

Nirmala V., Shashank H. S., Manoj M. M., Satish Royal G., and Premaladha J.

School of Computing, SASTRA Deemed to be University, Thanjavur, India

1.1 Introduction

Image classification modalities play a significant role in the health sector. Early diagnosis of fatal diseases using various imaging techniques [1] has positively impacted people's lives. Our work describes classification of skin cancer images using deep learning techniques [2]. Skin cancer attacks surrounding cells, resulting in the development of a mole on the external layer of the skin that can be categorized as malignant or benign. Many solutions using neural network architectures for diagnosis of the early stages of skin cancer have been proposed. The classification [3] metrics used include support vector machine (SVM), relevant vector machine (RVM), and neural network architectures. These machine learning algorithms pose several constraints for input data distribution, such as noise-free or high-contrast images, but these constraints do not apply to the skin cancer classification problem. Instead, it

DOI: 10.1201/9781003371380-1

is colour, texture, and structural features that play an essential role in skin cancer classification. Traditional parametric approaches cannot be used for skin cancer classification problems since skin lesions have different patterns. Hence deep learning techniques are used.

The automatic classification process [4] includes preprocessing, feature extraction, segmentation, and classification, resulting in a handcrafted feature set. However, since lesions have visual resemblance and are highly correlated due to their colour, texture, and shape, handcrafted feature extraction is not appropriate for skin cancer classification. The deep learning approach is therefore preferred. We can feed the images directly to the model, removing the need for any preprocessing [5] to be implemented before passing the image to the model. Neural network models are very effective in extracting specific features from the image. Even though deep learning models are efficient for classifying skin cancer, the various elements present in skin lesion images make identifying skin cancer [6] challenging for the following reasons:

- The ISIC 2016 and ISIC 2017 skin cancer datasets are highly imbalanced, with many benign samples.
- Many skin lesion images are highly similar, and classifying [7] them into benign and malignant images is challenging.

The novel modified LCNet model is designed for model training for boosted classification results even for the less accurate lesions of human skin. An optimization algorithm is improved with the repeated blocks of batch normalization.

The remainder of this chapter is organized as follows. Section 1.2 describes significant earlier work in this area. Section 1.3 explains our research in detail, the datasets involved and the model architecture. Sections 1.4 and 1.5 present our results with their comparative analysis and conclusion.

1.2 Related Works

Skin cancer is a deadly disease that can affect nearby cells of the body. Early detection and diagnosis is important [8]. Initially, handcrafted feature-based approaches were used on dermoscopic images. However, since there is a high correlation between skin texture and colour in skin images, such approaches are not regarded as suitable for skin classification problems [9]. As preprocessing operations are unnecessary, deep convolutional neural networks (DCNNs) have proved helpful. The first time DCNN was applied to skin cancer images [10] used 129,450 skin disease images to classify 2032 diseases. The researcher designed a deep learning framework with two fully convolutional residual networks, one to produce the segmentation result and the other to produce a coarse classification result. A lesion index calculation [11] unit was introduced to produce a heat map and refine the coarse classification results. Iqbal et al. [12] describe the contribution of each pixel towards the classification of another model, a convolution model consisting of multiple layers used for multi-class classification. It had 68 convolutional layers, passing the features from top to bottom. Zhang et al. proposed an attention residual neural network [13] that consisted of multiple ARL blocks, which was further followed by global average pooling and classification layers.

To improve classification efficiency, ensembles of CNNs, consisting of outputs from the layers of four different models, Google Net, AlexNet, VGG and ResNet, were created by Barata et al. [14]. Another approach using multiple imaging modalities was also proposed to increase the modularity of a self-supervised topology clustering network that could classify the unlabeled data without needing class-based information. The model learnt features at different levels of variations, such as the illumination, the background and the point of view.

Some models applied transfer learning [15] using pre-trained models for dermoscopic classification. Nevertheless, a small dataset with high accuracy does not fit all scenarios, especially with medical images, since each piece of information is highly sensitive in the diagnosis. Hyperparameter tuning was performed to achieve better results. Gessert et al. developed an ensemble model from Efficient Nets, SENet, and ResNet WSL which was used to perform a multi-class classification task [16] on the ISIC 2019 dataset. A cropping strategy was implemented to deal with different input resolutions. With the earlier reports for melanoma classification, many researchers carried out different trials. They achieved reasonable accuracy, and some of the results are inspiring. However, the status of early diagnosis of melanoma skin cancer is not generalized and, as we have seen in the Introduction, there are two major problems.

1.3 Materials and Methods

1.3.1 Dataset

The skin cancer images were obtained from the ISIC 2016 [17], ISIC 2017 [18] and ISIC 2020 [19] challenges. Since the skin samples were highly imbalanced, they were augmented by datasets from the ISIC archive. The ISIC challenge provides two datasets – training and testing. We divided our model learning and estimation process into three parts: training, validation and testing. We chose 20% for the validation process. Since the given skin cancer samples were highly imbalanced, data augmentation was carried out on classes with fewer samples to prevent the deterioration of the model learning process.

Data were classified into two classes: MEL (malignant) and BEN (benign). Other lesion types, such as seborrheic keratosis and nevus, are also considered benign. The total number of training samples and validation samples is shown in Table 1.1. The data distribution over ISIC 2016, 2017 and 2020 datasets is shown in Figure 1.1.

Table 1.1   Size of the Datasets

Dataset	Total Number of Samples	Training Samples (80%) of Total Samples	Validation (20%) of Total Samples	Samples Under Test Data
ISIC 2016	900	720	180	379
ISIC 2017	1620	1296	324	600
ISIC 2020	33126	26500	6626	439

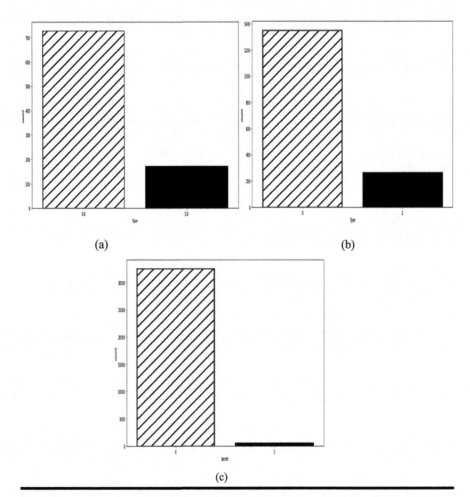

(a)   (b)

(c)

Figure 1.1   Data distribution over ISIC 2016, 2017 and 2020 datasets; cross-hatched – benign samples, shaded – malignant samples.

1) The proposed model uses a DCNN for classifying images into benign and malignant. The model consists of multiple blocks bonded together to facilitate the processing of many features in the convolutional neural network architecture.
2) Each block consists of varying parameters having different values. Parameters include stride, number of kernels, and kernel size.
3) The model consists of 11 blocks, each having its sequence of operations performed over the image.

1.3.2 Preprocessing Operations

For the given data sets, preprocessing was carried out to make them suitable for passing through the model. The images were normalized to make the computations effective. The normalization of images was carried out using pixel normalization. The pixel values were scaled to 0–1. Normalization is essential because it ensures that each input parameter has a similar data distribution.

Furthermore, data augmentation – rotation, shifting, flipping, and scaling – was carried out since the image samples were highly imbalanced [20]. A random rotation of 0° to 90° was applied to the image. The image was shifted by 10% of the entire width and height. Horizontal and vertical flipping was carried out on all the images. These augmentation operations [21] were applied only to the training and validation sets. Sample augmentation operations are shown in Figure 1.2. Since the model accepts a (128, 128, 3) image, all the images in the dataset were resized [22] to (128, 128, 3).

For the model, we stored all the images in HDF5 format and organized them into folders depending on the type and category of the image [23].

1.3.3 LCNet Architecture

The proposed DCNN model, Lesion Classification Network (LCNet), is formulated using 11 blocks, as shown in Figure 1.3. The model also has the following specification:

- Block 4 and 5 – repeated twice
- Block 7 and 8 – repeated 4 times
- Blocks 10 and 1 – repeated twice

The network accepts a (128 × 128 × 3) image as an input, after which a convolution operation is performed over the image using a (3 × 3) kernel having a stride of 2 to learn 8 features. A convolution is an approach to identifying and learning the features from the image by using an odd-sized kernel and sliding it over the image. The convolution operation is performed as follows

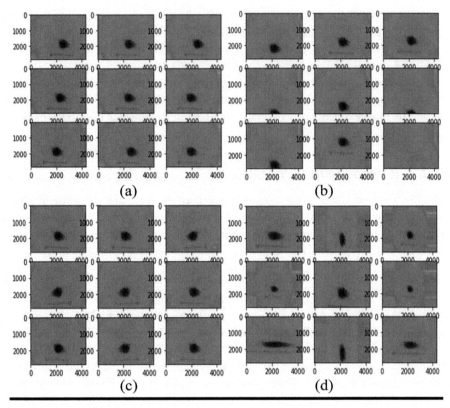

Figure 1.2   Augmentation operation on skin images (a) width shift, (b) height shift, (c) flipping, and (d) zooming.

$$\text{Conv}(u,v) = \sum_{i=-k}^{k} h(i,j).F(u-i,v-j) \tag{1.1}$$

Here $\text{Conv}(u, v)$ is the output of the convolution operation on the image using a kernel whose pixel positions are identified by using (i, j). Moreover, "k" determines the maximum size of the kernel in positive and negative axes. The $h(i, j)$ is the kernel, and $F(u, v)$ represents the pixel locations of the original image. The output of a convolution is a feature map that is reduced by passing to a max-pooling layer.

The max-pooling layer takes a pool size of (2, 2) and identifies the maximum pixel value in each pool. Further, each block has three essential layers:

1) Convolution
2) Batch normalization
3) LeakyReLU (leaky rectified linear unit)

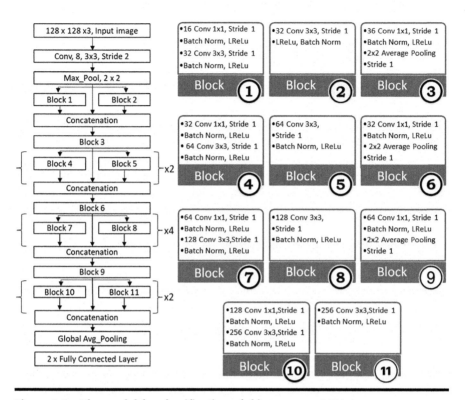

Figure 1.3   The model for classification of skin cancer – LCNet.

The input features to the subsequent blocks are normalized using batch normalization, a technique used for training deep neural network architecture. Here the inputs to a layer from the previous one are standardized for each mini-batch. These servers increase the learning process and speed up the training. The activation function used here is 'LeakyReLU' – leaky rectified linear unit as given by

$$f(x) = \begin{cases} s * x, & x < 0 \\ x, & x \geq 0 \end{cases} \tag{1.2}$$

The LeakyReLU overcame the 'dying ReLU' problem when x is less than zero. This blocks the process of learning in the ReLU. LeakyReLU speeds up the training process, as having a mean activation close to zero makes the training faster. Moreover, the LeakyReLU does not have a zero slope. The main advantage of LeakyReLU can be seen when during backpropagation, the weights are to be updated.

In ReLU, some dead neurons may never activate again, so training them wastes time. Our model uses a scaling factor 's' value of 0.3.

Figure 1.3 shows the LCNet architecture. Block 1 comprises two convolution layers, two batch-normalization and two LeakyReLU layers. The convolution layers consist of the following:

- First convolution layer – 16 kernels of size (1,1) and stride 1
- Second convolution layer – 32 kernels of size (1,1) and stride 1.

The stride determines the number of pixels by which the kernel moves. A batch normalizer and LeakyReLU succeed in each convolution layer. Block 2 consists of the following:

- Single convolution layer – 32 kernels, size (3,3), and stride 1

The result of the previous convolution is a feature map succeeded by LeakyReLU and batch normalizer. The output features of max-pooling, Block1 and Block2 are combined and are then passed to Block 3. Other blocks of the DCNN are constructed in a similar manner, having a different number of filters and kernel sizes. Towards the end of the neural network, a global average pooling layer is used, followed by a 2x fully connection layer.

The model uses the stochastic gradient descent (SGD) algorithm for the optimization of the model's parameters. The SGD algorithm is used to minimize the loss function, and to reach a global minimum such that the output is closest to the required value. The model has a learning rate of 0.0005. The learning rate is required for the reduction of the loss of the model in SGD, which is achieved by modifying the model weights. A very high learning rate may increase loss, while a low learning rate may require more iterations. Furthermore, the model uses a categorical-cross entropy loss function.

The proposed model uses an SGD optimizer to modify and update the neural network's weights during backpropagation. It is essential to minimize the error gradient, find the model parameters that produce an outcome and be closely related to the actual output. Table 1.2 shows all the hyperparameters used in the model training.

Table 1.2 Hyperparameters of the Model

Mini-Batch Size	Data Augmentation	Regularization Value	Optimization Algorithm	Learning Rate	Momentum	Activation Function	Epochs
32	Flipping, Rotation, Shifting, Scaling	0.0005	SGD	0.0005	0.99	LeakyReLU	50

1.4 Results and Discussion

We notice a higher training accuracy over the ISIC 2020 dataset, because it has more samples and can learn many more features from the dermoscopic images than other datasets. We have also implemented regularization techniques, specifically L2 regularization [21], to prevent the model's overfitting. Figure 1.4 shows the graphical representation of the LCNet model on the adopted datasets that include ISIC 2016, ISIC 2017 and ISIC 2020 for training. It displays the performance of the model

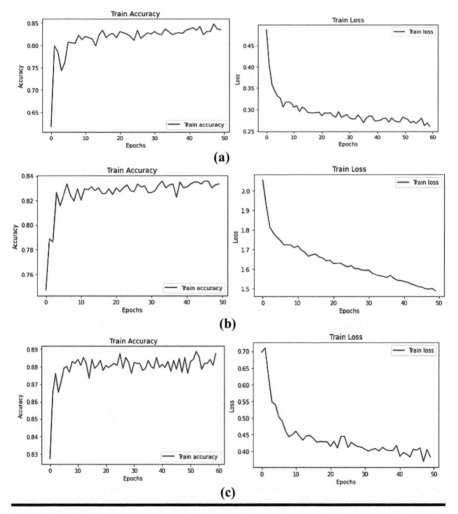

Figure 1.4 Train accuracy and loss curves for LCNet on training data. (a) Benign vs malignant classification for ISIC 2016, (b) benign vs malignant classification for ISIC 2017, and (c) benign vs malignant classification for ISIC 2020.

on the training data. We observe that, as the training accuracy increases, the loss reduces. The following models were trained over 50 epochs. Early stopping criteria were implemented to assess the model's result in case the training accuracy did not improve in successive epochs.

Figure 1.5 shows the graphical representation of the LCNet architecture on the validation data. It displays the network's performance on the validation set in terms of accuracy and loss. We observe that the validation accuracy is a constant curve in most

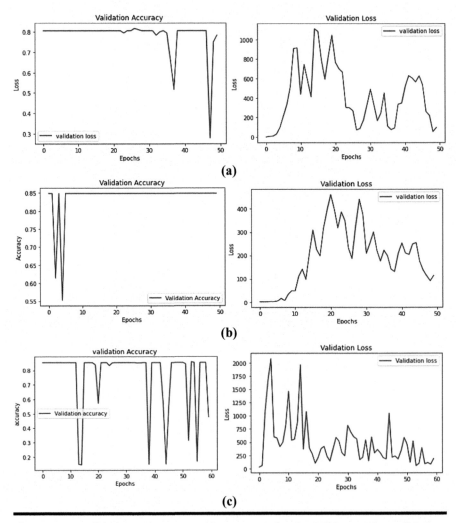

Figure 1.5 **Validation accuracy and loss curves for the LCNet on the validation. (a) Benign vs malignant classification for ISIC 2016, (b) benign vs malignant classification for ISIC 2017, and (c) benign vs malignant classification for ISIC 2020.**

cases. This is because the data distribution of the adopted datasets was imbalanced. However, we achieve an optimal accuracy nearing 0.8. Also, we can confirm that the model can learn, as the validation loss is minimal towards the end of the epochs.

In this work, we have used major four classification metrics:

1. Accuracy (ACC)
2. Precision (PRE)
3. Recall (REC)
4. F1-Score (F1)

The mathematical formulae defining the above metrics are as follows:

$$ACC = \frac{TP + TN}{TP + TN + FP + FN} \tag{1.3}$$

$$PRE = \frac{TP}{TP + FP} \tag{1.4}$$

$$REC = \frac{TP}{TP + FN} \tag{1.5}$$

$$F1 = \frac{2 \times PRE \times REC}{PRE + REC} \tag{1.6}$$

We observe that the first two confusion matrices are highly biased in identifying benign skin cancers since the data distribution used to train the model was imbalanced. However, in the last confusion matrix, we observe an optimal performance where 49 skin samples were correctly classified as malignant, and 160 were classified as benign.

Figure 1.6 displays a confusion matrix that consists of four boxes. This evaluation is used to measure the performance of our classification, which shows the true and false results.

- The *first box* (top left corner) exhibits the number of skin lesion images classified correctly as benign, which depicts the valid positive rate.
- The *second box* (top right corner) represents the number of input lesions mispredicted as malignant. It represents the false negative rate.
- The *third box* (bottom left corner) depicts the number of lesion images incorrectly predicted as benign. It represents the false positive rate.
- The *fourth box* (bottom right corner) represents total image lesions correctly classified as malignant and eventually represents the valid negative rate.

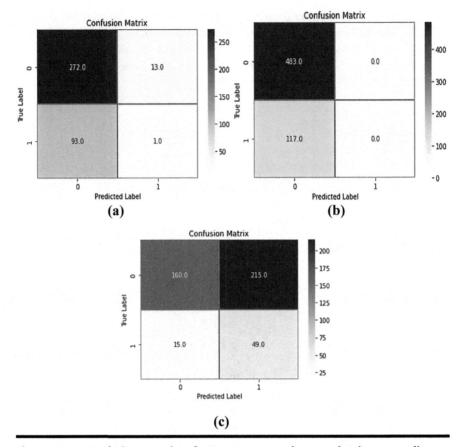

Figure 1.6 Confusion matrix of LCNet on test data (a) benign vs malignant classification for ISIC 2016, (b) benign vs malignant classification for ISIC 2017, and (c) benign vs malignant classification for ISIC 2020.

Since in the ISIC 2016 and ISIC 2017 datasets, the total number of benign samples was far greater than the number of malignant samples, the model could learn the benign features accurately. Hence, the confusion matrix for ISIC 2016 and ISIC 2017 is biased towards benign samples. Table 1.3 shows the performance metrics of classification using the LCNet architecture. Table 1.4 compares our proposed model with other state-of-the-art models.

The experimental results in Table 1.4 show that the model performs relatively well in classifying benign and malignant skin cancers. We observe a better accuracy in ISIC 2017 dataset compared to the remaining models. However, with oversampling, much better accuracy can be achieved as the model can learn more features regarding the malignant samples. Our model requires many samples to distinguish between malignant and benign. An advantage that our model has over other models is its significantly smaller number of parameters, which make it a low-weight model.

Table 1.3   Performance Evaluation of LCNet on the Adopted Dataset

Without Oversampling	ISIC 2020	ISIC 2017	ISIC 2016
ACC%	91.43	91.5	92.031
PRE%	86.8	80.5	74.52
REC%	43.0	98.0	95.43
F1%	57.421	89.19	83.69

Table 1.4   Experimental Results of Our Proposed Work on the Adopted Dataset

Approach	ISIC 2020 ACC PRE REC	ISIC 2017 ACC PRE REC	ISIC 2016 ACC PRE REC
ResNet18	0.908 0.898 0.888	0.750 0.640 0.571	0.809 0.789 0.809
Inceptionv3	0.486 0.297 0.492	0.774 0.691 0.612	0.799 0.809 0.811
Alex Net	0.754 0.691 0.685	0.740 0.670 0.660	0.654 0.595 0.64
Proposed Model (LCNet)	**0.91 0.86 0.43**	**0.915 0.805 1.00**	**0.92 0.74 0.95**

1.5 Conclusion

The proposed LCNet architecture has been trained over several skin lesion samples to learn features and help detect melanoma skin cancer. The model has been trained and tested over three datasets: ISIC 2016, 2017 and 2020. The model has an accuracy of 92.130%, 91.5% and 91.43% on the given datasets. The model achieves good accuracy in terms of the classification of benign and malignant skin cancers. Since many benign samples greatly influenced the model's training over the ISIC 2016 and 2017 datasets, the model was seen to be biased towards benign samples. The model's learning rate can be further increased by adding more malignant samples to the dataset. This random oversampling can further improve the model's prediction.

References

1. American Cancer Society. Key Statistics for Melanoma Skin Cancer. 2021. Available online: https://www.cancer.org/cancer/%20melanoma-skin-cancer/about/key-statistics.html (accessed on 15 December 2020).

2. Rahi, Md. Muzahidul Islam; Khan, Farhan Tanvir; Mahtab, Mohammad Tanvir; Ullah, A. K. M. Amanat; Alam, Md. Golam Rabiul; Alam, Md. Ashraful. Detection of skin cancer using deep neural networks. 2019: https://ieeexplore.ieee.org/abstract/document/9162400/authors#authors

3. Jinnai, S.; Yamazaki, N.; Hirano, Y.; Sugawara, Y.; Ohe, Y.; Hamamoto, R. The development of a skin cancer classification system for pigmented skin lesions using deep learning. *Biomolecules*. 2020, 10, 1123: http://dx.doi.org/10.3390/biom10081123

4. Liu, L.; Mou, L.; Zhu, X.X.; Mandal, M. Automatic skin lesion classification based on mid-level feature learning. *Comput. Med. Imaging Graph*. 2020, 84, 101765: http://dx.doi.org/10.1016/j.compmedimag.2020.101765

5. Kwasigroch, A.; Grochowski, M.; Mikołajczyk, A. Neural architecture search for skin lesion classification. *IEEE Access* 2020, 8, 9061–9071: http://dx.doi.org/10.1109/ACCESS.2020.2964424

6. Tharwat, A. Classification assessment methods. *Appl. Comput. Inform*. 2020, 17, 168–192: http://dx.doi.org/10.1016/j.aci.2018.08.003

7. Tang, P.; Liang, Q.; Yan, X.; Xiang, S.; Zhang, D. GP-CNN-DTEL: Global-part CNN model with data-transformed ensemble learning for skin lesion classification. *IEEE J. Biomed. Health Inform*. 2020, 24, 2870–2882: http://dx.doi.org/10.1109/JBHI.2020.2977013, http://www.ncbi.nlm.nih.gov/pubmed/32142460

8. International Agency for Research on Cancer. Cancer – World Health Organization. 2020. Available online: https://www.who.int/cancer/PRGlobocanFinal.pdf (accessed 15 December 2020).

9. Thomsen, K.; Iversen, L.; Titlestad, T.L.; Winther, O. Systematic review of machine learning for diagnosis and prognosis in dermatology. *J. Dermatol. Treat*. 2020, 31, 496–510: http://dx.doi.org/10.1080/09546634.2019.1682500

10. Al-Masni, M. A.; Kim, D. H.; Kim, T. S. Multiple skin lesions diagnostics via integrated deep convolutional networks for segmentation and classification. *Comput. Methods Programs Biomed*., 2020, 190, 105351.

11. Li, Y.; Shen, L. Skin lesion analysis towards melanoma detection using deep learning network. *Sensors (Basel)*. 2018 February. 11, 18(2), 556. 10.3390/s18020556. PMID: 29439500; PMCID: PMC5855504.

12. Iqbal, I.; Younus, M.; Walayat, K.; Kakar, M.U.; Ma, J. Automated multi-class classification of skin lesions through deep convolutional neural network with dermoscopic images. *Comput. Med. Imaging Graph*. 2021, 88, 101843.

13. Zhang, J.; Xie, Y.; Xia, Y.; Shen, C. Attention residual learning for skin lesion classification. *IEEE Trans. Med. Imaging* 2019, 38, 2092–2103.

14. Subramanian, R Raja; Achuth, Dintakurthi; Kumar, P Shiridi; Kumar Reddy, Kovvuru Naveen; Amara, Srikar; Chowdary, Adusumalli Suchan. Skin cancer classification using convolutional neural networks. 2020: https://ieeexplore.ieee.org/document/9377155/authors

15. Ashraf, R.; Afzal, S.; Rehman, A.U.; Gul, S.; Baber, J.; Bakhtyar, M., et al. Region-of-interest based transfer learning assisted framework for skin cancer detection. *IEEE Access*, 2020, 8, 147858–147871.

16. Rotemberg, V.; Kurtansky, N.; Betz-Stablein, B.; Caffery, L.; Chousakos, E.; Codella, N.; Combalia, M.; Dusza, S.; Guitera, P.; Gutman, D.; et al. A patient-centric dataset of images and metadata for identifying melanomas using clinical context. *Sci. Data*. 2021, 8, 34: http://dx.doi.org/10.1038/s41597-021-00815-z

17. Gutman, David; Codella, Noel C. F.; Celebi, Emre; Helba, Brian; Marchetti, Michael; Mishra, Nabin; Halpern, Allan. Skin Lesion Analysis toward Melanoma Detection: A Challenge at the International Symposium on Biomedical Imaging (ISBI) 2016, hosted by the International Skin Imaging Collaboration (ISIC). eprint arXiv:1605.01397. 2016.

18. Codella, N.; Gutman, D.; Celebi, M.E.; Helba, B.; Marchetti, M.A.; Dusza, S.; Kalloo, A.; Liopyris, K.; Mishra, N.; Kittler, H.; Halpern, A. Skin Lesion Analysis Toward Melanoma Detection: A Challenge at the 2017 International Symposium on Biomedical Imaging (ISBI), Hosted by the International Skin Imaging Collaboration (ISIC). arXiv: 1710.05006, 2018.

19. International Skin Imaging Collaboration. SIIM-ISIC 2020 challenge dataset. *International Skin Imaging Collaboration*, 2020, https://doi.org/10.34970/2020-ds01

20. Premaladha, J.; Surendra Reddy, M.; Hemanth Kumar Reddy, T.; Sri Sai Charan, Y.; Nirmala, V. Recognition of Facial Expression Using Haar Cascade Classifier and Deep Learning. In: Ranganathan, G., Fernando, X., Shi, F. (eds) *Inventive Communication and Computational Technologies*. Lecture Notes in Networks and Systems, vol. 311. Springer, Singapore, 2022. https://doi.org/10.1007/978-981-16-5529-6_27

21. Medhat, Sara; Abdel-Galil, Hala; Aboutabl, Amal Elsayed; Saleh, Hassan. Skin cancer diagnosis using convolutional neural networks for smartphone images: A comparative study. *J. Radiat. Res. Appl. Sci.* 2022, 15(1), 262–267, ISSN 1687-8507, https://doi.org/10.1016/j.jrras.2022.03.008

22. Jayaraman, P., Veeramani, N., Krishankumar, R., Ravichandran, K. S., Cavallaro, F., Rani, P., & Mardani, A. Wavelet-based classification of enhanced melanoma skin lesions through deep neural architectures. *Information*, 2022, 13(12), 583.

23. Prabu, S.; Jawali, N.; Sundar, K. J. A.; Sharvani, K.; Shanmukhanjali, G.; Nirmala, V. Indian Coin Detection and Recognition Using Deep Learning Algorithm. In *2022 6th Asian Conference on Artificial Intelligence Technology (ACAIT)* (pp. 1–6). IEEE, 2022, December.

Chapter 2

Trusted Location Information Verification Using Blockchain in Internet of Vehicles

Ritesh Yaduwanshi and Sushil Kumar
Jawaharlal Nehru University, New Delhi, India

2.1 Introduction

In advanced vehicular adhoc networks (VANETs), a vehicle's driver can connect to other vehicles' drivers, to pedestrians, roadside units and others parts of the urban infrastructure. VANETs are an intelligent transportation system (ITS) that uses communication to reduce traffic congestion. VANETs can be driven by vehicle-to-roadside unit (RSU) and/or vehicle-to-vehicle communication [1]. A processing center (PC) can be an RSU (or a reliable vehicle with a predetermined position). Before giving directions to the vehicles inside its coverage area, the PC checks the communication data. Location-based approaches and services are becoming commonplace in today's wireless networks, so that location data verification has attracted a lot of coverage in recent years [1–9]. Generally vehicles get their location from GPS or GNSS, but the reported location information may be incorrect as the result of either faulty location data recording/forwarding technology, or deliberate misinformation. Undesirable network outcomes like insufficient toll payments, traffic congestion or traffic delays may result if the vehicle's position information is not validated and the location inaccuracy is not recognized. In extreme situations, the lack of location

DOI: 10.1201/9781003371380-2

verification could result in disastrous events such as vehicle accidents. These various location verification systems (LVSs) that have been developed use a range of physical layer signal parameters to evaluate the vehicle's reported location information [2–11]. The constraint of all LVSs is that they typically perform well for the channel conditions that were considered throughout the design process [2], usually only working if all of the a priori channel data supplied to them is true. They can also only properly address the threat-model scenarios for which they were designed [12]. Because of these limitations, their real-world application is limited. The network can be disrupted simply by vehicles falsifying their location with location-based access control protocols [10] or geographic routing protocols [11]). A malicious vehicle can also falsify its location to seriously impair other vehicles [12] and to enhance its own network capabilities [13]. Accuracy of stated locations in VANETs is therefore critical and necessitates the use of an LVS. (See [14, 15] for an overview of IEEE 1609.2 certificate revocation.) This paper is organized as follows: related work is covered in Section 2.2, Section 2.3 presents the system model, Section 2.4 discusses results, and conclusions are offered in Section 2.5.

2.2 Related Work

Location verification systems are required to overcome the problem of location falsification in VANETs. There are two types of existing verification systems: infrastructure-based and infrastructure-less [5, 6]. Every location verification operation in this method involves four base stations. Each one counts the time it takes to issue a challenge to the appropriate node and receive an individual response. However, the large number of verification requests from automobiles creates a network bottleneck at the base station. The cost of deploying and maintaining infrastructure also rises, making VANET an expensive network An infrastructure-based approach is therefore not suitable for VANETs. Most infrastructures-less verification systems use various distance measuring techniques to safely and transparently approve location assertions. For example, in ref. [7], the solution places verifiers at certain sites, each with its own allowable distance. The primary constraint of these techniques is the usage of non-RF range technology, which in turn increases the cost of building these networks. [8] proposes a method for achieving location verification based solely on logic beacon reception. Autonomous location verification was implemented in [9] without assuming different trust levels of nodes. For location verification, [10] uses location-limited channels.

2.3 Trusted Location Information Verification Using Blockchain

In this section, we present a blockchain-based location verification system model focusing on location region and location sharping, location sharing and verification methods, together with the required assumptions.

Table 2.1 Location Verification for Internet of Vehicles

Articles	Filtering	Cryptography	Infra-structure	Verification	Detection
Hubauz et al. [13]	—	—	Yes	Verifiable multilateration	—
Galle et al. [18]	—	—	No	Data-processing model	Errors explained
Xiao et al. [19]	—	Digital signature	Yes	Signal analysis	Statistical model
Leinmuller et al. [7]	—	—	No	Trust model using sensors	—
Yan et al. [20]	—	—	No	Radar	Movement history
Song et al. [22]	—	Symmetric keys	No	Signal analysis	Distance enlargement
Ren et al. [21]	Grid map	—	No	Filtered data	—
Ren et al. [21]	—	—	No	Directional antenna	—

2.3.1 Assumptions

Vehicle-to-everything (V2X) and vehicle-to-vehicle (V2V) communications [11] are expected, as is the capacity for automobiles to connect to the internet efficiently. All vehicles are assumed to have the essential equipment, which includes sensors, GPS and on-board units (OBUs). It is believed that the number of valid roadside units (RSUs) outnumbers the number of malicious RSUs. We suppose that a valid RSU constructs a genesis block based on local events to initiate the block chain. We presume that important event alerts are disseminated within a certain geographic region of interest (RoI). We presume that the crucial signals are not encrypted, and that any adjacent vehicles will be able to read them. We assume that 15 messages are required to validate the occurrence, and that the message is correct.

2.3.2 System Model

Figure 2.1 shows the two stages of the system model according to their functions of location sharing and location verification. By disclosing the real location coordinates and the real location region during the location sharing step, our suggested technique ensures that only Owner vehicles can pass location verification. A full description of the procedure follows.

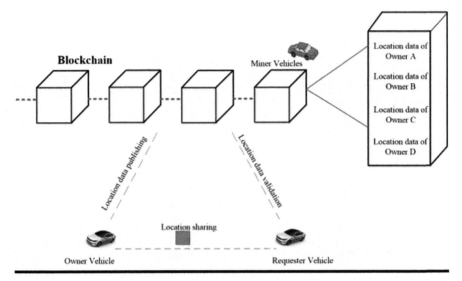

Figure 2.1 System model of block chain location verification in internet of vehicles.

2.3.3 *Location Sharing*

When a Requester asks for the Owner vehicle's location information, there are two possibilities: either the Owner vehicle has complete faith in the Requester vehicle and hence provides precise coordinates (x_i, y_i), or the Owner vehicle does not completely trust the Requester vehicle, in which case the Owner vehicle returns the rectangle location region with location coordinates (x_i, y_i). The pseudo code for the location sharing method is shown in Algorithm 1. The Owner vehicle will initially transmit the public key and session key by asymmetrically encrypting it, computing Res $\leftarrow$ SE($k_{session}$, $x_i \| y_i$) [23, 24, 25, 26, 27] to encrypt the exact position: Res $\leftarrow$ conRes$\|$ASE(Pub$_o$, $k_{session}$). Finally, the session key $k_{session}$ is retrieved using the Requester's private key to decrypt the Owner vehicle's location coordinates, i.e., $x_i' \| y_i' \leftarrow$ SD($k_{session}$, conRes). The privacy-preserving process for location coordinates is essential when the Owner vehicle does not have total trust in the Requester vehicle (x_i, y_i). Through the underchain channel, the Owner vehicle computes fuzRes $\leftarrow$ Enc($k_{session}$, ciph$_i\|$borInfo$\|$nodes$^x\|$ nodes^y) and provides Res $\leftarrow$ fuzRes$\|$ASE(Pub$_i$, $k_{session}$) to the Requester vehicle. Finally, using the session key $k_{session}$ produced by the Requester vehicle's private key Prir, the Owner vehicle's location information is decrypted. The Requester vehicle obtains the privacy-preserving location area because the border plaintext information $\{x_{id1}', x_{id2}', y_{id3}', y_{id4}'\}$ is present in borInfo'. The remainder of fuzRes is used during the Requester vehicle's location verification. The location sharing operation for the Owner vehicle and Requester vehicle is now complete.

ALGORITHM 1   LOCATION SHARING

Input: Privacy-preserving level n; Owner Vehicle's Location $l_i = (x_i, y_i)$; Owner vehicle's public key Pub_o
Output: Shared Location Information (LS)

a. Owner vehicle executes:
b. If $n = 0$ then   // trust level is maximum
c. conRes ← SE($k_{session}$, $x_i||y_i$);
d. Res ← conRes||ASE (pub$_o$, $k_{session}$);   // exact coordinates are sent
e. if N ≥ n ≥ 1 then   // trust level is not maximum
f. Find the border $\{x_{id1}, x_{id2}, y_{id3}, y_{id4}\}$ in level n;   //rectangular region sent
g. borInfo$_{id1}$ ← id$_1$|| x_{id1}|| ciph$^x_{id}$;
h. borInfo$_{id2}$ ← id$_2$|| x_{id2}|| ciph$^x_{id}$;
i. borInfo$_{id3}$ ← id$_3$|| x_{id3}|| ciph$^x_{id}$;
j. borInfo$_{id4}$ ← id$_4$|| x_{id4}|| ciph$^x_{id}$;
k. borInfo ← borInfo$_{id1}$|| borInfo$_{id2}$|| borInfo$_{id3}$|| borInfo$_{id4}$;
l. node^x ← {node$^x_{x1}$, node$^x_{x2}$,.....};
m. node^y ← {node$^y_{y1}$, node$^y_{y2}$,.....};
n. fuzRes ← Enc($k_{session}$,ciph$_i$,||borInfo||nodes^x||nodes^y);
o. Res ← fuzRes||ASE(Pub$_r$, $k$session);
p. End if
q. Requester vehicle executes:
r. If $n = 0$ then   // trust level is maximum
s. ||$x_i'y_i'$ ← SD($k$session,conRes);
t. LS ← x_i'|| y_i';
u. Else if $1 ≤ n ≤ N$ then   // trust level not maximum
v. nodes$'^y$ ||nodes$'^x$|| borInfo$'$|| ciph$_i'$ ← SD($k$session,fuzRes)
w. LS ← nodes$'^y$ || borInfo$'$|| nodes$'^x$|| Ciph$_i'$;
x. End if
y. Return LS

2.3.4 Location Verification

If the Requester vehicle confirms the Owner vehicle's ith location information during location sharing, location verification takes place in two steps. The pseudocode for the location verification technique is shown in Algorithm 2. After the Requester decodes conRes, the Owner's precise location coordinates $l_i' = (x_i', y_i')$ can be obtained if the Owner has complete trust in the Requester. The Requester then obtains the location record LR_i created during the location record phase from the block chain.

If Hash $(x_i'||y_i') = LR_i \cdot LI_i \cdot LH_i$, it shows that $xi' = xi$ and $yi' = yi$. When the Owner vehicle has doubts about the Requester, ciphi'||borInfo'||nodes'x||nodes'ySD(ksess ion, fuzRes) is acquired after the Requester decodes fuzRes; nodes'x and nodes'y are needed nodes on the root node authentication path for recovering xTree and yTree. When the Owner has doubts about the Requester, ciph$_i$'||borInfo'||nodes'^{x}||nodes'^{y} $\leftarrow$ SD($k_{session}$, fuzRes) is acquired after the Requester decodes fuzRes. The required nodes on the root node authentication path for recovering xTree and yTree are nodes'^{x} and nodes'^{y}. First, the Requester checks the received region boundary information borInfo' for integrity. If genMT(Hash (borInfoid1'), Hash(borInfoid2'), nodes'x) = xTreeroot' and genMT(Hash (borInfoid1'), Hash(borInfoid2'), nodes'y) = yTreeroot', the regional integrity verification is successful, indicating that the Owner has returned the proper region information borInfo' = borInfo. If Hash(ciph$_i$') = $LR_i \cdot LI_i \cdot OpeHash_i$, (borInfo$_{id1}$'$\cdot$ciph$^x_{id1}$) $\leq$ (ciph$_i$'$\cdot$ciph^x_i) $\leq$ (borInfo$_{id2}$'$\cdot$ciph$^x_{id2}$), and (borInfo$_{id3}$'$\cdot$ciph$^y_{id3}$) $\leq$ (ciph$_i$'$\cdot$Ciph^y_i) $\leq$ (borInfo$_{id4}$'$\cdot$ciph$^y_{id4}$), it shows that $x_{id1} \leq x_i \leq x_{id2}$ and $y_{id2} \leq y_i \leq y_{id4}$; location l_i is in the region surrounded by {x_{id1}, x_{id2}, y_{id3}, y_{id4}} that the Requester receives. The region verification is then complete. Finally, the Owner and Requester's location verification operation is accomplished. The above algorithms have computational complexity of O(1) and O(1), respectively. With increasing N, the compute overhead of Algorithm 1 grows exponentially. Large plaintext spaces have a high computing overhead, although they can be implemented offline during the startup process. Furthermore, [28, 29, 30, 31, 32] Algorithm 1 is only used once throughout the entire procedure. The computing overhead of Algorithm 2 increases as plaintext space grows, with the value of N having no effect. In the location record phase, it also has a low computing overhead. The two elements of N and plaintext space have essentially no effect on the processing cost of Algorithm 1. For Owners, the location sharing phase takes less time. Algorithm 4's calculation overhead is approximately linear with N's size. The plaintext space size has no bearing on it. Because the location verification phase only involves a hash operation, the computing overhead is minimal.

ALGORITHM 2   LOCATION VERIFICATION

Input: Location record in the Blockchain (LR); session key Ksession; Location sharing information (LS)
Output: Boolean variable (LV)

a. Initialize LV $\leftarrow$ False
b. If $n = 0$ then   // trust level is maximum
c. $x_i'||y_i' \leftarrow$ LS;

d. If $Hash(x_i'||y_i')LR_i \cdot Ll_i \cdot LH_i$ then

e. LV ← True;

f. End if

g. Else if $1 \leq n \leq N$ then   // trust level is not maximum

h. $ciph_i'||borInfo'||nodes'^x||nodes'^y ← borInfo'$;

i. $borInfo ← borInfo_{id1}|| borInfo_{id2}|| borInfo_{id3}|| borInfo_{id4}$;

j. $xTree_{root}' ← genMT(Hash(broinfo_{id1}'), Hash(broinfo_{id2}'), nodes'^x)$;

k. $yTree_{root}' ← genMT(Hash(broinfo_{id1}'), Hash(broinfo_{id2}'), nodes'^y)$;

l. If $xTree_{root}' = xTree_{root}$ and $yTree_{root}' = yTree_{root}$ then

m. If $Hash(ciph_i') = LR_i \cdot Ll_i \cdot OpeHash_i$ and $borInfo_{id1}' \cdot ciph_{id1}' < ciph_i' \cdot ciph_i^x < borInfo_{id2}' \cdot ciph_{id2}^x$ and $borInfo_{id3}' \cdot ciph_{id3}' < ciph_i' \cdot ciph_i^y <$ and $borInfo_{id4}' \cdot ciph_{id4}^y$

n. LV ← True;

o. End If

p. End If

q. End If

r. Return LV

2.4 Results and Simulation

2.4.1 Location Leakage

The likelihood of location leakage for each graph, as shown in Figure 2.2, is 0.075–0.0125 for distributed architecture and 0.125 for centralized architecture. Our suggested architecture can lower the probability to around 0.03%, significantly increasing location privacy safeguarding capability.

2.4.2 Channel Capacity Utilization

The system adopts a cooperative approach, requiring message transmission between cars in close proximity. We looked at how often the system uses a wireless communication channel and how many messages are transferred between vehicles. We employed a 152 B packet payload that comprised request information as well as location information for the questioned node. The average channel utilization is shown in Figure 2.3.

2.4.3 Message Delivery Success Rate

Single-hop delivery should allow vehicles within the same communication range to exchange messages. However, because of moving barriers, this may not always be the case. Figure 2.4 shows delivery of a message using a direct single-hop strategy to

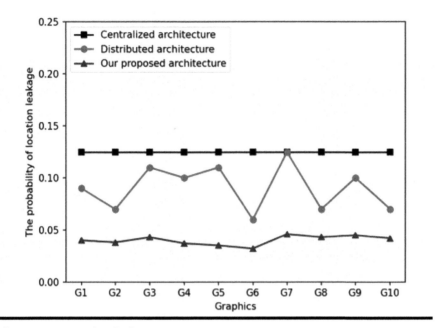

Figure 2.2   Location leakage.

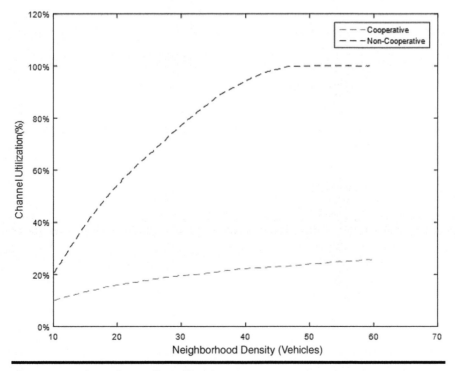

Figure 2.3   Channel capacity utilization.

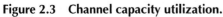

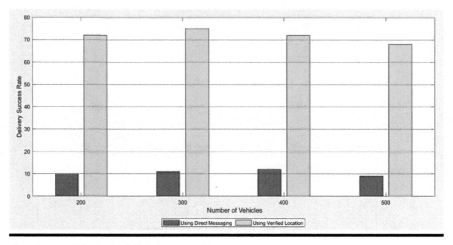

Figure 2.4   Message delivery success rate.

one that incorporated location verification and NLOS condition information. The sender can assess whether it can forward the message directly or whether it needs the help of other nodes by knowing the destination node. The results reveal that the delivery success rate has improved, as has the influence of moving impediments on direct messaging.

2.4.4 Processing Time

The usual processing time from generation to verification response is depicted in Figure 2.5. A verification request typically takes less than 200 milliseconds to process, depending on vehicle density.

2.4.5 Security Attack Resilience

We included malicious vehicular nodes in our simulations to evaluate our model's security mechanisms. The malicious vehicular nodes carried out a variety of attacks that might disrupt the protocol. The results (see Figure 2.6) indicated that the technique was not vulnerable to attacks. Malicious nodes accounted for between 25% and 75% of all nodes. These safeguards helped protect our protocol against the majority of the threats discovered.

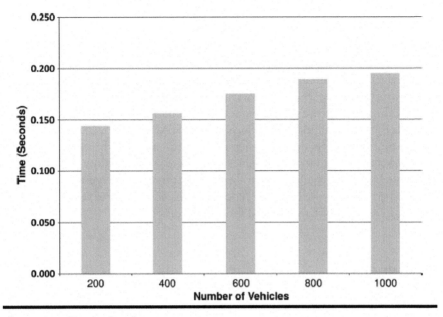

Figure 2.5   Processing time.

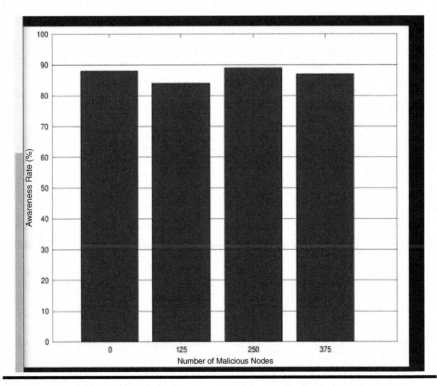

Figure 2.6   Security attack resilience.

2.5 Conclusion

This study investigates the decentralized architecture of an internet of vehicles based on block chain technology, and proposes a system model that includes block chain setup, vehicle registration, SBMs upload, and block chain record. Centralization and trustworthiness issues can be efficiently addressed by using a block chain-based VANET. In our proposed system model, there is no third central entity. The hash of SBMs is stored in block chain, which ensures SBM integrity while also speeding up data processing. The identity is then partitioned into more than k sub-identities in a blockchain-based internet of vehicles to ensure vehicle identity privacy, which will be updated on a regular basis using dynamic threshold encryption. The results of the experiments showed that our block chain-based internet of vehicles was very efficient in terms of system time and privacy protection.

References

1. Kumar, S., Dohare, U., Kumar, K., Dora, D. P., Qureshi, K. N., & Kharel, R. (2018). Cybersecurity measures for geocasting in vehicular cyber physical system environments. *IEEE Internet of Things Journal, 6*(4), 5916–5926.
2. Kumar, S., Singh, K., Kumar, S., Kaiwartya, O., Cao, Y., & Zhou, H. (2019). Delimitated anti jammer scheme for Internet of vehicle: Machine learning based security approach. *IEEE Access, 7,* 113311–113323.
3. Kaiwartya, O., Cao, Y., Lloret, J., Kumar, S., Aslam, N., Kharel, R., ... & Shah, R. R. (2018). Geometry-based localization for GPS outage in vehicular cyber physical systems. *IEEE Transactions on Vehicular Technology, 67*(5), 3800–3812.
4. Kasana, R., Kumar, S., Kaiwartya, O., Yan, W., Cao, Y., & Abdullah, A. H. (2017). Location error resilient geographical routing for vehicular ad-hoc networks. *IET Intelligent Transport Systems, 11*(8), 450–458.
5. Malaney, R. A. (2004, November). A location enabled wireless security system. In *IEEE Global Telecommunications Conference, 2004. GLOBECOM'04.* (Vol. 4, pp. 2196–2200). IEEE.
6. Malandrino, F., Borgiattino, C., Casetti, C., Chiasserini, C. F., Fiore, M., & Sadao, R. (2014). Verification and inference of positions in vehicular networks through anonymous beaconing. *IEEE Transactions on Mobile Computing, 13*(10), 2415–2428.
7. Leinmüller, T., Schoch, E., Kargl, F., & Maihöfer, C. (2005, July). Influence of falsified position data on geographic ad-hoc routing. In *European Workshop on Security in Ad-hoc and Sensor Networks* (pp. 102–112). Springer, Berlin, Heidelberg.
8. Čapkun, S., Čagalj, M., Karame, G., & Tippenhauer, N. O. (2010). Integrity regions: authentication through presence in wireless networks. *IEEE Transactions on Mobile Computing, 9*(11), 1608–1621.
9. Raya, M., & Hubaux, J. P. (2007). Securing vehicular ad hoc networks. *Journal of Computer Security, 15*(1), 39–68.
10. Yu, B., Xu, C. Z., & Xiao, B. (2013). Detecting sybil attacks in VANETs. *Journal of Parallel and Distributed Computing, 73*(6), 746–756.
11. Zhang, T., & Delgrossi, L. (2012). *Vehicle safety communications: protocols, security, and privacy.* John Wiley & Sons.

12. Čapkun, S., Buttyán, L., & Hubaux, J. P. (2003, October). SECTOR: secure tracking of node encounters in multi-hop wireless networks. In *Proceedings of the 1st ACM Workshop on Security of Ad hoc and Sensor Networks* (pp. 21–32).

13. Hubaux, J. P., Capkun, S., & Luo, J. (2004). The security and privacy of smart vehicles. *IEEE Security & Privacy, 2*(3), 49–55.

14. Sastry, N., Shankar, U., & Wagner, D. (2003, September). Secure verification of location claims. In *Proceedings of the 2nd ACM Workshop on Wireless Security* (pp. 1–10).

15. Vora, A., & Nesterenko, M. (2006). Secure location verification using radio broadcast. *IEEE Transactions on Dependable and Secure Computing, 3*(4), 377–385.

16. Xue, X., Lin, N., Ding, J., & Ji, Y. (2010). A trusted neighbor table based location verification for VANET Routing.

17. Bd, S. (2002). SP, and WHC. In *Talking to strangers: Authentication in adhoc wireless networks*, in *Symposium on Network and Distributed Systems Security (NDSS'02)*.

18. Golle, P., Greene, D., & Staddon, J. (2004, October). Detecting and correcting malicious data in VANETs. In *Proceedings of the 1st ACM International Workshop on Vehicular Ad hoc Networks* (pp. 29–37).

19. Xiao, B., Yu, B., & Gao, C. (2006, September). Detection and localization of sybil nodes in VANETs. In *Proceedings of the 2006 Workshop on Dependability Issues in Wireless Ad hoc Networks and Sensor Networks* (pp. 1–8).

20. Yan, G., Olariu, S., & Weigle, M. C. (2008). Providing VANET security through active position detection. *Computer Communications, 31*(12), 2883–2897.

21. Ren, Z., Li, W., & Yang, Q. (2009, October). Location verification for VANETs routing. In *2009 IEEE International Conference on Wireless and Mobile Computing, Networking and Communications* (pp. 141–146). IEEE.

22. Song, J. H., Wong, V. W., & Leung, V. C. (2008, December). Secure location verification for vehicular ad-hoc networks. In *IEEE GLOBECOM 2008-2008 IEEE Global Telecommunications Conference* (pp. 1–5). IEEE.

23. Yan, G., Chen, X., & Olariu, S. (2009, October). Providing VANET position integrity through filtering. In *2009 12th International IEEE Conference on Intelligent Transportation Systems* (pp. 1–6). IEEE.

24. Bucci, G., Ciancetta, F., Fiorucci, E., Fioravanti, A., Prudenzi, A., & Mari, S. (2019, September). Challenge and future trends of distributed measurement systems based on Blockchain technology in the European context. In *2019 IEEE 10th International Workshop on Applied Measurements for Power Systems (AMPS)* (pp. 1–6). IEEE.

25. Joy, J., & Gerla, M. (2017, July). Internet of vehicles and autonomous connected car-privacy and security issues. In *2017 26th International Conference on Computer Communication and Networks*.

26. Joy, J., Cusack, G., & Gerla, M. (2017, October). Poster: time analysis of the feasibility of vehicular blocktrees. In *Proceedings of the 3rd Workshop on Experiences with the Design and Implementation of Smart Objects* (pp. 25–26).

27. Dorri, A., Kanhere, S. S., & Jurdak, R. (2017, April). Towards an optimized blockchain for IoT. In *2017 IEEE/ACM Second International Conference on Internet-of-Things Design and Implementation (IoTDI)* (pp. 173–178). IEEE.

28. Sharma, P. K., Moon, S. Y., & Park, J. H. (2017). Block-VN: A distributed blockchain based vehicular network architecture in smart city. *Journal of Information Processing Systems, 13*(1), 184–195.

29. Lei, A., Cruickshank, H., Cao, Y., Asuquo, P., Ogah, C. P. A., & Sun, Z. (2017). Blockchain-based dynamic key management for heterogeneous intelligent transportation systems. *IEEE Internet of Things Journal, 4*(6), 1832–1843.

30. Amoretti, M., Brambilla, G., Medioli, F., & Zanichelli, F. (2018, July). Blockchain-based proof of location. In *2018 IEEE International Conference on Software Quality, Reliability and Security Companion (QRS-C)* (pp. 146–153). IEEE.
31. Chen, S., Hu, J., Shi, Y., Peng, Y., Fang, J., Zhao, R., & Zhao, L. (2017). Vehicle-to-everything (V2X) services supported by LTE-based systems and 5G. *IEEE Communications Standards Magazine, 1*(2), 70–76.
32. Mittag, J., Thomas, F., Härri, J., & Hartenstein, H. (2009, September). A comparison of single-and multi-hop beaconing in VANETs. In *Proceedings of the Sixth ACM International Workshop on VehiculAr InterNETworking* (pp. 69–78).

Chapter 3

Comparative Analysis of Word-Embedding Techniques Using LSTM Model

Mohd Danish and Mohammad Amjad

Jamia Millia Islamia University, New Delhi, India

3.1 Introduction

Feature extraction or sentiment analysis has been a hot topic in natural language processing for the last couple of years. The main objective of sentiment analysis is to obtain adequate knowledge from the vast pool of unstructured text data in order to overcome the problem of information overload. Many studies have been conducted on feature extraction to increase the performance of classification tasks [1]. In NLP, one of the techniques for extracting features involves compressing the input into vector space representations. This approach uses a term frequency matrix to convert unstructured data. Traditional text representation algorithms such as bag-of-words (BOW), term frequency (TF), and inverse document frequency (TF-IDF) only transform text into a set of terms according to the frequency of their occurrence within a document. All these text representations lack semantic information. Deep learning performs much better at sentiment classification than conventional machine learning techniques [2]. This paper examines the word-embedding techniques word2vec, GloVe, fastText and BERT for sentiment classification and evaluates their performance using LSTM as a classifier. Relevant literature is discussed

DOI: 10.1201/9781003371380-3

in Section 3.2, methodology is explained in Section 3.3, results are presented in Section 3.4, and future work is discussed in the concluding Section 3.5.

3.2 Related Works

The scope of natural language processing (NLP) has increased dramatically with deep learning techniques. Word representation through deep learning is an effective roadmap. The implementation of sentiment classification using deep learning models has become extremely popular. Word2vec was used by Zhang et al. [3] to analyze consumer sentiment toward Chinese clothing products based on lexicon and parts of speech; word2vec was found to perform well. Word2vec with convolution neural network (CNN) was applied using the Twitter election dataset [4]. Better results than SVM with text representation TF-IDF and SVM along with word embedding were achieved. Using the news and tweets dataset, [5] applied word2vec. Their findings had the best accuracy, scoring 93.41% for the news dataset and 90.81% for the tweets dataset. Authors in [6] applied BERT with a GloVe to study sarcasm in Twitter data. Their experiment showed the highest precision at 98.5%. [7] conducted citation intent classification using GloVe, BERT and Infersent.

In ref. [8] the combined word-embedding techniques of fastText and word2vec were applied to explore people's awareness during COVID-19, using the Twitter dataset. In ref. [9], fastText was applied to analysis of the identical question on Quora. They used 100,000 pairs for testing, and their proposed model achieved 91.14% accuracy. FastText N-grams were used to examine DNA sequences in ref. [10], after which they were added to a deep neural network for categorization. At two layers, this method produced cross-validation estimator accuracy of 85.42% and 73.2%. Word2vec, CBOW, GloVe, and Colbert & Weston were assessed by ref. [11] for cross-lingual Chinese and English word meaning disambiguation. They discovered that word2vec performed the best.

Researchers investigated three word-embedding algorithms for Twitter crisis classification: fastText, GloVe, and word2vec [12]. GloVe delivered the finest results across all three datasets, according to their experiment outcomes (CrisisLexT6, CrisisLexT26, and 2CTweets). Word2vec, GloVe, and LSA were used to study topic segmentation in Arabic and English [13]. For both languages, word2vec and GloVe were found to perform better than LSA.

The Yelp reviews dataset was used for an aspect-based sentiment analysis task using deep learning, machine learning and transfer learning models [14]. Using the ALBERT model, the highest accuracy of 98.30% was attained. Researcher in ref. [15] applied a Bi-LSTM model incorporated with word2vec to perform a sentiment analysis task on datasets from micro-blogging sites like Twitter and Tumblr. Their model enhanced accuracy up to 85%. The structure, feasibility, performance and results of LSTM and RNN models for a sentiment analysis task using Twitter data were studied in ref. [16].

3.3 Methodology

This section will discuss the IMDB movie review dataset, word-embedding techniques and LSTM classifier (see Figure 3.1 for the different stages).

3.3.1 Dataset

This work used the IMDB movie review dataset, which contains 50,000 movie text reviews. The dataset contains two attributes: textual review and sentiment score (positive or negative). Preprocessing was performed on the entire dataset. Preprocessing steps include removing HTML tags and punctuation, converting all text to lowercase, and removing stopwords. The dataset was split in a ratio of 80:20, i.e., 40,000 for training and 10,000 for testing the model.

3.3.2 Word-Embedding Techniques

3.3.2.1 Word2vec

Word embeddings are created using the word2vec (W2V) model, an unsupervised learning technique comprising a collection of linked models. It has a fully connected, or linear, layer employing stochastic gradient descent and back-propagation method, as well as a hidden layer called the projection layer. W2V depends on language-specific local knowledge [17]. The words around a word have an impact on the semantics that are learned from that word. W2V shows that linguistic patterns can be studied as linear relationships between word vectors. Continuous bag-of-words (CBOW) and Skip-gram are the two architecture models upon which word2vec is based. Figure 3.2 displays both models. CBOW attempts to estimate words using the context of a word as input. The opposite is true with Skip-gram, which gathers a word as input and determines its context. A window is set up in the act of kernel in order to gather input and select target words.

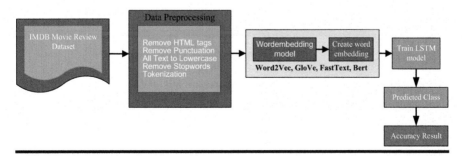

Figure 3.1   Systematic stages of this work.

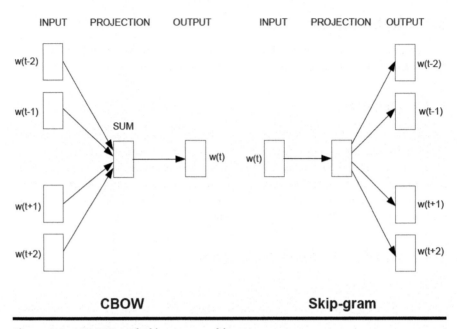

Figure 3.2 CBOW and Skip-gram architecture.

3.3.2.2 GloVe

GloVe uses global vectors for word representations. It is an unsupervised learning approach designed to construct word embeddings through integrating a global word co-occurrence matrix from a given corpus. Using statistics, GloVe determines the link between the words. GloVe makes use of the global matrix factorization strategy, which uses a matrix to demonstrate whether a term in a document is present or not [18]. GloVe learns the association between words by calculating the frequency with which terms emerge in the same corpus. The probability ratio of a word's occurrence has the potential to encode meaning and contribute to solving the problem of word analogy.

GloVe can be expressed as [18]:

$$F\left(w_i, w_j, w_k\right) = \frac{P_{ik}}{P_{jk}} \qquad (3.1)$$

where W represent word vector and $\bar{W}$ is context word

3.3.2.3 FastText

FastText is a vector representations technique developed by Facebook AI research. It is efficient for learning sentence classification and word embeddings [19]. Skip-gram and CBOW techniques can be trained using FastText, which uses a neural

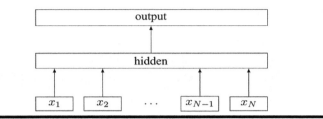

Figure 3.3   Architecture of fastText model.

network for word embeddings. It is unique because it can derive word vectors for unknown words or out-of-vocabulary words, whereas word2vec and GloVe lack vector representations for words not in the model dictionary. In addition, as seen in Figure 3.3, there is a hidden layer between the input and output layers of fastText. FastText offers representations for words that might not have appeared in the initial training data phase and can train models quickly on large data sets. Splitting a word into n-grams allows one to determine its vector embedding even if it was not used during model training.

3.3.2.4 BERT

In Bidirectional Encoder Representations from Transformers (BERT), the main objective is to pre-train deep bidirectional representation from unlabeled text by conditioning both left and right contexts [20]. BERT has two models: BERT base and BERT large. The base model has bidirectional self-attention and 12 encoders; the large model has 24 encoders and 16 bidirectional heads. Pre-training of the BERT model is done on a huge corpus of unlabeled text, such as Wikipedia (25 billion words) and book corpora (800 million words). This allows it to be tuned for small datasets specifically for NLP purposes. Both the earlier and later contexts of a statement are represented by the BERT model. The context-free GloVe and word2vec models, on the other hand, create word representations for each vocabulary word.

3.3.3 LSTM Deep Learning Classifier

Deep learning techniques facilitate its importance in the domain of NLP. In this research, long short-term memory (LSTM) is employed to measure the performance of the sentiment analysis task. LSTM is commonly utilized for sentence-level text classification due to its ability to understand context-dependent sequences. Additionally, the LSTM features feedback connections in contrast to conventional feed-forward neural networks. A typical LSTM architecture comprises an output gate, input gate, and a forget gate in addition to a cell, which serves as the LSTM unit's memory. These gates regulate the inflow and outflow of information, and the cell retains values for any length of time.

3.3.4 Evaluation Metric

In this work, the system's performance is measured by its accuracy, defined as the proportion of accurate estimates to all other estimates.

It can be represented as:

$$\text{Accuracy} = \frac{TP + TN}{TP + TN + FP + FN} \tag{3.2}$$

where TP, TN, FP, and FN are used to denote true positive, true negative, false positive and false negative respectively.

3.4 Results and Discussion

This work was implemented on Google Colab with the IMDB movie review dataset. The dataset was split into training (40,000) and testing (10,000) data for accuracy-based performance evaluation. The LSTM parameters used in this work can be seen in Table 3.1.

Our analysis shows that word2vec and GloVe cannot overcome the out-of-vocabulary problem, hence do not produce good results in testing. On the other hand, fastText solves unseen word or out-of-vocabulary problems, as words that could not originate in the course of the training process are broken down into n-grams and hence may be found in its vector embedding.

The BERT model outperformed all other word-embedding approaches and achieved the results in fewer epochs than other models. However, BERT takes much time to train because of the many parameters used. Table 3.2 shows the experimental results.

Experiments and research comparing the performance of word2vec, GloVe, fast-Text, and BERT have demonstrated that these state-of-the-art word-embedding techniques have comparable performance. The word-embedding performance depends on the dataset utilized and the issue domain (Figure 3.4).

Table 3.1   LSTM Parameters Applied

Parameter	Value
Epochs	1–10
Learning Rate	0.0001
Dropout	0.6
Optimizer	Adam

Table 3.2 Accuracy Result of Word Embeddings Models

Word Embedding	Accuracy in %
Word2vec	88
GloVe	89
Fasttext	86
BERT	**93**

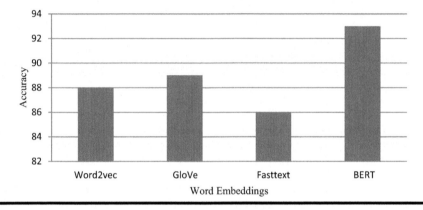

Figure 3.4 Experiment results of word-embedding models.

3.5 Conclusion and Future Work

Word embedding is one of the ways available for representing text in vector format. In this work, LSTM was used as a classifier to accomplish various word-embedding algorithms, namely word2vec, GloVe, fastText, and BERT. Unfortunately, word2vec and GloVe could not solve the out-of-vocabulary problem, whereas fastText does. Results were compared using the IMDB movie review dataset and it was found that the BERT model with an accuracy of 93% outperformed all the other word-embedding models; word2vec achieved 88, GloVe 89% and the fastText model 86%.

In future work, we will try out this word embedding on other dataset domains and analyze the combination of word-embedding models.

References

1. Kulkarni, N. (2021). A comparative study of word embedding techniques to extract features from text. *Turkish Journal of Computer and Mathematics Education (TURCOMAT)*, *12*(12), 3550–3557.

2. Liao, S., Wang, J., Yu, R., Sato, K., & Cheng, Z. (2017). CNN for situations understanding based on sentiment analysis of twitter data. *Procedia Computer Science, 111,* 376–381.

3. Jang, B., Kim, I., & Kim, J. W. (2019). Word2vec convolutional neural networks for classification of news articles and tweets. *PLoS One, 14*(8), e0220976.

4. Xu, Y. F. (2015). Chinese comments sentiment classification based on word2vec and SVM. *Expert Systems with Applications, 42*(1857), 1863.

5. Yang, X., Macdonald, C., & Ounis, I. (2018). Using word embeddings in twitter election classification. *Information Retrieval Journal, 21*(2), 183–207.

6. Eke, C. I., Norman, A. A., & Shuib, L. (2021). Context-based feature technique for sarcasm identification in benchmark datasets using deep learning and BERT model. *IEEE Access, 9,* 48501–48518.

7. Dhiman, A., & Toshniwal, D. (2020). An approximate model for event detection from Twitter data. *IEEE Access, 8,* 122168–122184.

8. Hasanah, N. A., Suciati, N., & Purwitasari, D. (2021). Identifying degree-of-concern on COVID-19 topics with text classification of Twitters. *Register: Jurnal Ilmiah Teknologi Sistem Informasi, 7*(1), 50–62.

9. Imtiaz, Z., Umer, M., Ahmad, M., Ullah, S., Choi, G. S., & Mehmood, A. (2020). Duplicate questions pair detection using Siamese Malstm. *IEEE Access, 8,* 21932–21942.

10. Le, N. Q. K., Yapp, E. K. Y., Nagasundaram, N., & Yeh, H. Y. (2019). Classifying promoters by interpreting the hidden information of DNA sequences via deep learning and combination of continuous fasttext N-grams. *Frontiers in Bioengineering and Biotechnology, 7,* 305.

11. Kang, H. J., Chen, T., Chandrasekaran, M. K., & Kan, M. Y. (2016). A comparison of word embeddings for English and cross-lingual Chinese word sense disambiguation. *arXiv preprint arXiv:1611.02956.*

12. Li, H., Li, X., Caragea, D., & Caragea, C. (2018). Comparison of word embeddings and sentence encodings as generalized representations for crisis tweet classification tasks. *Proceedings of ISCRAM Asia Pacific.*

13. Naili, M., Chaibi, A. H., & Ghezala, H. H. B. (2017). Comparative study of word embedding methods in topic segmentation. *Procedia Computer Science, 112,* 340–349.

14. Alamoudi, E. S., & Alghamdi, N. S. (2021). Sentiment classification and aspect-based sentiment analysis on yelp reviews using deep learning and word embeddings. *Journal of Decision Systems, 30*(2–3), 259–281.

15. Uikey, S., Singh, D. P., & Choudhary, J. (2022). Sentiment analysis: A comparative analysis. In *Data Intelligence and Cognitive Informatics* (pp. 795–807). Springer, Singapore.

16. Pradhan, R., Agarwal, G., & Singh, D. (2022). Comparative analysis for sentiment in tweets using LSTM and RNN. In *International Conference on Innovative Computing and Communications* (pp. 713–725). Springer, Singapore.

17. Ganegedara, T. (2019). Intuitive guide to understanding GloVe embeddings. *Towards Data Science [online].*

18. Pennington, J., Socher, R., & Manning, C. D. (2014, October). Glove: Global vectors for word representation. In *Proceedings of the 2014 Conference on Empirical Methods in Natural Language Processing (EMNLP)* (pp. 1532–1543).

19. Joulin, A., Grave, E., Bojanowski, P., & Mikolov, T. (2016). Bag of tricks for efficient text classification. *arXiv preprint arXiv:1607.01759.*

20. Devlin, J., Chang, M. W., Lee, K., & Toutanova, K. (2018). Bert: Pre-training of deep bidirectional transformers for language understanding. *arXiv preprint arXiv:1810.04805.*

Chapter 4

A Deep Learning Approach for Mask-Based Face Detection

Heta S. Desai and Atul M. Gonsai

Saurashtra University, Rajkot, Gujarat, India

4.1 Introduction

The transmission of the COVID-19 virus can be reduced by correct hygiene practices such as the use of hand sanitizer, hand washing after touching potentially contaminated surfaces, and face covering. According to the World Health Organization, face masks are one of the most effective protections against Coronavirus. However, fewer individuals are now using face masks in public areas such as shopping centers, restaurants, markets, and on public transport. Physically checking individuals for mask wearing in public places requires vast human resources. The alternative solution is automated face detection utilizing CCTV or a web camera [1]. Face detection and recognition using image processing supports numerous activities including observing criminal activity, automated attendance in education, passport identification, at air terminals, and in many other places [2]. While traditional face detection systems are highly accurate, there are numerous applications in which recognizing the occluded part of the face is extremely challenging when only part of the face is visible due to a face covering.

The system proposed in this study is designed to detect whether or not an individual is wearing a face mask. Data input is extracted from web or surveillance cameras and from video image frames. There are two steps: first, to train the model, and second, to apply the algorithm to the images for detection purposes by matching the

DOI: 10.1201/9781003371380-4

featured image with the dataset images. The system uses deep learning techniques such as Keras and TensorFlow for detection purposes, a convolutional neural network (CNN) for image classification, and a dataset from Kaggle for training and testing purposes. The dataset contains 3725 images of faces with face coverings and 3828 images without face coverings.

4.2 Related Work

A good deal of research has been done on identification of human faces utilizing Keras, TensorFlow, OpenCv and MobileNetV2. The model proposed in ref. [3] was trained with a huge dataset of images of people with and without face masks. Using deep learning to recognize faces in a crowd, the proposed algorithm achieved close to 99% accuracy over 3850 images. A framework proposed in ref. [2] works with still images from live recordings by CCTV camera and uses Python's DIP libraries. The system proposed in ref. [4] identifies and distinguishes the occluded part of faces covered with face masks. Three CNN-based procedures were chosen: (1) CNN-based YOLOv3; (2) CNN-based SSD utilizing MobileNetV2; and (3) VGG-16 descriptor.

The solution in ref. [5] implements segmentation at pixel level. RCNN techniques solved the occlusion problem. The model was tested on the Plasmodium Vivax dataset as well as a customized dataset. The object detection phase included localization and image classification of objects by marking bounding box. The model was tested and obtained 94% mean average precision.

Another study analyzed several face detection methods and applied them to different types of face mask [6]. Five different feature-based techniques were applied to different face masks: Haar cascade, histogram of oriented gradients (HOG), TinyFace, MTCNN and MMOD. The experimental results suggest that feature-based detectors have low accuracy rate; TinyFace achieved the highest recognition accuracy of 81.9% on the wider face dataset.

The system proposed in ref. [1] worked with three main processes: (1) preprocessing (2) detection and (3) classification. CNN was used to detect more than one face in a single video frame with higher detection accuracy. The Caffe model in combination with CNN achieved the highest accuracy in large-scale applications. The Haar cascade algorithm was used in a grayscale image to identify if a human face is present in a frame or not. If the frame contains a human face, the grayscale image is converted into an RGB image for the CNN classifier.

Table 4.1 Review of Different Face Detection Algorithms

Sr No	Theme	Methodology	Result	Future Scope
1.	Evaluation of face-covering methods using deep learning [7].	DETR algorithm on customized dataset.	Achieves 92.38% of accuracy.	Algorithm will be applied on a greater variety of data, including angle change, size, color and pixels.
2.	Occlusion-based face detection network [8].	MTCNN, RetinaFace and DLIB.	Used CFP dataset, modified by removing different parts of the face. RetinaFace performs better than other two.	Applied this algorithm on other dataset with live streaming.
3.	Person re-identification using deep learning [9].	Viola–Jones and MTCNN on cropped images of faces.	MTCNN achieves better result but works better if the faces are in correct pose.	Will work with other classifiers as well to test accuracy.
4.	Deep learning-based face detection [10].	HOG and CNN for face and mask detection, respectively.	Achieves 97% accuracy.	LSTM can be used for distance measurement purposes.
5.	Face detection using Max pooling [11].	Deep learning using Max pooling.	Training accuracy was 95.72% on LFW dataset.	Can be applied on any automated system for detection.
6.	Mask-based face detection using deep transfer [12].	DCNN + OpenCV +VGG19.	Validation accuracy was 98.7%.	Will work on speed and accuracy with surveillance camera.
7.	Study of face detection and distance measurement on different dataset [13].	CNN + YOLOv3 +DSFD + MobileNetv2.	91.20% accuracy.	Can be applied on distance measurement. System confused beard with mask.

4.3 Dataset

The dataset used in our model was imported from Kaggle. The dataset images are arranged in two sections: one section with face coverings and the other without. There are 3725 images with face masks (examples in Figure 4.1) and 3828 without (examples in Figure 4.2).

4.4 Proposed System

4.4.1 TensorFlow

The graph-based programming language TensorFlow provides an assortment of work processes to create and train models utilizing Python [3]. Newly developed TensorFlow libraries make the deep learning model more straightforward [2].

4.4.2 Keras

Keras is an open-source neural network library. It is easy to understand, extensible, and particularly suitable for quick investigations with deep learning methods [15]. Convolutional networks and recurrent networks are used both separately and together [3].

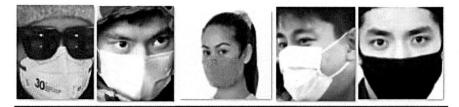

Figure 4.1   Some illustrative images from dataset with face mask.

Figure 4.2   Some illustrative images from dataset without face mask.

4.4.3 OpenCV

OpenCV contains an abundance of algorithms focused on real-time computer processing [3].

4.4.4 Numpy

Numpy is an open-source Python built-in library that works with machine learning and deep learning applications involving complex numerical operations with large datasets.

4.4.5 Convolution Neural Network (CNN)

CNN was used for the classification process. It concentrates on useful data within the image rather than on the whole image [11, 14]. A CNN classifier categorizes images into two groups: those with face masks and those without. CNN divides video into a number of frames and takes one RGB frame as an input in the form of a 3D matrix which includes width and height of the images and the number of pixels. The sequential CNN model has hidden layers: convolution layer, MaxPooling layer, dropout layer, flatten layer and dense layer. The convolution layer avoids overfitting and reduces errors by fitting the function. The MaxPooling layer calculates the largest pixel value from the feature map. The dropout layer is typically inserted between the fully connected layers or after a convolutional layer. It is commonly used to prevent overfitting and improve the generalization capability of the model. The flatten layer generates one sequential vector from the 2D feature map. The dense layer outputs one vector which is used to predict two classes (Figure 4.3).

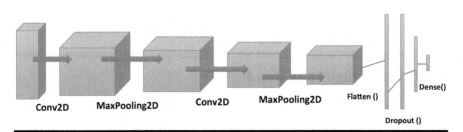

Figure 4.3 CNN model for mask-based face detection.

4.5 System Flow Chart

The system has two main parts: Phase 1 is about training the model and Phase 2 is about detecting whether an individual face is covered with a mask. If a person is wearing a face mask, a green rectangular box appears on the face, and if not a red box appears.

In the pre-processing step, video frames are taken from the CCTV camera or web camera. The video is divided into frames which are stored inside the system. The next process is segmentation, in which the facial images are divided into many specific and unique regions. In our system, segmentation delivers differentiation between the two categories of mask and no-mask. Faces covered with a face mask are assigned number 0 and if a face mask is not present, number 1 is assigned to them. This is followed by marking the unknown category with a proper name and storing it inside another vector memory.

Feature extraction is a process in which special features are extracted from the vector. In this case the feature vector has been generated by measuring different facial features such as the distance between the eyebrows, height and width of the lips and ears, the height and size of the nose, etc.

The extracted features are stored inside the vectors and memory and these vectors and memory are stored inside the dataset for future use. The neural network's binary cross-entropy classifier computes the cross-entropy loss between the true label which is stored inside the trained dataset and the predicted label. This classifier compares each predicted label with the actual label, which can be either 0 or 1. If the match result is 0 then a person is detected with face mask and if the result is 1 then a person is detected without face mask. Figure 4.4 is a flowchart of the proposed system.

4.6 Evaluating Performance Using Performance Matrix

After completing training and validation accuracy, we evaluated the system performance for accuracy.

$$\text{Accuracy} = \frac{\text{TP} + \text{TN}}{\text{TP} + \text{FP} + \text{TN} + \text{FN}} \tag{4.1}$$

4.6.1 Experiments and Result

Significantly, our model was able to recognize the individual regardless of the fact that the person was wearing a mask. The model has shown effectiveness in detecting face, with red color boundaries indicating "face without mask detected" and green boundaries indicating "face with mask detected" (Figure 4.5–4.7).

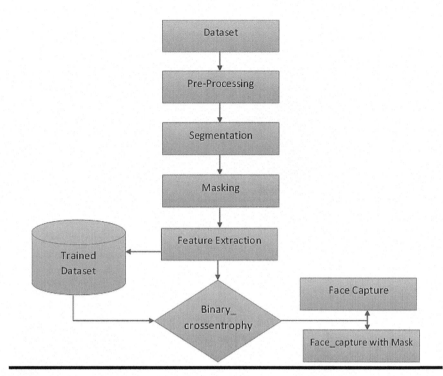

Figure 4.4   Proposed system flowchart.

Figure 4.5   Face detection without any occlusion.

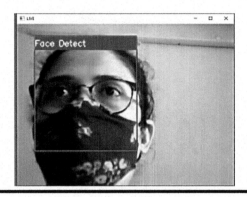

Figure 4.6   Face detection with face mask.

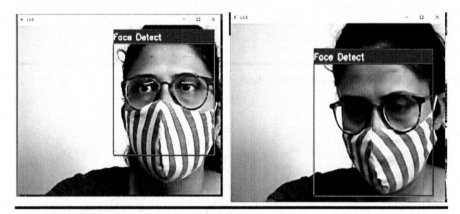

Figure 4.7   Face mask detection with angle variation.

Figure 4.8, the training loss/accuracy chart for the face mask detector, indicates high detection accuracy. Table 4.2 describes the training loss and accuracy, validation loss and accuracy. The proposed model achieves training accuracy of 95.94% and validation accuracy of 99.48%. Table 4.3 compares accuracy with other deep learning approaches.

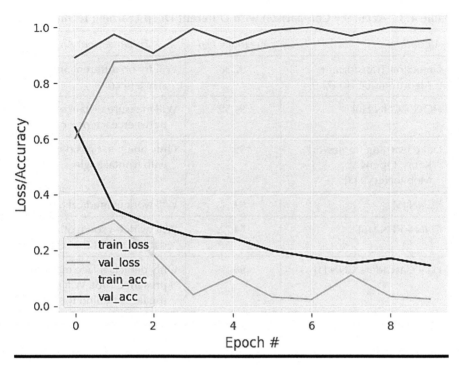

Figure 4.8   Accuracy and training loss on dataset.

Table 4.2   Result of Training and Validation Loss and Accuracy on Dataset

Epochs	Training Loss (%)	Training Accuracy (%)	Validation Loss (%)	Validation Accuracy (%)
1	69.46	52.94	25.00	89.18
2	34.16	88.97	30.73	97.42
3	31.09	88.12	18.33	90.72
4	26.00	88.46	04.11	99.48
5	20.11	92.80	10.74	94.33
6	19.29	93.03	3.20	98.97
7	15.59	95.14	2.40	100
8	14.82	94.54	11.05	96.91
9	16.56	94.68	3.44	100
10	14.44	95.94	2.53	99.48

Table 4.3 Accuracy Comparison with Different Deep Learning Techniques

Algorithm	Accuracy (%)	Enhancement Area
Detection Transformer Algorithm (DETR) [7]	92.38	Will try on different angle, size and color.
HOG + CNN [10]	94.59	Will measure distance between each person.
Deep learning framework: Keras, OpenCV, MobileNetV2 [3]	99	Only one person is detected with frontal angle.
RCNN [5]	94	Will work in medical field.
CNN + RPN [16]	64.72	Will work on some other dataset to test the result.
Haar Cascade + CNN [1]	98	Only detects if face mask is present or not. Will detect the faces behind the mask.
CNN + DSFD and MoileNetV2 classifier [13]	91.2	Sometimes confuses beard with face mask.

4.7 Conclusion and Future Scope

Facial recognition and detection is today a significant part of life, since it supports such activities as identification of criminals, tracking missing persons, and many more. However, in public places it is harder to identify faces because of occlusion and overlapping of faces. This paper presents a model to distinguish whether or not people are wearing face coverings. CNN is used to recognize faces from surveillance cameras and the CNN classifier classifies the images as with mask and without mask. Video frames containing human faces are input to a CNN classifier which detects faces with and without face masks. A green rectangle is drawn over the faces where a face mask has been detected and a red rectangle indicates no face mask detected.

References

1. G. Saranya, D. Sarkar, S. Ghosh, L. Basu, K. Kumaran and N. Ananthi, Face Mask Detection using CNN, *2021 10th IEEE International Conference on Communication Systems and Network Technologies (CSNT)*, 2021, pp. 426–431, doi: 10.1109/CSNT51715.2021.9509556.
2. S. I. Ali, S. S. Ebrahimi, M. Khurram and S. I. Qadri, Real-Time Face Mask Detection in Deep Learning using Convolution Neural Network, *2021 10th IEEE International Conference on Communication Systems and Network Technologies (CSNT)*, 2021, pp. 639–642, doi: 10.1109/CSNT51715.2021.9509704.

3. M. Chandraprabha, T. Akilan, Y. Garg, S. Yadav and V. Sanoriya, Deep Learning Based Face Mask Detection System in OpenCV, *2021 3rd International Conference on Advances in Computing, Communication Control and Networking (ICAC3N)*, 2021, pp. 1968–1973, doi: 10.1109/ICAC3N53548.2021.9725710.

4. O. Ibitoye, A Brief Review of Convolutional Neural Network Techniques for Masked Face Recognition, *2021 IEEE Concurrent Processes Architectures and Embedded Systems Virtual Conference (COPA)*, 2021, pp. 1–4, doi: 10.1109/COPA51043.2021.9541448.

5. D. Triphena Delight and V. Karunakaran, Deep Learning based Object Detection using Mask RCNN, *2021 6th International Conference on Communication and Electronics Systems (ICCES)*, 2021, pp. 1684–1690, doi: 10.1109/ICCES51350.2021.9489152.

6. J. Prinosil and O. Maly, Detecting Faces with Face Masks, *2021 44th International Conference on Telecommunications and Signal Processing (TSP)*, 2021, pp. 259–262, doi: 10.1109/TSP52935.2021.9522677.

7. M. N. A. Aziz, S. Mutalib and S. Aliman, Comparison of Face Coverings Detection Methods using Deep Learning, *2021 2nd International Conference on Artificial Intelligence and Data Sciences (AiDAS)*, 2021, pp. 1–6, doi: 10.1109/AiDAS53897.2021.9574318.

8. P. Hofer, M. Roland, P. Schwarz, M. Schwaighofer and R. Mayrhofer, Importance of different facial parts for face detection networks, *2021 IEEE International Workshop on Biometrics and Forensics (IWBF)*, 2021, pp. 1–6, doi: 10.1109/IWBF50991.2021.9465087.

9. E. Zangeneh, M. Rahmati, Y. Mohsenzadeh, Low resolution face recognition using a two-branch deep convolutional neural network architecture, Expert Systems with Applications, *2020 ELSEVIER Expert System with Applications*, 2020, Vol. 139, doi: 10.1016/j.eswa.2019.112854.

10. M. Sarma, A. K. Talukdar and K. K. Sarma, Deep Learning Based Face Mask Detection System for COVID-19 Control, *2021 Sixth International Conference on Image Information Processing (ICIIP)*, 2021, pp. 87–92, doi: 10.1109/ICIIP53038.2021.9702636.

11. F. M. J. Mehedi Shamrat, M. A. Jubair, M. M. Billah, S. Chakraborty, M. Alauddin and R. Ranjan, A Deep Learning Approach for Face Detection using Max Pooling, *2021 5th International Conference on Trends in Electronics and Informatics (ICOEI)*, 2021, pp. 760–764, doi: 10.1109/ICOEI51242.2021.9452896.

12. E. Zhang, A Real-Time Deep Transfer Learning Model for Facial Mask Detection, *2021 Integrated Communications Navigation and Surveillance Conference (ICNS)*, 2021, pp. 1–7, doi: 10.1109/ICNS52807.2021.9441582.

13. S. Srinivasan, R. Rujula Singh, R. R. Biradar and S. Revathi, COVID-19 Monitoring System using Social Distancing and Face Mask Detection on Surveillance video datasets, *2021 International Conference on Emerging Smart Computing and Informatics (ESCI)*, 2021, pp. 449–455, doi: 10.1109/ESCI50559.2021.9396783.

14. M. S. Ejaz and M. R. Islam, Masked Face Recognition Using Convolutional Neural Network, *2019 International Conference on Sustainable Technologies for Industry 4.0 (STI)*, 2019, pp. 1–6, doi: 10.1109/STI47673.2019.9068044.

15. M. S. Mazli Shahar and L. Mazalan, Face Identity for Face Mask Recognition System, *2021 IEEE 11th IEEE Symposium on Computer Applications & Industrial Electronics (ISCAIE)*, 2021, pp. 42–47, doi: 10.1109/ISCAIE51753.2021.9431791.

16. J. Gathani and K. Shah, Detecting Masked Faces using Region-based Convolutional Neural Network, *2020 IEEE 15th International Conference on Industrial and Information Systems (ICIIS)*, 2020, pp. 156–161, doi: 10.1109/ICIIS51140.2020.9342737.

Chapter 5

A Scalable System Architecture for Smart Cities Based on Cognitive IoT

Nabeela Hasan and Mansaf Alam
Jamia Millia Islamia University, New Delhi, India

5.1 Introduction

Smart cities are seeing a substantial increase in the amount of data generated by IoT-enabled devices. These linked gadgets offer information on how people interact with each other and with them individually as well as on how they can be improved. Conventional approaches have failed to offer consumers customized answers with a human touch. The combination of cognitive science and artificial intelligence (AI) has attracted the attention of both the academic community and industry. Cognitive computing is based on the idea of teaching AI to think like a human brain. It uses smart objects such as headgear, phones and other devices to learn about people's psychology, surroundings, speech, and social networks in order to offer reasoning skills comparable to those of humans. IBM's Watson cognitive computing technology demonstrated the ability of computers to perceive rationally like humans. Watson extricates data from documents without any human involvement or oversight and uses natural language processing to communicate as if it were a person.

DOI: 10.1201/9781003371380-5

The purpose of this chapter is to examine the problem of data scalability and flexibility in the context of cognitive computing systems implemented in a smart city setting. The chapter is structured as follows. Section 5.2 covers work related to the internet of things and cognitive IoT architectures, including their characteristics and essential components. Section 5.3 examines the architecture of smart cities in relation to IoT. In Section 5.4 we consider the technologies that allow the effective deployment of cognition-based systems and in Section 5.5 we explore new opportunities, problems, and advantages associated with implementing the proposed architecture. Section 5.6 concludes and discusses future work.

5.2 Related Work

This section describes the internet of things, elements of smart city design, IoT platforms and cognitive IoT architecture, all of which are relevant to the creation of scalable IoT systems.

5.2.1 IoT Architectural Design

In the internet of things, also identified as network architecture, material objects such as sensors, smart industries, actuators and other smart advances are linked to storage systems and share data [1]. Studies by Hwang et al. and Min Chen et al. [2], based on many previously established IoT designs, concluded that gathering diverse useful insights in the IoT issues of objects in the quantifiable environment through the internet creates a huge web of linked networks, while Sheth et al. [3] state that the IoT connects tremendous sensory devices in order to perform convergence of the data and physical worlds.

IoT architectures are designed to meet the massive and rapid data-processing needs for deep-data extraction utilizing cognitive computing functions.

In the new era of big data, the substantial rise in data and the constant upgrading of machine processing capability are inevitable [5]. As illustrated in Figure 5.1, the positioning of analyzers inside the IoT network is a distinctive characteristic of IoT systems. Each element of the architecture of the internet of things is described in Table 5.1.

The primary aim is to enhance the resilience of cities via the development of cognitive monitoring systems for the smart city which find and link those items that are important for the application at hand [6]. Research provides examples of IoT-related applications in which a cognitive system that enables collaboration among multiple devices is proposed [7]. The IoT architecture needs an identification framework where the mechanism for the management of different components and applications on IoT is coordinated and controlled [8]. The architecture is recognized as the critical component of the cohesive IoT service provider information center.

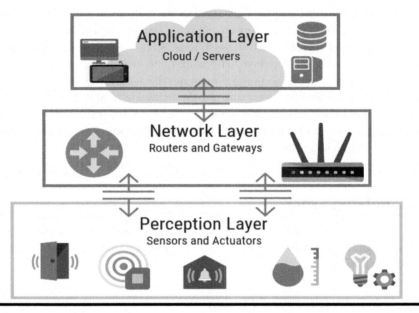

Figure 5.1   IoT layers [4].

Table 5.1   Different Layers in IoT Architecture

Layers	Responsibilities
Application layer	Creates technologically advanced environment such as intelligent home, smart devices, intelligent health and industries. Authenticity of data, plausibility and confidentiality.
Network layer	Collects data from perception layer (the bottom layer) and communicates to the application layer.
Perception layer	IoT sensor layer for packet collection, object identification, and transformation into a digital signal.

5.3 Cognitive Computing-based IoT Architecture

Today the internet of things is expanding quickly, with regular connections for more devices [9]. The CIoT is recognized as a structure or ecosystem in which everything and everyone are linked, Based on studies from LIDA [6] and SOAR [10], the presence of various kinds of structures based on significant architectures and agents in cognitive systems has also been explored. Zucker et al. [11] describe a cognitive design for buildings which utilizes these structures.

The idea of the cognitive IoT is to integrate, boost efficiency and attain cognition. CIoT is used to evaluate observed information, make smart choices, operate adaptively and monitor activities based on previous information. The IoT gathers vital items of information in real time from the physical realm to create comprehensive networking via the internet [12].

A study by Lin [13] presents decision making which includes semantic knowledge and cognition; Kawsar et al. [14] suggest health and safety management systems as well as other frameworks in IoT applications aimed at improving intellectual intelligence, for example in smart communities [15].

There are three main elements of the CIoT architecture for the smart city network: semantic modeling, machine learning and sensor components.

5.3.1 Cognitive Computing-based Smart City Architecture

Numerous data streams from multiple sensors are used to support diverse cognitive computing purposes. Fast and realistic tools can effectively serve the volatility of data generated by intelligent cities. The architecture suggested by CIoT has five layers.

Smart applications layer. This layer comprises several sub-layers, including intelligent buildings, housing, power, transit, industry and agriculture. The huge amount of data produced here includes both organized and unstructured data. Smart houses and apartments offer sensor data including various human characteristics such as sentiment, speech, neural activity, etc.

IoT layer. The IoT layer describes the sensor data on the number of devices. These sensors not only provide preliminary data to create cognitive computing techniques, but also provide a constant real-time image of the devices working effectively in various fields including IT, agriculture, transportation, construction, electricity and households. The collected data from all these devices are used to enhance various urban city services on the smart city application layer (Table 5.2).

Data layer. The data layer specifies the kind of knowledge collected from the sensors for human activities. These are essential for the development of the cognitive computer capacity AI system. The data layer includes components such as brain activity, emotions, environment, social media, speech recognition, gesture recognition and spatial-temporal data (Table 5.3).

Cognitive computing layer. This layer describes the design process for cognitive computing algorithms which includes data pre-processing, data analysis, cognitive feature identification and machine learning. We focus on data preparation, data analysis, extraction of cognitive characteristics, and machine

Table 5.2 Sub-layers of Smart Applications Layer

Sub-Layers	Functions
Smart buildings	Optimized service in elevators, light and HVAC systems. Also collects environmental and emotional data. Optimized energy utilization and air quality control using thermal analysis.
Smart home	Home activities management. Set temperature preferences.
Smart energy	Detects operational risks and maximizes uptime
Smart transport	Optimized real-time data on direction and speed. Service on time and more reliable.
Smart agriculture	Uses sensors to collect data. Locates crops ready to harvest, picks them and uses robots in place of labor.
Smart industry	Real-time optimized and productive decisions and better management of stocks and resources.

Table 5.3 Elements of Data Layer

Elements	Functions
Brain activity	Offers human brain-like analysis and approach towards any challenge.
Emotions	Detects facial expressions like dilated pupils, muscle spasms, etc.
Environment	Decisions are based on proper contextual environment with conditions like tasks, position, goals, etc.
Social media	By integrating human analysis from social networks with cognitive-based AI, we may achieve a deeper study of organizational emotions.
Speech recognition	Training cognitive AI from speech has numerous uses, particularly in customer support. Human speech tones, eagerness, and tension may be captured and utilized to teach AI to offer customized customer assistance.

(Continued)

Table 5.3 (Continued)

Elements	Functions
Gesture recognition	When integrating movements with AI, there are many applications, such as controlled systems and assistance for individuals with physical problems, stroke patients, etc.
Spatial-temporal data	Such data is used to teach robots navigation and build location and time understanding. Humans utilize this ability to solve puzzles and organize themselves by first picturing the issue and afterwards tackling it with determination.

Table 5.4 Cognitive Computing Algorithm Design Process

Design Step	Function
Data pre-processing	Source data may be inaccurate or imprecise. Inclusion of this data will result in ineffective cognitive computing AI models. The missing value is either deleted if it is irrelevant to the result, or restored to prevent data loss.
Data analysis	Data analysis is the identification of cognitive characteristics important to our model's training. Rather than developing a single cognitive model for every use case in the smart city, multiple characteristics are chosen.
Cognitive feature identification	Spatial-temporal, feelings, speech, and neural activity data are collected as psychological data. Activity features are gathered from the user's surroundings and actions. Brain function, sentiments, and social networks derive social characteristics.
Machine learning	Cognitive computing has moved it a level further by combining people and machines thinking in a more natural manner.

learning processes. This layer generates an algorithm based on selected features, allowing for more customized smart city solutions. We offer a cognitive computing-based AI model (Table 5.4).

Service layer. This layer addresses CIoT implementation in a smart city, including legal, fire safety, police, healthcare, autonomous cars, retailing, and journalism (see Table 5.5). Unlike earlier organized data-oriented machine learning techniques or database systems, cognitive computing employs complex data.

Table 5.5   Application of Cognitive Computing Architecture in Smart City

Applications	Benefits
Legal	Cognitive computing uses historical legal texts, voice recognition and spatial-temporal information to help legal firms find better answers. It provides legal organizations with advice on how to continue with a case and is regarded as a complement rather than a substitute.
Fire prevention	In addition to detecting and alerting the degree of danger, the system may offer real-time evaluation should the potential risk rise. Cognitive applications can help save the lives of firemen and others.
Police	It gives investigators a better sense of what to expect and can locate suspects. Providing historical and contextual information about a crime scene may help detectives.
Healthcare	The algorithm will propose a diagnosis based on the research of indicators that may have been missed by human negligence.
Autonomous cars	Spatial-temporal, brain activity and environmental data are utilized to offer real-time traffic analysis and improve personal security.
Retailing	It predicts demand for goods based on user preferences and the surroundings. This contains climate and location data.
Journalism	Businesses may utilize sources like social networks, sentiments, and speech to create ads that engage customers. Advertisers may offer more customized material that peaks user interest by using environmental data.

5.4   Assistive Technologies in Cognitive Computing

This section discusses the technological innovations that are necessary for the effective deployment of the cognitive architectures shown in Figure 5.2.

Earlier versions of machine learning have supported many applications, including image analysis, pattern identification and information security. However, it is not suitable for contemporary AI systems based on cognitive computing [16]. Reinforcement learning can acquire data from its surroundings and enhance its algorithm while learning in depth can learn numerous high-level characteristics

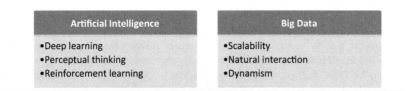

Figure 5.2   Cognitive computing technologies.

[14, 17]. The enormous amount of data produced in structured and unstructured form from IoT-based smart sensors, digital technologies and software applications is growing.

Cognitive systems are fundamental needs when data processing, convergence and accumulation take effect [18]. Interpretation of the data set will help with better identification and settlement of a complicated set of issues when a wide range of sources of information exist [19]. This information may be regarded as unorganized, organized, text and multimedia.

5.5   Conclusion

In this study, we have proposed a novel cognitive IoT systems architecture. The proposed system has numerous cognitive characteristics that not only handle diverse applications but also provide solutions in real time on a smart city framework. The need for individual setups is minimized for different and dynamic intelligent city-based applications. The cognitive computing architecture suggested tackles the contemporary challenge of the complexity and scalability of massive IoT data, which impacts intelligent cities. A CIoT-based network architecture for intelligent cities is proposed, and its possibilities and difficulties are examined.

References

1. Xu H, Yu W, Griffith D, Golmie N (2018). A survey on industrial internet of things: a cyber-physical systems perspective. *IEEE Access* 6:78238–78259.
2. Chen M, Herrera F, Hwang K (2018). Cognitive computing: architecture, technologies and intelligent applications. *IEEE Access* 6:19774–19783.
3. Sheth A (2016). Internet of things to smart IoT through semantic, cognitive, and perceptual computing. *IEEE Intell Syst* 31(2):108–112.
4. Calihman, A (2019). Architectures in the IoT Civilization. NetBurner. Available at: https://www.netburner.com/learn/architectural-frameworks-in-the-iot-civilization
5. Ramírez S, Fernández A, García S, Chen M, Herrera F (2018). Big data: tutorial and guidelines on information and process fusion for analytics algorithms with MapReduce. *Inf Fusion* 1(42):51–61.
6. Vanus J, Belesova J, Martinek R, Nedoma J, Fajkus M, Bilik P, Zidek J (2017). Monitoring of the daily living activities in smart home care. *Hum-Centric Comput Inf Sci* 7:30.

7. Chiang M, Zhang T (2016). Fog and IoT: an overview of research opportunities. *IEEE Internet Things J* 3(6):854–864.
8. Ammar M, Russello G, Crispo B (2018). Internet of Things: a survey on the security of IoT frameworks. *J Inf Secur Appl* 1(38):8–27.
9. Zhang M, Zhao H, Zheng R, Wu Q, Wei W (2012). Cognitive internet of things: concepts and application example. *Int J Comput Sci Issues (IJCSI)* 9:151.
10. Franklin S, Madl T, D'Mello S, Snaider J (2014). LIDA: a systems-level architecture for cognition, emotion, and learning. *IEEE Trans Auton Ment Dev* 6:19–41.
11. Zucker G, Habib U, Blöchle M, Wendt A, Schaat S, Siafara LC (2015). Building energy management and data analytics. In: *2015 international symposium on smart electric distribution systems and technologies (EDST)*, Vienna
12. Chen M, Miao Y, Hao Y, Hwang K (2017). Narrow band internet of things. *IEEE Access* 5:20557–20577.
13. Reisenzein R, Hudlicka E, Dastani M, Gratch J, Hindriks K, Lorini E, Meyer JJ (2013). Computational modeling of emotion: toward improving the inter-and intradisciplinary exchange. *IEEE Trans Affect Comput* 4:246–266.
14. Zhang L, Tan J, Han D, Zhu H (2017). From machine learning to deep learning: progress in machine intelligence for rational drug discovery. *Drug Discov Today* 22:1680–1685.
15. Foschini L, Taleb T, Corradi A, Bottazzi D (2011). M2M-based metropolitan platform for IMS-enabled road traffic management in IoT. *IEEE Commun Mag* 49:50–57.
16. Liu Q, Li P, Zhao W, Cai W, Yu S, Leung VC (2018). A survey on security threats and defensive techniques of machine learning: a data driven view. *IEEE Access* 6:12103–12117.
17. Nguyen ND, Nguyen T, Nahavandi S (2017). System design perspective for human-level agents using deep reinforcement learning: a survey. *IEEE Access* 5:27091–27102.
18. Chen Y, Argentinis JE, Weber G (2016). IBM Watson: how cognitive computing can be applied to big data challenges in life sciences research. *Clin Ther* 38:688–701.
19. Santos MY, Oliveira e Sá J, Andrade C, Lima FV, Costa E, Costa C, Martinho B, Galvão J (2017). A big data system supporting Bosch Braga Industry 4.0 strategy. *Int J Inf Manag* 37:750–760.

Chapter 6

Bagging-Based Ensemble Learning for Imbalanced Data Classification Problem

M. Govindarajan
Annamalai University, Annamalai Nagar, India

6.1 Introduction

Machine learning plays an important role in many prediction problems by constructing a model from an explored dataset. The most common task in the learning process is classification. Classification is the process of assigning an input item in a collection to predefined classes by discovering relationships between instances in the training set. Classification learning becomes complicated if the class distribution of the data is imbalanced. The class imbalance problem occurs when the number of representative instances is much less than that of other instances. In order to solve the imbalance problemand improve classification accuracy, this paper proposes new ensemble classification methods. The paper describes application of homogeneous ensemble classifiers to a standard automobiles dataset. Organization of this paper is as follows. Section 6.2 describes related work. Section 6.3 presents the proposed methodology and Section 6.4 explains the performance evaluation measures.

DOI: 10.1201/9781003371380-6

Section 6.5 focuses on the experimental results and discussion. A summary of results and conclusions is presented in Section 6.6.

6.2 Related Work

Jianhong Yan and Suqing Han [1] proposed a novel RE-sample and cost-sensitive stacked generalization (RECSG) method based on two-layer learning models. The first step is Level0 model generalization, including data pre-processing and base model training. The second step is Level1 model generalization, involving a cost-sensitive classifier and logistic regression algorithm. In the learning phase, pre-processing techniques can be embedded in imbalanced data learning methods. In the cost-sensitive algorithm, the cost matrix is combined with both data characters and algorithms. In the RECSG method, the ensemble algorithm is combined with imbalance data techniques.

Pelin Yıldırım et al. [2] proposed a novel ensemble-based ordinal classification (EBOC) approach which suggests bagging and boosting methods (AdaBoost algorithm) as a solution to the ordinal classification problem in the transportation sector. Here we compare the proposed EBOC approach with ordinal class classifier and traditional tree-based classification algorithms (i.e., C4.5decision tree, RandomTree, and REPTree) in terms of accuracy.

Goksu Tuysuzoglu and Derya Birant [3] proposed a novel modified version of bagging, called enhanced bagging (eBagging), which uses a new mechanism (error-based bootstrapping) when constructing training sets, in order to cope with this problem. In the experimental setting, the proposed eBagging technique was tested on 33 well-known benchmark datasets and compared with both bagging, random forest and boosting techniques using well-known classification algorithms: support vector machine(SVM), decision trees (C4.5), k-nearest neighbor (kNN) and naive Bayes (NB).

Cui Yin Huang and Hong Liang Dai [4] provided a review of class-imbalanced learning methods from data-driven methods and algorithm-driven methods based on numerous published papers studying class imbalance learning. Their preliminary analysis shows that class-imbalanced learning methods find their mainapplications in management and engineering.

Tebogo Bokaba et al. [5] performed a comparative analysis of ensemble methods using road traffic congestion data. Ensemble methods are capable of enhancing the performance of weak classifiers. The comparative analysis was conducted using a real-world dataset and bagging, boosting, stacking and random forest ensemble models to compare the predictive performance of the methods. Ensemble prediction models were developed to predict road traffic congestion, and evaluated using the following performance metrics: accuracy, precision, recall, F1-score, and the misclassification cost viewed as a penalty for errors incurred during the classification process.

6.3 Proposed Methodology

6.3.1 Pre-processing

Before performing any classification method, the data has to be preprocessed. In the data pre-processing stage, it has been observed that the datasets contain many missing value attributes. Eliminating the missing attribute records may lead to misclassification because the dropped records may contain some useful patterns. The dataset is preprocessed by removing missing values using supervised filters.

6.3.2 Existing Classification Methods

6.3.2.1 Radial Basis Function Neural Network

The radial basis function network (RBF) is in its simplest form a three-layered feedforward neural network with one input layer, one hidden layer and one output layer [6]. It differs from an MLP in the way the hidden layer performs its computation. The connection between the input layer and the output layer is nonlinear, while the connection between the hidden layer and the output layer is linear. RBF networks are instance based, meaning that each training case is compared and evaluated against the previously examined training cases. In an MLP all instances are evaluated once, while in an RBF network the instances are evaluated locally [7]. Instance-based methods use nearest neighbor and locally weighted regression methods. An RBF network can be trained more efficiently than a neural net using backpropagation, since the input and output layers are trained separately.

6.3.2.2 Support Vector Machine

Support vector machines were introduced by Vapnik and colleagues [8]. SVM models are very similar to classical multilayer perceptron neural networks used for classification [9], but recently they have been extended to solve regression problems [10]. SVM is very similar to an ANN since both receive input data and provide output data. For regression, the input and output of SVM are identical to those of the ANN. However, what makes the SVM better is that, unlike the ANN, it does not suffer from overfitting. So the ANN memorizes the input data at the training stage and will not perform well on the testing data.

6.3.3 Homogeneous Ensemble Classifiers

6.3.3.1 Dagging

This meta-classifier creates a number of disjoint, stratified folds out of the data and feeds each chunk of data to a copy of the supplied base classifier. Predictions are made via majority vote, since all the generated base classifiers are put into the Vote meta-classifier. It is useful for base classifiers that are quadratic or worse in time behavior, regarding the number of instances in the training data.

6.3.3.2 ECOC

Error-correcting output codes (ECOC) are commonly used in information theory for correcting bit reversals caused by noisy communication channels, or in machine learning for converting binary classifiers such as support vector machines to multi-class classifiers by decomposing a multi-class problem into several two-class problems [11]. Dietterich and Bakiri introduced ECOC to be used within the ensemble setting. The idea is to use a different class encoding for each member of the ensemble [12].

6.3.3.3 Proposed Bagged RBF and SVM Classifiers

Given a set D, of d tuples, bagging [13] works as follows. For iteration i ($i = 1, 2, \ldots, k$), a training set, D_i, of d tuples is sampled with replacement from the original set of tuples, D. The bootstrap sample, D_i, created by repeatedly sampling D with a replacement from the given training data set D. Each example in the given training set D may appear repeatedly or not at all in any particular replicate training data set D_i. A classifier model, M_i, is learned for each training set, D_i. To classify an unknown tuple, X, each classifier, M_i, returns its class prediction, which counts as one vote. The bagged RBF and SVM, M^*, counts the votes and assigns the class with the most votes to X.

ALGORITHM   RBF AND SVM ENSEMBLE CLASSIFIERS USING BAGGING

Input:

- D, a set of d tuples.
- $k = 2$, the number of models in the ensemble.
- Base classifiers (radial basis function, support vector machine)

Output: Bagged RBF and SVM, M^*

Method:

(1) For $i = 1$ to k do // create k models
(2) Create a bootstrap sample, D_i, by repeatedly sampling D with a replacement from the given training data set D. Each example in the given training set D may appear repeatedly or not at all in any particular replicate training data set D_i
(3) Use D_i to derive a model, M_i;

(4) Classify each example d in training data D_i and initialize the weight, W_i for the model, M_i, based on the accuracies of the percentage of correctly classified examples in training data D_i.

(5) endfor

To use the bagged RBF and SVM models on a tuple, X:

1. if classification then
2. let each of the k models classify X and return the majority vote;
3. if prediction then
4. let each of the k models predict a value for X and return the average predicted value.

6.4 Performance Evaluation Measures

6.4.1 Cross-Validation Technique

Cross-validation [14], sometimes called rotation estimation, is a technique for assessing how the results of a statistical analysis will generalize to an independent data set. It is mainly used in settings where the goal is prediction and one wants to estimate how accurately a predictive model will perform in practice. 10-fold cross-validation is commonly used. In stratified K-fold cross-validation, the folds are selected so that the mean response value is approximately equal in all the folds.

6.4.2 Criteria for Evaluation

The primary metric for evaluating classifier performance is classification accuracy: the percentage of test samples that a given classifier can correctly predict the label of new or previously unseen data (i.e., tuples without class label information). Similarly, the accuracy of a predictor refers to how well a given predictor can guess the value of the predicted attribute for new or previously unseen data.

6.5 Experimental Results and Discussion

6.5.1 Vehicle Dataset Description

This dataset classifies a given silhouette from four different vehicle types, with a set of features that are extracted from the silhouette by the hierarchical image processing system extension BINATTS.

6.5.2 Experiments and Analysis

In this section, new ensemble classification methods are proposed with homogeneous ensembles using bagging, and their performances are analyzed in terms of accuracy.

In this research work, new ensemble classification methods are proposed with homogeneous ensembles using bagging, and their performances are analyzed in terms of accuracy. Here, the base classifiers are constructed using radial basis function and support vector machine. Bagging is performed with radial basis function classifier and support vector machine to obtain a very good classification performance. Table 6.1 show classification performances for a standard dataset of automobiles using existing and proposed bagged radial basis function neural network and support vector machine.

The results show that the proposed bagged radial basis function and bagged support vector machine classifiers are shown to be superior to individual approaches for a standard dataset of automobile problems in terms of classification accuracy. According to Figure 6.1, the proposed combined models show a significantly larger improvement of classification accuracy than the base classifiers, and the results are found to be statistically significant. This means that the combined methods are more accurate than the individual methods in the field of automobiles. Table 6.1 compares the performance of the proposed bagged RBF and SVM to the performance of ECOC and Dagging with RBF and SVM. The proposed bagged RBF and SVM performs significantly better than ECOC and Dagging on a standard automobiledataset.

Table 6.1 The Performance of Base Classifiers and Homogeneous Ensemble Classifiers for Automobiles

Dataset	Classifiers	Classification Accuracy (%)
Vehicle	RBF	66.66
	Proposed Bagged RBF	78.36
	ECOC RBF	66.43
	Dagged RBF	73.28
	SVM	74.34
	Proposed Bagged SVM	76.83
	ECOC SVM	69.62
	Dagged SVM	66.66

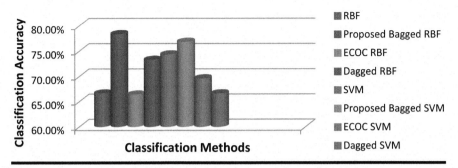

Figure 6.1 Accuracy for homogeneous ensemble classifiers in vehicle dataset.

6.6 Conclusion

In this research work, new combined classification methods are proposed with homogeneous ensembles using bagging, and their performance accuracy has been compared using a standard automobile dataset. Here, the proposed bagged radial basis function and bagged support vector machine combine the complementary features of the base classifiers. The performance of the proposed homogeneous ensemble classifiers are compared to the performance of other standard homogeneous ensemble methods. The standard homogeneous ensemble methods include ECOC andDagging. The experiment results lead to the following observations.

- SVM exhibits better performance than RBF in the important respect of accuracy.
- The proposed bagged methods showsignificantly higher classification accuracy than the base classifiers.
- The proposed ensemble methods provide significantly improved accuracy compared to individual classifiers, and the proposed bagged RBF and SVM perform significantly better than ECOC and Dagging.

Future research will be directed towards developing more accurate base classifiers, particularly for the automobile problem.

Acknowledgment

The author gratefully acknowledges the authorities of Annamalai University for the use of its facilities and the encouragement to carry out this work.

References

1. Jianhong Yan and Suqing Han, (2018). Classifying imbalanced data sets by a novel RE-sample and cost-sensitive stacked generalization method, *Mathematical Problems in Engineering*, 2018:1–13.
2. Pelin Yıldırım, Ula GK Birant, and Derya Birant, (2019). EBOC: Ensemble-based ordinal classification in transportation, *Journal of Advanced Transportation*, 2019:1–17.
3. Goksu Tuysuzoglu and Derya Birant, (2020). Enhanced bagging (eBagging): A novel approach for ensemble learning, *The International Arab Journal of Information Technology*, 17(4):515–528.
4. Cui Yin Huang and Hong Liang Dai, (2021). Learning from class-imbalanced data: Review of data driven methods and algorithm driven methods, *DSFE*, 1(1):21–36.
5. Tebogo Bokaba, Wesley Doorsamy and Babu Sena Paul, (2022). A comparative study of ensemble models for predicting road traffic congestion, *Applied Sciences*, 12:1337.
6. Robert Callan, (1998). *Essence of Neural Networks*. Prentice Hall PTR Upper Saddle River, NJ, USA.
7. Tom M. Mitchell, (1997). *Machine Learning*, New York, McGraw-Hill.
8. Cortes Corinna and Vladimir Vapnik, (1995). Support vector networks, *Machine Learning*, 20(3):273–297.
9. Ruan Hua and Dai Liankui, (2010). Support vector machine classification and regression based hybrid modeling method and its application in Raman spectral analysis, *Chinese Journal of Scientific Instrument*, 11:2440–2446.
10. Vapnik Vladimir, Steven Golowich, and Alex Smola, (1997). Support vector method for function approximation, regression estimation, and signal processing, *Advances in Neural Information Processing Systems*, 9:281–287.
11. Erin L. Allwein, Robert E. Schapire, and Yoram Singer, (2000). Reducing multiclass to binary: A unifying approach for margin classifiers, *Journal of Machine Learning Research*, 1:113–141.
12. Thomas G. Dietterich and Ghulum Bakiri, (1995). Solving multiclass learning problems via error-correcting output codes, *Journal of Artificial Intel Research*, 2:263–286.
13. Leo Breiman, (1996). Bagging predictors, *Machine Learning*, 24(2):123–140.
14. Jiawei Han and Micheline Kamber, (2003). *Data Mining – Concepts and Techniques*. Morgan Kaufman Publishers, Inc. San Francisco, CA.

Chapter 7

Design and Implementation of a Network Security Model within a Local Area Network

Aderonke J. Ikuomola, Kehinde S. Owoputi, and Stephen O. Johnson-Rokosu

Olusegun Agagu University of Science and Technology, Okitipupa, Nigeria

7.1 Introduction

Security on the internet and networks is a crucial issue in a computer network [1]. With advances in networking and the internet, the threats to information and networks and damage to the network infrastructure have been on the increase due to vulnerabilities arising from misconfiguration of hardware/software, poor network design, technology flaws and carelessness on the part of end users. Information is a valuable asset that needs to be secured so the user does not risk losing it [2, 3].

Network security is an important area of interest [4, 5] and the most vital element of information security, because it is responsible for securing all information that passes through the computer network [6]. The aims of security are protection of confidentiality, maintenance of integrity and assurance of availability [3].

DOI: 10.1201/9781003371380-7

Network administrators for companies, organizations and institutions need to implement secure models in order to prevent information loss within a network. These models will help to secure information stored within the network, provide protection against fortuitous data corruption, and assist with sharing information with people who are authorized to have access to the network.

Routers and switches are important parts of network operations and their security needs to be properly managed. Proper management of these components can help reduce network downtime, improve security, prevent attacks, reduce network threats and contribute to the analysis of suspected security breaches.

The present work describes a network security model within a LAN using VLAN, access control list and port security, designed to provide solutions for the protection and security of information assets and networks in an organization. This network security model was tested within a simulated environment using Olusegun Agagu University of Science and Technology (OAUSTECH) Virtual Local Area Network (VLAN), which consists of the Faculty of Science (VLAN 100), Faculty of Engineering (VLAN 200) and Faculty of Agriculture (VLAN 300).

The work is organized as follows. A literature review is provided in Section 7.2. Section 7.3 describes the design methodology for a network security model within a local area network. Implementation is described in Section 7.4. Section 7.5 concludes the research work.

7.1.1 Problem Statement

Threats to information and networks have been on the increase due to vulnerabilities arising from misconfiguration of hardware/software, poor network design, technology flaws and carelessness on the part of end users which can cause a lot of damage to network infrastructure. Insecurity has become a major threat to companies, organizations and institutions, resulting in the need for network administrators to implement secure models to prevent information loss within a network. These models will help to secure information stored within the network and provide protection against fortuitous data corruption.

7.2 Literature Review

The authors of Alabady [3] developed a network security model with routers and firewall. The network operations were examined using different steps to test the robustness of the network security against different types of attacks and scanning tools were used to simulate real network attacks. Although the security performance of the model is very effective and it has a high network speed and services, the network security can be reduced due to poor router filtering configuration exposing internal network components to scans and attacks.

In Poonam et al. [7] a way of securing a private network using ACL was proposed. They simulated the network using a Cisco Packet Tracer. The private network was configured using the standard ACL to either grant or deny packets based on source IP address within the network. The system allowed the flow of network packets *in/out* of router interfaces. The limitation is that it prevents telnet communications within the network.

The author of Tambe [8] proposed a means of segmenting a network using VLAN. The system provides greater flexibility and an easy way of partitioning resources in a network, and is cost-effective, but the network is not 100% secured and is vulnerable to some attacks.

In Alimi and Mufutau [9], a method of enhancing network performance using VLAN and implementing the IEEE 802.1Q trunking protocol frame-tagging mechanism was put forward. The model enhances security within the network and improves network management. The network is not scalable and there is no inter-communication between the VLANs.

Implementation of a VLAN using a network simulator was carried out by Ali [10]. VLANs were used as a substitute for routers for broadcast containment. The network is cost-effective but there is no inter-communication between different VLANs and the network is vulnerable to attack.

Research in Maddipatla and Agarwal [11] proposed a switch port security model for reducing the traffic on LANs. It regulates network traffic by providing security to the switch interfaces. The strength of this model is that network reliability and port bandwidth are guaranteed and security of the network is certain. The limitation is that flooding attacks can occur within the switch when more than one MAC address is being assigned to the switch port.

The authors of Agrawal et al. [12] designed and implemented an internet protocol traffic management using ACL to analyze and simulate the network. The design reduces network traffic and improves network performance but packet loss does occur within the network.

An LAN using a network simulator was implemented in Isaac et al. [13], which also explained various concepts such as the topology design, IP configuration, information transmission and the use of VLANs. The network model is robust and easy to implement but it is vulnerable to attacks due to some security configurations (access control list and port security) that were not implemented within the network.

In Varsha [14], a network security model using various securities was designed and implemented. Multiple routing protocols were used in different areas. The network design follows Cisco standard three-layer architecture and it can prevent different attacks. The network memory requirements are high and it uses expensive layer 3 switches.

The researchers in Kulkarni et al. [15] proposed an ACL which was configured on all routed network protocols to filter packets as they pass through a router. Although the network provides additional security by denying host or IP addresses, it is difficult to manage and packet loss occurs within the network.

Table 7.1 Comparison of Reviewed Network Security Models

Author (s)	VLAN	ACL	Port Security	Security	Connectivity
Alabady (2009) [3]	No	No	No	Medium	Yes
Poonam et al. (2014) [7]	No	Yes	No	High	No
Alimi and Mufutau (2015) [9]	Yes	No	No	Medium	No
Ali (2015) [10]	Yes	No	No	Low	No
Maddipatla and Agarwal (2015) [11]	Yes	No	Yes	Medium	Yes
Tambe (2015) [8]	Yes	No	No	Low	Yes
Agrawal et al. (2016) [12]	No	Yes	No	Medium	No
Kulkarni et al. (2017) [15]	No	Yes	No	High	No
Varsha (2017) [14]	No	No	No	Medium	Yes
Isaac et al. (2017) [13]	Yes	No	No	Low	Yes

In our study a network security model within a local area network (LAN) was designed and implemented. The model is cost-effective, and provides an easy way of partitioning resources and preventing unauthorized users within the network. Table 7.1 compares the reviewed network security models.

7.3 Design Methodology

7.3.1 Design Consideration

The following are included in the network security model.

1) *VLAN* is a group of devices on one or more LANs that are configured to communicate as if they were on the same LAN segment when actually they are on different LAN segments.

2) *Access Control Lists* are sets of commands used to filter incoming/outgoing traffic within the network. They tell the operating system the access rights to be given to each user.
3) *Port Security* is used to restrict input to an interface. It restricts and identifies the MAC addresses of the workstations that are allowed to access the port within the network.

7.3.2 Architecture of a Network Security Model within a LAN

The architecture of a network security model is shown in Figure 7.1. The system comprises a switch, router, network server, network printer, and networking cable. The proposed system supports the use of VLAN, ACL and port security.

During the setup of the network, VLAN was used to logically segment the network to save cost and for easy maintenance. ACL was used to protect the network. The port security prevented packets being forwarded to the network by an unknown device and also reduced the number of MAC addresses on a given port.

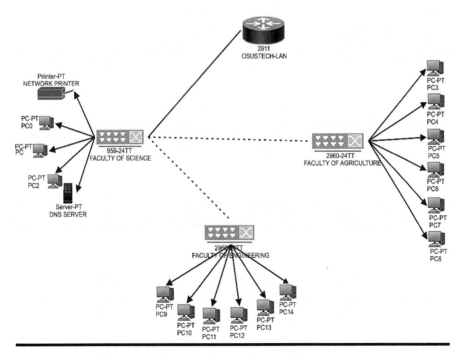

Figure 7.1   Architecture of a network security model.

7.3.3 Software Specification

Packet Tracer, a simulation tool, was used to create simulated network topologies. It can run on Linux, Microsoft Windows and MacOS.

7.4 Implementation

The system was implemented using Cisco Packet Tracer and was tested with a network security model within a simulated environment using Olusegun Agagu University of Science and Technology, Okitipupa (OAUSTECH).

7.4.1 Network Security Model Implementation Requirements

The network model requirement is defined in terms of the hardware, software components and IP addresses used in configuring various devices within the model that contribute to the effectiveness of the implementation process. Table 7.2 shows the configuration device requirements.

Table 7.3 gives information on the IP addresses used in setting up and configuring the network model.

7.4.2 The Implemented Local Area Network (LAN) Model and its Configurations

This section describes how the network security model was configured within a LAN. Figure 7.2 shows the network design model of the OAUSTECH which consists of several sections. Each section represents VLAN, with the Faculty of Science representing VLAN 100 with IP address **198.165.10.0** 255.255.255.0, the Faculty of Engineering representing VLAN 200 with IP address **198.165.20.0** 255.255.0.0, and finally the Faculty of Agriculture representing VLAN 300 with IP address **198.165.30.0** 255.255.255.0. This network model consists of three switches and a

Table 7.2 Device Requirements

Device	Quantity	Model
PCs	15	Generic
Switches	3	Cisco 2960
Router	1	Cisco 2911
Network Printer	1	Generic
Network Server	1	Generic

Table 7.3   IP Table

VLAN/Interface	IP Address/ Network Address	Subnet Mask
VLAN 100	198.165.10.0	255.255.255.0
VLAN 200	198.165.20.0	255.255.255.0
VLAN 300	198.165.30.0	255.255.255.0
Interface G0/0.1	198.165.10.1	255.255.255.0
Interface G0/0.2	198.165.20.1	255.255.255.0
Interface G0/0.3	198.165.30.1	255.255.255.0

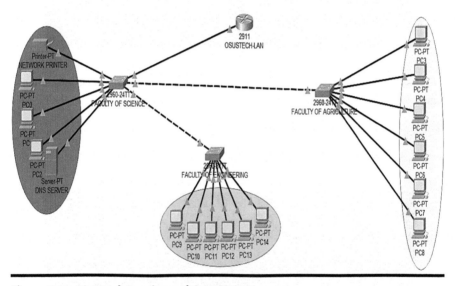

Figure 7.2   Network topology of OAUSTECH.

router. The switches in the various faculties were used to create its VLANs while the router played the role of inter-communication between the different VLANs created in the network.

Figure 7.3 is a screenshot of the configuration when setting up the VLAN within the LAN and also the VLAN trunking protocol (VTP), which allows the core switch to act as a server while other switches connected to it acts as clients.

Figure 7.4 is a screenshot of the inter-VLAN commands configured in the router to enhance communication between the different configured VLANs within the LAN network security model.

```
SCIENCE                                              —    □    ×

  Physical    Config    CLI    Attributes

                    IOS Command Line Interface

  Switch>enable
  Switch#configure terminal
  Enter configuration commands, one per line.  End with
  CNTL/Z.
  Switch(config)#hostname SCIENCE
  SCIENCE(config)#VTP MODE SERVER
  Device mode already VTP SERVER.
  SCIENCE(config)#VTP DOMAIN OSUSTECH
  Changing VTP domain name from NULL to OSUSTECH
  SCIENCE(config)#VLAN 100
  SCIENCE(config-vlan)#NAME SCIENCE
  SCIENCE(config-vlan)#VLAN 200
  SCIENCE(config-vlan)#NAME ENGINEERING
  SCIENCE(config-vlan)#VLAN 300
  SCIENCE(config-vlan)#NAME AGRICULTURE
  SCIENCE(config-vlan)#

  Ctrl+F6 to exit CLI focus                    Copy      Paste
```

Figure 7.3   VLAN configuration.

```
OSUSTECH-LAN                                         —    □    ×

  Physical    Config    CLI    Attributes

                    IOS Command Line Interface

  Router#CONF T
  Enter configuration commands, one per line.  End with
  CNTL/Z.
  Router(config)#INT G0/0.1
  Router(config-subif)#encapsulation dot1q 100
  Router(config-subif)#ip address 198.165.10.1
  255.255.255.0
  Router(config-subif)#no shut
  Router(config-subif)#INT G0/0.2
  Router(config-subif)#encapsulation dot1q 200
  Router(config-subif)#ip address 198.165.20.1
  255.255.255.0
  Router(config-subif)#no shut
  Router(config-subif)#INT G0/0.3
  Router(config-subif)#encapsulation dot1q 300
  Router(config-subif)#ip address 198.165.30.1
  255.255.255.0
  Router(config-subif)#no shut
  Router(config-subif)#
```

Figure 7.4   Inter-VLAN configuration.

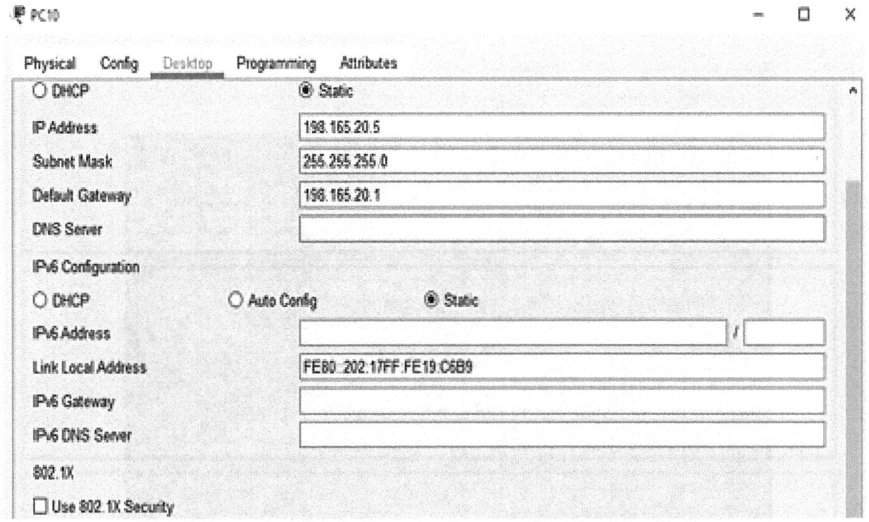

Figure 7.5   PC configuration.

Figure 7.5 is a screenshot of the PC configuration showing how an IP and gateway addresses are assigned to a host or personal computer within the network, which makes them easily identifiable within their segmented VLANs and able to communicate with other VLANs within the network security model.

Figure 7.6 shows the port security commands that have been configured in one of the VLANs within the network model. Each PC has its port number connected to the switch and its MAC address.

Figure 7.7 shows the access control list command configured on the router. The ACL command was used as a packet filter firewall within the LAN model which helps to check the incoming packet IP addresses against a list of trusted addresses and rejects unmatched addresses.

7.4.3 Results

7.4.3.1 Ping Test

A ping command was used to test the network connectivity and communication, followed by the IP address of the device. The ping test was performed between the Faculty of Agriculture and the Faculty of Science, and between the Faculty of Engineering and the Faculty of Agriculture, as shown in Figures 7.8 and 7.9 respectively. The test shows that the devices connected to the VLANs were communicating with other devices on the network.

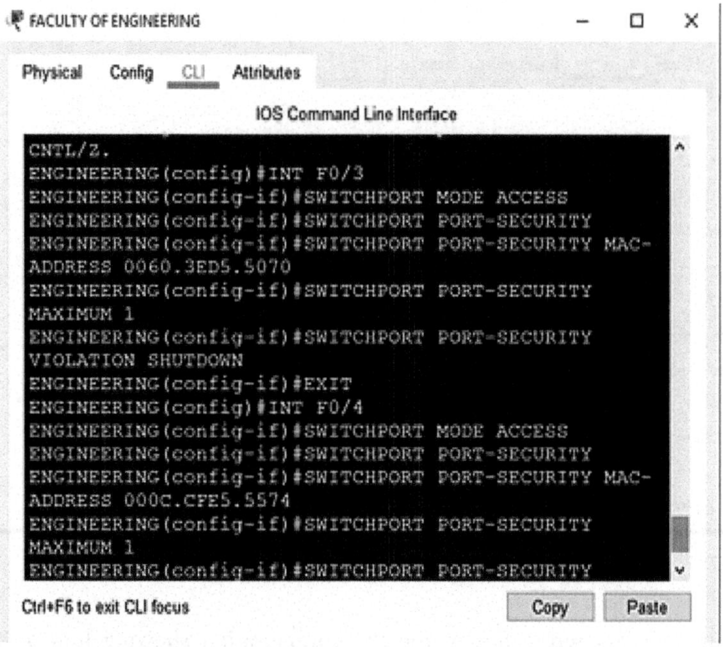

Figure 7.6   Port security configuration.

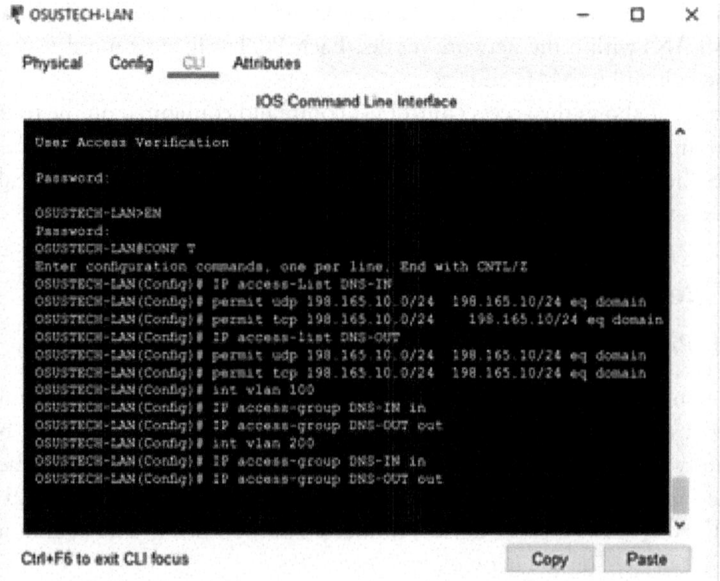

Figure 7.7   Access control list command.

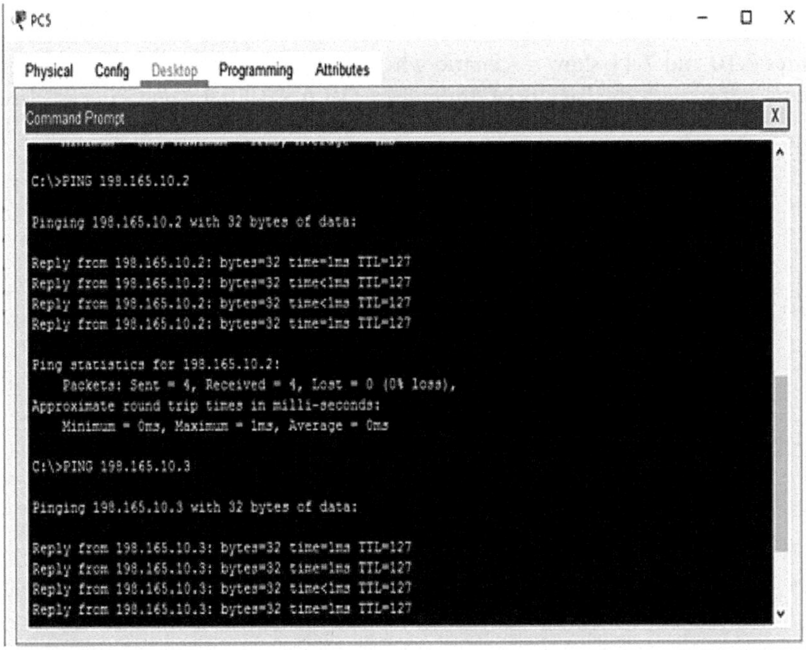

Figure 7.8 Inter -LAN communication between Faculty of Agriculture and Faculty of Science.

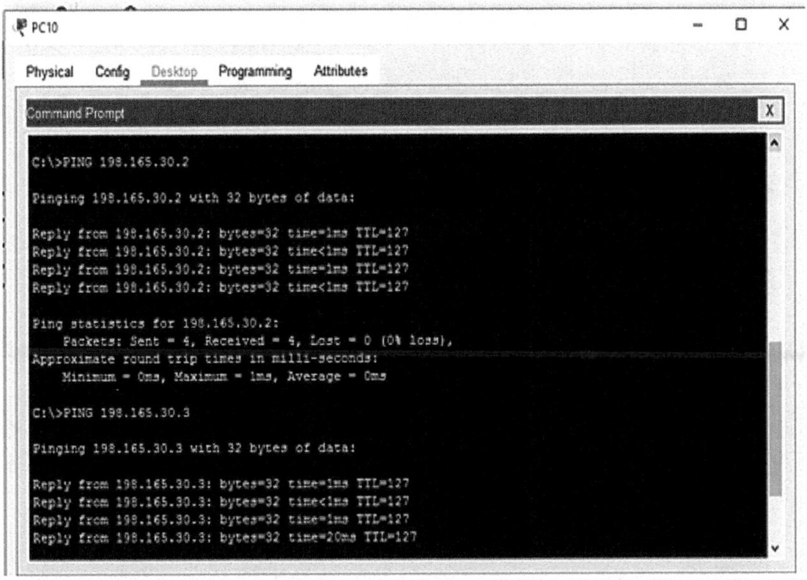

Figure 7.9 Inter-VLAN communication between Faculty of Engineering and Faculty of Agriculture.

7.4.3.2 Port Security

Figures 7.10 and 7.11 show a scenario whereby an unauthorized user tries to connect its laptop with the Faculty of Agriculture (VLAN 300), by replacing an already

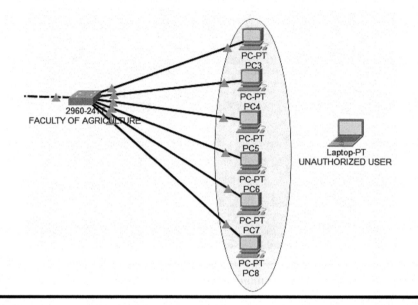

Figure 7.10   Port security 1.

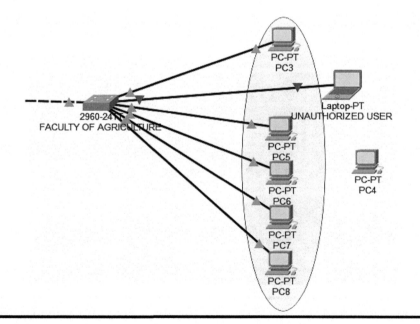

Figure 7.11   Port security 2.

configured PC. Figure 7.10 shows that when the laptop of the unauthorized user was connected to a switch port which has port security commands already configured on it, the switch port automatically shut down. The port in which the unauthorized user tries to connect is colored red because the unknown laptop MAC address has not been included on the switch port MAC address table.

7.5 Conclusion

This work described a network security model implemented within a LAN using Cisco Packet Tracer. Using this model can give network administrators of an organization or a company more insight on how to prevent unauthorized access to its resources or loss of vital data/information to hackers/intruders, and it can also save costs when setting up a network. The most prominent feature of the model is that it provides an easy way of partitioning resources within the network, and the techniques implemented in the network model help to improve network security significantly.

In future, it might be necessary to implement network security model using Internet Protocol Version 6 (IPv6) and routing protocols if the size of the network is increased or expanded. The network address translation can also be configured within the network to strengthen security and safeguard the network.

References

1. T. Akin (2002). Hardening Cisco Routers, *O'Reilly and Associates*, 45(2), 110–119.
2. J. Kim, K. Lee and C. Lee (2004). Design and Implementation of Integrated Security Engine for Secure Networking, *In Proceedings International Conference on Advanced Communication Technology*, 2(5), 120–126.
3. S. Alabady (2009). Design and Implementation of a Network Security Model for Cooperative Network, *International Arab Journal of e-Technology*, 1(2), 26–36.
4. A. Sathiyavaishnavi, R. Mohammed and D. Dhammearatchi (2013). Access Agent: Improving the Performance of Access Control Lists, *International Journal of Scientific and Technology Research*, 5(4), 143–150.
5. S. Gaigole, L. Monali and M. Kalyankar (2015). The Study of Network Security with its Penetrating Attacks and Possible Security Mechanisms, *International Journal Computer Science and Mobile Computing*, 4(5), 728–735.
6. S. Chen, R. Iyer and K. Whisnant (2002). Evaluating the Security Threat of Firewall Data Corruption Caused by Instruction Transient Errors. In *Proceedings of the 2002 International Conference on Dependable Systems and Network*, Washington, D.C., 2002, 2(4), 50–59.
7. D. Poonam, A. Samek and K. Dong (2014). Access Control List Implementation in a Private Network, *International Journal of Information and Computation Technology*, 4(14), 1361–1366.
8. S.S. Tambe (2015). Understanding Virtual Local Area Networks, *International Journal of Engineering Trends and Technology*, 25(4), 174–176.

9. I.A. Alimi and A.O. Mufutau (2015). Enhancement of Network Performance of an Enterprises Network with VLAN, *American Journal of Mobile Systems, Applications and Services*, 1(2), 82–93.

10. S.Y. Ali (2015). Implementation of Virtual Local Area Network using Network Simulator, *International Journal of Scientific Research Engineering and Technology*, 4(10), 1060–1065.

11. K. P. Maddipatla and S. Agarwal (2015). Limiting Traffic on Local Area Networks through Switch Port Security, *International Journal of Advanced Research in Computer Science and Software Engineering*, 5(8), 385–390.

12. A. Agrawal, H. Parasei and R. Debnar (2016). IP Traffic Management with Access Control List using Cisco Packet Tracer, *International Journal of Science, Engineering and Technology Research (IJSETR)*, 5(5), 1557–1561.

13. T. Isaac, S. Edwin and P. Jonah (2017). Design and Simulation of Local Area Network Using Cisco Packet Tracer, *The International Journal of Engineering and Science (IJES)*, 6(10), 63–77.

14. T. K. Varsha (2017). Design and Implementation of a Network Security Model for Campus Network using Various Securities, *International Journal of Innovative Research in Computer and Communication Engineering*, 5(6), 11082–11090.

15. W. Kulkarni, S. Agawral and B. Jackie (2017). Access Control List: Route-Filtering and Traffic Control, *International Journal of Advanced Research on Computer and Communication Engineering*, 6(7), 364–369.

Chapter 8

Review of Modern Symmetric and Asymmetric Cryptographic Techniques

Anupam Bhatia and Naveen Naveen
CRSU, Jind, India

8.1 Introduction

Cybercrime is rising rapidly around the world, including in India, with criminals making widespread use of the internet to commit a wide variety of crimes. Cybercrime is a problem in every part of society [1]. A wide variety of practices fall under the umbrella of computer crime, including ad fraud, financial crimes, scams, and computer fraud. Unlike other types of assets, cyber assets are potentially accessible to criminals in distant locations. This distance provides the criminal with significant protection; thus, the risks are low, and with cyber assets and activities amounting to trillions of dollars, the payoff is high. When we talk about cybercrime, we often focus on the loss of privacy and security. But cybercrime also results in significant economic losses, creating a heavy burden on law enforcement agencies worldwide.

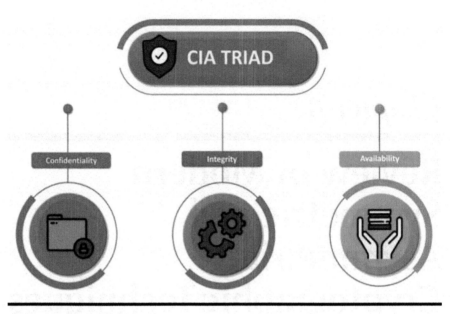

Figure 8.1 CIA triad [3].

In general, information security programs are built around three objectives, known as the CIA (confidentiality, integrity, availability) triad [2]. Figure 8.1 shows CIA triad of security.

Confidentiality. is the most common perspective on information security. It permits authorized users to access sensitive information.

Integrity. Integrity means that the changes can only be made by authorized entities through authorized mechanisms and no one else should alter the information.

Availability. Data/information must be available to authorized users.

8.1.1 Security Services

Data Confidentiality is the basic security service provided by cryptography and keeps the information from an unauthorized person, meanings it protects the data from attackers. It is sometimes known as privacy or secrecy. Confidentiality can be achieved through mathematical algorithms for data encryption.

Data Integrity is a security service that protects data from modification.

Authentication deals with the verification of the actual person. It confirms that data has been sent by a verified sender.

Non-Repudiation is a security service that provides proof of the origin of information and integrity of data.

Access Control deals with access to data, and to whom the access to data should be given.

8.1.2 Cryptography in Data Security

Historically, among humanity's basic needs have been, first, communicating or sharing information, and second, communicating selectively. These two needs have developed a system whereby only the desired people can access data or information unauthorized persons cannot read encrypted messages. Cryptography is the term used to describe this method of introducing information security. The word 'cryptography' combines two Greek words, *ryptos*, meaning hidden, and *graph*, meaning writing.

Data can be scrambled or disguised using a variety of techniques in cryptography, making it only accessible to those with the ability to reconstruct the data into its original form. Cryptography offers a solid, practical foundation for data secrecy and integrity checks in modern computer systems.

The two primary types of cryptographic processes that ICSF supports are:

i. symmetric algorithms, using the same key value for both the encryption and decryption calculations.
ii. asymmetric algorithms, where a distinct key is utilized for the encryption and decryption calculations.

8.1.3 Types of Cryptography

Symmetric Key Encryption. Both the sender and the receiver use the same key to encrypt and decode data. Tools for generating random numbers and PINs as well as payment apps use symmetric encryption methods like AES and DES.

Asymmetric Key Encryption. The opposite of symmetric encryption. For both encryption and decryption, it employs a pair of keys. While a private key is needed for decryption, a public key is utilized for encryption. Figure 8.2 shows the process of symmetric and asymmetric techniques.

Hash functions. The most popular kind of cryptography that does not use a key is hash functions. The primary operation of the hash function algorithm is to transform an input value into a compressed numerical value, rendering it hard to reconstruct the plain text's original content. The plain text is utilized in situations like comparing passwords without saving them because it will hash to the same output. The primary goal of hash functions is to prevent data tampering. IT administrators utilize this one-way encryption to encrypt their credentials.

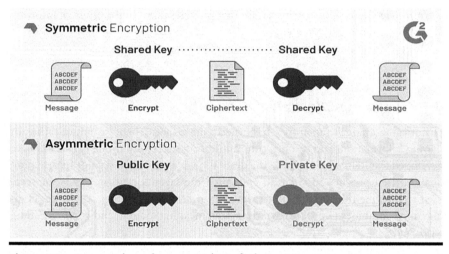

Figure 8.2   Symmetric and asymmetric techniques [4].

Some of the common solutions used to secure citizens' information, are provided by cryptographic encryption methods like secure hash algorithms (SHA-1 and SHA-256 bits), RSA (Ron Rivest, Adi Shamir, and Leonard Adleman), and Advanced Encryption Standard (AES) for encrypting information.

Some hybrid encryption techniques with fuzzy systems and other machine-learning techniques can be used to improve speed and security. The major concern of the proposed research is to develop an efficient algorithm to secure sensitive data such as Aadhaar with speedy execution (Figure 8.3).

8.2 Review of Literature

Arpana Chaturvedi, Vinay Kumar, and Meenu Dave, in "Performance Analysis of Implementation of AES(XTS)-MR in HDFS and its Suitability in UIDAI" [6], concluded that the proposed algorithm provides better security against external attacks and resolves the demerit of Kerberos. Based on observations, they concluded that this algorithm is appropriate to secure the important data stored in HDFS.

In addition to improving the AES algorithm, Shaomin Zhang, Yufang Gan, and Baoyi Wang, in "Parallel Optimization the AES Algorithm Based on MapReduce" [7], implemented the MapReduce framework on the AES encryption algorithm to ensure confidentiality and integrity. Experiments proved that the new scheme reduces the time consumption compared to the conventional method and is feasible to protect the security of cloud data.

Mustafa Emad Hameed, Masrullizam Mat Ibrahim and Nurulfajar Abd Manap, in "Review on Improvement of Advanced Encryption Standard (AES) Algorithm based on Time Execution, Differential Cryptanalysis and Level of Security" [8],

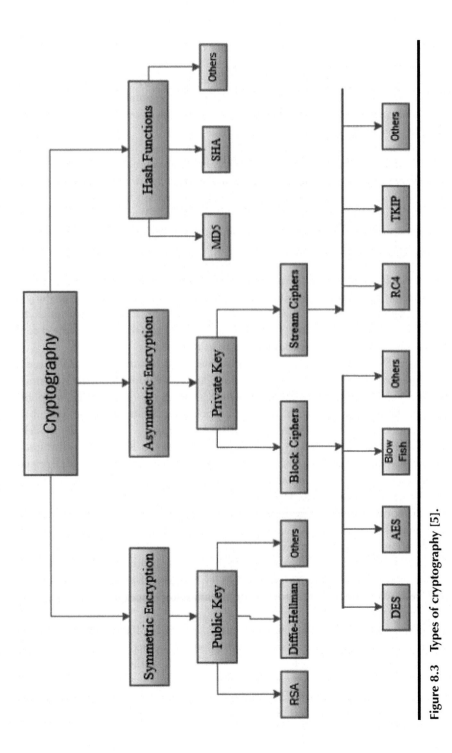

Figure 8.3 Types of cryptography [5].

surveyed improvements to AES made by authors worldwide between 2011 and 2016. The authors found that the maximum data size that can be encrypted using AES cannot exceed 1 GB.

Puneet Kumar and Shashi B. Rana studied AES in "Development of modified AES algorithm for data security" [9]. They increased the number of rounds to 16 for both encryption and decryption to secure the data. improvement in the security of the system was observed.

Mohammed N. Alenezi, Haneen Alabdulrazzaq, and Nada Q. Mohammad, in "Symmetric Encryption Algorithms: Review and Evaluation study" [10], present an overview of common symmetric encryption algorithms and explain how they work. The authors made a comparative study of ten encryption algorithms AES, DES, IDEA, SEED, RC2, RC4, RC6, XTEA, DESede, and BlowFish – on the basis of encryption time, CPU utilization, and throughput. concluded that AES, RC4, and RC6 produced the best results in terms of throughput and encryption time.

Fatma Mallouli, Aya Hellal, Nahla Sharief Saeed, and Fatimah Abdulraheem Alzahrani, in "A Survey on Cryptography: comparative study between RSA vs ECC Algorithms, and RSA vs El-Gamal Algorithms" [11], made a comparative study of RSA and ECC algorithms, and of RSA and El Gamal algorithms. They concluded that the RSA algorithm is not very efficient and has no scalability, compared to El Gamal. ECC is more secure and efficient than RSA.

Rasha Samir Abdeldaym, Hatem Mohamed Abd Elkader, and Reda Hussein, in "Modified RSA Algorithm Using Two Public Key and Chinese Remainder Theorem" [12], proposed a model in which an RSA algorithm sends two public keys to the receivers instead of one. the proposed model uses Chinese Remainder Theorem (CRT) to increase the speed of RSA decryption. The proposed model is compared ith the original RSA, RSA with multi keys, and RSA-CRT and is found to be more secure than standard RSA and RSA - CRT. It enhanced the performance of RSA, decreased the computation cost, and was faster than RSA with multi keys, but it took a long time to perform compared to standard RSA.

To modify the RSA algorithm, Kamilah Abdullah, Sumarni Abu Bakar, Nor Hanimah Kamis and Hardi Aliamis, in "RSA Cryptosystem with Fuzzy Set Theory for Encryption and Decryption" [13], proposed a model that integrates a fuzzy set into a standard RSA asymmetric encryption algorithm to improve security. Cipher text and plain text are obtained in TFN (triangular fuzzy number) terms. This research shows that fuzzy set theory is an appropriate tool for securing other cryptosystems.

Zeyad Al-Odat, Assad Abbas, and Samee U. Khan, in "Randomness Analyses of the Secure Hash Algorithms, SHA-1, SHA-2 and Modified SHA" [14], proposed a modified SHA design to improve the randomness of the internal rounds. The Bayesian and odd ratios are used to analyze the randomness of rounds of SHA-1 and SHA-2 hash functions. The authors used CUDA platform for experimental purposes and found that modified SHA produces more random rounds than other functions [15].

Maxrizal, Syafrul Irawadi, and Sujono, in "Discrete Logarithmic Improvement for El Gamal Cryptosystem Using Matrix Concepts" [16], improved El Gamal encryption by modifying key pair generation. The proposed algorithm works well and is relatively safe at a small prime number.

Adeshina, Adekunle Micheal, in "Evaluation of Elliptic Curve El-Gamal and RSA Public-Key Cryptosystems for Digital Signature" [17], presented an evaluation of digital signature algorithms, i.e., Elliptic Curve El Gamal and RSA. The author concluded that RSA is suitable for most applications that have signature verification. On the other hand, Elliptic Curve El Gamal generates keys of shorter length for a shorter time with high security but the proposed algorithm takes more time to verify.

Hari Murti, Endang Lestariningsih, Rara Sriartati Redjeki, and Eka Ardhianto, in "Systematic Literature Review of the Role of Fuzzy Logic in the Development of Cryptographic and Steganographic Techniques" [18], studied the literature to find a combination of fuzzy logic with cryptographic techniques to improve information security. They found that the use of fuzzy logic not only improves information security but also plays an important role in selecting the best and most secure key and improves the quality of random numbers in PRNGs (pseudo random number generators).

8.3 Discussion

Symmetric key cryptography is a faster and more straightforward process but it is more vulnerable to security risks because of the private key involved [19]. Symmetric cryptography techniques are computationally inexpensive [20]. Meanwhile, asymmetric key cryptography may be a more complex and slower process, but it is ultimately a far more secure encryption method and it also can authenticate identities [21].

The AES algorithm uses an algebraic structure to generate keys that are too simple. So generating and encrypting new fresh keys is very slow. Every block of message is always encrypted in the same manner. It is very hard to implement AES with software [22].

The main disadvantage of RSA encryption technique is its slow processing. Generation of keys is very slow and it is also very slow when there is a large quantity of data to be encrypted [11, 17].

The demerits of SHA256 are that it is difficult to handle because of its size and its hash function is less secure than the MD5 hash function. Another disadvantage of SHA256 is that its processing is slow compared to MD5.

The demerits of ECC are that it increases the size of the encrypted message significantly more than RSA encryption. The ECC algorithm is more complex and more difficult to implement than RSA, which increases the likelihood of implementation errors, thereby reducing the security of the algorithm. It is much slower than other symmetric cryptographic algorithms [11].

Table 8.1 Shortcomings of Encryption Techniques

Encryption Techniques	Shortcomings
AES	■ Uses algebraic structure to generate keys that are too easy and simple. ■ Slow algorithm to generate new fresh keys. Slow to encrypt. ■ Hard to implement AES with software [22].
RSA	■ Slow processing, when a large quantity of data is to be encrypted. ■ Generation of keys is very slow [11, 17].
SHA256	■ Difficult to handle because of its size. ■ Hash function is less secure than MD5 hash function. ■ Processing is slow.
ECC	■ Increases the size of the encrypted message significantly more than RSA encryption. ■ More complex and more difficult to implement. ■ Much slower [11].
El Gamal	■ Not secure against common modulus attacks and known-plaintext attacks. ■ Need for randomness. ■ Message expansion by a factor of two takes place during encryption [23].

The main disadvantage of El Gamal is the need for randomness, and its slower speed (especially for signing). Another potential disadvantage is that message expansion by a factor of two takes place during encryption. However, this message expansion is negligible if the cryptosystem is used only for the exchange of secret keys. It is not secure against common modulus attacks and known-plaintext attacks [23]. Table 8.1 shows shortcomings of the encryption techniques.

8.4 Conclusion

The rapid increase in cybercrime around the world including in India means that securing sensitive information using encryption and decryption techniques is essential. The main purpose of this survey is to introduce different types of encryption and decryption techniques and to discuss their shortcomings. Previous studies have almost exclusively focused on AES, RSA, and SHA encryption algorithms to secure sensitive data such as Aadhaar data. Some modern algorithms like El Gamal and ECC encryption schemes are also used to secure data. These algorithms are good enough to secure the information but the literature review shows that they have some shortcomings.

References

1. D. A. S. Poonia, "Cyber Crime: Challenges and its Classification," *International Journal of Emerging Trends & Technology in Computer Science*, vol. 3, no. 6, pp. 119–121, 2014.
2. S. S. Dhanda, B. Singh, and P. Jindal, "Demystifying Elliptic Curve Cryptography: Curve Selection, Implementation and Countermeasures to Attacks," *Journal of Interdisciplinary Mathematics*, vol. 23, no. 2, pp. 463–470, Feb. 2020.
3. CIA-Triad-What-is-cybersecurity-Edureka.png (2048 × 1162).
4. https://learn.g2.com/hs-fs/hubfs/G2CR_B050_What-isEncryption_V1.png?width= 2000&name=G2CR_B050_What-is-Encryption_V1.png
5. https://www.researchgate.net/profile/Maghrib_Alrammahi2/publication/323369289/ figure/download/fig4/AS:668895320997896@1536488480770/Types-of-Cryptography-Various-Cryptographic-Algorithms-a-Data-Encryption-Standard.ppm
6. A. Chaturvedi, V. Kumar, and M. Dave, "Performance Analysis of Implementation of AES (XTS)-MR in HDFS and Its Suitability in UIDAI," *International Journal of Computer Trends and Technology*, vol. 60, pp. 161–168, Jun. 2018.
7. S. M. Zhang, Y. F. Gan, and B. Y. Wang, "Parallel Optimization the AES Algorithm Based on MapReduce," *Applied Mechanics and Materials*, vol. 644–650, pp. 1911–1914, 2014.
8. M. Hameed, M. Mat Ibrahim, and N. Abd Manap, "Review on Improvement of Advanced Encryption Standard (AES) Algorithm Based on Time Execution, Differential Cryptanalysis and Level Of Security," *Journal of Telecommunication, Electronic and Computer Engineering*, vol. 10, pp. 139–145, Jan. 2018.
9. P. Kumar and S. B. Rana, "Development of Modified AES Algorithm for Data Security," *Optik*, vol. 127, no. 4, pp. 2341–2345, Feb. 2016.
10. M. Alenezi, H. Alabdulrazzaq, and N. Mohammad, "Symmetric Encryption Algorithms: Review and Evaluation study," *International Journal of Communication Networks and Information Security*, vol. 12, pp. 256–276, Aug. 2020.
11. F. Mallouli, A. Hellal, N. Sharief Saeed, and F. Abdulraheem Alzahrani, "A Survey on Cryptography: Comparative Study between RSA vs ECC Algorithms, and RSA vs El-Gamal Algorithms," in *2019 6th IEEE International Conference on Cyber Security and Cloud Computing (CSCloud)/ 2019 5th IEEE International Conference on Edge Computing and Scalable Cloud (EdgeCom)*, pp. 173–176, Jun. 2019.
12. R. S. Abdeldaym, H. M. A. Elkader, and R. Hussein, "Modified RSA Algorithm Using Two Public Key and Chinese Remainder Theorem," *International Journal of Electronics and Information Engineering*, vol. 10, pp. 51–64, Mar. 2019.
13. K. Abdullah, S. A. Bakar, N. H. Kamis, and H. Aliamis, "RSA Cryptosystem with Fuzzy Set Theory for Encryption and Decryption," *AIP Conference Proceedings*, vol. 1905, no. 1, pp. 030001-1–030001-6, Nov. 2017.
14. Z. Al-Odat, A. Abbas, and S. U. Khan, "Randomness Analyses of the Secure Hash Algorithms, SHA-1, SHA-2 and Modified SHA," in *2019 International Conference on Frontiers of Information Technology (FIT)*, pp. 316–3165, Dec. 2019.

15. P. Shingote and A.M. Shah, "Secure Hash Algorithms for Securing IOT," in *Proceedings of International Conference on Cyber Security and Ethical Hacking in Blockchain Technology*, pp. 68–76, 2021.

16. Maxrizal, S. Irawadi, and Sujono, "Discrete Logarithmic Improvement for ElGamal Cryptosystem Using Matrix Concepts," in *2020 8th International Conference on Cyber and IT Service Management (CITSM)*, pp. 1–5, Oct. 2020.

17. A. M. Adeshina, "Evaluation of Elliptic Curve El-Gamal and RSA Public-Key Cryptosystems for Digital Signature," *Journal of Information Science*, vol. 4, pp. 36–49, Feb. 2020.

18. H. Murti, E. Lestariningsih, R. Redjeki, and E. Ardhianto, "Systematic Literature Review of the Role of Fuzzy Logic in the Development of Cryptographic and Steganographic Techniques," *Asian Journal of Research in Computer Science*, pp. 25–30, Dec. 2021.

19. R. B. Marqas, S. M. Almufti and R. R. Ihsan "Comparing Symmetric and Asymmetric Cryptography in Message Encryption and Decryption by Using AES and RSA Algorithms," *Journal of Xi'an University of Architecture & Technology*, vol. XII, no. III, pp. 3110–3116, Mar. 2020.

20. F. Maqsood, M. Ahmed, M. Mumtaz, and M. Ali, "Cryptography: A Comparative Analysis for Modern Techniques," *International Journal of Advanced Computer Science and Applications*, vol. 8, no. 6, pp. 442–448, 2017.

21. F. Maqsood, M. Ahmed, M. Mumtaz, and M. Ali, "Cryptography: A Comparative Analysis for Modern Techniques," *International Journal of Advanced Computer Science and Applications*, vol. 8, no. 6, 442–448, 2017.

22. A.-L. Sousi, D. Yehya, and M. Joudi, *"AES Encryption: Study & Evaluation"* 2020.

23. G. Sahni and G. Singh, "Modern Cryptographic Technique – A Literature Review," *International Journal for Scientific Research and Development*, vol. 1, pp. 2657–2658, 2014.

Chapter 9

Quantum Computing-Based Image Representation with IBM QISKIT Libraries

Barkha Singh, S. Indu, and Sudipta Majumdar
Delhi Technological University (AICTE), Delhi, India

9.1 Introduction

In 1982 Feynman [1] explained the challenges of manipulating large-scale qubits in quantum computing.

$$| I(\theta) \rangle = \frac{1}{2^n} \sum_{i=0}^{2^{2n}-1} (\cos\theta_i)|0\rangle + \sin\theta_i|\rangle \otimes |i\rangle$$

$$\theta_i \in \left[0, \frac{\pi}{2} \right], i = 0,1,\cdots,2^{2n}-1 \tag{9.1}$$

Today noisy intermediate-scale quantum (NISQ) is very much used to understand "quantum supremacy". Llyod et al. describe how maps can be trained for quantum states from data. The quantum state has the power of distinguishing images at a very precise level. Quantum properties can also be exploited to achieve higher efficiency through quantum image processing [6]. Flexible representation of quantum images (FRQI) represents a quantum state of the image using the following equation:

$\cos\theta_i|0\rangle + \sin\theta_i|1\rangle$: encoding equation for color information. The theta shows the angle for encoding of color and the encoding for position is represented by ket notation as: $\theta_0|00\rangle$, $\theta_1|01\rangle$, $\theta_2|10\rangle$, $\theta_3|11\rangle$ [33] [34] [35],

$$
\begin{aligned}
|I\rangle = \frac{1}{2}[&(\cos\theta_0|0\rangle + \sin\theta_0|1\rangle)\otimes|00\rangle \\
+&(\cos\theta_1|0\rangle + \sin\theta_1|1\rangle)\otimes|01\rangle \\
+&(\cos\theta_2|0\rangle + \sin\theta_2|1\rangle)\otimes|10\rangle \\
+&(\cos\theta_3|0\rangle + \sin\theta_3|1\rangle)\otimes|11\rangle]
\end{aligned}
\tag{9.2}
$$

For color encoding (Figure 9.1), CNOT and X gates will be in use in the well-known Hadamard algorithm to increase the location of pixel 2 × 2 grayscale value image implementation. The work is concentrated on π, 0, values of Θ_i = 0 mean black pixel, minimum intensity pixel Θ_i = $\pi/2$ means white pixel, maximum intensity pixel Θ_i = $\pi/4$ means pixels at 50% intensity. $|i\rangle$: representing position of pixel respectively.

9.2 Objective

9.2.1 Main Objective

The main objective is to minimize CNOT gate depth and number to reduce complexity. This is achieved following experimental analysis by compressing the image by grouping pixels with same intensity by one conditional rotation, so that the binary string used to encode the pixel position can be reduced. Many pixels are associated with same angle – Θ_i – therefore the single-gate requirement will be considerably reduced [8] [26] [27] [28].

9.2.2 Algorithm Steps

The algorithm developed involves the following steps:

1. Import all standard QISKIT libraries [7]. For Θi = 0 pixels are at minimum intensity for all black pixels and similarly for other values of Θi, calculation is to be considered for only one value for intensity encoding to put all the values in quantum circuit [13] [21] [23] [24].
2. The image is retrieved during the second part of programming for all four equiprobable states. A 2 × 2 image will be considered according to the value of Θi which will equal zero for state $|1\rangle$. Since θ_i = $\pi/4$, [15] [17] [19].

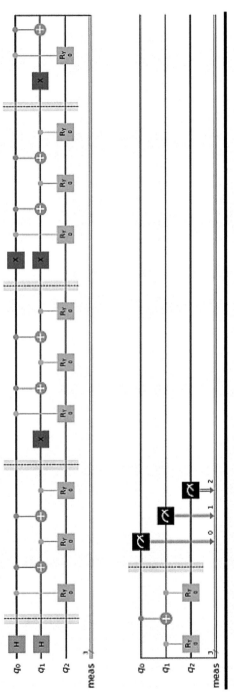

Figure 9.1 Quantum circuit visualization for theta = 0, which means all pixels are black [6].

∀i - all pixels at 50%. In the third state, measurements are performed using histogram plots. The depth and number of gates are the two main factors for various classes of image [2], according to the rotation angle [29] [30] [32].

3. For optimization, the depth size can be increased accordingly. All the operations on the quantum circuit can be performed using IBM quantum lab and libraries [7].

4. A further step is compression, in which pixels with the same intensity are grouped [33] [34] [35].

5. In this step, the binary string encodes the position, according to the compression technique.

In this representation the red pixels are at positions $|0\rangle$, $|4\rangle$, $|8\rangle$, $|12\rangle$.

Their respective binary representation (Figure 9.2) and Boolean expressions are represented in Table 9.1.

9.3 Review of Work Implemented

The NEQR process consists of preparation and compression. Here a 2 × 2 grayscale image is analyzed using the NEQR model.

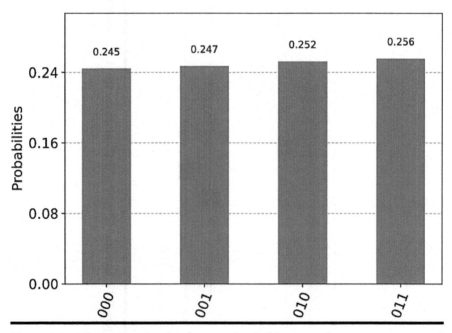

Figure 9.2 Histogram plot for four equiprobable states for measurement and image retrieval [4].

Table 9.1   Binary String and Boolean Expressions for Red Pixels [41]

Position	Binary String	Boolean expression
$|0\rangle$	$|0000\rangle$	$\overline{X_3 X_2 X_1 X_0}$
$|4\rangle$	$|0100\rangle$	$\overline{X_3}\ X_2 \overline{X_1 X_0}$
$|8\rangle$	$|1000\rangle$	$X_3\ \overline{X_2 X_1 X_0}$
$|12\rangle$	$|1100\rangle$	$X_3 X_2\ \overline{X_1 X_0}$

The first part of this implementation includes the color range of the image with **bitstring** as follows:

- black = 0 bit
- white = 1 bit

Encoding a 2 × 2 grayscale image involves the following steps:

1. The pixel position of the 2 × 2 image is represented in the first column.
2. The intensity value at the specified pixel position is encoded in the second column.
3. The third column describes the grayscale intensity (Table 9.1) (e.g., 01100100 = 100)
4. The intensity level is represented in tabular form (Figure 9.3).
    - First the pixel position is stored in a 2D image.
    - $f(Y, X)$: function denotes colored pixel value
    - The 0–255 value is regarded as the most common grayscale range [12].2^q denotes their values, where 256 is for $q = 8$. The number of bits required for the binary sequence of colors is represented by q: $C^0, C^1, \ldots C^{q-2}, C^{q-1}$

$$f(Y,X) = C_{YX}^0, C_{YX}^1, \cdots, C_{YX}^{q-2}, C_{YX}^{q-1} \in [0,1], f(Y,X) \in \left[0, 2^{q-1}\right] \qquad (9.3)$$

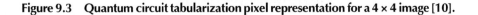

Figure 9.3   Quantum circuit tabularization pixel representation for a 4 × 4 image [10].

where the binary representation of the grayscale intensity value is done by C. For a 2×2 quantum image representation, the expression will be:

$$[I) = \frac{1}{2^n} \sum_{Y=0}^{2^{2n-1}} \sum_{X=0}^{2^{2n-1}} |f(Y,X)\rangle|YX\rangle = \frac{1}{2^n} \sum_{Y=0}^{2^{2n-1}} \sum_{X=0}^{2^{2n-1}} |\otimes_{i=0}^{q-1}\rangle|C_{YX}^i\rangle | YX\rangle$$

$$\Omega_{YX}|0\rangle^{\otimes q} = \frac{1}{\sqrt{2}}(|00000000\rangle|00\rangle + |01100100\rangle|01\rangle \qquad (9.4)$$

$$+ |11001000\rangle|10\rangle + |11111$$

where $\Omega_{YX}|0\rangle$ is the quantum operation representing the value of the pixel at position (Y, X).

9.3.1 Quantum Circuit of 2^n Qubits for a 2×2 Image

To encode an image, a quantum circuit with the specific number of qubits is created. Two separate quantum circuits are created for the pixel values: one for intensity, and the other for the pixel positions: **idx** [9]. Identity gates relate to the position qubits, and Hadamard gates to the intensity qubits [16].

9.3.2 Tabular Representation of Intensity Values

After introducing the Hadamard gate to the pixel positions and the identity gates to the intensity values, the quantum circuit is visualized using barriers.

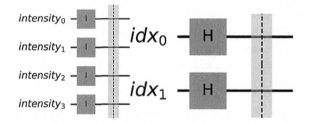

9.3.3 Grayscale Image Representation on a Quantum Circuit

Combine the pixel position circuit with its respective pixel intensity value to encode the pixel values as:

a. 00 = 00000000 for black pixels
b. 01 = 01100100 for value of grayscale = 100
c. 10 = 11001000 for value of Grayscale = 200
d. 11 = 11111111 for pixel having white intensity

e. For the first pixel at position (0,0) use identity gates

f. To encode the second pixel (0,1) whose value is (01010101), use a Control Not gate with two-qubit controls (2-CNOT), where the controls are triggered by the pixel position (*Y*, *X*), and the targets rotate the Ciyx qubit which represents the pixel value (Figure 9.4).

g. For the CNOT gate to trigger, the control is a combination of 0 and 1, surrounding the qubit with *X* gates so it will trigger when the specified control is 0.

h. Encode the next pixel at position (1,0) with a value of (10101010) by encoding the adding of the 0 CNOT gates, where 0 is on *X* pixel.

i. Encode the third pixel whose value is (10101010): value11 = '11111111' by adding the CNOT gates.

j. Encode the last pixel position (1,1), with the value 11111111 by adding Toffoli gates to all the pixel image values.

For the circuit analysis the decompose function is used and the results are obtained in the form of circuit dimensions (Figure 9.5) as: depth 148; size 244. Where data is usable but extremely noisy and with low quantum volume, the noise from results can be minimized [18].

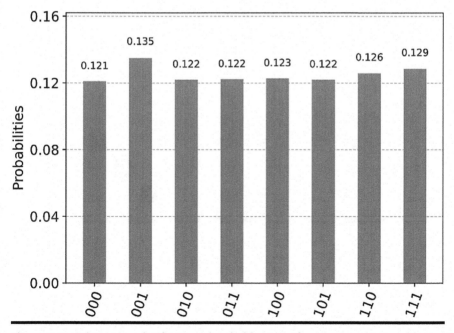

Figure 9.4   Histogram plot for 8 equiprobable states for measurement and image retrieval [3] [11].

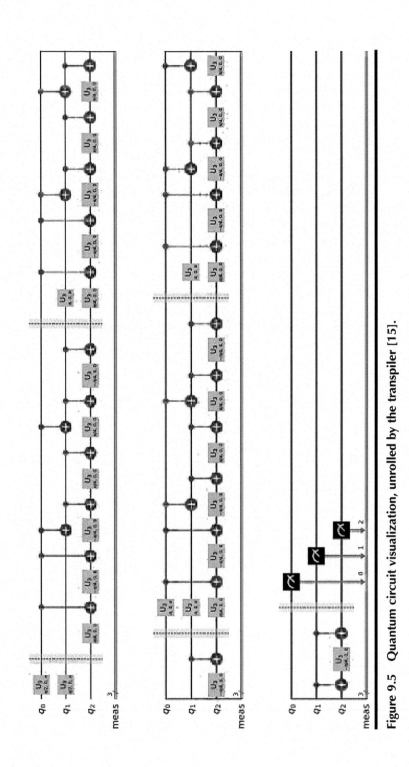

Figure 9.5 Quantum circuit visualization, unrolled by the transpiler [15].

$$| I \rangle = \frac{1}{2}[(\cos\theta_0 |0\rangle + \sin\theta_0 |1\rangle) \otimes |00\rangle$$
$$+ (\cos\theta_1 |0\rangle + \sin\theta_1 |1\rangle) \otimes |01\rangle$$
$$+ (\cos\theta_2 |0\rangle + \sin\theta_2 |1\rangle) \otimes |10\rangle \qquad (9.5)$$
$$+ (\cos\theta_3 |0\rangle + \sin\theta_3 |1\rangle) \otimes |11\rangle]$$

```
Encoded: 00 = 0
Encoded: 01 = 01100100
Encoded: 10 = 11001000
Encoded: 11 = 1
{'0101100100': 2003, '0000000000': 2055, '1011001000'
```

9.4 Advantages

The main advantage of using optimizers is time efficiency.

NEQR has the following advantages over FRQI: [38] [39].

- *Quadratic speed:* increases with the complexity [31] [37].
- *Compression value:* will reach up to 1.5 times compression of optical image ratio [1].
- *Retrieval:* accurate image retrieval.
- *Operations:* achieves complex color operations [35].

$$[I\rangle = \frac{1}{2^n} \sum_{Y=0}^{2^{2n-1}} \sum_{X=0}^{2^{2n-1}} \left| f(Y, X)\rangle \right| YX\rangle = \frac{1}{2^n} \sum_{Y=0}^{2^{2n-1}} \sum_{X=0}^{2^{2n-1}} \left| \otimes_{i=0}^{q-1} \right\rangle \left| C_{YX}^i \right\rangle | YX\rangle$$

$$\Omega_{YX} | 0\rangle^{\otimes q} = \frac{1}{\sqrt{2}} (\left|00000000\rangle | 00\rangle + \left|01100100\rangle | 01\rangle \qquad (9.6)$$

$$+ \left|11001000\rangle | 10\rangle + |11111$$

9.5 Result Analysis

The two left-most bits (00,01,10,11) are represented by pixel position and the 8-bit binary representation is achieved using the remaining bit values of the grayscale intensity values shown in the following encoded results [20] [22].

00 = 00000000, **01** = 01100100, **10** = 11001000, **11** = 11111111

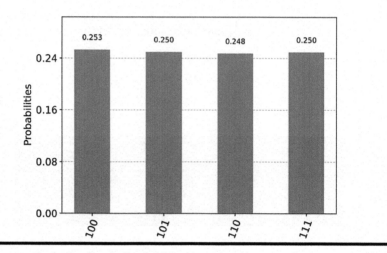

Figure 9.6   Ideal stimulated circuit histogram plot [5] [14].

Table 9.2   Pixel Position is Stored in 2D Image [38]

Intensity 0	— — —
Intensity 1	— — —
Intensity 2	— — —
Intensity 3	— — —
Idx 0	— — —
Idx 1	— — —

This problem is solved by mapping classical data to quantum data using the FRQI format, in which each pixel is measured to obtain the final optimum result using operations such as the geometric and color operation of transformation (Figure 9.6). Further research could be carried out to eliminate noise value [25].

9.6 Conclusions

The main purpose of this research is to implement all image processing-based application tasks on a quantum computer. Control Not gates for quantum image representation by reducing depth is implemented; in a quantum circuit, reduction of depth helps to minimize the number of controlled gates. In such applications, FRQI plays a very important role since it stores and captures all the information such as position and color transformation of an image which is important as a quantum state in its normalized condition. Processing color images on quantum computer involves:

1. FRQI extension method [40] [41] [42].
2. MCQI method for which three operators are used. They are:
   ▪ Channel of Interest Operator (CIO) is used to shift the grayscale value of color channels like R, G, B or Alpha.
   ▪ The information is encoded from R, G, B, or alpha channel.

References

1. S. Chakraborty, S. H. Shaikh, A. Chakrabarti, and R. Ghosh, "An image denoising technique using quantum wavelet transform," *International Journal of Theoretical Physics*, vol. 59, no. 11, pp. 3348–3371, 2020.
2. S. Dutta, A. Basarab, B. Georgeot, and D. Kouamé, "Quantum mechanics-based signal and image representation: Application to denoising," *IEEE Open Journal of Signal Processing*, vol. 2, pp. 190–206, 2021.
3. T. Barbu, "Variational quantum denoising technique for medical images," in *2020 International Conference on e-Health and Bioengineering (EHB)*. IEEE, 2020, pp. 1–4.
4. Y. Liu, M. Sun, Z. Jia, J. Yang, and N. K. Kasabov, "Denoising of fluorescence image on the surface of quantum dot/nanoporous silicon biosensors," *Sensors*, vol. 22, no. 4, p. 1366, 2022.
5. P. Agarwal and M. Alam, "Quantum-inspired support vector machines for human activity recognition in industry 4.0," in *Proceedings of Data Analytics and Management*. Springer, 2022, pp. 281–290.
6. M. Krelina, "Quantum technology for military applications," *EPJ Quantum Technology*, vol. 8, no. 1, p. 24, 2021.
7. F. Phillipson, R. S. Wezeman, and I. Chiscop, "Indoor–outdoor detection in mobile networks using quantum machine learning approaches," *Computers*, vol. 10, no. 6, p. 71, 2021.
8. A. Shokry and M. Youssef, "Quantum computing for location determination," *arXiv preprint arXiv:2106.11751*, 2021.
9. M. Bhatia and S. Sood, "Quantum computing-inspired network optimization for IoT applications," *IEEE Internet of Things Journal* 7 (6), 5590–5598, 2020.
10. L. Banchi, J. Pereira, and S. Pirandola, "Generalization in quantum machine learning: A quantum information standpoint," *PRX Quantum*, vol. 2, no. 4, p. 040321, 2021.
11. S. Endo, Z. Cai, S. C. Benjamin, and X. Yuan, "Hybrid quantum-classical algorithms and quantum error mitigation," *Journal of the Physical Society of Japan*, vol. 90, no. 3, p. 032001, 2021.
12. J. J. Meyer, J. Borregaard, and J. Eisert, "A variational toolbox for quantum multi-parameter estimation," *npj Quantum Information*, vol. 7, no. 1, pp. 1–5, 2021
13. D. Bachtis, G. Aarts, and B. Lucini, "Quantum field-theoretic machine learning," *Physical Review D*, vol. 103, no. 7, p. 074510, 2021.
14. J. Alcazar, V. Leyton-Ortega, and A. Perdomo-Ortiz, "Classical versus quantum models in machine learning: Insights from a finance application," *Machine Learning: Science and Technology*, vol. 1, no. 3, p. 035003, 2020.

15. R. Babbush, J. R. McClean, M. Newman, C. Gidney, S. Boixo, and H. Neven, "Focus beyond quadratic speedups for error-corrected quantum advantage," *PRX Quantum*, vol. 2, no. 1, p. 010103, 2021.
16. K. H. Wan, O. Dahlsten, H. Kristjánsson, R. Gardner, and M. Kim, "Quantum generalisation of feedforward neural networks," *npj Quantum Information*, vol. 3, no. 1, pp. 1–8, 2017.
17. S. Y.-C. Chen, C.-M. Huang, C.-W. Hsing, H.-S. Goan, and Y.-J. Kao, "Variational quantum reinforcement learning via evolutionary optimization," *Machine Learning: Science and Technology*, vol. 3, no. 1, p. 015025, 2022.
18. H.-Y. Hsieh, J. Ning, Y.-R. Chen, H.-C. Wu, H. L. Chen, C.-M. Wu, and R.-K. Lee, "Direct parameter estimations from machine learning-enhanced quantum state tomography," *Symmetry*, vol. 14, no. 5, p. 874, 2022.
19. C. H. Alderete, M. H. Gordon, F. Sauvage, A. Sone, A. T. Sornborger, P. J. Coles, and M. Cerezo, "Inference-based quantum sensing," *Physical Review Letters*, vol. 129, no. 19, p. 190501, 2022.
20. Y. Wang, K.-Y. Lin, S. Cheng, and L. Li, "Variational quantum extreme learning machine," *Neurocomputing*, vol. 512, pp. 83–99, 2022.
21. J. L. Beckey, M. Cerezo, A. Sone, and P. J. Coles, "Variational quantum algorithm for estimating the quantum fisher information," *Physical Review Research*, vol. 4, no. 1, p. 013083, 2022.
22. E. Tang, "Dequantizing algorithms to understand quantum advantage in machine learning," *Nature Reviews Physics*, pp. 1–2, 2022.
23. H.-Y. Huang, M. Broughton, J. Cotler, S. Chen, J. Li, M. Mohseni, H. Neven, R. Babbush, R. Kueng, J. Preskill et al., "Quantum advantage in learning from experiments," *Science*, vol. 376, no. 6598, pp. 1182–1186, 2022.
24. D. Aharonov, J. Cotler, and X.-L. Qi, "Quantum algorithmic measurement," *Nature Communications*, vol. 13, no. 1, pp. 1–9, 2022.
25. H.-Y. Huang, R. Kueng, G. Torlai, V. V. Albert, and J. Preskill, "Provably efficient machine learning for quantum many-body problems," *Science*, vol. 377, no. 6613, p. eabk3333, 2022.
26. M. Nakahara and Y. Sasaki, *Quantum Information and Quantum Computing - Proceedings of Symposium*. World Scientific, 2012, vol. 6.
27. M. A. Nielsen and I. Chuang, "Quantum computation and quantum information," 2002.
28. H. M. Wiseman, "Benjamin Schumacher and Michael Westmoreland: Quantum processes, systems, & information," 2010.
29. D. P. DiVincenzo, "Book review on quantum computation quantum information," *Quantum Information & Computation*, vol. 1, no. 2, pp. 95–96, 2001.
30. E. Cavalcanti, "Christopher A. Fuchs: Coming of age with quantum information: notes on a Paulian idea," *Quantum Inf Process* **11**, 633–636 (2012). https://doi.org/10.1007/s11128-011-0343-x2012
31. N. Nguyen and K.-C. Chen, "Quantum embedding search for quantum machine learning," *IEEE Access*, vol. 10, pp. 41444–41456, 2022.
32. M. Larocca, P. Czarnik, K. Sharma, G. Muraleedharan, P. J. Coles, and M. Cerezo, "Diagnosing barren plateaus with tools from quantum optimal control," *Quantum*, vol. 6, p. 824, 2022.
33. M. Lytras, A. Visvizi, X. Zhang, and N. R. Aljohani, "Cognitive computing, big data analytics and data driven industrial marketing," *Industrial Marketing Managemen*, vol. 90, pp. 663–666, 2020.

34. S. S. Nisha, H. Patil, A. Bag, A. Singh, Y. Kumar, and J. S. Kumar, "Critical information framework against cyber-attacks using artificial intelligence and big data analytics," in *2022 2nd International Conference on Advance Computing and Innovative Technologies in Engineering (ICACITE)*. IEEE, 2022, pp. 533–537.

35. Q. Meng, K. Wang, X. He, and M. Guo, "Qoe-driven big data management in pervasive edge computing environment," *Big Data Mining and Analytics*, vol. 1, no. 3, pp. 222–233, 2018.

36. A. Singh, S. Ahmad, and M. I. Haque, "Big data science and exasol as big data analytics tool," *International Journal of Innovative Technology and Exploring Engineering*, vol. 8, no. 9S, pp. 933–937, 2019.

37. K. Bajaj, B. Sharma, and R. Singh, "Implementation analysis of IoT-based offloading frameworks on cloud/edge computing for sensor-generated big data," *Complex & Intelligent Systems*, vol. 8, no. 5, pp. 3641–3658, 2022.

38. C. Aradau and T. Blanke, "The (big) data-security assemblage: Knowledge and critique," *Big Data & Society*, vol. 2, no. 2, p. 2053951715609066, 2015.

39. A. K. Sandhu, "Big data with cloud computing: Discussions and challenges," *Big Data Mining and Analytics*, vol. 5, no. 1, pp. 32–40, 2021.

40. M. Ghasemaghaei, "The role of positive and negative valence factors on the impact of bigness of data on big data analytics usage," *International Journal of Information Management*, vol. 50, pp. 395–404, 2020.

41. A. Goscinski, F. C. Delicato, G. Fortino, A. Kobusińska, and G. Srivastava, "Special issue on distributed intelligence at the edge for the future internet of things," *Journal of Parallel and Distributed Computing*, vol. 171, pp. 157–162, 2023.

42. M. Mallow, A. Hornung, J. N. Barajas, S. S. Rudisill, H. S. An, and D. Samartzis.

43. A. E. Azzaoui, P. K. Sharma, and J. H. Park, "Blockchain-based delegated quantum cloud architecture for medical big data security," *Journal of Network and Computer Applications*, vol. 198, p. 103304, 2022.

Chapter 10

Source Authentication of Videos Shared on Social Media

Mohd Shaliyar and Khurram Mustafa

Jamia Millia Islamia University, New Delhi, India

10.1 Introduction

Over the course of the past few years, OSM has developed into a mature and significant global medium of communication. It has digitally deep ties to everything from computers to mobile devices to webpages. As a result, a complex online social structure exists, in which users are digitally linked together irrespective of their religion, location, race, caste, or language. However, the main driving force behind the momentum of various online social media (OSM) systems is user-created multimedia content such as images, videos, text, or audio. The impact of such media extends far beyond the realm of mere communication and can permeate diverse cultural, political, and economic spheres. Further, the practice of uploading enormous volumes of data via OSM is causing sufficiency issues. These kinds of behavior have the potential to turn OSM into an epicenter for spreading misinformation or disinformation.

OSM are an adaptable and low-cost platform for sharing information vital to many fields, including national security, business, society, citizen evaluations, and online advertising. According to ref. [1], there were around 4.26 billion users linked to OSM in the year 2021, and by the year 2027, it is expected that this number will have increased to 6 billion. However, the potential drawbacks include risks to users' privacy and safety, malware and phishing scams, hate speech, harm to relationships

DOI: 10.1201/9781003371380-10

and health, bullying and harassment, and more. In addition to these issues, the OSM community's reliance on communication services may be jeopardized by the prevalence of numerous messaging apps like WhatsApp, Facebook, Instagram, and others.

"Rumormongers", so runs the proverb, are among the most dangerous foes a country may have. Disruption caused by hoaxes can have significant effects on the progress of the nation as a whole. Researchers have found that the authenticity of the online source is more important than the reliability of its content. In 2013, a bogus video on OSM ignited riots in Muzzaffar Nagar, Uttar Pradesh's northern district, killing more than 60 civilians and rendering 1,000 homeless. In 2018, due to the proliferation of fake WhatsApp messages, a gang of tribal men attacked a poor, elderly, and mentally ill woman with rods and bars. In 2018, residents in Murki (Telangana) attacked and severely injured five tourists after a false story of a child kidnapping circulated on WhatsApp. However, in each of these cases the source of the misinformation is obscure. Nevertheless, there is no upper bound to such incidents. Moreover, the literature [2] explains in depth how WhatsApp spreads false information within the field of OSM.

How to identify the first user of shared content in OSM has therefore become the most pressing concern when it comes to message-forwarding apps. Since OSM is being used by a large number of individuals and the web is so accessible, information can be openly distributed and uploaded without checking the credibility of the source. Such digital data transmission/sharing practices may have significant social, political, and domestic growth repercussions if they are not evaluated in light of the veracity of the epicenters. This, however, necessitates identifying the source of the rumor, since it facilitates the propagation of numerous hoaxes inside the OSM. To examine the authenticity of a source in OSM, this research investigates and propounded a methodology in digital watermarking.

Digital watermarking has many applications, including but not limited to content authentication [3], copyright protection [4], and telemedicine [5]. Watermarking involves the incorporation of one digital signal as a watermark into another digital signal as a carrier or host (image, text, video, or audio). Although multiple digital watermarking techniques to address issues in several applications have been proposed by researchers, further issues remain to be resolved. Improved watermarking technologies are required to deal with the current concerns.

There are two distinct types of watermarking: spatial and transform. Digital watermarking can also be classified as text, image, audio, or video watermarking according to the type of carrier signal used. There are three distinct variants of digital image watermarking, based on its resilience: robust, semi-fragile, and fragile.

10.2 Literature Review

The optimal keyframe selection using IGSA and HT in the LWT domain is based on the lossless efficient video-watermarking system propounded for copyright protection [6]. In this method, keyframes include a scrambled watermark logo followed by an LWT. The IGSA algorithm obtains a collection of MSF that remains imperceptible and robust. The proposed technique's security is improved by conducting Arnold transform on the watermark logo before embedding. Comparing imperceptibility and robustness properties with other studies shows that IGSA-LH is more resistant to attack.

The fundamental innovation of the approach proposed in ref. [7] is the combination of zero watermarking and blockchain. The suggested approach does not alter keyframes, so detecting and removing conventional watermarks is not required. Since the blockchain is used in the authentication and copyright tracking process, using it in conjunction with zero watermarking provides a solution to the rights tracking problem and enables tamperproof storage. The suggested technique provides better copyright protection than video fingerprinting for video information.

The research in ref. [8] proposes a robust video watermarking method to blindly embed a watermark in complex frames for copyright protection. However, optimization strategies based on Firefly are used to extract these complex frames. For selected video frames, adaptive histogram bit shifting has been used to conceal the cryptographic watermark in the LL band of DWT. In terms of PSNR, MSE, and BER, the final result demonstrates that the suggested method outperformed state-of-the-art methods for digital video watermarking.

A blind semi-fragile watermarking approach was proposed in ref. [9] to authenticate video content in the multi-SVD-DWT domain. The watermarks created are based on features extracted from regions of interest in conjunction with the QR code technique. Furthermore, the watermark is encoded using Arnold transform and then embedded into the DWT mid-frequency sub-bands via the SVD coefficients. However, this methodology is highly vulnerable to semantic content modifications such as cropping and object manipulation, producing drastically lower and higher NC and BER values of 0.9 and 0.1 respectively. The suggested technique achieves a large capacity and imperceptibility, as indicated by its strong PSNR and SSIM values.

The study in ref. [10] proposes a method for implementing secure digital video watermarking via compression. The selected frames are decomposed by DT-CWT. The encrypted watermarks are embedded at locations that are optimally chosen with an adaptive cuttlefish optimization technique to bolster the system's security. To decrease the size of the video, H.265 compression is applied to the video sequence. The proposed methodology outperforms other existing studies in respect of PSNR, NCC, and MSE.

Secure and robust video watermarking combining DWTs, SVD, and the Laplacian Pyramid is proposed in ref. [11]. The Laplacian Pyramid divides the watermark image into low- and high-frequency images. The images used as watermarks are then all embedded in the SVD of HH and HH1 DWT sub-bands. Experimental and comparative results reveal that watermarked videos have very high watermark transparency and robustness in terms of PSNR and signal processing attacks. Furthermore, watermarks extracted by the suggested approach, without transmission assaults, have a higher PSNR.

10.3 Proposed Methodology

The lack of searchability, ways of viewing viral videos, and ease of "deep-fake" content creation all make video among the most difficult types of misinformation to fact-check. This study aims to develop a watermark-based mechanism to facilitate authentication by introducing traceability. The proposed transform-based video watermarking comprises the two steps of watermark insertion and removalEffectiveness of its application has been experimentally assessed with the two promising watermarking methods DWT and SLT.

10.3.1 Watermark Insertion

In the watermark embedding process, the authors introduced a 10-digit telephone number, an AADHAAR number, a social security number (SSN), and GPS coordinates as a watermark into the carrier signal. Each time a user tries to share a video on social media, the system will check for the presence of a watermark. If a watermark is already present, the system will not overwrite it with the current sender's information. If no watermark is found, the system will insert the current sender's information as a watermark. This allows us to trace the information back to its epicenter and authenticate the source. The embedding procedure consists of the following steps:

1. Convert the individual watermark into its corresponding binary form.
2. Merge all watermarks into a single watermark (W1) by employing four copies of a watermark in the host video W = (W1 + W2 + W3 + W4) to enhance reliability. Even if the watermarked video is attacked, at least one watermark can be used to retrieve information about the source.
3. Convert the video from RGB to grayscale.
4. Divide the video sequence into its respective frames.
5. Select the frames with maximum entropy.
6. Transform each selected frame into size 512 × 512.
7. Divide each selected frame into non-uniform blocks of size 16 × 16. Each block is used to embed a single watermark binary bit.
8. Conduct transform domain technique (DWT and SLT) on each block of each selected frame to have (HH, LH, LL, and HL) sub-bands.
9. Modify the coefficients HL and LH using the watermark bit, embedding strength (ES), MF1 and MF2 using Equations (10.1) and (10.2)

$$MF1 = \frac{ES - \left(\text{Mean HL} - \text{Mean LH}\right)}{2} \tag{10.1}$$

$$MF2 = \frac{ES - \left(\text{Mean LH} - \text{Mean HL}\right)}{2} \tag{10.2}$$

10. Conduct inverse transform to get modified blocks
11. Perform steps 7–8 on each block to insert each watermark bit into the host-selected video frame.
12. The modified frames are re-transformed from 512 × 512 to their original frame size.

Finally, the watermarked video is created to be shared on OSM.

10.3.2 Watermark Extraction

The extraction technique covers watermark extraction and user identification via the retrieved 10-digit phone number, SSN or AADHAAR, and GPS coordinates in the following steps:

1. Divide the video sequence into its respective frames.
2. Select the frames with maximum entropy.
3. Each selected frame is transformed into size 512 × 512.
4. Each selected frame is divided into non-uniform blocks of size 16 × 16.
5. Conduct transform domain technique (DWT and SLT) on each block of each selected frame to have (HH, LH, LL, and HL) sub-bands.
6. Extract the watermark bits from each block using Equation (10.3).

$$\text{EWbit} = \begin{cases} 1 \text{ if Mean HL} > \text{Mean LH} \\ 0 \text{ if Mean LH} > \text{Mean HL} \end{cases} \quad (10.3)$$

7. Repeat steps 5–6 for each block to retrieve all watermark bits. Extracted and embedded watermark bits are compared to examine the performance of the proposed methodology. The proposed system assumes that the watermarked video is attacked.

10.4 Experimental Evaluation

The experimental results for robustness and imperceptibility were established using DWT and SLT transform domain strategies. The videos used for the experiment were downloaded from ref. [12]. To integrate a watermark and assess the efficacy of the proposed method, three host videos of sizes 386 × 288, 800 × 480, and 800 × 480 were utilized (Figure 10.1). The selected frames of maximum entropy were resized into 512 × 512 and then the respective frames were divided into 16 × 16 non-overlapping uniform blocks. Consequently, 1024 blocks were created. However, the size of the watermark is also equal to 1024 bits (960 bits + 64 bits of padding). Hence, each block is used to embed one bit. To measure the robustness of

| Host video 1 (Akiyo) | Host video 2 (Foreman) | Host video 3 (Hall of monitors) |

Figure 10.1 Host videos for watermarking process.

Table 10.1 Watermarked Videos with PSNR and SSIM for DWT and SLT

Host Video	Watermarked Video (DWT)	Watermarked Video (SLT)
PSNR	46.1424	46.1224
SSIM	0.9909	0.9908
PSNR	43.6886	43.6858
SSIM	0.9827	0.9827
PSNR	44.5973	44.5057
SSIM	0.9875	0.9871

the proposed approach, BER has been used between inserted and extracted watermark bits. Similarly, PSNR and SSIM were used to evaluate the imperceptibility between host and watermarked video. Table 10.1 shows the PSNR and SSIM values of all three watermarked videos with an embedding strength of 0.01.

10.5 Discussion

Multiple watermarking algorithms, including DWT and SLT, have been evaluated in this research to authenticate the source of shared video content in OSM. There is a trade-off between PSNR and BER among DWT and SLT based on the examination of several embedding strengths. For optimal results, we selected an embedding strength of 0.01. BER was used to compare extracted and embedded watermark bits from respective frames as shown in Tables 10.2, 10.3, and 10.4. For each

Table 10.2   Comparison of the Robustness of DWT and SLT in Terms of BER for Source Authentication

		For Video Akiyo.mp4 with ES = 0.01					
		BER					
		DWT			SLT		
S.no.	Attack	F263	F265	F266	F263	F265	F266
1	a	**0**	0.0019	**0**	0.0009	**0.0009**	0.0039
2	b	0.0039	0.0039	**0.0009**	0.0019	**0.0009**	0.0029
3	c	0	0	0.0009	0	0	**0**
4	d	**0**	0	**0**	0.0009	0	0.0009
5	e	0.8183	0.8164	0.8154	**0.0039**	**0.0039**	**0.0039**
6	f	0.8242	0.8232	0.8232	**0.0019**	**0.0019**	**0.0019**
7	g	0	0	**0**	0	0	0.0009
8	h	0.7753	0.7744	0.7744	**0**	**0**	**0**
9	i	**0**	0	**0**	0.0009	0	0.0009
10	j	0.0039	0.0039	0.0048	**0**	**0**	**0.0009**
11	k	**0**	**0**	**0**	0.0009	0.0019	0.0029
12	l	0.0957	0.0966	0.0976	**0.0058**	**0.0039**	**0.0048**
13	m	**0**	0	**0**	0.0009	0	0.0009
14	n	**0.3583**	**0.3535**	**0.3535**	0.4169	0.4257	0.4287
15	o	**0.2949**	**0.2988**	**0.2968**	0.3027	0.3027	0.3115
16	p	0.1982	0.1943	0.1933	**0.0302**	**0.0244**	**0.0224**

(Continued)

Table 10.2   (Continued)

		For Video Akiyo.mp4 with ES = 0.01					
		BER					
		DWT			SLT		
S.no.	Attack	F263	F265	F266	F263	F265	F266
17	q	0.0615	0.0585	0.0595	**0.0039**	**0.0039**	**0.0048**
18	r	0.0009	**0**	**0**	**0**	0	0.0009
19	s	0.0224	0.0224	0.0224	**0.0009**	**0**	**0.0009**
20	t	0.1787	0.1718	0.1806	**0.0009**	**0**	**0.0029**

Table 10.3   Comparison of the Robustness of DWT and SLT in Terms of BER for Source Authentication

		For Video Foreman.mp4 with ES = 0.01					
		BER					
		DWT			SLT		
S.No.	Attack	F217	F216	F218	F217	F216	F218
1	a	**0.0029**	0.0039	0.0048	0.0039	**0.0029**	**0.0039**
2	b	0.0078	0.0097	0.0107	**0.0029**	**0.0087**	**0.0107**
3	c	**0.0009**	**0.0009**	**0.0078**	0.0019	0.0029	0.0087
4	d	0	0.0009	0	0	**0**	0
5	e	0.6533	0.6562	0.6494	**0.0009**	**0.0009**	**0.0019**
6	f	0.6699	0.6865	0.6679	**0**	**0**	**0.0009**
7	g	0	0.0009	0	0	**0**	0
8	h	0.5859	0.6054	0.5517	**0**	**0**	**0**
9	i	0	0.0009	0	0	**0**	0
10	j	0.0009	0.0019	0.0039			
11	k	0	0.0019	0.0009	0	**0**	**0**
12	l	0.1298	0.1259	0.1171	0.0087	0.0146	0.0097

(*Continued*)

Table 10.3 (Continued)

For Video Foreman.mp4 with ES = 0.01							
BER							
		DWT			SLT		
S.No.	Attack	F217	F216	F218	F217	F216	F218
13	m	0	0.0009	0	0	0	0
14	n	**0.2509**	**0.2265**	**0.2382**	0.3671	0.4414	0.4042
15	o	**0.1767**	**0.164**	**0.1826**	0.2734	0.2949	0.2812
16	p	**0.083**	**0.0869**	**0.1005**	0.1005	0.0976	0.1044
17	q	0.016	0.0166	0.0136	**0.0068**	**0.0097**	**0.0107**
18	r	**0**	**0**	**0**	0.0009	0	0
19	s	0.0419	0.0468	0.0439	**0**	**0**	**0.0009**
20	t	0.0917	0.1015	0.0927	**0.04**	**0.0546**	**0.0429**

Table 10.4 Comparison of the Robustness of DWT and SLT in Terms of BER for Source Authentication

For Video Hall_of_monitors.mp4 with ES = 0.01							
BER							
		DWT			SLT		
S.no.	Attack	F29	F30	F31	F29	F30	F31
1	a	**0.0039**	**0.0009**	**0.0048**	0.0117	0.0029	0.0068
2	b	**0.0107**	**0.0039**	**0.0107**	0.0263	0.0126	0.0166
3	c	0.0097	**0.0019**	**0.0058**	**0.0087**	0.0078	0.0175
4	d	**0.0039**	**0.0009**	0.0019	0.0048	0.0019	**0.0009**
5	e	0.7548	0.7529	0.7539	**0.0185**	**0.0214**	**0.0205**
6	f	0.7783	0.7724	0.7753	**0.0078**	**0.539**	**0.0107**
7	g	0.0039	**0**	0.0009	**0.0029**	0.0019	0.0009
8	h	0.6308	0.6289	0.6308	**0.0048**	**0.0029**	**0.0029**

(Continued)

Table 10.4 (Continued)

		For Video Hall_of_monitors.mp4 with ES = 0.01					
		BER					
		DWT			SLT		
S.no.	Attack	F29	F30	F31	F29	F30	F31
9	i	**0.0039**	**0.0009**	0.0019	0.0048	0.0019	**0.0009**
10	j	0.0087	**0.0029**	0.0068	**0.0039**	0.0039	**0.0039**
11	k	**0.0068**	**0.0029**	**0.0039**	0.0107	0.0107	0.0097
12	l	0.163	0.163	0.1601	**0.0302**	**0.0273**	**0.0253**
13	m	0.0048	**0.0009**	0.0019	0.0048	0.0019	0.0019
14	n	**0.2626**	**0.2265**	**0.2597**	0.3974	0.4062	0.4082
15	o	**0.2187**	**0.207**	**0.2236**	0.247	0.2851	0.2744
16	p	0.1738	0.1718	0.1708	**0.0703**	**0.0986**	**0.0878**
17	q	0.0332	**0.0292**	0.0361	**0.0292**	0.0341	**0.0273**
18	r	**0.0058**	**0.0009**	**0.0019**	0.0087	0.0029	0.0039
19	s	0.1865	0.1855	0.1728	**0.0136**	**0.0146**	**0.0058**
20	t	0.2382	0.2529	0.2421	**0.1591**	**0.1308**	**0.1406**

watermarking technique, the BER was examined for each of the three host videos. SLT has been chosen for future experimentation, as it outperforms DWT in robustness with several signal processing attacks.

The attacks were as follows: (a) salt & pepper 0.05, (b) Gaussian noise 0.01, (c) speckle noise 0.01, (d) Poisson noise, (e) average filter [ones(3)/9], (f) median filter [3 × 3], (g) Gaussian filter [3 × 3], (h) Wiener filter [3 × 3], (i) adjust image contrast [0 0.8] [0 1], (j) sharpening (0.2), (k) adaptive equalization, (l) motion blur (theta = 7, len = 10), (m) Gamma correction 0.8, (n) compression (QF = 50), (o) compression (QF = 60), (p) compression (QF = 70), (q) compression (QF = 80), (r) compression (QF = 90), (s) JPEG 2000 compression (QF = 10), and (t) JPEG 2000 compression (QF = 15).

The experiment results were obtained using a Matlab (2018 a) environment with a 2.20 GHz Xenon processor and 64 GB RAM.

10.6 Limitation

This study propounds a methodology for source authentication of shared videos on social media using the watermarking technique. However, the study was a limited one in that the experimental videos were free from frame dropping, frame swapping, translation, and cropping attacks.

10.7 Conclusion

This research suggested a persistent video watermarking mechanism based on the transform domain as a means of identifying the first user of shared video on social media. The implementations were found to be feasible and effective via both SLT and DWT. A comparative study of DWT and SLT-based implementations was performed with 10-digit mobile phone numbers, SSN or AADHAAR numbers, and GPS as an embedded watermarks. Four copies of the watermark are inserted into the frame of maximum entropy. The overall comparison against several parameters/attacks revealed that SLT-based implementation outperforms DWT-based implementation in terms of various signal processing attacks along with similar PSNR values. The immediate extensions may include generalization by extending the scope of attacks, and optimization to achieve higher imperceptibility and robustness.

References

1. Number of social media users 2025 | Statista. [Online]. Available: https://www.statista.com/statistics/278414/number-of-worldwide-social-network-users/. [Accessed: 25-June-2022].
2. Banaji, S., Bhat, R., Agarwal, A., Passanha, N., & Sadhana Pravin, M. (2019). "WhatsApp vigilantes: An exploration of citizen reception and circulation of WhatsApp misinformation linked to mob violence in India." Department of Media and Communications, London School of Economics.
3. C. Kumar, A. K. Singh, and P. Kumar, "Dual watermarking: An approach for securing digital documents," *Multimed. Tools Appl.*, vol. 79, no. 11–12, pp. 7339–7354, Mar. 2020, doi: 10.1007/s11042-019-08314-5.
4. N. Tarhouni, M. Charfeddine, and C. Ben Amar, "Novel and Robust Image Watermarking for Copyright Protection and Integrity Control," *Circuits, Syst. Signal Process.*, vol. 39, no. 10, pp. 5059–5103, Oct. 2020, doi: 10.1007/s00034-020-01401-1.
5. A. Benoraira, K. Benmahammed, and N. Boucenna, "Blind image watermarking technique based on differential embedding in DWT and DCT domains," *EURASIP J. Adv. Signal Process.*, vol. 2015, no. 1, Dec. 2015, doi: 10.1186/s13634-015-0239-5.
6. R. Singh, H. Mittal, and R. Pal, "Optimal keyframe selection-based lossless video-watermarking technique using IGSA in LWT domain for copyright protection," *Complex Intell. Syst.*, vol. 8, no. 2, pp. 1047–1070, Apr. 2022, doi: 10.1007/s40747-021-00569-6.
7. X. Wu, P. Ma, Z. Jin, Y. Wu, W. Han, and W. Ou, "A novel zero-watermarking scheme based on NSCT-SVD and blockchain for video copyright," *Eurasip J. Wirel. Commun. Netw.*, vol. 2022, no. 1, Dec. 2022, doi: 10.1186/s13638-022-02090-x.

8. M. Kumar, J. Aggarwal, A. Rani, T. Stephan, A. Shankar, and S. Mirjalili, "Secure video communication using firefly optimization and visual cryptography," *Artif. Intell. Rev.*, vol. 55, no. 4, pp. 2997–3017, Apr. 2022, doi: 10.1007/s10462-021-10070-8.

9. A. Hammami, A. Ben Hamida, and C. Ben Amar, "Blind semi-fragile watermarking scheme for video authentication in video surveillance context," *Multimed. Tools Appl.*, vol. 80, no. 5, pp. 7479–7513, Feb. 2021, doi: 10.1007/s11042-020-09982-4.

10. G. Dhevanandhini and G. Yamuna, "An effective and secure video watermarking using hybrid technique," *Multimed. Syst.*, vol. 27, no. 5, pp. 953–967, Oct. 2021, doi: 10.1007/s00530-021-00765-x.

11. R. Shoitan, M. M. Moussa, and S. M. Elshoura, "A robust video watermarking scheme based on Laplacian pyramid, SVD, and DWT with improved robustness towards geometric attacks via SURF," *Multimed. Tools Appl.*, 2020, doi: 10.1007/s11042-020-09258-x.

12. "Xiph.org:: Derf's Test Media Collection." [Online]. Available: https://media.xiph.org/video/derf/. [Accessed: 28-Aug-2022].

Chapter 11

Task Scheduling Using MOIPSO Algorithm in Cloud Computing

Rajeshwari Sissodia, Manmohan Singh Rauthan, and Varun Barthwal

Hemvati Nandan Bahuguna Garhwal University, Srinagar, India

11.1 Introduction

Cloud computing is a promising technology through which consumers receive a variety of services with rapid response and scalability over the internet. Virtualization is the process of partitioning the resources of a physical machine (PM) to enable multiple execution environments in cloud computing. Various principles, including time-sharing, machine simulation, and emulation, are employed in virtualization to virtualize computing, storage, network, and memory. This enables the multi-tenancy idea in cloud computing, whereby virtualized resources are pooled to serve multiple users through the same PM (Figure 11.1). Virtualization, load balancing, fault tolerance, security, and scheduling are the most critical problems to address.

Virtualization consists of a hypervisor or VM monitor that presents a guest operating system with a virtual operating platform. Some popular hypervisors are VMW's ESX/ESXi, Oracle VM Server, Citrix XenServer, Xenhypervisor, and KVM. A hypervisor or VM monitor virtualizes a guest OS with a virtual OS platform. Virtualization, task scheduling, reusability, privacy, and scheduling are crucial. Scheduling tasks is one of the greatest challenges in cloud computing. The technique for searching for required resources is identical to the procedure for searching for various VMs, because it is the required resources that collectively constitute VMs.

DOI: 10.1201/9781003371380-11

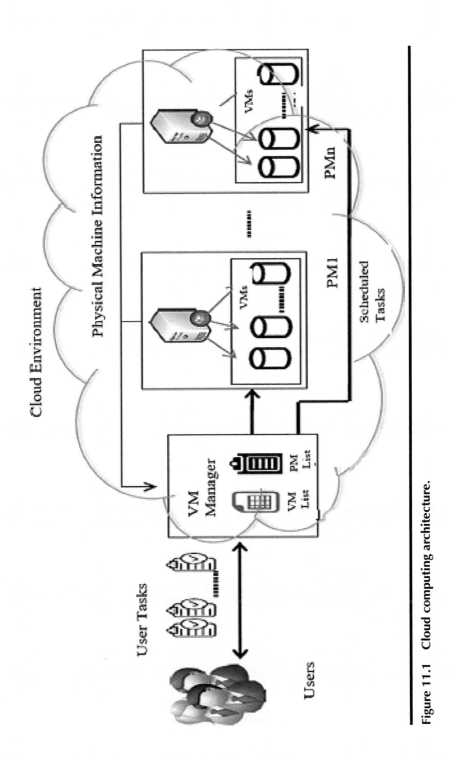

Figure 11.1 Cloud computing architecture.

Cloud-based tasks are carried out by VMs. Users send requests to the data center to have their jobs executed. A task may entail data entry and processing, software access, or storage-related operations. The execution of these tasks is contingent on the task-to-VM mapping. To achieve the highest quality of service (QoS) in the cloud, it is essential to map tasks to virtual machines. Both independent and dependent tasks are possible. The nature of task scheduling is an NP-hard issue involving several jobs and machines. Task-to-resource mapping is successfully achieved if the cloud has achieved the minimal makespan, the minimum execution time of tasks and VMs, and the maximum use of resources, among other criteria. In addition to the task being carried out, a response must be delivered to the user.

There is much academic interest in task scheduling practice for load balancing, energy efficiency, resource usage, work migration, and QoS. The challenge remains to build unique algorithms for task scheduling in a cloud context. The following are important contributions to task scheduling research.

- A Multi-objective Improved Particle Swarm Optimization Algorithm (MOIPSO) using ranking method is proposed to address task scheduling problems.
- This method satisfies multi-objective optimization in the cloud by minimizing the makespan, average cost and average completion time required to execute it.

11.2 Related Work

Using a cloud platform, Sourabh Budhiraja et al. [1] presented a modified genetic algorithm (MOGA) for CPU task scheduling. The MOGA method was compared to standard genetic algorithm (SGA). Tsai et al. [2] presented the improved differential algorithm (IDEA), which combines Taguchi's method with a differential evolution algorithm (DEA). The proposed IDEA method identifies the cost associated with processing and receiving. Atul Vikas Lakra et al. [3] developed a multi-objective job scheduling strategy to boost physical server efficiency and preserve SaaS application. It reduces CPU execution time. Jena et al. [4] introduced job scheduling using multi-objective nested particle swarm optimization (TSPSO). This approach reduces EC and ET.

Awad et al. [5] created the multi-objective load balancing particle swarm optimization (MLBMPSO) algorithm to increase speed and productivity by simultaneously executing multiple tasks. Liyun Zuo et al. [6] presented an improved ant method for cost-based scheduling. This method reduce cost and makespan. Hua He et al. [7] present an ideal approach to adaptive multi-objective task scheduling (AMTS) that can increase productivity, optimize resources, and shorten task completion times. The AMTS algorithm based on particle swarm optimization (PSO) has been demonstrated to be a viable technique for achieving the best job outputs, minimizing cost and conserving energy. Majid Habibi et al. [8] aim to improve the imperialistic competitive algorithm (ICA) by optimizing the use of time, bandwidth, and resources. This study shows that the upgraded ICA model outperforms both genetic algorithm (GA) and traditional ICA.

The responsive multi-objective load balancing transformation (RMOLBT) approach developed by V.G. Ravindhren et al. [9] can be employed in a multi-cloud scenario based on abstraction. The RMOLBT algorithm is compared with load-balanced algorithm (LBA) and PSO. The group task scheduling (GTS) algorithm was designed by V.G. Ravindhren et al. [10] to meet the needs of cloud users and their QoS. The GTS algorithm was compared with min-min and task scheduling (TS). The GTS algorithm prioritizes jobs based on their processing time. The cuckoo gravitational search algorithm (CGSA) was introduced by Pradeep et al. [11]. Comparisons show that the proposed CGSA outperforms other algorithms such as the GSA, CS, PSO and GA. Pradeep et al. [12] suggest a cuckoo harmony search algorithm (CHSA) to provide effective scheduling. The CHSA is compared to hybrid CGSA, CS, and HS algorithms. The suggested CHSA algorithm achieves excellent performance by minimizing cost, memory use, penalty, EC, and credit.

Dr T. Jacob et al. [13] developed the oppositional cuckoo search algorithm (OCSA), which optimizes scheduling time and cost. The OCSA outperforms other cloud simulation tools such as PSO, IDEA, and GA. N. Gobalkrishnan et al. [14] proposed the novel genetic gray wolf optimization (GGWO) algorithm that combines the GA and gray wolf optimizer (GWO) algorithms to help lower load demand, EC, migration expenses, and time. The GGWO algorithm perform better than the GA and GWO.

Sajjad Jaber et al. [15] presented a multi-objective improved cuckoo search algorithm (MOICS) to optimize reduced makespan and cost.

11.3 Problem Formulation

The primary objective of task scheduling algorithms is to bind a set of user tasks to a set of remote resources in order to achieve multiple objectives, including the minimization of makespan, total completion time and average waiting. Therefore, an effective scheduling algorithm that focuses on many objectives is necessary. In this paper, the objective problems listed below are addressed for the development of efficient task scheduling.

1. Makespan (Mi)
   The makespan is the final time to finish the task. The makespan is calculated using Equation (11.1).

$$Mi = maximum \left(completion\ time \right) \tag{11.1}$$

2. Average completion time (ACT)
It is calculated using Equation (11.2)

$$ACT = \frac{Cloudlet.getCostPerSec\,()\times Cloudlet.getWaitingTime()}{size} \qquad (11.2)$$

3. Average cost
It is calculated by using Equation (11.3)

$$Average\ Cost = \frac{Cloudlet.getCostPerSec\,()\times Cloudlet.getActualCPUTime()}{size} \qquad (11.3)$$

4. Fitness function fi(x)
To evaluate particle positions, a fitness function is used, as illustrated in Equation (11.4).

$$Fitness\ Function\ fi(x) = minimum\left(Mi + ACT, average\ Cost\right) \qquad (11.4)$$

11.4 System Model

In this model, the task manager accepts the tasks, manages the tasks, and asks the users to submit the information to the scheduler. The task scheduling architecture is represented schematically in Figure 11.2. Cloud computing setups have a local resource manager for each physical node. CPU, memory load, and individual task execution time are provided periodically to a global resource manager to determine resource cost. The scheduler collects task and resource data from the task manager and global resource management to achieve efficient task scheduling. The MOIPSO algorithms assign each task to the most appropriate available resource to execute tasks based on the multi-objective parameters such as makespan, average cost and average completion time.

11.5 Traditional Approach

A swarm of particles, each representing a different solution, is used in traditional PSO. It has two main characteristics, a position x and a velocity v, which represent the intended position and velocity of movement. The various jobs are represented by virtual machines (VMs). Individual articles are referred to as having the best personal experience (p_{best}), whereas entire populations are referred to as having the best group experience (g_{best}). The position of a particle in the global problem space at any given time is defined by its personal best (p_{best}) and the positions of many

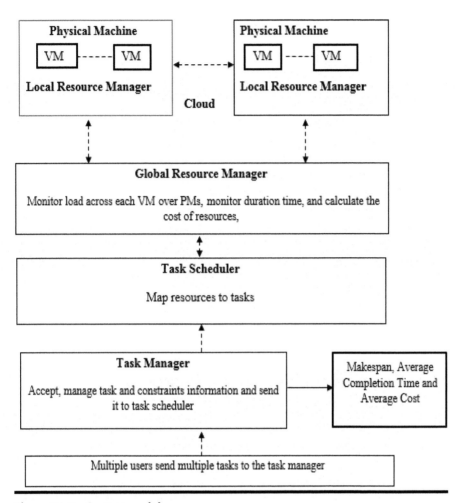

Figure 11.2   System model.

identical best particles (g_{best}). The PSO uses adaptive movement, which involves particle movement during each iteration. At iteration t, PSO updates particle x_i as

$$x_i(t) = x_i(t-1) + v_i(t) x_i(t) = x_i(t-1) + v_i(t) \tag{11.5}$$

Here
    t denotes iteration
    i denotes particle
    x_i denotes particle current position
    $x_i(t-1)$ denotes location of particle
    $v_i(t)$ denotes particle velocity

Equation (11.6) specifies the velocity of particle i at time t.

$$v[i] = \omega \times v[i] + C \times \left(p_{\text{best}}[i] - x[i] \right) + C \times \left(g_{\text{best}}[i] - x[i] \right) \tag{11.6}$$

where
  v denotes particle velocity
  x denotes particle position
  p_{best} denotes particle best position
  g_{best} denotes swarm best position
  r_1, r_2 are random integers between 0 and 1
  C_1 and $C_2 = C$ denote acceleration coefficient
  ω denotes inertia weight

Equation (11.6) makes use of w to direct the particle's motion and enhance the convergence of PSO. For better PSO convergence, ω in Equation (11.6) controls particle mobility. In the search space, the values r_1 and r_2 control particle movement. C_1 and C_2 are both positive constants that govern the best particles for both individuals and the global. Since a particle's best position (p_{best}) affects the best locations of its neighbors, their values are equal.

11.6 Proposed Multi-objective Improved Particle Swarm Optimization

The proposed approach determines the makespan, average cost and average completion time for each task in each VM using Equations (11.1), (11.2) and (11.3). Now initialize the swarm, velocity, position, and p_{best} values. Calculate fitness function using Equation (11.4) based on the rank of average cost, makespan and average completion time. Select the particle (VMs) which has minimum rank value (i.e., p_{best}) by considering the multi-objective parameters (i.e., average cost, makespan and average completion time).

**ALGORITHM   MULTI-OBJECTIVE IMPROVE PARTICLE
SWARM OPTIMIZATION (MOIPSO)**

Input: Number of tasks (t), Number of virtual machine (VMs)
Output: p_{best}
Begin MOIPSO (t, VMs)
for $t \in$ T do
for $v \in$ VMS do
Calculate makespan (t,v) using Equation (11.1)

Calculate average completion time (t,v) using Equation (11.2)
Calculate average cost (t,v) using Equation (11.3)
end for
Initialize each swarm particles, velocity, position and p_{best}
for $i \in$ T do
for $v \in$ VMs do
Calculate fitness function (VMs, (mi, average cost and average completion time)) using Equation (11.4)
{
Sort v in ascending order based on makespan, average cost and average completion time
Sort v in ascending order based on the rank
Select v with smallest rank value
}
$p_{best}(i)$ = Evaluate (fitness function) update (velocity (i), position (i))
end for
end for
return p_{best}
end

11.7 Experiment

This section contains the proposed approach's experiment results, discussion and a detailed comparison with existing methods to demonstrate the proposed method's efficiency.

11.7.1 Experimental Set-Up

The CloudSim is a Java-based cloud simulation toolkit. It is a structure for developing and implementing cloud infrastructure systems and services that supports big cloud nodes and environments. Simulations were performed in heterogeneous cloud environments in order to compare the proposed method with existing heuristic techniques (i.e., RR and FCFS).

11.7.2 Experimental Parameters

Table 11.1 gives the experimental parameters and values.

Table 11.1   Experimental Parameters

Cognitive constant (C_1)	2
Social constant (C_2)	2
Inertia weight (ω)	0.9
Number of cloudlets	1000–4000
Population size	30
Number of iterations	4000
Number of VMs	20
Number of hosts	2
Type of policy	Time shared
Number of datacenter	2

11.7.3 Experiment, Result and Discussion

1. Makespan

Assume there are 1000–4000 cloudlets in the experiment, running on 20 VM. Equation (11.1) is used to compute the makespan. The RR and FCFS are two well-known techniques for comparing the performance of the MOIPSO algorithm. As shown in Figure 11.3, the MOIPSO algorithm has the lowest makespan while the FCFS algorithm has the highest makespan.

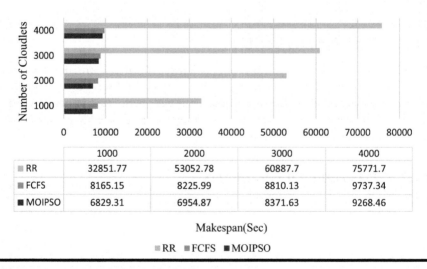

	1000	2000	3000	4000
RR	32851.77	53052.78	60887.7	75771.7
FCFS	8165.15	8225.99	8810.13	9737.34
MOIPSO	6829.31	6954.87	8371.63	9268.46

Makespan(Sec)

RR   FCFS   MOIPSO

Figure 11.3   Comparative analysis of makespan.

2. Average Completion Time

Assume there are 1000–4000 tasks in the experiment, running on 20 VMs. Equation (11.2) is used to compute the average completion time. The RR and FCFS are two well-known techniques for comparing the performance of the MOIPSO algorithm. As shown in Figure 11.4, the MOIPSO algorithm has the lowest completion time, while the FCFS algorithm has the highest completion time.

3. Average Cost

Assume there are 1000–4000 tasks in the experiment, running on 20 VMs. Equation (11.3) is used to compute the average completion time. The RR and FCFS are two well-known techniques for comparing the performance of the MOIPSO algorithm. As shown in Figure 11.5, the MOIPSO algorithm has the lowest cost, while the FCFS algorithm has the highest cost.

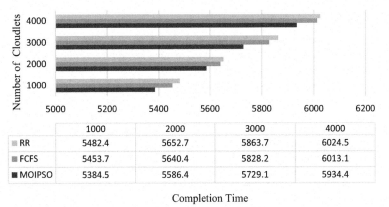

	1000	2000	3000	4000
RR	5482.4	5652.7	5863.7	6024.5
FCFS	5453.7	5640.4	5828.2	6013.1
MOIPSO	5384.5	5586.4	5729.1	5934.4

Completion Time

RR FCFS MOIPSO

Figure 11.4 Comparative analysis of average completion time.

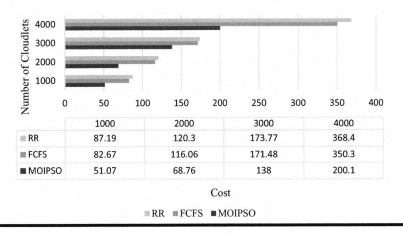

	1000	2000	3000	4000
RR	87.19	120.3	173.77	368.4
FCFS	82.67	116.06	171.48	350.3
MOIPSO	51.07	68.76	138	200.1

Cost

RR FCFS MOIPSO

Figure 11.5 Comparative analysis of average cost.

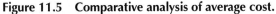

11.8 Conclusion and Future Work

This paper presents a multi-objective improved particle swarm optimization algorithm (MOIPSO) using the ranking method to solve the multi-objective task scheduling problem. The proposed MOIPSO algorithm allocated tasks to the VM which has minimum rank value by considering three conflicting parameters (i.e., makespan, average cost, and average completion time). Following experiments using the CloudSim tool, the proposed MOIPSO algorithm provided an optimal solution for reducing makespan, average cost and average completion time. In future, the proposed MOIPSO will include other multi-objective parameters such as wall clock time and submission time.

References

1. Budhiraja, S. and Singh, D. An Efficient Approach for Task Scheduling Based on Multi-Objective Genetic Algorithm in Cloud Computing Environment, *International Journal of Computer Science and Communication (IJCSC)*, vol. 4, ISSN-0973-7391, pp. 74–79, 2012.
2. Tsai, J.-T., Fang, J.-C., and Chou, J.-H. Optimized Task Scheduling and Resource Allocation on the Cloud Computing Environment Using An Improved Differential Evolution Algorithm, *Computers & Operations Research*, vol. 40, pp. 3045–3055, 2013.
3. Lakra, A. and Yadav, D. Multi-Objective Tasks Scheduling Algorithm for Cloud Computing Throughput Optimization, *Procedia Computer Science*, vol. 48, pp. 107–113, 2015.
4. Jena, R. Multi-objective Task Scheduling in Cloud Environment Using Nested PSO Framework, *Procedia Computer Science*, vol. 57, pp. 1219–1227, 2015.
5. Awad, A., Hefnawy, N., and Elkader, A. Dynamic Multi-objective Task scheduling in Cloud Computing based on modified particle swarm optimization, *Advances in Computer Science(ACSIJ): An International Journal*, vol. 4(5), No. 17, ISSN: 2322-5157, pp. 110–117, 2015.
6. Zuo, L. and Shoo, L. A Multi-Objective Optimization Scheduling Method Based on the Ant Colony Algorithm in Cloud Computing, *IEEE Access*, vol. 3, ISSN: 2169–3536, pp. 2687–2699, 2015.
7. He, H., Guangquan, X., Shenzhen, P., and Zhao, Z. AMTS: Adaptive Multi-Objective Task Scheduling Strategy in Cloud Computing, *China Communications*, vol. 13, ISSN: 1673-5447, pp. 162–171, 2016.
8. Habibi, M. and Navimipour, M. Multi-Objective Task Scheduling in Cloud Computing Using an Imperialist Competitive Algorithm, *International Journal of Advanced Computer Science and Applications (IJACSA)*, vol. 7(5), pp. 289–293, 2016.
9. Ravindhren, V.G. and Ravimaran, S. Responsive Multi-objective Load Balancing Transformation Using Particle Swarm Optimization in Cloud Environment, *Journal of Advances in Chemistry*, vol. 12, ISSN: 2321-807X, pp. 4815–4816, 2016.
10. Ali, H. G. E. D. H., Saroit, I. A., and Kotb, A. M. Grouped tasks scheduling algorithm based on QoS in the cloud computing network, *Egyptian Informatics Journal*, vol. 18, pp. 11–19, 2016.
11. Pradeep, K. and Jacob, T.P. CGSA scheduler: A multi-objective-based hybrid approach for task scheduling in a cloud environment, *Information Security Journal*, vol. 27, pp. 77–91, 2017.

12. Praveen, K. and Prem Jacob, T. A Hybrid Approach for Task Scheduling Using the Cuckoo and Harmony Search in Cloud Computing Environment, *Wireless Personal Communication*, vol. 101, pp. 2287–2311, 2018.

13. Jacob, T. and Kumar, P. OCSA: Task scheduling algorithm in the cloud computing environment, *International Journal of Intelligent Engineering and Systems*, vol. 11(3), pp. 271–279, 2018.

14. Gopalakrishnan, N. and Arum, C. A New Multi-Objective Optimal Programming Model for Task Scheduling using Genetic Grey Wolf Optimization in Cloud Computing, Computer And Communications Networks Systems, *The Computer Journal*, vol. 61(10), pp. 1523–1536, 2018.

15. Jaber, S., Ali, Y., and Ibrahim, N. An Automated Task Scheduling Model Using a Multi-objective Improved Cuckoo Optimization Algorithm, *International Journal of Intelligent Engineering and Systems*, vol. 15, No. 1, 2022. DOI: 10.22266/ijies2022.0228.27.

Chapter 12

Feature Selection-Based Comparative Analysis for Cardiovascular Disease Prediction Using a Machine Learning Model

Smita and Ela Kumar

Indira Gandhi Delhi Technical University for Women, New Delhi, India

12.1 Introduction

According to WHO statistics, cardiovascular disease is one of the leading causes of mortality worldwide. In 2019, an estimated 17.9 million people died from cardiovascular disease worldwide, with 85% of the deaths attributed solely to heart attack and stroke [1]. Detecting symptoms of cardiovascular disease as early as possible is essential so that cardiologists can advise patients and treatment can begin [12, 17]. This work investigates heart disease issue using publicly available data from the cardiology department, Excelcare Hospital, Guwahati, Assam, and the Cleveland Heart Disease dataset at UCI.

Artificial intelligence (AI) is playing an increasingly important role in healthcare decision making, with computer technologies aiding digital diagnosis of patients [8, 10, 16]. With machine learning come new opportunities for healthcare practitioners in the field of medical data collection [7, 9, 18]. This paper uses two different

DOI: 10.1201/9781003371380-12

datasets to provide a comparative analysis of a set of machine learning models with and without feature selection to predict the chances of cardiovascular disease.

12.2 Related Work

Ayon et al. [3] used seven machine learning models for comparative analysis of the Statlog and Cleveland datasets with 270 and 303 samples respectively. In the first part of implementation, five-fold and ten-fold cross-validation techniques were used on both datasets before evaluating matrices such as accuracy, sensitivity, specificity, precision and F1 score, etc. The objective of the cross-validation method is to examine both training and test, and after examination to test exactly once. The result shows that out of seven deep learning models for both datasets, SVM performs well with 98.15% accuracy in the Statlog dataset and 97.36% in the Cleveland dataset.

In [4], Spencer et al. concentrate on predicting the accurate results for cardiovascular disease by applying chi-square feature selection and principal component analysis (PCA) feature extraction to the combination of four heart disease datasets from the UCI ML repository. The four datasets were combined in order to analyze a large number of samples using various ML techniques and thus provide a realistic predictive model.

Yadav, Dhyan Chandra et al. in [2] consider feature elimination and feature selection methods for predicting the chances of cardiovascular disease occurrence, using various matrix-like classification accuracy, sensitivity, and graphical analysis. Strong features were identified by Pearson correlation (PC) on the various ML models, then recursive features elimination (RFE) methods were added to their algorithms. Finally, Pearson correlation and Lasso regularization with RF ensemble showed 99% accuracy, the highest of the four algorithms with comparative analysis of two different PC scenarios.

Ghosh, Pronab et al. in [5] performed comparative analysis of various basic ML models with feature selection using relief-based trained models and found the random forest bagging method (RFBM) achieved the highest accuracy of 99.05% with ten features.

Latha, et al. [6] proposed various machine learning models for prediction of heart disease using feature selection for performance enhancement. Their research focuses mainly on comparative analysis using ensemble models such as bagging, boosting, stacking and majority voting. Comparative analysis of the results showed that majority voting generates the highest score in terms of accuracy (85.48%) with NB, Bayes net (BT), RF, and multilayer perception (MP).

12.3 Proposed Methodology

Figure 12.2 illustrates the workflow of the present research paper. The steps undertaken are data pre-processing, data scaling, feature selection, and algorithmic computation using various ML models, followed by analysis of the results predicting cardiac complications in male and female patients. Python 3 was used to carry out this overall task. In the data cleaning phase, most of the common methods for removal of all null values fill the missing values with mean or most probable values within their range [13]. Once data have been cleaned, chi-square feature selection techniques are added to select the most prominent features for predicting the possibility of disease, with min-max scaling techniques for data transformation within a range between 0 and 1. The model incorporates nine ML techniques with their associated prominent performance measure such as confusion matrix, precision, recall, F1-score and accuracy [14, 15].

Figure 12.1 shows the basic principle of majority voting as an ensemble classifier in the final steps of implementation. The ensemble classifier uses an estimator to append various classifiers for voting, then each classifier prepares a prediction regarding each instance and the final output prediction is the one that obtains more than 50% of the total votes.

12.3.1 Dataset

Two datasets are used for comparative analysis with binary values. The first was obtained from the Cardiology Department at Excelcare Hospital, Guwahati, Assam, and the second from the Cleveland Heart Disease data at the UCI repository [3]. Table 12.1 shows the number of records in each dataset that come under the headings of cardiovascular disease and non-cardiovascular disease.

Excelcare Heart Disease datasets contained 17 parameters, such as body mass index (BMI), body surface area (BSA), total cholesterol, sodium serum, etc. Here label 0 is used for the absence of cardiac complications, whereas label 1 is for the presence of cardiac complications in the patients.

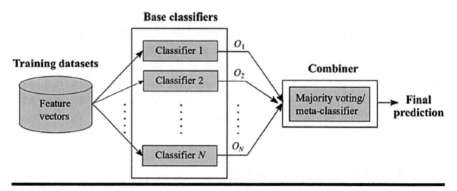

Figure 12.1 Ensemble Classifier [11].

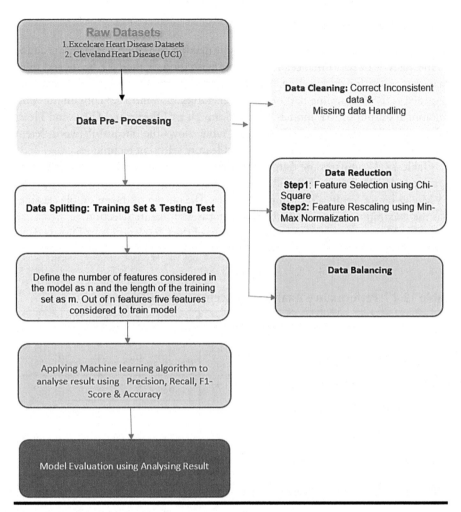

Figure 12.2   Model for predicting cardiovascular disease.

Table 12.1   Description of Heart disease Data Sets

Dataset Name	Total Number of Patients	Number of Parameters	Number of Non-Cardiac Patients	Number of Cardiac Patients
Excelcare Heart Disease datasets	2079	16	988(47%)	1091 (53%)
Cleveland Heart Disease dataset (UCI)	1025	13	499 (48%)	526 (52%)

12.4 Result Analysis

In the analysis of the computational decision-making part, nine classifiers are added to the analysis of performance, and two normalization methods, Z-score and min-max, are added for data scaling. Since min-max definitely gives good results, it is regarded as the data scaling part of this paper. Tables 12.2 and 12.3 contain the computational output of ML models for Excelcare Heart Disease and Cleveland Heart Disease (UCI) datasets respectively. Each table shows the output of two different scenarios of ML algorithms with associated feature selection techniques.

Table 12.2 compares the output from the Excelcare Heart Disease dataset with specified classifiers from two different AI environments. All classifiers except the SVM give better results after using chi-square. The output of the ensemble classifier has the maximum accuracy, which is 87% in cases of feature selection.

Table 12.3 contains the algorithmic output of the Cleveland Heart Disease dataset using specified models. Ensemble gives the best output of 96% accuracy with

Table 12.2 Performance Analysis of Excelcare Heart Disease

Models		Without Feature Selection				With Feature Selection			
		Precision	Recall	F1 score	Acc. (%)	Precision	Recall	F1 score	Acc. (%)
LR	0	.74	.76	.70	77	.67	.71	.69	79
	1	.59	.69	.75		.71	.67	.78	
KNN	0	.69	.76	.72	73	.75	.88	.81	80
	1	.73	.67	.67		.84	.72	.79	
NB	0	.81	.83	.82	84	.86	.89	.87	85
	1	.79	.78	.84		.88	.86	.86	
ANN	0	.82	.83	.89	85	.86	.85	.87	86
	1	.80	.86	.81		.88	.89	.84	
SVM	0	.88	.84	.86	86	.88	.85	.89	85
	1	.85	.83	.85		.84	.81	.83	
RF	0	.74	.76	.75	77	.80	.79	.79	81
	1	.79	.78	.73		.79	.81	.79	
DT	0	.81	.83	.79	83	.83	.85	.79	85
	1	.83	.80	.79		.84	.81	.84	

(Continued)

Table 12.2 (Continued)

Models		Without Feature Selection				With Feature Selection			
		Precision	Recall	F1 score	Acc. (%)	Precision	Recall	F1 score	Acc. (%)
SGD	0	.80	.78	.77	79	.83	.80	.84	84
	1	.81	.77	.78		.79	.76	.84	
Ensemble	0	.84	.79	.83	**85**	.88	.86	.88	**87**
	1	.83	.82	.81		.86	.82	.86	

Table 12.3 Cleveland Heart Disease

Models		Without Feature Selection				With Feature Selection			
		Precision	Recall	F1-Score	Acc. (%)	Precision	Recall	F1-Score	Acc. (%)
LR	0	.91	.79	.84		.87	.81	.89	89
	1	.82	.93	.87		.71	.67	.78	
KNN	0	.83	.89	.86	86	.75	.88	.81	85
	1	.89	.83	.86		.84	.75	.79	
NB	0	.88	.81	.84	85	.86	.89	.87	85
	1	.83	.90	.86		.88	.86	.86	
ANN	0	.90	.83	.86	87	.86	.86	.87	89
	1	.85	.92	.88		.88	.89	.84	
SVM	0	.92	.79	.85	85	.88	.85	.89	85
	1	.83	.93	.88		.84	.81	.83	
RF	0	.93	.99	.95	94	.90	.89	.95	96
	1	.96	.97	.99		.89	.91	.98	
DT	0	.96	.94	.94	92	.93	.95	.96	95
	1	.91	.96	.97		.94	.91	.94	
SGD	0	.97	.39	.55	75	.83	.82	.84	84
	1	.64	.99	.78		.89	.86	.84	
Ensemble	0	1.00	.93	.94	95	.98	.96	.98	**96**
	1	.98	.89	.97		.96	.92	.95	

chi-square feature selection. The results in Table 12.3 show that RF, LR, ANN, SGD, and DT classifiers perform well with feature selection, whereas only KNN gives a good result in the absence of feature selection. The accuracy of naïve Bayes and SVM remains the same for both scenarios (Figure 12.3).

Figure 12.4 shows the learning curves of classifiers that give the highest accuracy in each dataset. In Figure 12.4, the curve shows the performance of the ensemble on

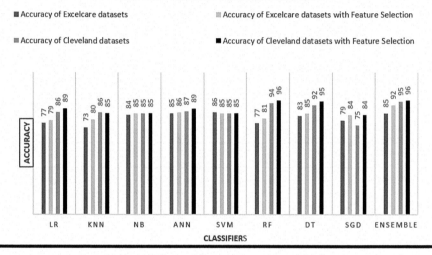

Figure 12.3   Comparative performance analysis of both datasets.

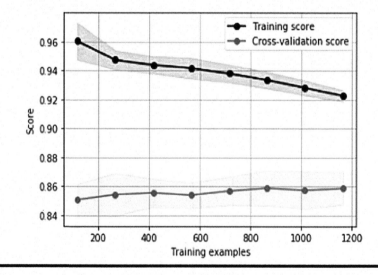

Figure 12.4   Learning curves of model having the highest accuracy of the Excelcare Heart Disease dataset.

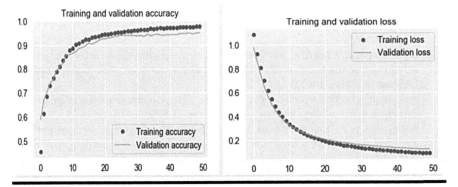

Figure 12.5 Training and validation accuracy and loss curve of the model having the highest accuracy of the Cleveland dataset.

the Excelcare Heart Disease dataset, and Figure 12.5 shows the training and validation accuracy and loss curve of the Cleveland Heart Disease dataset.

12.5 Conclusion

The research in this paper focuses on accurate prediction of major cardiovascular disease in the early stages. Various basic ML models are considered for two different cardiac patient datasets. To enhance the prediction models, initially Z-score data scaling is implied, and the comparative performances of all the measuring parameters such as precision, recall, F1score, and accuracy are studied in respect of the two different AI scenarios. This work seeks to enhance prediction of the occurrence of cardiac disease in order to improve the survival rate of cardiac patients worldwide regardless of cultural and socio-economic parameters.

References

1. Gárate-Escamila, Anna Karen, Amir Hajjam El Hassani, and Emmanuel Andrès. "Classification models for heart disease prediction using feature selection and PCA." *Informatics in Medicine Unlocked* 19 (2020): 100330.
2. Yadav, Dhyan Chandra, and Saurabh Pal. "Prediction of heart disease using feature selection and random forest ensemble method." *International Journal of Pharmaceutical Research* 12.4 (2020): 56–66.
3. Ayon, Safial Islam, Md Milon Islam, and Md Rahat Hossain. "Coronary artery heart disease prediction: a comparative study of computational intelligence techniques." *IETE Journal of Research* (2020): 1–20.
4. Spencer, Robinson, et al. "Exploring feature selection and classification methods for predicting heart disease." *Digital health* 6 (2020): 2055207620914777.

5. Ghosh, Pronab, et al. "Efficient prediction of cardiovascular disease using machine learning algorithms with relief and LASSO feature selection techniques." *IEEE Access* 9 (2021): 19304–19326.

6. Latha, C. Beulah Christalin, and S. Carolin Jeeva. "Improving the accuracy of prediction of heart disease risk based on ensemble classification techniques." *Informatics in Medicine Unlocked* 16 (2019): 100203.

7. Patel, Jaymin, Dr Tejal Upadhyay, and Samir Patel. "Heart disease prediction using machine learning and data mining technique." *Heart Disease* 7.1 (2015): 129–137.

8. Bashir, Saba, et al. "Improving heart disease prediction using feature selection approaches." *2019 16th International Bhurban Conference on Applied Sciences and Technology (IBCAST)*. IEEE, 2019.

9. Kamble, Sharyu U., et al. "Heart disease prediction using machine learning techniques." *IJETT* 6.1 (2019).

10. Abdar, Moloud, et al. "A new machine learning technique for an accurate diagnosis of coronary artery disease." *Computer Methods and Programs in Biomedicine* 179 (2019): 104992.

11. Raza, Khalid. "Improving the prediction accuracy of heart disease with ensemble learning and majority voting rule." *U-Healthcare Monitoring Systems*. Academic Press, 2019. 179–196.

12. Ali, Liaqat, et al. "An automated diagnostic system for heart disease prediction based on χ_2 statistical model and optimally configured deep neural network." *IEEE Access* 7 (2019): 34938–34945.

13. Chen, Min, et al. "Disease prediction by machine learning over big data from healthcare communities." *IEEE Access* 5 (2017): 8869–8879.

14. Khan, Younas, et al. "Machine learning techniques for heart disease datasets: A survey." *Proceedings of the 2019 11th International Conference on Machine Learning and Computing*, 2019.

15. Rong, Guoguang, et al. "Artificial intelligence in healthcare: Review and prediction case studies." *Engineering* 6.3 (2020): 291–301.

16. Lei, Zhenfeng, et al. "A novel data-driven robust framework based on machine learning and knowledge graph for disease classification." *Future Generation Computer Systems* 102 (2020): 534–548.

17. Gonsalves, Amanda H., et al. "Prediction of coronary heart disease using machine learning: an experimental analysis." *Proceedings of the 2019 3rd International Conference on Deep Learning Technologies*, 2019.

18. Gavhane, Aditi, et al. "Prediction of heart disease using machine learning." *2018 Second International Conference on Electronics, Communication, and Aerospace Technology (ICECA)*. IEEE, 2018.

Chapter 13

Use of Cryptography in Networking to Preserve Secure Systems

Kamal Kumar
Baba Mastnath University, Rohtak, India

Vinod Kumar
Shyam Lal Collage, University of Delhi, New Delhi, India

Seema
Baba Mastnath University, Rohtak, India

13.1 Introduction

With data becoming so important across all industries, it is necessary to prevent unauthorized access to data and information. The word "cryptography" is a combination of two Greek words – *kryptos*, meaning hidden, and *graph*, signifying writing. Typically, cryptography is the process of sending a secret message or conducting a secret conversation between two people or two organizations in order to keep their communications hidden from third parties. In other words, it refers to the use of codes, cyphers, and hidden messages. An oral or written message, a broadcast, or a collection of digital data could all represent the original communication. The success of concealed messages depends on them going unnoticed, whether they are written in invisible way or concealed otherwise. The messages concealed are generally simple to understand once found. Without the proper codebook, it's usually impossible to decipher words, numbers, or symbols that represent words or sentences in a code.

In a general communication network or software system, there are several endpoints, including multiple clients and back-end servers. These client–server exchanges occur over unreliable networks. Communication takes place over private networks that can be hacked by outside adversaries or nefarious insiders, or over open, public networks like the internet. Encryption ensures confidentiality, integrity and authenticity, making the communication very secure.

Leon Battista Alberti created the first cypher machine, which utilized a wheel. Blaise de Vigenère created the intriguing Vigenère cypher, a poly-alphabetic cypher that used a Caesar cypher modification [1]. German engineer Arthur Scherbius created the Enigma machine at the close of World War I to safeguard military communications [2]. During World War II, German forces used the Enigma machine to transmit vital information [3]. It was among the best rotor machines at the time. Due to the development of electronic machines like computers, modern cryptography makes substantial use of mathematics, including elements of information theory, computational complexity and statistics. Nowadays many computer cyphers are classified according to their binary bit sequences. Public key cryptography became a new sort of cryptography in the 1970s. The digital signature is the most recent addition to the cryptography arena and was first outlined by Diffie-Hellman in his work "New Directions in Cryptography" [4].

Cryptography is the use of codes to transform computerized data in such a way that only a specified recipient will be able to read it using a key. It also refers to the process or skill of communicating in or interpreting secret writings including codes, ciphers etc. Cryptographers call a communication's initial form the cleartext or plaintext. The outcome of enciphering the original transmission is known as the ciphertext. A key and an algorithm are frequently used in the enciphering procedure. A specific technique for encrypting a computer program or a written set of instructions is called an encryption algorithm. The exact scrambling procedure is described in the key. There are two types of keys – public keys and private keys [5].

Encryption is the process of hiding the data by converting plaintext into cipher text so that it is unintelligible. Decryption is the process of translating encrypted text into readable form. Decryption converts the ciphertext back to the plaintext [6]. The codes used to encrypt plaintext messages are known as cyphers. The algorithm used in cryptography to convert the inputs into fixed length encrypted text is known as cryptographic hash function [7]. Hash ensures integrity and security of the data [8]. Hash can be 128-bit, 160-bit or 256-bit in size [9].

13.1.1 Characteristics of Cryptography

Cryptography is an algorithm-based method of securing communication between participants. It has the following characteristics:

Privacy. Privacy is one of the most important requirements in any communication network. Cryptography maintains the privacy of the senders and receivers and keeps the data safe.

Reliability. The data sent using cryptography is reliable and is assumed to be free from any unauthorized access.

Non-repudiation. Neither senders nor receivers can later deny their participation in the communication network after the connection is established. This improves the audit and accountability in the communication process.

Authentication. Cryptography ensures the authentication of the senders and receivers in the communication network. This increases the trust of the users in the network.

Non-alteration. Cryptography does not let any unauthorized third party access or alter the data. Only the sender and receiver can make the required changes.

No obstruction in transmission. There are no hurdles or obstructions like third-party verification in a cryptography-based communication network.

Secret transmission. The data is transmitted in encrypted form and hence kept secret from attacks by unauthorized parties.

Transmission integrity. Integrity in transmission is sometimes more important than secrecy alone.

Storage secrecy and integrity. The information is stored in a very authentic manner, ensuring the utmost security and integrity for the users [10].

13.1.2 Types of Cryptography

Cryptography is primarily of two types: symmetric and asymmetric [11].

Symmetric cryptography, also known as private key cryptography. In this type of cryptography, a private key is used between the parties. The same private key is used both for encryption and decryption of the data. Only the sender and receiver have access to the private key. The sender encrypts the message to be transmitted using a private key. The receiver uses the same private key to decrypt the message into plaintext form [12] (Figure 13.1).

Asymmetric cryptography, also known as public key cryptography. In this type of cryptography, the processes of encryption and decryption take place using two different keys – a public key and a private key. These two keys are related to each other but only mathematically. The public key is available in the public domain but no one can guess or derive the private key from the public key. Any sender who wishes to send a message can encrypt the message using the public key of the destined receiver. The encrypted message can be decrypted by the receiver using the private key. Even if someone accesses the transmitted encrypted message, the message will not be in readable form and there is no way that the hacker can derive the private key from the public key available [13] (Figure 13.2).

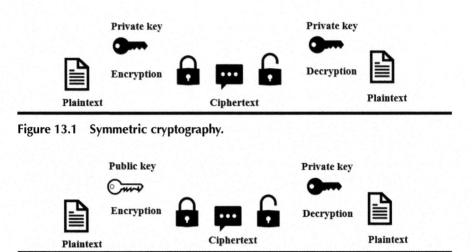

Figure 13.1   Symmetric cryptography.

Figure 13.2   Asymmetric cryptography.

13.1.3 Cryptanalysis

Cryptanalysis is the study or art of understanding and analyzing ciphers, ciphertext and cryptosystems in order to assess how the codes have been formed and find out ways to weaken the encryption logics [14]. The main significance of cryptanalysis is to improve existing algorithms so that the chance to crack the encrypted data can be minimized [15]. The attackers may discover ways to decrypt the encrypted data even without using the decryption keys. Cryptanalysis tries to discover anomalies that can be used by hackers to convert the ciphertext back to plaintext without the use of the required private key [16]. Cryptanalysis is an ongoing process: the entities involved in cryptography and in cryptanalysis keep on moving forward along parallel lines [17].

There are various types of cryptanalysis attacks:

Ciphertext-only attack. In this type of attack, the analyst manages to get access to the encrypted message. The attacker has no access to the plaintext or the original text but has ciphertext available. The analyst may try to decrypt the message or may transfer the encrypted message to a third unauthorized party.

Known-plaintext attack. In this type of attack, the analyst has access to some or all of the original text of the ciphertext. The analyst may use that information to understand the logic of the encryption and crack the key to encrypt and decrypt the data. After deriving the key, the analyst may decrypt the entire ciphertext and thus create a security risk in the communication network.

Chosen plaintext attack. In this type of attack, the analyst has the device or system used to encrypt the data or may also have access to the algorithm used for encryption. The analyst can encrypt the original message using the compromised system or algorithm or the derived key.

Differential cryptanalysis attack. In this type of attack, the analyst tries to analyze the block ciphers and understand the logic by which the algorithm works from the pair of original texts rather than from one plaintext.

Integral cryptanalysis attack. This type of attack is quite similar to a differential cryptanalysis attack. The analyst tries to analyze the sets of original texts instead of the pair of plaintexts. In the sets of plaintexts, some of the plaintexts are kept the same while others are changed.

Side-channel attack. As the name suggests, this type of attack is not based on either the plaintext or the ciphertext but on side channels like the electromagnetic radiations coming from the system, the power consumed by the system for encryption, the time taken by the system when it comes across any new data set, etc.

Dictionary attack. This type of attack is used in those cases where password protected files are involved. It works on the logic that people keep easy-to-guess passwords to protect the data so that they can easily remember the password. In this type of attack, all the words are encrypted in a dictionary and then the analyst sees if the output matches the encrypted password in the file.

Man-in-the-middle attack. As the name suggests, in this type of attack, the analyst tries to access the communication channel between the parties who might share the keys with each other for securing the communication. The analyst exchanges keys with each of the users, making them believe that they are exchanging the keys with each other. But in reality, the analyst is in communication with the users and the users have no idea that they are communicating with the analysts [18].

13.2 Cryptographic Primitives

Cryptographic primitives refers to various ways, methods and tools to ensure security in communication. The various types are shown in Figure 13.3.

The primitives should satisfy the following basic requirements:

Security. The primitives should ensure information security. Although it is very difficult to quantify the level of security that should be provided by the cryptographic primitives, these primitives should provide optimum level of security.

Functionality. The cryptographic primitives should be functional in nature and should be able to combine with each other to meet the required needs.

Operations methods. The cryptographic primitives provide different types of outputs based on the operation method and hence the primitives should be able to provide the desired outputs for a given method of operation.

Performance. The efficiency of the cryptographic primitives should be high. It can be measured in terms of speed, number of failures, etc.

Implementation ease. A cryptographic primitive might look very helpful but it might not be practical to implement and hence not be of much use. It is pertinent that the cryptographic primitives should be easily implementable in the practical environment [19].

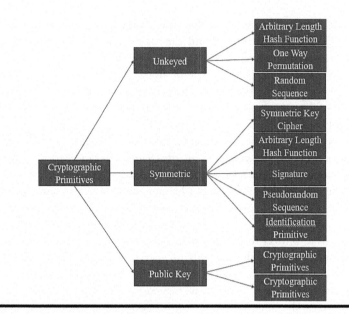

Figure 13.3   Cryptographic primitives.

13.3 Applications of Cryptography

The latest encryption technologies have multiple applications across different areas. The various applications of cryptography are listed below [20]:

Computer security. Computers need to be kept safe from various threats via antivirus applications, which are these days developed using cryptography.

Network security. Network security is related to both software and hardware. Cryptographic algorithms are used to secure the network from analysts.

Internet security. This relates to securing the data during transmission. Cryptography is used to secure the data across various interconnected internet networks.

Digital signatures. Cryptography helps add the authentication layer through digital signatures and adds to the integrity and confidentiality of the documents.

Secure online banking. Safe encryption techniques are a must for secure online banking. The number of online banking frauds is increasing daily, with analysts using newer ways of deceiving customers. Cryptography provides ways to authenticate the identity of users and keep the data safe, secure and confidential and minimize fraud risk.

Safe chatting services. Chat applications like Telegram, WhatsApp, etc. use end-to-end encryption technologies to ensure that no unauthorized party gets access to the messages of the authorized users. This boosts the confidence of the users in these applications.

Secure emailing. Emails are very important to users and contain a lot of personal data. Cryptography-based encryption tools are used to secure emails so that the data can be safeguarded against any threat from analysts.

Cryptocurrency. Cryptocurrencies are gaining momentum with the passage of time and the trading volumes are experiencing exponential growth. Cryptocurrency is based on cryptographic encryption technologies [21].

13.4 Issues in Network Security

With the growing competition across all sectors, the threats to information security have increased multifold. There are various types of issues that create concerns around the network security. Some of the issues are due to internal factors while some others pertain to external threats. The various types of issues that threaten network security are:

Viruses in the network. Viruses are pieces of code that pose huge dangers to network security. Common examples include mails from unknown sources which include some suspicious links. When the user tries clicking on the link, the virus gets installed on the device and spreads throughout compromising all the data available.

Trojan Horse. This is a very dangerous attack by hackers. The harmful code is stored in apparently safe programming algorithms so that basic security tools cannot detect it. After getting installed on a device, it tampers with all the data and gains unauthorized access to confidential data.

Spams. Spams are basically the flooding of useless messages in such a way that the user might miss important messages. In spams, there are no direct attacks on the information available in the network, but indirectly the user is denied access to important information.

Phishing. Phishing basically involves sending fraudulent mails by the attackers that look genuine to the users asking the users to share their confidential information. The existing set of security tools might not be able to predict that the email is not genuine and hence should be blocked.

Packet sniffers. These are tools or devices that tamper with the data during transfer. These devices can filter out confidential personal information from the compromised network systems.

Websites with fraudulent intent. Some websites contain code that has been created with malicious intent. When users visit these websites and click on the code, they come under the hackers' control and end up getting their confidential information compromised by the attackers.

Loss of hardware. The threat to information also comes from the physical threat to hardware devices, such as damaging or stealing computers. If the information is saved on the hardware device and there is no other backup, the user might lose important data and information.

Sharing of computers. In those cases where the same devices are used by multiple users, there is a high network security risk. One of the users might steal or try to access confidential information of other users.

Zombie Computers and Botnet. Any device of which the hacker has managed to gain control is a zombie device and the hacker can access all the confidential information stored on it. A botnet is a device used by hackers to transmit information without the knowledge of the actual owner.

Old software and applications. Old systems and applications are unsafe and more prone to hacker attack. All the time attackers are working out methods to crack the codes for the existing applications. Hence there is a need to constantly update applications and software.

Web cookies. The hackers may try to derive personal information about the users by getting access to the unencrypted cookies available in the system. The cookies may not directly help the attackers but can be indirectly used to predict information about the users.

Shared hosting. In shared hosting, multiple websites are based on a single network server. This is normally done to save operational costs. However, shared hosting leads to the risk of websites being compromised due to attacks on the server.

Cryptography provides the benefits of strong encryption and decryption algorithms that make it extremely difficult for hackers to enter the network in an unauthorized manner. Even if the attacker gets access to the information in the network, it will be available in encrypted form and the attacker will not be able to derive any meaning from the ciphertext. Hence, cryptography provides a very strong mechanism to safeguard the information on the network against potential attacks by hackers. As cryptography addresses most network security concerns, it is regarded as very important and useful for dealing with threats. [22].

13.5 Issues in Cryptography

Cryptography has many benefits and provides solutions to security needs while transferring the information. Listed below are some issues related to cost and ease of use.

Difficult to use for users. Any data or record which is encrypted with strong encryption logics and algorithms using cryptography might be difficult to access or use by even the legitimate users. Legitimate users might not find the encrypted information in urgent and important circumstances [23].

Cost-inefficient. The setting up of cryptosystems in any organization is very costly and maintenance costs are high. Systems need upgrading at regular intervals and will involve huge costs. From a cost perspective, cryptosystems might not meet the required return on investment.

Prone to poor design. If the design of the cryptosystems is inadequate, data and information may not be safeguarded from external threats. Poor design will lead to loopholes in the architecture and might fall prey to the hackers trying to steal information from the network.

Bad password management. There are multiple encryption methods of which the password-based method is the most common. So it becomes very important to manage passwords in a secure manner. In many cases, for the sake of ease, people store passwords in plaintext and the same may be compromised.

Poor random number generation. The algorithms are dependent on the generation of random numbers for the creation of public and private keys to encrypt and decrypt the data and information. If the hacker is able to guess or predict the logic behind the random number generation, then they will be able to predict the private keys of the users.

Insecure encryption and decryption. A strong standard cryptosystem will be very strong against any potential threat or attack by hackers. But any customized cryptography with loose ends might not be able to secure the network architecture against unauthorized access or external threats [24].

Key-related issues. Poor key combinations, inefficient use of keys, non-rotation, insecure storage of keys, compromised transfer of keys, less protection of keys, non-destruction of keys, etc. are some of the issues related to encryption and decryption keys [25].

13.6 Conclusion and Future Directions

In the current digital world, information is key. There is a serious need to secure information against unauthorized access. Hackers use innovative methods to tamper with confidential information, constantly developing new ways to compromise network security. Encryption has emerged as one of the best ways to secure the network from any kind of unauthorized access or attack by hackers. The information is encrypted in such a way that only the designated user can decrypt it. It is difficult for hackers to enter the network architecture due to strong cryptographic password-based algorithms. Even if attackers manage to access data, it will be available in encrypted form and it is extremely difficult for attackers to decrypt the information as they cannot derive the private key from any available source. Ciphertext is of no use to the hacker and is equivalent to not getting access to the network.

Although there is no doubt that cryptography can solve issues of network security, there are concerns around practical implementation. Encryption is a complex technology which is difficult for small organizations to understand and implement. It is also a very costly technology and not all entities can afford to incur such heavy costs for network security. Encryption technology is relatively new and has not yet reached saturation point. Hidden challenges may appear in future, so it is necessary that both private and government entities make sufficient efforts to discover all the possible hidden nuances of this technology and make it much more effective and implementable than the current capacity. With large-scale implementation, the benefits of scale will decrease costs and make cryptographic technology affordable to everyone.

References

1. Bruen A.A. and Forcinito M. A. *Cryptography, information theory, and error correction: A Handbook for the 21st Century,* John Wiley & Sons Inc., New Jersey, p. 21 (2004).
2. Thawte, http://book.itep.ru/depository/crypto/Cryptography_history.pdf
3. Binance Academy, https://academy.binance.com/en/articles/history-of-cryptography
4. Naser, S.M. Cryptography: From the Ancient History to Now, Its Applications and a New Complete Numerical Model. *International Journal of Mathematics and Statistics Studies,* vol. 9, pp. 11–30, (2021). Researchgate.
5. Preveil, https://www.preveil.com/blog/public-and-private-key/
6. Simplileran, https://www.simplilearn.com/tutorials/cryptography-tutorial/what-is-cryptography
7. Geeksforgeeks, https://www.geeksforgeeks.org/cryptographic-hash-function-in-java/
8. Hashed Out, https://www.thesslstore.com/blog/what-is-a-hash-function-in-cryptography-a-beginners-guide/
9. Section, https://www.section.io/engineering-education/understand-hashing-in-cryptography/
10. Rao, C., Rath, A.K., Kabat, M.R., Cryptography And Network Security Lecture Notes. http://dx.doi.org/10.2139/ssrn.2741776
11. Elprocus, https://www.elprocus.com/cryptography-and-its-concepts/
12. Rawat, S. Characteristics, Types and Applications of Cryptography. Analyticsteps (2021).
13. Pgp Corporation, https://www.cs.unibo.it/babaoglu/courses/security/resources/documents/intro-to-crypto.pdf
14. Tutorialspoint, https://www.tutorialspoint.com/what-is-cryptanalysis-in-information-security
15. Paar, I.C., Pelzl, I.J. *Understanding Cryptography.* Springer, Heidelberg (2010).
16. Rosencrance, L. Cryptanalysis. Techtarget (2021).
17. Claret, O.A. Overview of Cryptography. Researchgate (2011).
18. Geeksforgeeks, https://www.geeksforgeeks.org/cryptanalysis-and-types-of-attacks/
19. Stack Exchange, https://crypto.stackexchange.com/questions/39735/whats-a-cryptographic-primitive-really
20. Tutorialspoint, https://www.tutorialspoint.com/what-are-the-applications-of-cryptography-in-information-security
21. Ronan The Writer, https://ronanthewriter.com/applications-of-cryptography-in-daily-life/
22. Vadicherla, P. Security Issues on Cryptography and Network Security. *International Journal of Computer Science and Information Technologies,* vol. 7(3), pp. 1648–1654 (2016).
23. Tutorialspoint, https://www.tutorialspoint.com/cryptography/benefits_and_drawbacks.htm
24. Ubiq, https://www.ubiqsecurity.com/cryptographic-issues-top-three-application-flaw/
25. Stubbs, R. Cryptographic Key Management - the Risks and Mitigation. Cryptomathic (2018).

Chapter 14

Issues and Challenges of Blockchain in Healthcare

Bhavna Sethi, Harish Kumar, and Sakshi Kaushal

Panjab University Chandigarh, Chandigarh, India

14.1 Introduction

Block chain is an immutable digital ledger widely used for storing information or records, such that no duplicate code can quickly change or modify the whole record. The block chain concept, which was invented by Satoshi Nakamoto in 2008 for crypto currency, offers an innovative way to maintain records, in particular patient data [1].

14.1.1 Reasons for Adopting Block Chain

This paper outlines a proposed approach to management of their personal health data by patients. Block chain is both highly secure and accessible to the patients, who are able to manage their files and mark availability of data more easily and efficiently.

14.2 Design

14.2.1 Terms and Definitions

Block: A data fingerprint created using cryptography from the data in the block is included in each block in the block chain. The hash locks blocks in time and order [1], therefore, the block content cannot be altered in any way.

DOI: 10.1201/9781003371380-14

Chain: A hash links one block to another, mathematically tying them together. The data in the previous block is used to create the block chain hash.

Network: A linkage of nodes. Every node in the block chain contains a record of every transaction.

Cryptography: A way of exposing information (encrypting and decrypting) through advanced mathematics. Only the authorized / intended recipients can view it.

Smart Contracts: An electronic automated protocol which uses artificial intelligence and specifies the rules that a transaction must follow. Runs on block chain and uses algorithms to create and measure execution conditions.

Distributed Ledger: Capable of running multiple sites, organizations, or locations throughout a network with privileges.

Crypto-Tokens: These belong to a specific category of virtual currency present on their block chains that represent an object and its worth [1].

Proof of work (POW): The protocol's main goal is to recognize faults like distributed denial-of-service (DDoS) attacks, which cause a computer system to become overloaded with resources by sending out numerous unauthorized fake requests.

Proof of stake (PoS): The more coins a node owns, the more probable it is that it will be necessary to validate the blocks on the bitcoin network. Validations are decided based on the number of network participants.

Practical Byzantine Fault Tolerance (PBFT): A term that refers to the ability to tolerate faults. It passes through a number of stages when validating transactions. To authenticate its activities, each approved node sends a message to the network.

Ethereum: A public and hybrid-based block chain technology that has the ability to send and receive data. It provides transparency, security, and immutability for all data in the form of transactional units or tokens. Ethereum works on smart contracts that are the foundation of decentralized applications (dApps). It provides automatic execution when a condition or trigger is met. Through decentralized databases, it allows medical institutions to share structured data securely [2].

14.2.2 Interplanetary File System

A distributed file system acts as the nodes in this peer-to-peer data distribution technology. The system divides the file into N fragments while we upload it to the IPFS network. Each fragment further generates a hash value, and all the fragment hashes are merged as one to get the whole file's hash value [3].

14.3 Related Work

Hao Wang proposed a system named EHR that combines the IAM protocol for a health record management system using Hyperledger Fabric. The system is easy to implement without major modifications. Muhammad Usman et al. [4] proposed an electronic medical records management system powered by block chain and also using Hyperledger, enabling patients to view their medical history, store and share records efficiently. Leila Ismail [5], in a study of effective healthcare at the lowest possible cost, utilized a block chain-based system for managing medical records. It allows allied health professionals to upload patients' medical data and patients to upload their social/lifestyle data. It also supports diagnosis and prognosis. Shuaib et al. [6] proposed a decentralized electronic health record system offering improved security and more effective sharing compared to current systems. It combines three different systems: permission block chain based on a decentralized file system, a threshold signature technique, and the IBFT consensus algorithm. Sharma et al. [7] deployed a block chain-based EHR network and implemented basic functionalities in the network. They focused on securing EHRs and protecting the privacy of patients with cryptography/hashing and decentralization. Innab [8] states the key issues with deploying electronic health records are accessibility, privacy, and safety. International information security standards such as the HIPAA are recommended for electronic medical records. Aiden Feng [9] designed a permission block chain-based method for managing medical data and built a platform using vaccination clearance during the COVID-19 pandemic. In terms of performance, it focuses on the improvement of the PBFT protocol of the original Hyperledger Fabric. Irfan Maulana Akbar [10] focuses on implementation of a system proven to handle heavy workloads using Ethereum block chain. B. Narendra Kumar Rao [11] found potential uses of block chain technology in several social insurance contexts. Lei Li [12] proposed HF and IPFS as the foundation for an EMR sharing system. Saira Afzal [12] analyzed literature on the ethics of electronic medical records and found that most of the issues raised are about the impact of inaccurate electronic data on therapy and the doctor–patient relationship, as well as issues relating to privacy, anonymity, security, and informed consent. Leonard [13] examined the possibility of developing an electronic medical file unification framework with a third layer for unification and a second layer to record data without a biometric tag. Through the newly established FIRD biometric check point system, this framework produced a check-and-balances mechanism. Saha et al. [14] conducted a comparative analysis and proposed a system based on electronic medical records where patient data security and privacy are the main issues. Priti Tagde [15] states that AI requires cryptographic documents to make judgments, and block chain makes it possible to store these records. Through the use of these recent innovations, healthcare programs have increased service effectiveness, reduced costs and democratized healthcare.

14.4 Applications and Challenges of Block Chain in Healthcare

14.4.1 Applications

- *Patient monitoring:* Block chain can increase the level of security for information flow. It provides a valid method for transmitting information between network nodes and incorporates concepts such as privacy and intransience. Wearable device technologies (WBANs) and gateways are examples that can help increase monitoring quality.
- *Drug supply chain management:* It is one of the best methods for business development. Several industries, such as healthcare, use block chain technology to manage their supply chains.
- *Health asset tracking in the supply chain:* It is used for tracking health assets across the supply chain. One in every ten medications sold in poorer nations was counterfeit or of poor standard in 2017. These crimes result in enormous financial losses for the healthcare system.
- *Privacy and security in block chain for healthcare:* The increasing growth in volume of health data is due to the digitization of physical documents and the use of sensors and other technical equipment. Data is generated from a variety of sources, including hospital records and monitoring equipment. The Healthcare Insurance Portability and Accountability Act (HIPAA) guarantees the privacy of medical information [16].
- *Electronic medical records:* Saved electronically to give private and sensitive information linked to patient diagnostics and therapeutics. Must be shared regularly among peers, but this can give rise to difficulties, since there is a risk that the data will be altered or compromised [17].

14.4.2 Challenges

Researchers are working to overcome or mitigate the following challenges [16, 17]:

- *Throughput:* It is a concern when working with healthcare systems because without it, a potential life-saving diagnosis or problem could be missed.
- *Latency:* Block validation takes a few minutes, which might be problematic for system security services.
- *Security:* If a single entity gains control of 51% of the capacity of an organization's network, this can lead to serious and widespread damage to the health system [18].
- *Resource consumption:* Managing costs is a major challenge for companies trying to use this technology in the private and public sector.

- *Usability:* Because these technologies are so hard to handle, usability is also a concern. Health professionals lack technical expertise and the systems are simple and can lead to intrusion. A user-friendly API (application programming interface) must be created.
- *Centralization:* Block chain is a decentralized architecture, as opposed to some implementations that rely on a centralized architecture and lowering network vulnerability toward attacks.
- *Privacy:* Block chain-based solutions must adhere to the General Data Protection Regulation (GDPR).

14.4.3 Strategies and India-centric Outcomes Targeted towards Block Chain

- *AI in healthcare: past, present and future:* It is applied to different types of healthcare data that can be either structured or unstructured. It focuses on reasons and data types and examines the diseases that are being addressed [19]. AI technologies are important and essential innovations in medical research, but there are many obstacles during real-life implementation. There are no rules and regulations with respect to the safety and efficiency of AI systems.
- *Use of block chain ecosystem (technological and management challenge):* Block chain technology is being used more frequently in a variety of industries, including manufacturing, banking and finance, energy, transportation, and more [20]. Supply chain and logistics, financial technology (fintech), decision support systems, internet of things (IoT), smart cities, healthcare, construction, security, and privacy are just a few of the difficulties it faces.
- *Decentralized secure storage of medical records using block chain and IPFS:* Data about patients is typically stored locally in hospitals, and sometimes there is even lack of backup storage. Data loss or corruption is an emerging risk [21]. Cloud storage is becoming more and more popular in hospitals, but is also not without certain drawbacks [22]. According to one source, the dApp professional system distributes a patient's record throughout hospitals for tracking and auditing purposes. Another proposed solution is called "Heal Chain," and it uses a prototype IPFS [23] to transport data gathered from smart wearable devices.
- *Interoperability: past, present and future trends:* It is defined as "the semantic relation between ledgers to transfer data or value, with assurances of validity." [24] This initiative aims to make it easier for developers and researchers to complete their job, which will make the block chain ecosystem more useful.
- *Scalability Challenges:* Block chain technology addresses scalability issues and offers solutions in the healthcare industry. It is divided into two main categories: block chain redesign and storage optimization. Various solutions, including block chain modeling, read mechanisms, write mechanisms and

bi-directional networks, have been proposed for storage optimization and redesign of the block chain [25].

■ *Privacy and security:* Medical history records are the most sought-after records online and are regarded as sensitive and important information. The most crucial aspects of cryptography and encryption are security and privacy. They lessen the amount of patient and healthcare data that is available in a digital health system. The existing block chain-based healthcare provides solution for a data-sharing framework, but at same time faces issues of security and privacy [26].

14.5 Differences between Current and Proposed Systems

14.5.1 Current System

India, a nation with a vast range of geographical, social, ethnic, linguistic, and religious diversity, undoubtedly needs a healthcare infrastructure that allows for the efficient and secure processing of each citizen's health data. To facilitate patient information exchange between hospitals, pharmacies, and insurers, the medical chain uses dual block chain and technological advances [27]. At present, medical records are extremely centralized and it can be difficult for doctors to obtain critical data about a patient. The medical chain would allow insurers, clinicians, and patients to access medical records with the ease, speed, and security of block chain.

14.5.2 Proposed System

Currently, several institutions and organizations maintain numerous patient medical records. The proposed system uses transactions in medical records hosted over block chain to build an intelligent balancing system to address issues now occurring in the healthcare industry. It offers the capability of searching, validating and storing encrypted EMRs based on block chain. The objective is to protect patient data from unauthorized access by third parties. EMR architecture is used to safely save documents and keep a single version of reality. Stakeholders or participants need to go through a number of permission processes in order to obtain patient medical data and add the transaction to the distributed ledger's history. A full view of a system's trustworthiness, cost-effectiveness, data confidentiality, and availability is provided by block chain.

14.5.3 Benefits

■ Immediate access to patient medical records
■ Reduction in communication errors

- Chronicle organization of data
- Scheduling of appointments and automatic reminders
- Increased patient involvement in management of medical billing and accounting

14.5.4 Implementation

- Create and insert data into a new EMR platform built on block chain that offers validating patient record.
- Apply the cloud storage and interplanetary file system (IPFS), which helps reduce the cost.

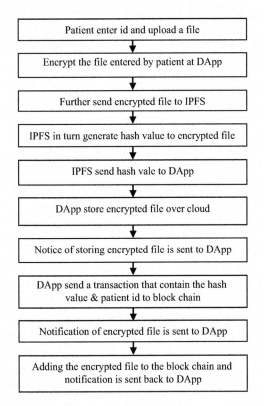

14.6 System Architecture

User application (decentralized application): It offers a user application that medical personnel and patients can access. It provides three functions linked to the patient records and two related to the patients (add patients and verify patients). Add the patient's medical records first. The second step is a technique for verifying the saved files validation so that no modification or tampering with original data is done by

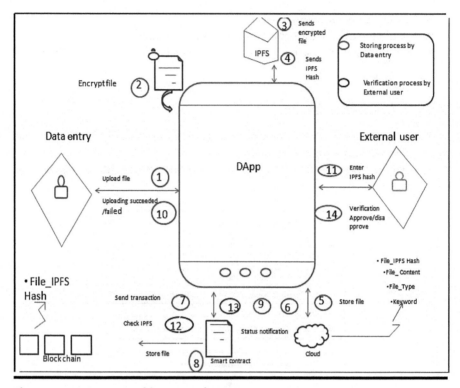

Figure 14.1 System architecture of EMR.

unauthorized persons based on the block chain. The third step is scanning or searching for all saved files in the system. One of the most important tasks is encryption.

Interplanetary file system (IPFS): There is difficulty storing large files directly on the block chain. It provides users with the capacity to locate the file using its hash address (Figure 14.1).

Cloud computing storage: All encrypted data of patients' personal information, file type, keywords, and IPFS hash of the encrypted file is stored by system. The system stores the medical files' actual content once they have been encrypted to ensure data protection and confidentiality.

14.7 Conclusion

Modern life revolves around digitization in every domain including the medical. Previously, medical data was recorded on paper, which led to damage or modification as there was no access-based database or storage on permanent criteria. This new system will ensure privacy of information along with storage and access.

References

1. Vardhini, B., Dass, S. N., Sahana, R., and Chinnaiyan, R., "A Blockchain based Electronic Medical Health Records Framework using Smart Contracts," 2021, *International Conference on Computer Communication and Informatics (ICCCI), 2021*, pp. 1–4. doi: 10.1109/ICCCI50826.2021.9402689.
2. ethereum in-vs-ethereum-driven-different-purposes.asp.
3. IPFS: https://ipfs.io/
4. Usmana, Muhammad, & Qamarb, Usman, "Secure Electronic Medical Records Storage and Sharing Using Blockchain Technology," 2020, *International Conference on Identification, Information and Knowledge in the Internet of Things* Volume 174, pp. 321–327.
5. Ismail, Leila, Materwala, Huned, and Khan, Moien AB, "Performance Evaluation of a Patient-Centric Blockchain-based Healthcare Records Management Framework," 2020, *In Proceedings of the 2nd International Electronics Communication Conference (IECC '20)*. Association for Computing Machinery, NewYork, NY, USA, pp. 39–50. https://doi.org/10.1145/3409934.3409941
6. Shuaib, K., Abdella, J., Sallabi, F. et al., "Secure decentralized electronic health records sharing system based on blockchains," *Journal of King Saud University – Computer and Information Sciences*, https://doi.org/10.1016/j.jksuci.2021.05.002
7. Sharma, Yogesh and Balamurugan, Balamurugan, "Preserving the Privacy of Electronic Health Records using Blockchain," 2020, *Procedia Computer Science*. 173, pp. 171–180. 10.1016/j.procs.2020.06.021.
8. Innab, Nisreen, "Availability, Accessibility, Privacy and Safety Issues Facing Electronic Medical Records," 2018, *International Journal of Security, Privacy and Trust Management*. 7. pp. 1–10. 10.5121/ijsptm.2018.7101.
9. Feng, Aiden, "A Design of Electronic Medical Record System based on Permissioned Blockchain," 2022, UWSpace. http://hdl.handle.net/10012/18053
10. Akbar, Irfan Maulana, Bhawiyuga, Adhitya, and Siregar, Reza, "An Ethereum Blockchain Based Electronic Health Record System for Inter-Hospital Secure Data Sharing," 2021, *6th International Conference on Sustainable Information Engineering and Technology 2021 (SIET '21)*. Association for Computing Machinery, New York, NY, USA, pp. 226–230. https://doi.org/10.1145/3479645.3479699
11. Sathyanarayanan M.E., Ramyadevi, N., Deebika, S., and Soumiya, R., "Block Chain based Implementation of Electronic Medical Health Record," 2020, *International Journal Of Engineering Research & Technology (IJERT) RTICCT – 2020* (Volume 8 – Issue 12).
12. Akbar, Irfan Maulana, Bhawiyuga, Adhitya, and Siregar, Reza, "An Ethereum Blockchain Based Electronic Health Record System for Inter-Hospital Secure Data Sharing," 2021, *6th International Conference on Sustainable Information Engineering and Technology 2021 (SIET '21)*. Association for Computing Machinery, New York, NY, USA, pp. 226–230. https://doi.org/10.1145/3479645.3479699
13. Afzal, Saira, and Arshad, Amber, "Ethical Issues among Healthcare Workers Using Electronic Medical Records: A Systematic Review," 2021, *Computer Methods and Programs in Biomedicine Update*. https://doi.org/10.1016/j.cmpbup.2021.100030
14. Leonard, D.C., Pons, A.P., Asfour, S.S., "Realization of a Universal Patient Identifier for Electronic Medical Records through Biometric Technology," 2009, *IEEE Transactions on Information Technology in Biomedicine* July;13(4), pp. 494–500. doi: 10.1109/TITB.2008.926438. Epub 2008 May 30. PMID: 19273015.

15. Saha, Arijit, Amin, Ruhul, Kunal, Sourav, Vollala, Satyanarayana, and Dwivedi, Sanjeev K., "Review on Blockchain Technology based Medical Healthcare System with Privacy Issues," 2019, Wiley. https://doi.org/10.1002/spy2.83

16. Tagde, P., Tagde, S., Bhattacharya, T. et al, "Blockchain and Artificial Intelligence Technology in e-Health," 2021, *Environmental Science and Pollution Research* 28, pp. 52810–52831. https://doi.org/10.1007/s11356-021-16223-0

17. De Aguiar, Erikson Júlio, Faiçal, Bruno S., Krishnamachari, Bhaskar, and Ueyama, Jó, "A Survey of Blockchain-Based Strategies for Healthcare," 2020, *ACM Computing Surveys*. 53, 2, Article 27 (March 2021), p. 27. https://doi.org/10.1145/3376915

18. Government of India Ministry of Electronics and Information Technology (MeitY) "National Strategy on Block chain," Global Efforts January 2022, https://www.meity.gov.in/writereaddata/files/NationalStrategyBCT_%20Jan2021_final.pdf

19. Stafford, Thomas F. and Horst Treiblmaier. "Characteristics of a Blockchain Ecosystem for Secure and Sharable Electronic Medical Records," 2020, *IEEE Transactions on Engineering Management* 67, pp. 1340–1362.

20. Jiang, Fei, Jiang, Yong, Zhi, Hui, Dong, Yi, Li, Hao, Ma, Sufeng, Wang, Yilong, Dong, Qiang, Shen, Haipeng, and Wang, Yongjun, "Artificial Intelligence in Healthcare: Past, Present and Future," 2017, *BMJ*. 2, p. svn-2017. 10.1136/svn-2017-000101.

21. Choo, K.K.R., "Editorial: Blockchain Ecosystem—Technological and Management Opportunities and Challenges," 2020, *IEEE Transactions on Engineering Management*, 67(4), November, pp. 982–987.

22. El Faqir, Youssef, Arroyo, Javier, and Hassan, Samer, "An Overview of Decentralized Autonomous Organizations on the Blockchain," 2020, *Proceedings of the 16th International Symposium on Open Collaboration (OpenSym '20)*. Association for Computing Machinery, New York, NY, USA, Article 11, pp. 1–8. https://doi.org/10.1145/3412569.3412579

23. Kumar, Shivansh, Bharti, Aman, and Amin, Ruhul, "Decentralized Secure Storage of Medical Records using Blockchain and IPFS: A Comparative Analysis with Future Directions," 2021, *Security and Privacy*. 4. 10.1002/spy2.162.

24. Belchior, Rafael, Vasconcelos, André, Guerreiro, Sérgio, and Correia, Miguel, "A Survey on Blockchain Interoperability: Past, Present, and Future Trends," 2021, *ACM Computing Surveys* 54, 8, Article 168 (November 2022), p. 41. https://doi.org/10.1145/3471140

25. Mazlan, A. A., Mohd Daud, S., Mohd Sam, S., Abas, H., Abdul Rasid, S. Z., and Yusof, M. F., "Scalability Challenges in Healthcare Blockchain System—A Systematic Review," 2020, *IEEE Access*, vol. 8, pp. 23663–23673. doi: 10.1109/ACCESS.2020.2969230.

26. Ali, Aitizaz, Hasliza A. Rahim, Pasha, Muhammad Fermi, Dowsley, Rafael, Masud, Mehedi, Ali, Jehad, and Baz, Mohammed, "Security, Privacy, and Reliability in Digital Healthcare Systems Using Blockchain," 2021, *Electronics*, 10. 10.3390/electronics10162034

27. Alrebdi, Norah, Alabdulatif, Abdulatif, Iwendi, Celestine, and Lian, Zhuotao, "SVBE: Searchable and Verifable Blockchain-based Electronic Medical Records System," 2022. https://doi.org/10.1038/s41598-021-04124-8

Chapter 15

Accident Prediction by Vehicle Tracking

Giddaluri Bhanu Sekhar, Javvaji Srinivasulu,
M. Bhargav Chowdary, and M. Srilatha

Jawaharlal Nehru Technological University, Kakinada, India

15.1 Introduction

In developing countries like India, the number of both vehicles and accidents is increasing day by day. The main cause of the annual growth of the accident rate is the lack of appropriate surveillance. Traffic monitoring has become a popular method of gathering data on traffic conditions [1]. In real-time monitoring, human-controlled CCTV video streams can be inefficient, unreliable, and involve high potential for human error [8]. Calculating the number of vehicles passing through a specific location is difficult and inefficient for humans, who are unable to analyze all monitors simultaneously or maintain constant focus. Efficient traffic management requires a user-friendly intelligent traffic tracking system, for which new concepts in machine learning are extremely useful.

Several technologies for accurate vehicle monitoring and detection have been developed over the last decade. Traditional methodologies for object detection like the Gaussian mixed model (GMM) [10], implemented using CNN and RNN layers, can give promising experimental results, but may fail to work in real time. For speed and accuracy, YOLO performed better than other object detection models.

Most of the methodologies that use machine learning involve training the model with the accidents that have occurred in previous years and predicting the occurrence of accidents with a rough estimation using regression mechanisms. A countable number of features or methods in deep learning are considered for estimating the occurrence of accidents instantly.

From multi-object tracking through discriminative label propagation [11, 12], to real-time anomaly recognition via neural networks [13], and the integration of deep learning for crowd analysis [14, 15], these advancements redefine surveillance and safety. Simultaneously, vehicle detection via spatio-temporal features [16] and 3D model-based tracking for accident prediction [17] reflect innovative road safety strategies, complemented by machine learning's role in severity assessment [19] and citywide traffic risk prediction [20], including uncertain traffic flow insights [21]. A novel 3D LiDAR-based vehicle detection and tracking system [5] segments vehicles using a dual-view representation, with convolutional neural networks independently trained on LiDAR data. Similarly, a 3D LiDAR-based system [6] employs Convolutional Neural Networks (CNNs) to classify vehicle points from Velodyne HDL-64 sensor data. Geometric processing produces inputs for a multi-object tracking system using Multi-Hypothesis Extended Kalman Filters (MH-EKFs).

The system proposed here uses YOLO object detection with an improved version of the DeepSORT tracking mechanism to track vehicles that are entering and leaving a junction. The model is able to predict the occurrence of accidents by comparing speeds in successive frames. YOLO is a real-time object detection technique that use deep neural networks. This algorithm is particularly popular because of its speed and accuracy. It has been used to recognize traffic lights, people, parking meters, and cars. DeepSORT overcomes the challenges faced by other tracking mechanisms such as CentroidTracking, etc. The DeepSORT model is modified so that it is capable of computing the speeds of each tracked vehicle. An automatic mechanism comprising a listener and handler is attached to predict accident occurrence by comparing vehicle speeds. Traditional methods for calculating the speed of a vehicle in a video stream are insufficiently accurate. The proposed model is able to calculate the speed of vehicles in the video stream with an accuracy of 92.74%.

15.2 Related Work

Xuezhi Xiang et al. [1] propose a UAV-based multi-vehicle recognition and tracking framework that can be used to count vehicles and can work with both static and dynamic backgrounds. The expense of this system is substantial since a large number of sensors will be required in urban areas. Surveillance video cameras are one of the most widely utilized sensors in the field of traffic monitoring as they can offer vehicle detection and counting using video feed. However, they have a number of drawbacks, including occlusion, shadows, and a limited field of vision.

Lin et al. [2] resolved the occlusion problem with occlusion detection and queue detection. Several solutions for traffic monitoring utilizing aerial video have been developed in recent years.

Ruimin Ke et al. [3] developed a method for extracting interest points from a pair of frames to calculate vehicle speed and for monitoring interest points in aerial videos using the Kanade–Lucas optical flow algorithm.

Shastry et al. [4] developed an approach for detecting vehicles from aerial videos using video registration, utilizing the KLT (Kanade–Lucas–Tomasi) characteristics tracker to automatically estimate traffic flow parameters.

Muhammad Azhad bin Zuraimi et al. [7] proposed a convolutional neural network method. With human sight, calculating the number of vehicles passing through a specific location is difficult and inefficient. Their system is designed to identify a vehicle in a video and categorize it by type. Vehicles include motorcycles, cars, buses, and trucks. The system counts the vehicle passthrough line if it is visible in the video. The vehicle's speed and accuracy will be assessed to create a YOLO model with many versions. The most recent version of YOLO should be the most accurate in terms of speed and accuracy.

Madhusri Maity [9] organized a survey on R-CNN and its proposed versions. Several technologies for accurate vehicle monitoring and detection have been developed over the last decade. Traditional vehicle identification algorithms, such as the Gaussian mixed model (GMM) [10], generate promising results, but when lighting changes occur in the presence of cluttered backgrounds and other circumstances, they may not function effectively. Deep learning methods include built-in feature extraction capabilities, which makes them more appealing to researchers than traditional approaches, as they reduce the number of classification errors caused by erroneous handmade feature extraction. Convolutional neural networks (CNNs) outperform older methods in a range of computer vision tasks because they are made to closely resemble the functioning capabilities of the human brain. As a result, we have concentrated our efforts in this survey on deep neural networks such as the Faster R-CNN and the YOLO network.

Xuezhi Xiang et al. [1] developed a framework which counts vehicles based on detecting and tracking them from airborne recordings. They used a foreground detector for static backgrounds since it can overcome small noise. By modifying the model, they got different variations of the real scene. Image registration is used to create a moving background and camera motion is calculated to detect a vehicle in a reference frame. Furthermore, an online-learning tracking method was developed to deal with the form and scale of vehicles in photos.

Sreyan Ghosh et al. [18] developed a system that can detect a potential accident in seconds by analyzing the video footage provided by the camera. The system is powered by deep learning algorithms that are mainly used by CNN. These algorithms are able to analyze the frames taken from the video. The camera used for the system is a Raspberry Pi 3 B+ model. The proposed system can notify police and hospitals of an accident by sending a text message alert. The system can also provide details about the accident, such as location.

15.3 Methodology

The main objective of the system is to predict accident occurrence by detecting and classifying vehicles using YOLOv4, which is implemented using a convolution neural network, tracking vehicles using simple online real-time tracking (SORT)

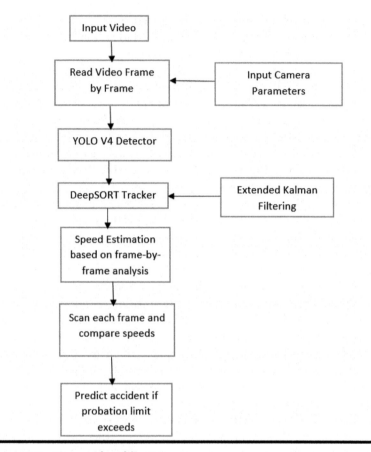

Figure 15.1 Proposed architecture.

with deep correlation metric, and finding their speeds frame by frame accurately and efficiently. The system is an improvised version of current tracking architectures which is capable of classifying vehicles and calculating their speeds.

Initially we capture the surveillance video at a suitable frame rate. Then the video is divided into frames. At the same time, the well-known object detector You Only Look Once (YOLO v4) is used to detect the objects in a frame. Yolov4 combined with Darknet has a pre-trained classifier which classifies the detected vehicles using custom weights. Each detected object is assigned a simple online real-time tracking (SORT) tracker to track it until it disappears from the current frame. Each tracker assigned to an object collects the pixels regarding the object in the previous frame and the current frame and calculates the speed of the object using mathematical formulae. The speeds calculated on each frame are compared so that accident occurrence is estimated when the risk factor is high.

The proposed system consists of four modules: object detection and classification, object tracking, speed estimation and accident prediction (Figure 15.1).

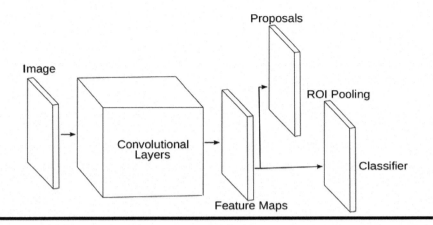

Figure 15.2   Internal architecture of YOLO.

15.3.1 *Object Detection and Classification*

Object detection was originally performed using sliding window techniques. The proposed system uses the YOLO v4 algorithm to detect and classify the objects. YOLO, in use since 2018, is an object detection algorithm based on a convolution neural network. The YOLO v4 algorithm can detect the objects in one forward pass, which is why it is called You Only Look Once.

In order for the YOLO v4 algorithm to detect the objects, it needs to be trained. Training occurs by taking the input vector of the object. The input vector consists of the probability of class, co-ordinates of the bounding boxes, and height and width of the bounding boxes. Then we train the neural network to classify the object as well as the bounding box.

The YOLO v4 algorithm divides the input frame into multiple grid cells, each of which will be encoded, and objects have been detected if the input frame consists of multiple objects (Figure 15.2).

The intersection over union (IOU) approach is used by the YOLO v4 algorithm in cases where the algorithm detects multiple bounding rectangles for a single object.

Intersection Over Union = Intersect area / Union area.

If the value of the IOU is more than 0.6 or 0.7 we can say that the bounding boxes are overlapping; if they are completely overlapping the value will be 1. If the bounding boxes are not overlapping the value will be 0. This technique is also called non-max supression.

15.3.2 *Object Tracking*

Tracking involving only detection fails, due to many disturbances that might arise in the video feed, such as atmospheric conditions. If a vehicle is lost between frames it looks like a new object. While single-frame detection can work, there must be a

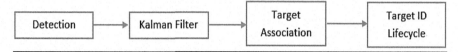

Figure 15.3   Phases in tracking.

correlation of monitored features between subsequent images of the video for detection to work.

Traditional methods like meanshift and optical flow perform well in tracking. They are complex in computational terms and prone to noise in case of optical flow.

The proposed system uses SORT with a deep association metric which uses extended Kalman filtering for correlation measurement frame by frame. The great advantage of Kalman filtering is that it works recursively. Using SORT involves estimation, association and track identity creation (Figure 15.3).

Kalman filters are used to evaluate states in a state space format based on linear dynamic systems. However, using linear dynamic equations for object identification to estimate vehicle states in a video analytics procedure gives inappropriate measurement vectors. We therefore improved Kalman filtering by turning it into a non-linear version that linearized the model in terms of current estimate. The models for state transition and measurement are as follows:

$$Y(X) = F(Y_{X-1}, k_{X-1}) + Z_{X-1} \tag{15.1}$$

$$A(X) = H(Y_X) + B_X \tag{15.2}$$

where F is a function of the prior state, Y_{X-1}, and the control input, K_{X-1}, which generates the current state, Y_X. For the process model and the measurement model with covariance P and Q, respectively, H is the measurement function, Z_{X-1} and B_X are the Gaussian noises.

All we need is the Jacobian matrix of each model at each time step, which is the first-order partial derivative of a vector function with respect to a vector. We linearized the model regarding the current estimate in this way, which is similar to the Kalman filter.

So now we need to propagate the detection from one frame to the next using a non-linear velocity model. When a detection is linked to a vehicle, the detected bounding box is utilized to update the target state, where the velocity components are solved using the extended Kalman filter framework (Figure 15.4).

To assign detection, each target's bounding box geometry is calculated by estimating its new location in the most recent frame in comparison to previous targets. The assignment cost matrix is then computed as IOU distance between each detection and all predicted bounding boxes from the existing targets. A Hungarian algorithm is used to solve optimally.

Assign a single-object tracker to each of the vehicles detected. All the single-object trackers are combined together so that each object is tracked uniquely with a key.

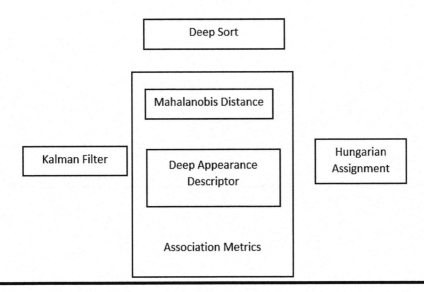

Figure 15.4   Subcomponents involved in DeepSORT.

15.3.3 Speed Estimation

Estimating vehicle speed looks simple but it involves a specific task. Many results are obtained from the previous module (tracking of each vehicle identified and assigning a unique ID from the vehicle entering to vehicle leaving the camera's view), including the vehicle's previous location pixels, its centroid etc. The distance calculation is based upon the vehicle's position in the current frame and previous frame and mathematical formulae are applied for calculating the speed of the vehicle. The speeds of all vehicles calculated are combined to track all vehicle speeds, using parameters gained from the input such as:

1. Height of camera placed at the surveillance point (h_c)
2. Minimum angle of vision of camera (θ_{mv})
3. Maximum angle of vision of camera (θ_{Mv})
4. Output resolution of camera (width x height)
5. Frame rate (f_{ps})
6. Probation distance the camera unable to reach (D)

Unlike traditional methods that follow a Euclidean distance formula to find how far an object is displaced from the previous frame to the current frame, our proposed system maps the input parameters, i.e, θ_{mv} and θ_{Mv}, to find the actual displacement of the vehicle from previous to current frame (Figure 15.5).

These are then used to establish an equation that helps to find out the actual position of the vehicle.

$$Y_v = \theta_{mv} + \left(\left(\theta_{Mv} - \theta_{mv}\right)/\left(h_c - D\right)\right) \times x \qquad (15.3)$$

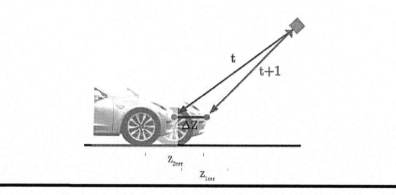

Figure 15.5   Vehicle at *t* and *t* + 1 frame.

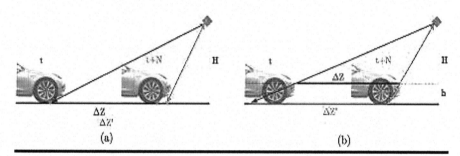

Figure 15.6   Displacement of vehicle on successive frame.

where
    x is an independent variable that holds the value of pixels information (vertical) when a vehicle is detected;
    y is a dependent variable that summarizes to gives angle of vision of vehicle from a camera associated with the vertical plane.

The above calculates the angle associated with the vertical alignment. Similarly, we obtain the angle involved with horizontal orientation (Figure 15.6).

$$X_h = (Y - \theta_{mv}) / ((\theta_{Mv} - \theta_{mv}) / (h_c - D)) \tag{15.4}$$

where
    Y represent the horizontal pixel location of vehicle;
    X_h is dependent variable that summarizes to give
    Angle of vision with horizontal plane.

The displacement $\Delta z'$ which represents the actual distance covered by the vehicle during the interval of a particular frame is calculated as

$\theta_1 = Y_v$ in previous frame
$\theta_2 = Y_v$ in current frame
$\theta_3 = X_h$ in previous frame
$\theta_4 = X_h$ in current frame

$$\Delta z' = \text{Height} \times \left(\left| \tan\theta_1 - \tan\theta_2 \right| + \left| \cot\theta_3 - \cot\theta_4 \right| \right) \tag{15.5}$$

It can be clearly observed that if $\theta_1 > \theta_2$ then the vehicle is moving towards the camera and vice versa.

If $\theta_3 > \theta_4$, then the vehicle is moving towards the right from the camera's point of view and vice versa.

As $\Delta z'$ holds the actual distance displaced by the vehicle in the particular frame interval, we can estimate the speed of the vehicle by applying mathematical formula

$$\text{Speed}_{(v)} = \Delta z' \times f_{ps} \times (18/5) \tag{15.6}$$

where
f_{ps} – frame rate in which the video feed is read by camera
18/5 is constant to convert the speed in m/sec to km/hr

The speed is calculated for all the detected vehicles in each frame as its accuracy from frame to frame is necessary for surveillance.

15.3.4 Accident Prediction

As we have seen, the speed of each vehicle in each frame is calculated and tracked simultaneously and updated in the upcoming frame. When each frame is processed, every vehicle's bounding boxes and their position with respect to each vehicle are checked.

1. To decrease the time taken to process each frame, certain similar patterns in the behavior of vehicles in motion are considered These include the fact that two stationary vehicles cannot collide with each other, so these are neglected in the comparison.
2. For any two vehicles which are traveling in the same direction there can be two critical possibilities:
   (a) A vehicle ahead of another vehicle and travelling faster than it is neglected for estimation on that frame.
   (b) A vehicle traveling faster than a following vehicle is considered.

3. Vehicles that are approaching a junction that are traveling faster than the speed limit at the junction have high importance for implementation of the listener.
4. A stationary person on the road might be responsible for an accident.
5. For any two vehicles, the distance between them is calculated, but if the distance between them is greater than probation distances, the estimation is ignored.

The possibility of collision between two vehicles is calculated applying the above considerations, and if it is greater than the risk factor, a message is printed on the screen.

15.4 Results Analysis

The proposed system is able to detect and classify vehicles that are entering and leaving the junction. We have extended the Kalman filter to a non-linear dynamic model which is able to assign a unique ID to each vehicle tracked from entering into the junction to leaving it. It is able to calculate the speed of each vehicle accurately frame by frame. It is able to compare speeds of vehicles and calculate the possibility of accident occurring through video footage. The proposed system generated useful results at high computing speeds with a good accuracy that could run at 12–14 fps according to how busy the junction is (Figure 15.7).

Figure 15.7   Output screenshot-1.

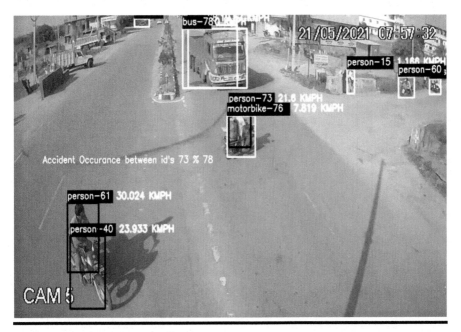

Figure 15.8   Output screenshot-2.

Figure 15.7 is the output screenshot of the real-time speed estimation system of a camera feed.

The camera is at 20 meters above ground level, and its angle of vision is between 20 degrees and 60 degrees. The output resolution of the camera in the above feed is 1920(width) × 1080(height) pixels. The camera is working at 25 frames per second. The probation distance the camera is unable to reach is 10 meters from the point of contact on the ground (Figure 15.8).

Figure 15.8 is the output screenshot of the accident estimation in the video that was analyzed.

15.5 Performance Analysis

Estimating speeds of vehicles in real time is a task that must be done quickly and accurately. The proposed system uses the concept of the distance displaced by a vehicle from frame to frame in order to calculate its speed. The SORT tracker is modified to the extent that it can also calculate the speeds of vehicles by tracking them simultaneously. Speeds are calculated with greater accuracy and are integrated with the active listener which identifies the possibility of accident before it occurs (Figure 15.9).

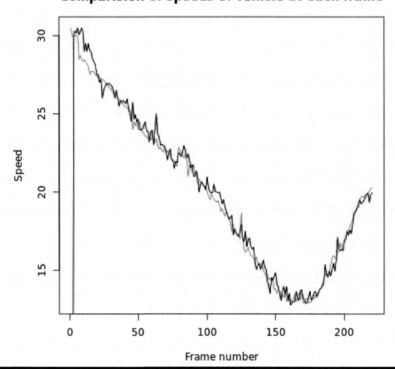

Figure 15.9   Comparison of speeds of vehicle at each frame.

Figure 15.9 shows a scenario of a vehicle that was tracked by the proposed system and its speed estimated on different frames. The graph compares the actual speeds of the selected vehicle with its estimated speeds at particular timestamps. The proposed system is able to calculate the speed of vehicles in the video stream with an accuracy of 92.74%.

15.6 Conclusion and Future Work

We implemented a new version of the SORT_YOLOv4 algorithm that improves the performance of its tracking architecture with some new approaches. One of these is the use of identity switches. This prevents YOLO object detection from being forwarded to SORT components, which leads to no tracking results. When YOLO detects an object in a subsequent frame, it will assign a new object ID to it. The DeepSORT tracker is used to solve this issue by only requiring a particular box in the first frame. After that, the tracker can track the entire frame without the

YOLO component. When a vehicle is detected by YOLO, it is immediately sent to the DeepSORT detection. This method ensures that the video is watched properly to predict accident occurrence.

In future, we can integrate the model with the IOT component to communicate the possibility of accident occurrence, if it is above a certain threshold, to the local police station and hospital for emergency attention.

References

1. Xiang, Xuezhi, Zhai, Mingliang, Lv, Ning, and El Saddik, Abdulmotaleb, "Vehicle Counting Based on Vehicle Detection and Tracking from Aerial Videos," *Sensors*, vol. 18, no. 8, p. 2560, 2018.
2. Lin, S. P., Chen, Y. H., and Wu, B. F., "A Real-Time Multiple-Vehicle Detection and Tracking System with Prior Occlusion Detection and Resolution, and Prior Queue Detection and Resolution," in *Proceedings of the 18th International Conference on Pattern Recognition (ICPR'06)*, Hong Kong, China, 20–24 August 2006; vol. 1, pp. 828–831.
3. Ke, R., Kim, S., Li, Z., and Wang, Y., "Motion-vector Clustering for Traffic Speed Detection from UAV Video," in *Proceedings of the 2015 IEEE First International Smart Cities Conference (ISC2)*, Guadalajara, Mexico, 25–28 October 2015, pp. 1–5.
4. Shastry, A. C. and Schowengerdt, R. A., "Airborne Video Registration and Traffic-flow Parameter Estimation," *IEEE Trans. Intell. Transp. Syst.*, vol. 6, pp. 391–405, 2005.
5. Vaquero, Victor, Pino, Ivan del, Moreno-Noguer, Francesc, Sola, Joan, Sanfeliu, Alberto, and Andrade-Cetto, Juan, "Dual-Branch CNNs for Vehicle Detection and Tracking on LiDAR Data," *IEEE Transactions on Intelligent Transportation Systems*, pp. 1–12, 2020.
6. Vaquero, V., del Pino, I., Moreno-Noguer, F., Sola, J., Sanfeliu, A., and Andrade-Cetto, J., "Deconvolutional Networks for Point-cloud Vehicle Detection and Tracking in Driving Scenarios," in *Proc. Eur. Conf. Mobile Robots (ECMR)*, Sep. 2017, pp. 1–7.
7. Bin Zuraimi, M. A. and Kamaru Zaman, F. H., "Vehicle Detection and Tracking using YOLO and DeepSORT," in *2021 IEEE 11th IEEE Symposium on Computer Applications & Industrial Electronics (ISCAIE)*, 2021, pp. 23–29, doi: 10.1109/ISCAIE51753.2021.9431784.
8. Velastin, S. A., "CCTV Video Analytics: Recent Advances and Limitations," in *1st International Visual Informatics Conference (IVIC)*, Kuala Lumpur, vol. 5857, Nov. 2009.
9. Maity, M., Banerjee, S., and Sinha Chaudhuri, S., "Faster R-CNN and YOLO based Vehicle Detection: A Survey," in *2021 5th International Conference on Computing Methodologies and Communication (ICCMC)*, 2021, pp. 1442–1447, doi: 10.1109/ICCMC51019.2021.9418274.
10. Stauffer, C. and Grimson, W. E. L., "Adaptive Background Mixture Models for Real-time Tracking," in *Proceedings. 1999 IEEE Computer Society Conference on Computer Vision and Pattern Recognition*, doi: 10.1109/CVPR.1999.784637.
11. Amit Kumar, K. C., Jacques, L., and de Vleeschouwer, C., "Discriminative and Efficient Label Propagation on Complementary Graphs for Multi-object Tracking," *IEEE Transactions on Pattern Analysis and Machine Intelligence*, vol. 39, no. 1, pp. 61–74, 2017.
12. Naiel, M. A., Ahmad, M. O., Swamy, M. N. S., Lim, J., and Yang, M. H., "Online Multi-object Tracking via Robust Collaborative Model and Sample Selection," *Computer Vision and Image Understanding*, vol. 154, pp. 94–107, 2017.

13. Singh, V., Singh, S., and Gupta, P., "Real-Time Anomaly Recognition Through CCTV Using Neural Networks," *Procedia Computer Science*, vol. 173, pp. 254–263, 2020. doi:10.1016/j.procs.2020.06.030.

14. Ullah, W., Ullah, A., Haq, I. U. et al., "CNN Features with Bi-directional LSTM for Real-time Anomaly Detection in Surveillance Networks," *Multimedia Tools and Applications*, vol. 80, pp. 16979–16995, 2021.

15. Sreenu, G. and Saleem Durai, M. A., "Intelligent Video Surveillance: A Review through Deep Learning Techniques for Crowd Analysis," *Journal of Big Data*, vol. 6, p. 48, 2019.

16. Wang, Y. et al., "Detection and Classification of Moving Vehicle from Video Using Multiple Spatio-Temporal Features," *IEEE Access*, vol. 7, pp. 80287–80299, 2019, doi: 10.1109/ACCESS.2019.2923199.

17. Weiming, H., Xuejuan Xiao, D. Xie, T. T., and Maybank, S., "Traffic Accident Prediction using 3-D Model-based Vehicle Tracking," *IEEE Transactions on Vehicular Technology*, vol. 53, no. 3, pp. 677–694, May 2004, doi: 10.1109/TVT.2004.825772.

18. Ghosh, S., Sunny, S. J., and Roney, R., "Accident Detection Using Convolutional Neural Networks," in *2019 International Conference on Data Science and Communication (IconDSC)*, 2019, pp. 1–6, doi: 10.1109/IconDSC.2019.8816881.

19. Labib, M. F., Rifat, A. S., Hossain, M. M., Das, A. K., and Nawrine, F., "Road Accident Analysis and Prediction of Accident Severity by Using Machine Learning in Bangladesh," in *2019 7th International Conference on Smart Computing & Communications (ICSCC)*, 2019, pp. 1–5, doi: 10.1109/ICSCC.2019.8843640.

20. Ren, H., Song, Y., Wang, J., Hu, Y., and Lei, J., "A Deep Learning Approach to the Citywide Traffic Accident Risk Prediction," in *2018 21st International Conference on Intelligent Transportation Systems (ITSC)*, 2018, pp. 3346–3351, doi: 10.1109/ITSC.2018.8569437.

21. An, J., Fu, L., Hu, M., Chen, W., and Zhan, J., "A Novel Fuzzy-Based Convolutional Neural Network Method to Traffic Flow Prediction With Uncertain Traffic Accident Information," *IEEE Access*, vol. 7, pp. 20708–20722, 2019, doi: 10.1109/ACCESS.2019.2896913.

Chapter 16

Blockchain-Based Cryptographic Model in the Cloud Environment

Pranav Shrivastava, Bashir Alam, and Mansaf Alam

JMI, New Delhi, India

16.1 Introduction

Cloud computing (CC) has provided numerous benefits in recent years, including high availability, efficiency, and flexibility. This platform provides exceptional performance in a multitude of areas, including compute and storage [1]. Because of advances in cloud platforms, many businesses and individuals have used and uploaded various cloud data for reasons of cost saving and ease of sharing. Blockchain (BC) is a centralized technology in which each block communicates a series of hash keys and transactions to the previous block. This is analogous to the connected list method, which is frequently distributed, replicated, and updated across all network nodes. The hash key is utilized to link blocks together, resulting in a chain of blocks [2].

Blockchain is a distributed system in which numerous nodes collaborate to preserve data using distributed ledger technology (DLT), and this type of work is difficult to edit, trace, and forge [3]. Nobody can update or alter the transaction data on this blockchain. This type of immutable method is only possible on blockchain. As a result, blockchain security is more efficient than traditional security methods.

Untrustworthy and unknown individuals have the potential to cause harm to federated systems [4, 5, 6]. Botnet assaults have occurred in some cases when the pool of resources is large [7]. Irrational malevolent actors can grow their mining capacity in order to disturb the actions of other honest miners. Opponents can utilize block-withholding attacks, causing the pool to lose block-finding competition [8, 9, 10].

Most CC outcomes are based on parallel and distributed computing, meaning anyone can access the cloud platform from anywhere, which can result in third parties acquiring people's personal information illegally. Blockchain is the most secure method to be used within the cloud platform; it also improves transaction speed while using fewer computational resources, thus solidifying its reputation as a stronger security method fit for cloud platforms. In this study, CC and blockchain security were merged. The proposed unique approach should meet all of the issues and needs associated with dynamic groups in a CC environment.

Section 16.2 presents relevant works on blockchain security. Section 16.3 is concerned with the suggested blockchain security in the cloud environment. Sections 16.4 and 16.5 describe future work and conclusions.

16.2 Related Works

Mayuranathan et al. [11] concentrated on progressing and applying blockchain security for cloud applications in order to improve and reinforce security. They built AuthPrivacyChain, based on blockchain-based access control, to provide greater security. This technique was also deployed on the cloud platform.

Yang and colleagues [12] proposed a system based on authorization, access control, and authorization revocation. Access-controlled data was encrypted and kept in blockchain identity. Finally, they created an Enterprise Operation System (EOS) based on the AuthPrivacyChain. The strategy ensures privacy and prevents hackers from gaining unauthorized access to resources.

Wang et al. [13] proposed a technique called the Electronic Health Record (EHR) Sharing Protocol. The data requester may seek the anticipated keyword from the provider in order to access appropriate EHRs in the EHR consortium blockchain, after which the encrypted text is obtained and the data owner's authorization is obtained. For data security, it includes conditional proxy re-encryption and searchable encryption. The consortium blockchain also ensures the system's availability.

Zhu et al. [14] suggested a controllable blockchain data management (CBDM) technique organized in a cloud platform. They also increased the efficiency of the cloud blockchain platform.

Deep et al. [15] developed a cloud-based approach using blockchain technology. Blockchain made it arduous to modify a user's login process. The insider cannot access the user's login data owing to the distributed ledger-based authentication system. Insider action was discovered and could not be changed. Inside and outside users' IDs and signatures are identical in this case. The database's user access control is also authenticated.

Zhang et al. [16] proposed what they called a certificate-less public verification technique against procrastinating auditors (CPVPA) using the blockchain concept. This method requires auditors to record every confirmation result as a transaction onto a blockchain. However, the blockchain transaction method is inefficient in terms of time. After entering the linked transaction into a blockchain, the confirmation can be time-stamped. This empowers users to see if auditors are carrying out the confirmations at the scheduled time. Furthermore, the CPVPA developed certificate-less cryptography that is free of certificate administration issues.

Eltayieb et al. [17] introduced the blockchain-based attribute-based signcryption approach for safe data exchange. To offer safe data allocation in the cloud, a combination of attribute-based signcryption and blockchain was advocated. The established approach in CC addresses security requirements such as unforgeability and confidentiality. Smart contracts were used to address cloud storage issues such as persistent erroneous outcomes in the traditional cloud server.

Gabriel et al. [18] proposed a blockchain-based security for network function virtualization orchestration (BSec-NFVO). The blockchain concept was proposed to ensure auditability, non-repudiation, and to safeguard orchestration processes in virtualized systems. This method provides a flexible structure for orchestration protection that is both simple and active. It was created for OPNFV (Open Platform for Network Function Virtualization), coupled with a version of the ordinary case of a collusion-resistant consensus mechanism. The developed scheme produced consistent results as the number of consensus members increased.

Neeraj et al. [19] proposed the concept of blockchain data aimed at cloud data reliability security. The mobile agent method was used to implement the distributed VM (virtual machine) agent concept. The VM agent enables several tenants to collaborate to secure data trust confirmation. The VM agent approach enabled consistent data storage, confirmation, and observation. This is an essential criterion to develop a blockchain reliability security approach. The blockchain-based reliability security structure was built using the VM proxy model. The exclusive hash estimate associated with the data is formed using the Merkel hash tree, and is used to witness the data interchange utilizing the smart contract in the blockchain.

Sheng et al. [20] created a cloud-based secure eHealth structure for EHR tamper-proofing using the blockchain concept. From unauthorized changes to safe outsourced EHRs, the blockchain approach created a secure cloud-based eHealth framework. The primary goal is to outsource EHRs utilizing verified applications. Every step for outsourcing EHRs is merged as a transaction on the public blockchain. The blockchain-based currencies provide a tamper-proof way of performing transactions with no need of a central authority. The EHRs cannot be updated after the linked transaction is registered in the blockchain concept. As a result, every applicant can validate their integrity for certain outsourced EHRs by verifying the linked transaction.

The literature review shows that numerous research solutions and algorithmic patterns based on statistical techniques have been proposed, methods that have great complexity. Only a few publications mention security predictions. This study introduces modified infinite chaotic cryptography for cloud security with blockchain.

16.3 Proposed Methodology

Cloud computing and its applications are rapidly expanding. However, cloud security is still a difficult problem. Several security systems are installed in a cloud environment, but they are not distributed and are less transparent, making it extremely challenging to deploy existing security policies. Furthermore, these measures are more costly and resource intensive. This study proposes blockchain security in the cloud context to address these challenges. Because of the enhanced properties of blockchain, such as its high cohesiveness and massively dispersed nature, this security solution is regarded as the finest approach in CC. With blockchain, the consumption of computer resources is reduced, and transactions are processed rapidly, improving security system performance in a cloud environment. Figure 16.1 depicts a cloud with a blockchain-based security system.

This method is used to connect each attribute type to the validation contract address. The primary purpose of this cloud-based blockchain security is to safeguard information flow while limiting the possibility of a third party having access to the user's sensitive data or ledger. Each user is given two major keys: the private key and the public key. When a user requests data, they must first provide the key; once the key is validated, the user is permitted access to the data.

16.3.1 Protection of Authentication

In this stage, authentication with blockchain is used to authenticate users. A pair of private and public keys is used for each user. The public key chain is stored on the blockchain created by the bitcoin structure to maintain key security. The blockchain has two nodes to build the chain of private blocks. A specific user saves his private key, and his public key is required with the address in the built blockchain. In blockchain, the system grants the user authorization to guarantee that users can retrieve the public keys of other users by address.

16.3.2 Ownership Protection

Users have secure and private ownership, which is validated via cloud-based blockchain identity management at various authentication stages. This secure technique is used for key generation as well as encryption. Addresses are assigned to identification features, and access can be expanded if certain conditions are met. Then, in a permissioned ledger, identity information is saved and kept totally decentralized.

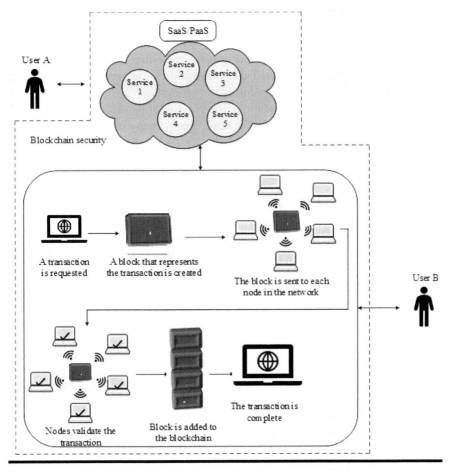

Figure 16.1   Cloud with blockchain security structure.

16.3.3 *Identity Mapping Validation*

In blockchain, the mechanism for confirming the hashes of the previous and next blocks is critical for safe data transmission. This approach proposes validation plans that are specifically related to a specific type of property. The matching cosine similarity criterion is used to determine the valid user in this case. The cosine similarity between users A_i and B_i is then computed using digests as described by:

$$\text{Cosine}\left(A_i, B_i\right) = \frac{\sum_{i=1}^{n}\left(A_i B_i\right)}{\sqrt{\sum_{i=1}^{n}\left(A_i\right)^2} \times \sqrt{\sum_{i=1}^{n}\left(B_i\right)^2}} \tag{16.1}$$

16.4 Future Work

The suggested blockchain-based cloud security system will be implemented in JAVA with the NetBeans IDE. The proposed system's processing time on the cloud and time consumption will be analyzed and compared to the present existing methods. The suggested security system considers three groups: authentication, ownership protection, and identity validation. The purpose of blockchain authentication is to validate the user's identity. At the same time, the use of approved and non-modifiable blockchain preserves the public key created in the blockchain to link the blockchain address to the public key to avoid forgery and interference from other people's public keys.

16.5 Conclusions

The major goal of this study is to provide blockchain security in cloud applications for safe data transmission. The proposed solution consists of three phases: authentication protection, ownership protection, and identity mapping validation. The entire operation is carried out with the JAVA programming language and the NetBeans IDE. The simulation results are expected to confirm that the proposed method delivers good security in the cloud environment and excellent performance when compared to existing strategies.

References

1. Park, Jin Ho, and Jong Hyuk Park. "Blockchain security in cloud computing: Use cases, challenges, and solutions." *Symmetry* 9, no. 8 (2017): 164.
2. Sadhu, Ram Basnet, and Shakya Subarna. "BSS: Blockchain securit yover software defined network." In *International Conference on Computing, Communication and Automation (ICCCA2017)*, IEEE.
3. Li, Zhi, Ali Vatankhah Barenji, and George Q. Huang. "Toward a blockchain cloud manufacturing system as a peer to peer distributed network platform." *Robotics and Computer-Integrated Manufacturing* 54 (2018): 133–144.
4. Hassan, M.M., A. Alelaiwi, and A. Alamri "A dynamic and efficient coalition formation game in cloud federation for multimedia applications." In *Proceedings of the International Conference on Grid Computing and Applications*, p. 71 (2015).
5. Esposito, Christian, Alfredo De Santis, Genny Tortora, Henry Chang, and Kim-Kwang Raymond Choo. "Blockchain: A panacea for healthcare cloud-based data security and privacy?." *IEEE Cloud Computing* 5, no. 1 (2018): 31–37.
6. Chen, H., B. An, D. Niyato, Y.C. Soh, and C. Miao "Workload factoring and resource sharing via joint vertical and horizontal cloud federation networks." *IEEE Journal on Selected Areas in Communications* 35, no. 3 (2017): 557–570.
7. Ray, B., A. Saha, S. Khatua, and S. Roy. "Quality and profit assured trusted cloud federation formation: Game theory based approach. *IEEE Transactions on Services Computing* 14, no. 3 (2018): 805–819.

8. Bairagi, A.K., M.G.R. Alam, A. Talukder, T.H. Nguyen, C.S. Hong, et al. "An overlapping coalition formation approach to maximize payoffs in cloud computing environment." In *2016 International Conference on Information Networking*, pp. 324–329 (2016).

9. Tosh, Deepak K., Sachin Shetty, Xueping Liang, Charles A. Kamhoua, Kevin A. Kwiat, and Laurent Njilla. "Security implications of blockchain cloud with analysis of block withholding attack." In *2017 17th IEEE/ACM International Symposium on Cluster, Cloud and Grid Computing (CCGRID)*, pp. 458–467. IEEE, (2017).

10. Taghavi, M., J. Bentahar, H. Otrok, and Bakhtiyari K. Cloudchain. "A blockchain-based coopetition differential game model for cloud computing." In *International Conference on Service-Oriented Computing* Nov. 12, pp. 146–161 (2018). Springer, Cham.

11. Mayuranathan, M., M. Murugan, and V. Dhanakoti. "Enhanced security in cloud applications using emerging blockchain security algorithm." *Journal of Ambient Intelligence and Humanized Computing* 27 (2020 Jul.): 1–3.

12. Yang, C., L. Tan, N. Shi, B. Xu, Y. Cao, and K. Yu. "AuthPrivacyChain: A blockchain-based access control framework with privacy protection in cloud." *IEEE Access* 6, no. 8 (2020 Apr.): 70604–70615.

13. Wang, Y., A. Zhang, P. Zhang, and H. Wang. "Cloud-assisted EHR sharing with security and privacy preservation via consortium blockchain." *IEEE Access* 23, no. 7 (2019 Sep.): 136704–136719.

14. Zhu, L., Y. Wu, K. Gai, K.K. Choo. "Controllable and trustworthy blockchain-based cloud data management." *Future Generation Computer Systems* 1, no. 91 (2019 Feb): 527–555.

15. Deep, G., R. Mohana, A. Nayyar, P. Sanjeevikumar, and E. Hossain. "Authentication protocol for cloud databases using blockchain mechanism." *Sensors*. 19, no. 20 (2019 Jan): 4444.

16. Zhang, Yuan, Xu Chunxiang, Xiaodong Lin, and Xuemin Sherman Shen. "Blockchain-based public integrity verification for cloud storage against procrastinating auditors." In *IEEE Transactions on Cloud Computing* (2019).

17. Eltayieb, Nabeil, Rashad Elhabob, Alzubair Hassan, and Fagen Li. "A blockchain-based attribute-based signcryption scheme to secure data sharing in the cloud." *Journal of Systems Architecture* 102 (2020): 101653.

18. Rebello, Gabriel Antonio F., Igor D. Alvarenga, Igor J. Sanz, and Otto Carlos MB Duarte. "BSec-NFVO: A blockchain-based security for network function virtualization orchestration." In *ICC 2019–2019 IEEE International Conference on Communications (ICC)*, pp. 1–6 (2019). IEEE.

19. Wei, PengCheng, Dahu Wang, Yu Zhao, Sumarga Kumar Sah Tyagi, and Neeraj Kumar. "Blockchain data-based cloud data integrity protection mechanism." *Future Generation Computer Systems* 102 (2020): 902–911.

20. Cao, Sheng, Gexiang Zhang, Pengfei Liu, Xiaosong Zhang, and Ferrante Neri. "Cloud-assisted secure eHealth systems for tamper-proofing EHR via blockchain." *Information Sciences* 485 (2019): 427–440.

Chapter 17

Big-Data Analytics in Disaster Management

Pallavi and Sandeep Joshi

Manipal University Jaipur, Jaipur, India

17.1 Introduction

Every year, a variety of natural disasters strike throughout the world, killing thousands of people, displacing millions more, and ruining billions of dollars' worth of property and infrastructure [2]. Natural disasters are mostly unpredictable phenomena that occur in a relatively short space of time, as is the case with earthquakes. Information technology (IT) plays a crucial role as an integrator in disaster management. This is especially true when it comes to catastrophe data [1], which need to be collected as soon as is humanly possible, then securely transmitted to a cloud storage facility for processing, and finally processed in real time. Data collected during catastrophic events such as floods, landslides, mudslides, soil erosion, and so on generally comes from a variety of sources [3] and in a large volume, presenting a considerable challenge for data management. Advanced and methodical techniques are needed to analyze the heterogeneity of credible data sources such as sensors, social networks, and other sources, enabling effective execution of disaster management plans. Real-time data analysis is required for the majority of natural catastrophes, including flash floods, earthquakes, landslides, hurricanes, cyclones, tornadoes, tsunamis, and storms, so that key events may be identified and human lives can be saved in the aftermath of the disaster. In these kinds of systems, maintaining a high level of data security is necessary for the system to function properly.

Sensor-generated data and user-generated information (such as that found on social media sites such as Twitter, Flickr, and Facebook) are the two types of data

DOI: 10.1201/9781003371380-17

used throughout the process (such as satellite images and drone footage). When these facts are thoroughly reviewed, the consequences of a crisis can be successfully mitigated [4].

17.2 A Disaster-resilience Strategy Based on Big Data

The concept of vulnerability relates to a social unit's capacity to withstand the negative consequences of the dangers that it faces. Resilience is defined as the ability to cope with a wider variety of shocks and risks, as well as the ability to help people and communities return to their previous condition [5]. In the aftermath of a disaster, disaster management is an integrated process that involves preparing for, responding to, recovering from, and mitigating the effects of the disaster. Each of the four processes is a tool that can be used to increase the adaptive, absorptive, and transformative capacities of an individual, a group, or an entire society, and any combination of these processes can be utilized to accomplish this goal (Figure 17.1).

The primary objective of disaster management is to lessen the harmful impacts and ramifications that natural and man-made disasters have on society, thus

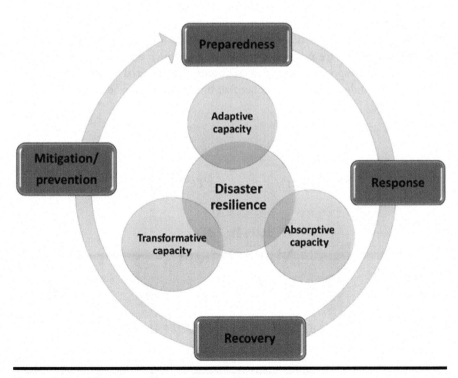

Figure 17.1   Disaster-resilience framework.

protecting individuals and social infrastructure [9]. There are three main aspects to disaster management:

- readiness and early warning
- impact and response
- mitigation, risk, and vulnerability modeling.

Emergency preparations are short term, but disaster mitigation is long term, and both are necessary for disaster management to function properly. The phases that take place during and immediately after the occurrence of a disaster are known as the reaction and recovery phases [6].

17.3 Disaster Management

Research on risk modeling and management in the context of disaster preparation and response has provided models of risk that are relevant to both man-made and natural disaster scenarios. Disaster management is defined as "the integration of all activities required to build, sustain and improve the capabilities to prepare for, respond to, recover from, or mitigate against a disaster" [7]. The disaster management cycle, seen in Figure 17.2, is a collection of four distinct but related tasks, each of which focuses on either risk management (prevention, readiness, and reaction), or crisis management (response and recovery), and which is organized into a single category [8]. The response and recovery stages are characterized by the fact that these actions are not independent and sequential, but begin immediately. In addition to

Figure 17.2 Disaster preparedness lifecycle phases.

this, populations can be subjected to separate long-term and short-term rehabilitation operations, which can take anything from a few days to many months.

The term "hazard" refers to the possibility that a specific catastrophic hazard may occur, which can include several different situations. Exposure data include information about the population and information about shelter requirements, while vulnerability data include information about the social and economic vulnerability indices. The evacuation of people and the control of road congestion risks are two areas that fall under the purview of disaster response operations [10].

Disaster management apps may be divided into two categories – "pre-disaster" and "post-disaster" – with varying requirements for reaction speed, accuracy, and effectiveness. Several pre-disaster applications, including catastrophe prediction, early warning systems, and simulation exercises, among others, place a strong emphasis on measured and comprehensive data analysis. However, applications such as evacuation, rescue operations, and monitoring (among others) that take place after a disaster require findings that are spontaneous and precise. But any disaster management system (DMS) application should be able to accommodate diverse and dispersed data sources, as well as enable decision-makers to derive valuable knowledge from such data sources in an interactive way. To be effective, DMSs must meet stringent technological standards in terms of dependability and availability as well as maintenance, correctness, and usability [11]. Table 17.1 lists the requirements that must be met by any DMS application. By ensuring that these objectives are met, app developers can establish benchmark quality attributes that can be used to validate the performance of the DMS and quantify its efficacy.

Table 17.1   Typical Use Cases and Requirements for DMS

Status of the Disaster	Applications of DMS	Requirements of DMS
Pre-Disaster	Prediction of disasters	Authenticity availability Maintainability efficiency Adoption
Post Disaster	Early warning experiments in simulation expulsion	
	Rescue assistance monitoring / surveillance	
	Logistics management	

17.4 Characteristics of Big Data

The "five Vs" are used to define the features of large amounts of data [12].

Value. It is impossible to exaggerate how significant the value of enormous amounts of data is. We do not process or store any data at this time. We are responsible for the storage, management, and analysis of reliable and helpful data.

Velocity. The most important factor is velocity. The speed of real-time data is created by velocity. It connects the speeds of the data sets, the change rates, and the activity bursts. Big data provide fast, demanding data. The speed at which data flow from many sources, such as application logs, business processes, networks, sensors, mobile devices, and so on, is referred to as "big data velocity".

Variety. Big data is a term that can apply to data that is structured, unstructured, or even semi-structured, and it can originate from a wide number of places.

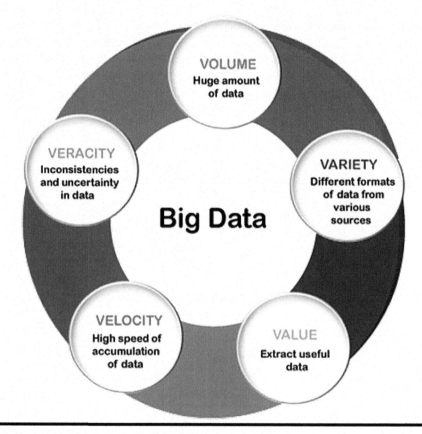

Figure 17.3 Characteristics of big data.

In the past, data was only collected from databases and spreadsheets; however, data is now received in a variety of formats, such as PDFs, emails, audio, social media postings, photos, videos, and so on.

Veracity. This concerns the data's reliability and the method of handling and maintaining data effectively and efficiently.

Volume. The term "big data" – coined by IBM in 2005 – refers to the enormous amounts of data that are generated daily from a wide variety of sources, including but not limited to corporate processes, machines, social media platforms, networks, and human interactions.

17.5 Application of Big Data in Disaster Management

Disasters such as snowmelt floods and earthquakes can be predicted with the help of geographic information systems (GIS), global positioning systems (GPS), and environmental monitoring devices that connect to the cloud.

Big-data platforms have been shown to be extremely useful resources for preparing for and responding to natural disasters. Big data allow authorities in charge of disaster risk management to better monitor individuals in the case of an emergency and make it simpler to carry out extra post-disaster responsibilities such as logistics and resource planning, as well as real-time communications [13, 14].

According to ref. [15], disaster risk management in emergency circumstances improved when data, location information, and real-time photos were merged. In addition, machine learning and image processing can generate heat maps of the affected area, which can contribute to the prompt and efficient provision of support to individuals who need aid [8].

17.6 Comparative Analysis of the Methods Employed

Learning machines are getting smarter all the time, which means we have more tools at our disposal to solve the world's problems. The ability to safely evacuate a building in an emergency is one of the most essential uses of the technology described above. The most remarkable consequences of the approach presented are its capacity to measure the attitudes of a community, to develop intelligently planned danger situation responses, and to provide the best emergency evacuation plot on 3D alerts as a new and different feature [5].

By employing real-time changing data and surveillance systems, projecting future impacts and reactions, and optimizing strategic and logistical decisions for effective response planning and execution, organizations want to accomplish the integration of data analytics into their operations. The use of IT has developed into enterprise resource planning (ERP) systems, which aim to integrate the reporting of organizations and provide real-time data from a single source. More research is required on the human element in the process of developing operational protocols with technologies powered by artificial intelligence [6].

Hadoop and Apache Spark are the two frameworks that are utilized the most frequently for data analysis. Applying both at the same time will provide superior results. As technology continues to advance at a rapid pace, methodologies based on machine learning will emerge as front-and-center players in the administration and analysis of big data. Studies are needed of more contemporary algorithmic and software systems that can be used for storing, organizing, managing, and analyzing massive volumes of data. In subsequent studies, it may be possible to investigate additional applications of big data in smart real estate, taking into consideration the degree to which businesses are prepared to use the technology, the degree to which the industry is ready for the disruptions that big data may cause, as well as barriers to and benefits of adoption and implementation [16].

Data handling can be broken down into four stages: the production of data, the capture of data, the storage of data, and the analysis of data. Applications of big data can boost the productivity of government organizations and encourage the advancement of human science and technology [17].

17.7 Conclusion

Effective catastrophe management is a worldwide problem that requires international cooperation. As the number and accessibility of varied datasets continue to grow at an alarming rate, the potential and value of the big-data paradigm for disaster management are becoming increasingly apparent. This study focused on the exploitation of big data to strengthen disaster management resilience, and on contemporary technologies that can be used throughout the entirety of the disaster management process. An individual's or a society's capacity to withstand and cope with the negative consequences of a catastrophe is a mixed function of their adaptive, absorptive, and transformational capacity to withstand and cope with such consequences. This holds whether it is the individual or the society that is attempting to endure and cope with the effects of the catastrophe. Our generation is growing up in an era in which data is the most precious asset. Improvements in machine learning are resulting in a greater number of potentially useful instruments for addressing humanity's concerns.

References

1. M. N. I. Sarker, Y. Peng, C. Yiran, R. C. Shouse, Disaster resilience through big data: Way to environmental sustainability, *International Journal of Disaster Risk Reduction* 51 (2020) 101769.
2. S. A. Shah, D. Z. Seker, M. M. Rathore, S. Hameed, S. B. Yahia, D. Draheim, Towards disaster resilient smart cities: Can internet of things and big data analytics be the game changers?, *IEEE Access* 7 (2019) 91885–91903.

3. M. F. Abdullah, M. Ibrahim, H. Zulkifli, Big data analytics framework for natural disaster management in Malaysia, in *International Conference on Internet of Things, Big Data and Security*, Vol. 2, SCITEPRESS, 2017, pp. 406–411.

4. D. Puthal, S. Nepal, R. Ranjan, J. Chen, A secure big data stream analytics framework for disaster management on the cloud, in *2016 IEEE 18th International Conference on High-Performance Computing and Communications; IEEE 14th International Conference on Smart City; IEEE 2nd International Conference on Data Science and Systems (HPCC/SmartCity/DSS)*, IEEE, 2016, pp. 1218–1225.

5. P. Alipour Sarvari, M. Nozari, D. Khadraoui, The potential of data analytics in disaster management, in *Industrial engineering in the big data era: Selected Papers from the Global Joint Conference on Industrial Engineering and Its Application Areas, GJCIE 2018*, June 21–22, 2018, Nevsehir, Turkey, Springer, 2019, pp. 335–348.

6. O. M. Araz, T.-M. Choi, D. L. Olson, F. S. Salman, Role of analytics for operational risk management in the era of big data, *Decision Sciences* 51 (6) (2020) 1320–1346.

7. D. Parry, A. Norris, S. Madanian, S. Martinez, L. Labaka, J. Gonzalez, Disaster e-health: A new paradigm for collaborative healthcare in disasters. Centre for Integrated Emergency Management, the University of Agder (2015).

8. M. Arslan, A.-M. Roxin, C. Cruz, D. Ginhac, A review on applications of big data for disaster management, in *2017 13th International Conference on Signal-Image Technology & Internet-Based Systems (SITIS)*, IEEE, 2017, pp. 370–375.

9. D. Velev, P. Zlateva, An innovative approach for designing an emergency risk management system for natural disasters, *International Journal of Innovation, Management and Technology* 2 (5) (2011) 407.

10. E. Regnier, Public evacuation decisions and hurricane track uncertainty, *Management Science* 54 (1) (2008) 16–28.

11. T. Bayrak, Identifying requirements for a disaster-monitoring system, *Disaster Prevention, and Management: An International Journal* 18 (2009) 86–99.

12. G. Kapil, A. Agrawal, R. Khan, A study of big data characteristics, in *2016 International Conference on Communication and Electronics Systems (ICCES)*, IEEE, 2016, pp. 1–4.

13. S. Fang, L. Xu, Y. Zhu, Y. Liu, Z. Liu, H. Pei, J. Yan, H. Zhang, An integrated information system for snowmelt flood early-warning based on internet of things, *Information Systems Frontiers* 17 (2) (2015) 321–335.

14. G. Buribayeva, T. Miyachi, A. Yeshmukhametov, Y. Mikami, An autonomous emergency warning system based on cloud servers and sns, *Procedia Computer Science* 60 (2015) 722–729.

15. H. S. Munawar, A. Hammad, F. Ullah, T. H. Ali, After the flood: A novel application of image processing and machine learning for post-flood disaster management, in *Proceedings of the 2nd International Conference on Sustainable Development in Civil Engineering (ICSDC 2019)*, Jamshoro, Pakistan, 2019, pp. 5–7.

16. H. S. Munawar, S. Qayyum, F. Ullah, S. Sepasgozar, Big data and its applications in smart real estate and the disaster management life cycle: A systematic analysis, *Big Data and Cognitive Computing* 4 (2) (2020) 4.

17. D. Emmanouil, D. Nikolaos, Big data analytics in prevention, preparedness, response and recovery in crisis and disaster management, in *The 18th International Conference on Circuits, Systems, Communications and Computers (CSCC 2015)*, Recent Advances in Computer Engineering Series, Vol. 32, 2015, pp. 476–484.

Chapter 18

Fuzzy Minimum Spanning Tree Calculation-Based Approach on Acceptability Index Method

Prasanta Kumar Raut, Siva Prasad Behera, and Debdas Mishra
C.V. Raman Global University, Bhubaneswar, India

Vinod Kumar
Shyam Lal College, University of Delhi, New Delhi, India

Kamal Lochan Mahanta
C.V. Raman Global University, Bhubaneswar, India

18.1 Introduction

The minimum spanning tree (MST) problem is extensively applied for connecting different cities via electricity lines or phone lines while optimizing the material costs

DOI: 10.1201/9781003371380-18

involving the use of available road infrastructures. Some of the very effective MST algorithms are due to the work of Kruskal and Prims [1].

In a classical network, the weights of the edges in an MST are expected to be actual values. However, in the majority of real-world applications, the various parameters used, such as costs, demand, and time, need not be accurate. In such situations, we can take advantage of the notion of fuzzy numbers for the purpose of simulation, which results in an FMST. Zadeh (1978) introduced the "fuzzy set theory" for dealing with uncertainty issues [2].

MST, first introduced by Graham and Hell, is among the most widely studied and applied concepts in combinatorial optimization and conventional graph optimization theory. The spanning tree of a graph in which the sum of the costs of the arcs is minimal is termed its MST. Several scholars of graph theory, such as Harel and Tarjan in 1984, Dijkstra in 1959, Prim in 1957, and Kruskal in 1956, suggested some good algorithms to compute the MST of weighted graphs [3, 4].

MST can be found in a variety of real-world applications, such as speech recognition, cluster analysis, image processing, wireless networks, telecommunications, and logistics. The massive expansion of telecommunications networks over the past several decades has made MST a hot topic. Consider the broadcasting problem, where identical messages must be sent to every node in the communication network. It is possible to model this kind of communication network as an MST problem [5, 6].

18.1.1 *Literature Review*

There are many types of algorithm that exist to evaluate the MST on networks. P. C. Pop suggested an MST on the basic clustering principle [7]. Carrabs, F. et al. suggested the MST on the basis of the α-cut method [8]. A. Dey et al. [9] suggested a new method for solving FMST along with several operations such that addition, defuzzification, and ranking method is used. The fuzzy minimum spanning tree (F-AMST) model, suggested by W. Gao et al. [10], federated the adaptive minimum spanning tree (AMST) method.

18.1.2 *Motivation and Contribution*

Many methods have been proposed to solve the FMST [11, 12]. In this chapter, we have developed an algorithm that evaluates the FMST based on an acceptability index in a fuzzy network. This algorithm has real-life applications and can be applied to various combinatorial optimization problems, such as distribution systems, transportation network problems, the design of telecommunications networks, energy infrastructure, airlines, and hydraulic systems, construction of highways and railroads, and laying pipelines. The algorithm is useful when there is uncertainty on the edge or vertices weight, or where the edge or vertices weight represents the time or cost or distance of a network.

Section 18.2 of this paper provides a definition of fuzzy set theory, Section 18.3 presents algorithms and methods with examples, and Section 18.4 provides a conclusion.

18.2 Preliminaries

18.2.1 Triangular Fuzzy Number

The membership function associated with a triangular fuzzy number $A = (a_1, a_2, a_3)$ is given as follows.

$$\mu_A(x) = \begin{cases} 0 & , & x \le a_1 - a_2 \\ \dfrac{x - (a_1 - a_2)}{a_2} & , & a_1 - a_2 < x < a_1 \\ 1 & , & x = a_1 \\ \dfrac{(a_1 + a_3) - x}{a_3} & , & a_1 < x < a_1 + a_3 \\ 0 & , & x \ge a_1 + a_3 \end{cases}$$

where a_1 is the center and a_2, a_3 represents the left and right spread respectively.

18.2.2 Trapezoidal Fuzzy Number

The membership function associated with a trapezoidal fuzzy number $A = (a_1, a_2, a_3, a_4)$ is given as follows.

$$\mu_A(x) = \begin{cases} 0 & , & x \le a_1 - a \\ \dfrac{x - (a_1 - a_3)}{a_3} & , & a_1 - a_3 < x < a_1 \\ 1 & , & a_1 \le x \le a_2 \\ \dfrac{(a_2 + a_4) - x}{a_4} & , & a_2 < x < a_2 + a_4 \\ 0 & , & x \ge a_2 + a_4 \end{cases}$$

18.2.3 Yager Index

The ranking index $I(A) = \int_0^1 \propto \left(A_\propto^L + A_\propto^U \right) d \propto$ where $[A_\propto^L, A_\propto^U]$ is the α-cut interval of fuzzy number A.

18.2.4 The π_2 Membership Function

Let π_2 membership function have four parameters, i.e. (lw, lp, rp, rw), then its membership function is defined by

$$\pi_2\left(x:\left(lw,lp,rp,rw\right)\right)=\begin{cases}\dfrac{lw}{lp+lw-x} & , & \text{if } x < lp \\[2mm] 1 & , & \text{if } lp \leq x \leq rp \\[2mm] \dfrac{rw}{x-rp+rw} & , & \text{if } x > rp\end{cases}$$

18.2.5 The Minimum Operation of Two π_2-Type Fuzzy Numbers

Let $L_1 = (lw_1, lp_1, rp_1, rw_1)$ and $L_2 = (lw_2, lp_2, rp_2, rw_2)$ are two π_2-shaped fuzzy numbers then its minimum operation is

$$L_{\min}\left(L_1,L_2\right)=\min\left(lw_1,lw_2\right),\min\left(lp_1,lp_2\right),\min\left(rp_1,rp_2\right),\min\left(rw_1,rw_2\right)$$

18.2.6 The Acceptability Index

For any proposition $L_{min} = (lw, lp, rp, rw)$ the acceptability index denoted as $L_i = (lw_i, lp_i, rp_i, rw_i)$ is given by $\text{AI}\left(L_{min} \leq L_i\right) = \dfrac{-\left(rw+lw_i\right)}{rp-rw-lp_i-lw_i}$. Making use of the notion of acceptability index, the concept of the ranking order is defined on the basis of highest acceptability index.

We have $L_1 < L_2 \Longleftrightarrow \text{AI}\left(L_{min} < L_1\right) > \text{AI}\left(L_{min} < L_2\right)$

Let y_d be the membership function

If $x > rp$, $y_d = \dfrac{rw}{x-rp+rw}$

$$rw = y_d\left(x-rp+rw\right)$$

$$rw = xy_d - rpy_d + rwy_d$$

$$xy_d = rw + rpy_d - rwy_d \tag{18.1}$$

$$x = \dfrac{rw+rpy_d-rwy_d}{y_d}$$

$$\text{If } x < lp_i,\ y_d = \frac{lw_i}{lp_i + lw_i - x}$$

$$lw_i = y_d \left(lp_i + lw_i - x \right)$$

$$lw_i = lp_i y_d + lw_i y_d - xy_d$$

$$xy_d = lp_i y_d + lw_i y_d - lw_i \tag{18.2}$$

$$x = \frac{lp_i y_d + lw_i y_d - lw_i}{y_d}$$

Equating Equation (18.1) and (18.2)

$$rw + rpy_d - rwy_d = lp_i y_d + lw_i y_d - lw_i$$

$$rpy_d - rwy_d - lp_i y_d - lw_i y_d = -rw - lw_i$$

$$y_d \left(rp - rw - lp_i - lw_i \right) = -\left(rw + lw_i \right)$$

$$y_d = \frac{-\left(rw + lw_i \right)}{\left(rp - rw - lp_i - lw_i \right)}$$

18.2.7 The α-Cut Interval for Fuzzy Number

(a) For trapezoidal fuzzy number $A = (a_1, a_2, a_3, a_4)_{LR}$ the expression $A_\alpha = [\alpha a_3 + (a_1 - a_3), a_2 + a_4 - \alpha a_4] = [A_\alpha^L, A_\alpha^U]$ represents the α-cut interval.

Moreover, we have

$$\frac{A_\alpha^L - \left(a_1 - a_3 \right)}{a_3} = \alpha$$

$$A_\alpha^L = \alpha a_3 + \left(a_1 - a_3 \right)$$

and

$$\frac{\left(a_2 + a_4 \right) - A_\alpha^U}{a_3} = \alpha$$

$$A_\alpha^U = \left(a_2 + a_4 \right) - \alpha a_4$$

18.2.8 On α-Cut Interval for Fuzzy Interval

For a fuzzy interval $A = [a_1, a_2]$, the expression $A_\alpha = \left[A_\alpha^L, A_\alpha^U \right] = \left[a_1 - \alpha a_3, \alpha a_4 + a_2 \right]$ represents the α-cut interval for representation.

The above α-cut interval of fuzzy interval is calculated for all $\alpha \in [0, 1]$

$$\frac{a_1 - A_\alpha^L}{a_3} = \alpha$$

$$A_\alpha^L = a_1 - \alpha a_3$$

$$\frac{A_\alpha^U - a_2}{a_4} = \alpha$$

$$A_\alpha^U = \alpha a_4 + a_2$$

18.2.9 On the Convex Index

The convex index of a trapezoidal fuzzy number $A = (x_1, x_2, x_3, x_4)_{LR}$ is given by $Col\,(A) = \lambda \left(A_\alpha^L \right) + (1 - \lambda) \left(A_\alpha^U \right)$, where $[A_\alpha^L, A_\alpha^U]$ is the α-cut interval of A.

Observe that

(i) $\mu_A \left[\lambda \left(A_\alpha^L \right) + (1 - \mu) \left(A_\alpha^U \right) \right] \geq \min \left\{ \mu_A \left(A_\alpha^L \right), \mu_A \left(A_\alpha^U \right) \right\} \forall \alpha, \lambda \in [0,1]$

(ii) For trapezoidal fuzzy numbers A and B, $A < B \iff Col(A) < Col(B)$.

18.3 Algorithm for Fuzzy Minimum Spanning Tree

18.3.1 Fuzzy Minimum Spanning Tree Based on the Acceptability Index

- Take a network $G = (V, E)$ with V as the set of vertices (nodes of the network G) and E as the set of edges (arcs of the network G).
- In order to determine the fuzzy minimum vertex, apply definition 18.2.5.
- Now vertex is ranked after acceptability index AI ($L_{min} \leq L_i$) is calculated using definition 18.2.6.
- Identify the minimum spanning tree based on highest acceptability index and then adding the vertices one by one into the growing spanning tree.
- If adding the vertex creating the cycle rejects this edge, keep adding vertex until we reach all vertices.

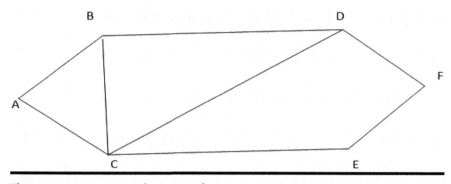

Figure 18.1 Transportation network.

The above process is represented by the numerical example in Figure 18.1:

Step 1 Consider a network with 6 vertices and 8 edges respectively.

Let us assume vertex (A) = (12, 36, 36, 6), (B) = (14, 30, 32, 5), (C) = (5, 36, 42, 7), (D) = (3, 30, 35, 6), (E) = (4, 34, 38, 8), (F) = (7, 32, 35, 8)

Step 2 Minimum vertex is B = (14, 30, 32, 5) using definition 2.9.

Step 3 Now find its vertex based on the acceptability index.

Step 4 Now add the vertex of minimum spanning tree based on highest acceptability index and then add the edges one by one into the growing spanning tree. And finally we get the spanning tree B–D–F–E–C–A

Table 18.1   Ranking on Acceptability Index

Vertex	Acceptability Index	Ranking
A	0.80	5
B	1.43	1
C	0.71	6
D	1.3	2
E	0.81	4
F	1	3

18.3.2 Fuzzy Minimum Spanning Tree Algorithm Using Convex Index

- Design a network $G = (V, E)$.
- Using definitions 18.2.7 and 18.2.8, determine the α-cut interval for every fuzzy trapezoidal number for all possible path lengths L_i, for $i = 1, 2. \ldots n$.
- Calculate convex index for all possible path lengths $Col(A) = \lambda\left(A_\alpha^L\right) + (1 - \lambda)\left(A_\alpha^U\right)$, L_i i.e. $i = 1$. m using definition 18.2.9.

Identify the minimum spanning tree based on convex index and then adding the vertex one by one into the growing spanning tree.

If adding the vertex creating the cycle rejects this edge, keep adding vertex until we reach all vertices.

Step 1 Design a network $G = (V, E)$.
Let us assume the edge lengths as
$(A) = (36, 36, 12, 6)$
$(B) = (30, 32, 14, 5)$
$(C) = (36, 42, 5, 7)$
$(D) = (30, 35, 3, 6)$
$(E) = (34, 38, 4, 8)$
$(F) = (32, 35, 7, 8)$

Step 2 Let $\alpha = 0.5$ and $\lambda = 0.7$, since $\alpha, \lambda \in [0, 1]$

$L_{1\alpha}, U_{1\alpha} = [30, 39]$, $L_{2\alpha}, U_{2\alpha} = [25, 34.5]$, $L_{3\alpha}, U_{3\alpha} = [49, 45.5]$, $L_{4\alpha}$, $U_{4\alpha} = [42, 38]$, $L_{5\alpha}, U_{5\alpha} = [32, 42]$, $L_{6\alpha}, U_{6\alpha} = [28.5, 39]$

Step 3 Now calculate the convex index by using formula
$$Col(A) = \lambda\left(A_\alpha^L\right) + (1 - \alpha)\left(A_\alpha^U\right)$$
Minimum convex index is vertex $B = 27.87$ so now we add the vertex according to the convex index.

Table 18.2 Ranking on Convex Index

Vertex	Convex Index	Ranking
A	43.7	5
B	27.87	1
C	47.95	6
D	30.8	2
E	35	4
F	31.65	3

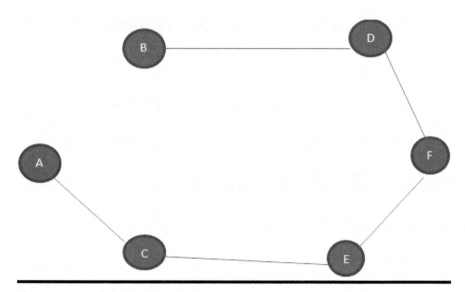

Figure 18.2   Minimum spanning tree.

Step 4   If adding the vertex creating the cycle rejects this edge, keep adding vertex until we reach all vertices. Finally, we get the resultant minimum spanning tree *B–D–F–E–C–A*.

18.3.3 Verification Using Yager's Index

We can verify minimum spanning tree using Yager's index. To find Yager's ranking index $I(A) = \int_{0}^{1} \propto \left(A_{\propto}^{L} + A_{\propto}^{U} \right) d \propto$ where $[A_{\propto}^{L}, A_{\propto}^{U}]$ is the $\propto$-cut interval of fuzzy number A.

Table 18.3   Ranking on Yager's Index

Vertex	Yager's Index	Ranking
A	43.5	5
B	29.75	1
C	47.25	6
D	30	2
E	37	4
F	33.75	3

Table 18.4 Comparison with Existing Methods

Proposed Method	Network	Parameter	Methodology	Advantages
A. Dey et al.[13]	MST	Neutrosophic number	Adding and ranking operation	Uncertainty information can't be defined
P.C Pop et al.[14]	MST	Crisp number	Clustering principle	Uncertainty information can't be defined
F. Corrabs et al.[15]	MST	Crisp number	A-cut methodology	Uncertainty information can't be defined
G Pandurangan et al.[16]	MST	Crisp number	Clustering principle along with centroid rule	Uncertainty information can't be defined
Our proposed method	FMST	Trapezoidal number	Acceptability index along with ranking index	Uncertainty information can be defined

Hence minimum Yager's index is $B = 29.75$. Now add the vertex according to the ranking of Yager's vertex and then finally we get the MST which is $B - D - F - E - C - A$.

18.3.4 Comparison

The fuzzy minimum spanning tree (FMST) problem is the optimization problem of finding the minimal length of the network. In this section, we compare our proposed method with the existing methods.

18.4 Conclusion and Future Scope

In this chapter, we designed two algorithms, the acceptability index-based algorithm and the convex index-based algorithm, for computing the MST of a network with a vertex as a fuzzy trapezoidal number. We note that the minimum spanning tree remains the same in both methods, which is also verified in Yager's index. Using this method, decision makers can identify the best possible path among different alternatives from the list. In future work, we will try to implement our suggested algorithm for real-life problems in transportation, supply chain management, and other important fields.

References

1. Chang, W. C., Chiu, Y. D., & Li, M. F. (2008, August). Learning Kruskal's Algorithm, Prim's algorithm and Dijkstra's algorithm by board game. In *International Conference on Web-based Learning* (pp. 275–284). Springer, Berlin, Heidelberg.

2. S. Wang et al. (2020). Semi-supervised PolSAR image classification based on improved tri-training with a minimum spanning tree. *IEEE Transactions on Geoscience and Remote Sensing*, vol. 58, no. 12, pp. 8583–8597, doi: 10.1109/TGRS.2020.2988982.

3. Kruskal, J. B. (1956). On the shortest spanning subtree of a graph and the traveling salesman problem. *Proceedings of the American Mathematical society*, 7(1), 48–50.

4. Harel, D., & Tarjan, R. E. (1984). Fast algorithms for finding nearest common ancestors. *SIAM Journal on Computing*, 13(2), 338–355.

5. Graham, R. L., & Hell, P. (1985). On the history of the minimum spanning tree problem. *Annals of the History of Computing*, 7(1), 43–57.

6. Graham, R. L., & Hell, P. (1985). On the history of the minimum spanning tree problem. *Annals of the History of Computing*, 7(1), 43–57.

7. Pop, P. C. (2020). The generalized minimum spanning tree problem: An overview of formulations, solution procedures and latest advances. *European Journal of Operational Research*, 283(1), 1–15.

8. Carrabs, F., Cerulli, R., Pentangelo, R., & Raiconi, A. (2021). Minimum spanning tree with conflicting edge pairs: a branch-and-cut approach. *Annals of Operations Research*, 298(1), 65–78.

9. Dey, A., Son, L. H., Pal, A., & Long, H. V. (2020). Fuzzy minimum spanning tree with interval type 2 fuzzy arc length: Formulation and a new genetic algorithm. *Soft Computing*, 24(6), 3963–3974.

10. Gao, W., Zhang, Q., Lu, Z., Wu, D., & Du, X. (2018). Modelling and application of fuzzy adaptive minimum spanning tree in tourism agglomeration area division. *Knowledge-Based Systems*, 143, 317–326.

11. Wang, K., Zhou, Y., Tian, G., & Goh, M. (2021). A structured solution framework for fuzzy minimum spanning tree problem and its variants under different criteria. *Fuzzy Optimization and Decision Making*, 20(4), 497–528.

12. Mohanta, K., Dey, A., Debnath, N. C., & Pal, A. (2019, September). An algorithmic approach for finding minimum spanning tree in a intuitionistic fuzzy graph. In *Proceedings of 32nd International Conference on* (Vol. 63, pp. 140–149).

13. Dey, A., Broumi, S., Son, L. H., Bakali, A., Talea, M., & Smarandache, F. (2019). A new algorithm for finding minimum spanning trees with undirected neutrosophic graphs. *Granular Computing*, 4, 63–69.

14. Pop, P. C. (2020). The generalized minimum spanning tree problem: An overview of formulations, solution procedures and latest advances. *European Journal of Operational Research*, 283(1), 1–15.

15. Carrabs, F., Cerulli, R., Pentangelo, R., & Raiconi, A. (2021). Minimum spanning tree with conflicting edge pairs: a branch-and-cut approach. *Annals of Operations Research*, 298(1–2), 65–78.

16. Pandurangan, G., Robinson, P., & Scquizzato, M. (2018). The distributed minimum spanning tree problem. *Bulletin of EATCS*, 2(125).

Chapter 19

Encoder/Decoder Transformer-Based Framework to Detect Hate Speech from Tweets

Usman and S. M. K. Quadri

Jamia Millia Islamia, New Delhi, India

19.1 Introduction

With the majority of corporate advertising and promotion moving online, firms are more worried than ever about hate speech material. Online hate speech may be described as written statements containing derogatory or discriminatory terminology. While companies control the material they produce and publish online through their social media channels and websites, they have no control over what online consumers post or remark about their brand.

Over the last decade, we have seen the development of what defines brand marketing; the rise of jobs such as Social Content Manager and Community Manager reflects the requirement for regulating the interaction around a brand's online content [9]. This has typically concentrated on community interaction, which entails generating online comments or postings about brand material. This has resulted in the development of social monitoring systems such as Stackla, Meltwater and Olapic, kla, which concentrate on increasing brand exposure and online engagement. With the increase in hate speech, however, brand building is facing new challenges: today's Community Managers and other similarly oriented roles must now examine their company's digital platforms for any possible hate speech.

In the absence of an appropriate technology, hate speech or objectionable language identification is a time-consuming and resource-intensive human operation. A Community Manager will not have the capacity to fully monitor all brand-associated material for hate speech and may need to add personnel to their team in order to meet the rising demand for this form of digital content management. It is also crucial to highlight that a human's capacity to effectively identify hate speech material depends on a variety of circumstances, such as their energy level, reading skills, and personal prejudices as to what constitutes unpleasant content. The use of AI will enable the automation of this labor-intensive procedure, improving efficiency and precision.

19.2 Related Work

Data augmentations primarily add to the generalizability and robustness of a model by supplying diverse data. Existing techniques often stress one side (i.e., generalizability or resilience), but hardly any of them include both in a single framework. In general, enhancing generalization will improve prediction accuracy in standard scenarios. Sometimes, increasing robustness may hinder effectiveness. However, it will assist in mitigating the effects of harmful attacks.

Augmentation methods may range from perturbation to generation [21, 27–39]. Perturbation techniques generate (typically) minor and manageable modifications to the original samples provided. Typically, they are cheap and scalable. However, artificial perturbations will inevitably cause inaccurate context, which might negatively impact the quality of the information. Changing some crucial terms may also result in label-flipping issues [40]. Generative approaches allow a deep learning network to record the behavior of a specific portion of the data and then produce comparable data from a specified beginning [41–45].

Recently, fairness has been examined and explored in a variety of fields, including corporate operations [46], general language models [48] and recommendation systems [47]. Previous research defined fairness as "equal opportunities" in broad classification issues [49, 50], and scholars have investigated theoretical arguments and methods for enhancing fairness [51–54]. Researchers in different fields have developed a variety of uncertainty assessment techniques, including dropout methods [56], ensemble models [55] and probability evaluation [57, 58]. However, scholars in the arena of hate speech have paid little attention to estimations of fairness and ambiguity.

Research in [14, 15] performed a comprehensive investigation of hate speech. Arango et al. [16] addressed a model validation challenge involving the identification of hateful speech. Nobata et al. [1] experimented with several kinds of features for produced relevant findings and classification tasks. Recent publications used lSTMs, CNNs and attention processes to improve detection outcomes [3–6, 17, 18]. Djuric et al. [2] explored embeddings at the paragraph level for hate speech identification. Mou et al. [19] used both LSTMs and CNNs for word/word-piece embeddings and character/phonetic embeddings, respectively. Posters of hate speech may use deliberate manipulation techniques to avoid previous hate speech detection technologies [20–21].

Researchers in [7, 8, 10–13] have made available their databases of hate speech. Others [22, 23, 24, 25, 26] supplied counter speech datasets for improved hate speech classification. In addition to these available datasets, Tran et al. [27] used Yahoo Finance and Yahoo News databases to construct a hate speech classifier. Most studies only collected data from a single platform (mostly Twitter), therefore their algorithms may not identify hate speech on some other sites.

19.3 Preliminaries

19.3.1 BERT (Bidirectional Encoder Representations from Transformer)

BERT is [59] a language model based on multi-layer bidirectional encoder transformer architecture [60], with enhancements to unidirectionality requirements via the use of the Masked Language Model approach (MLM). The model attained state-of-the-art performance in eleven natural language processing tasks at the time of its release, outperforming even task-specific approaches. In addition, the team trained models of varying sizes and proved the well-known premise that growing model size would result in continuous gains in downstream tasks. With 340 million parameters, BERT Large was the largest model trained.

The MLM method arbitrarily conceals input bits with a particular token, a randomized token, or with nothing at all (Figure 19.1). In addition, this method enables the model to train to anticipate the original message using simply the relevance of both ways while pretraining. BERT's architecture consists of two phases: a pretraining phase in which the model is programmed to estimate the result from

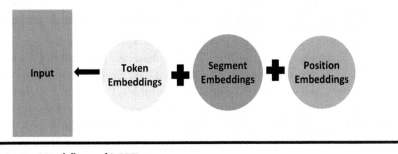

Figure 19.1 Workflow of BERT.

the input using a huge unlabeled dataset and a very basic binary Next Sentence Prediction task. Next is the fine-tuning stage, where the model is programmed with the purpose of the task using an annotated dataset. The first step is reusable whenever a particular activity is required.

In addition to tokenizing the text through embedding, several special tokens are also included. Similar to the original transformer, the token embedding may be supplied to the model together with a segment embedding showing to which pair the phrase relates and a position embedding showing the location of the token to construct the input for the model (Figure 19.1).

19.3.2 GPT-2 (Generative Pretrained Transformer)

GPT-2 [61], a modified version of GPT, is based on the design of decoder transformers [60]. The biggest model contains 1.5 billion parameters and was developed using no task-specific input. The authors demonstrated that a generic model may learn to execute tasks without training datasets, variable changes, or model modification. When it was released, it achieved state-of-the-art performance in seven out of eight tasks. Studies suggest that the model will have to train to exploit unsupervised data to accomplish specified tasks, resulting in more accurate forecasts. The model is capable of doing unsupervised multimodal learning. The training data was 40 GB in volume, and coincidences with the task data were examined to exclude the chance of the model achieving high scores by memory. N-gram and Bloom filters and overlaps were used to check for overlaps. The overall overlapping was just 6%, and it was determined that it delivers modest but continuous improvements to the findings. Furthermore, it is proven that the models were underfitted given the continual rise in model size-related confusion. When a big language model learns on a suitably huge and varied dataset, it may function well across a broad spectrum of applications and data. The word embedding employed included 50,000 tokens and is a combination of word-level Unicode strings and Byte-Pair Encoding (BPE). A greedy strategy is employed to prevent mixing text classes with byte series.

19.4 Framework of the System

This section provides a detailed description of the data source and the NLP tasks, such as text augmentation, text purification and sentiment analysis, using BERT and GPT-2 techniques (Figure 19.2). We have used data provided in [1] which contains 24,000 tweets from Twitter. The collected data received is not balanced: some tweets contain two words and some have around 50. Preferably, DL classifiers are trained using broad and varied datasets that more accurately reflect the actual prevalence of hate speech. Using the GPT-2 paradigm, we automatically generate large-scale datasets of hate speech text sequences and counterexamples from labeled seed instances. The Generative Pretrained Transformer (GPT-2) is a linguistic framework

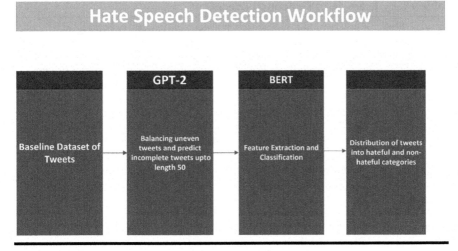

Figure 19.2   Architecture of proposed framework.

that has been developed to anticipate, or "produce," the next term in the sequence, given the preceding utterances. GPT-2, which was trained using 40GB of web text, produced text patterns of greater importance than ever. However, our goal is to construct hateful rather than generic text sequences. In particular, we want to construct hate (and non-hate) speech segments that: (a) introduce high language variety; (b) are regarded by humans as hate (or non-hate) speech with greater probability; and (c) demonstrate high language fluency. To satisfy the first criterion, we use accessible labeled samples and tune GPT-2 to generate hate (and non-hate) speech. Utilizing the complex language model provided in GPT-2 and producing a vast set of candidate sequences achieves a high level of variety. Last but not least, we maintain good quality of the data by dynamically analyzing the created candidate sequences using BERT, a state-of-the-art text classifier, where generated sequences that are determined as low-quality texts by BERT are deleted automatically. Next, we codify and describe each of these aspects of our methodology for generating hate speech. The data provided to it is extended with the help of GPT-2. Examples of the generated tweet and original tweet are shown in Table 19.1.

Here,

0 = hate speech
1 = offensive language
2 = neither should be considered

Text data preprocessing is a vital step since it prepares the unprocessed text for mining, making it simpler to retrieve meaning from text and use machine learning approaches. If this phase is skipped, there is a greater likelihood of dealing with

Table 19.1 Example of Generated Tweets

Class	Tweet	Generated Tweet
Two	@karmendanielle_ let the coons be great it's in the dream	@karmendanielle_ let the coons be great it's in the dream, the dream is to be in the coons, in the coons, in the coons, in the coons, in the coons, in
Two	#IndigenousPeoplesDay ....right. Because these #redskins had a lot of #queens, right? nomg. #sofunny	#IndigenousPeoplesDay.........right. Because these #redskins had a lot of #queens, right? nomg. #sofunny #indigenouspeoplesday #sadday #sodomit #s
Two	@AustinthaIntern Johnny football is trash man. Trash. Lol.	@AustinthaIntern Johnny football is trash man. Trash. Lol.\n\nI'm not a big football fan but I've watched every single game of this one so far. The first half was pretty much the same, the second half is
One	Twitter game is on point tonight btw guys, if you haven't caught on you're full retard.	Twitter game is on point tonight btw guys, if you haven't caught on you're full retard. #GoDucksGo #GoDucksGo pic.twitter.com/ Yj9qYq6K6z Ryan (@
One	Twitter your being a bitch	Twitter your being a bitch, you know, you're not going to be able to keep your job, you know? And I was like, you know what, you know, I'm going to be a little more vocal. I'm not going
One	U can't stay the same & expect change. U can't truly expect a good man if he call himself nigga, nigger. It means the same; A No Good Person!	U can't stay the same & expect change. U can't truly expect a good man if he call himself nigga, nigger. It means the same; A No Good Person! No Good Man! No Good Man! No Good
Zero	I hate when black people try and be white so bad ... Your a nigger	I hate when black people try and be white so bad... Your a nigger, you're not white," he said. The victim said the officer's response was "disrespectful." Police said the officer was taken to a

(Continued)

Table 19.1 (Continued)

Class	Tweet	Generated Tweet
Zero	I like Chinese buffets but I hate all the chinks	I like Chinese buffets but I hate all the chinks in the armor. I like Chinese buffets but I hate all the chinks in the armor. I like Chinese buffets but I hate all the chinks in the armor

distorted and ambiguous information. The primary purpose of this step is to remove irrelevant information in order to determine the emotion of Twitter posts, such as syntax, numerals, special characters and phrases of little weight.

Due to Twitter posts' character restriction, users often shorten words in various ways, such as 'u' for 'you'. In addition, they prefer to be casual and use non-standard phrases, neglect syntax, omit punctuation, or convey their emotions with many punctuation marks such as '!!!!' and emoticons. Twitter is used internationally, therefore users mix languages and write in various scripts. They also create new words and phrases according to the latest fads. Twitter is often used for advertising, which adds noise to data. To get. an accurate depiction of the text, the noise must be eliminated. The following are some of the procedures used in preprocessing data cleansing:

- Converting text into similar case, preferably lower case
- Removal of symbols from tweets
- Conversion of slang/punctuation into standard English
- Conversion of emoticons into text
- Correction of spelling mistakes
- Removal of numerals from the text
- Replacement of abbreviations

We avoided some of the conventional data cleansing methods, such as stemming, which removes the tail of the word and might alter its meaning, leading to erroneous sentiment classification. We only used those strategies that were essential and appropriate for our situation.

The following methods were used to compute each metric. "tp" is an abbreviation for "true positive," which refers to the count of events for which the model properly projected positive class. "fp" stands for "true negative," which shows the frequency in which the model erroneously identified the positive class. In contrast, true negative and false negative are identical to positive class, but aim the negative domain. All of these numbers are determined by comparing the forecast to the actual value.

$$\text{F1 score} = \frac{\text{tp}}{\left(\text{tp} + \frac{1}{2}\left(\text{fp} + \text{fn}\right)\right)}$$

$$Precision = \frac{tp}{\left(tp + fp\right)}$$

$$Recall = \frac{tp}{\left(tp + fn\right)}$$

$$Accuracy = \frac{tp + tn}{\left(tp + fp + tn + fn\right)}$$

A variant of the BERT approach was consistently the best in the deep learning category, most likely because the GPT-2 model was not intended for direct series categorization. We annotated the phrases in order to generate the model's inputs. Hugging Face auto tokenizer was used for BERT, and Hugging Face GPT-2 tokenizer was used for GPT-2. We ensured that all tweets had the same length by using padding. The truncation parameter was assigned to "true" to restrict phrase size to the allowable sequence length. We fitted the model to the training dataset and evaluated its accuracy using the validation dataset. For each of the models, the relevant assessment measures and loss curves were displayed. In terms of the testing phase precision, we discovered that the BERT model outperforms the GPT-2 model (see Table 19.2).

Table 19.2 Comparison of Models

Class	Evaluation Metrics	Model	
		BERT	GPT-2
Hate	Accuracy	0.78	0.88
	Precision	0.93	0.80
	Recall	0.74	0.71
	F1 Score	0.82	0.47
Offensive	Accuracy	0.78	0.79
	Precision	0.77	0.70
	Recall	0.89	0.81
	F1 Score	0.82	0.72
Neither	Accuracy	0.78	0.77
	Precision	0.89	0.85
	Recall	0.85	0.89
	F1 Score	0.81	0.79

19.5 Conclusion

The present status of the evaluated machine learning methods, especially deep learning models, offers enormous promise for detecting hate speech. These models are able to handle the vast volumes of data exchanged in media platforms. Even if the best models may not have a particularly high uncertainty, a more trustworthy model may be developed with more training sets or other designs. Even in their present condition, the models might be utilized to assist people with decision-making. In order to conduct a more comprehensive analysis of our tweets, it is necessary to refine the present assessment approaches and conduct new research.

References

1. C. Nobata, J. Tetreault, A. Thomas, Y. Mehdad, and Y. Chang, "Abusive language detection in online user content," in *WWW*, 2016. [Online]. Available: https://doi.org/10.1145/2872427.2883062

2. N. Djuric, J. Zhou, R. Morris, M. Grbovic, V. Radosavljevic, and N. Bhamidipati, "Hate speech detection with comment embeddings," in *WWW*, 2015. [Online]. Available: https://doi.org/10.1145/2740908.2742760

3. P. Badjatiya, M. Gupta, and V. Varma, "Stereotypical bias removal for hate speech detection task using knowledge-based generalizations," in *WWW*, 2019. [Online]. Available: https://doi.org/10.1145/3308558.3313504

4. H. Liu, P. Burnap, W. Alorainy, and M. L. Williams, "Fuzzy multi-task learning for hate speech type identification," in *WWW*, 2019. [Online]. Available: https://doi.org/10.1145/3308558.3313546

5. A. G. Chowdhury, A. Didolkar, R. Sawhney, and R. Shah, "Arhnetleveraging community interaction for detection of religious hate speech in arabic," in *ACL Student Research Workshop*, 2019. [Online]. Available: https://doi.org/10.18653/v1/p19-2038

6. Z. Zhang, D. Robinson, and J. Tepper, "Detecting hate speech on twitter using a convolution-gru based deep neural network," in *European Semantic Web Conference*, 2018. [Online]. Available: https://doi.org/10.1007/978-3-319-93417-4-48

7. O. de Gibert, N. Perez, A. García-Pablos, and M. Cuadros, "Hate speech dataset from a white supremacy forum," in *2nd Workshop on Abusive Language Online (ALW2)*. Brussels, Belgium: Association for Computational Linguistics, Oct. 2018, pp. 11–20. [Online]. Available: https://www.aclweb.org/anthology/W18-5102

8. M. Zampieri, S. Malmasi, P. Nakov, S. Rosenthal, N. Farra, and R. Kumar, "SemEval-2019 Task 6: Identifying and Categorizing Offensive Language in Social Media (OffensEval)," in *Proceedings of the 13th InternationalWorkshop on Semantic Evaluation*, Minneapolis, MN, USA, 6–7 July 2019, pp. 75–86.

9. E. Wulczyn, N. Thain, and L. Dixon, "Ex machina: Personal attacks seen at scale," in *WWW*, 2017, pp. 1391–1399. [Online]. Available: https://doi.org/10.1145/3038912.3052591

10. N. Ousidhoum, Z. Lin, H. Zhang, Y. Song, and D.-Y. Yeung, "Multilingual and multi-aspect hate speech analysis," in *EMNLPIJCNLP*. Hong Kong, China: Association for Computational Linguistics, Nov. 2019, pp. 4675–4684. [Online]. Available: https://www.aclweb.org/anthology/D19-1474

11. T. Davidson, D. Warmsley, M. Macy, and I. Weber, "Automated hate speech detection and the problem of offensive language," in *Proceedings of the International AAAI Conference on Web and Social Media*, vol. 11, no. 1, 2017.

12. Z. Waseem and D. Hovy, "Hateful symbols or hateful people? predictive features for hate speech detection on twitter," in *NAACL student research workshop*, 2016, pp. 88–93. [Online]. Available: https://doi.org/10.18653/v1/n16-2013

13. M. ElSherief, V. Kulkarni, D. Nguyen, W. Y. Wang, and E. Belding, "Hate lingo: A target-based linguistic analysis of hate speech in social media," in *ICWSM*, vol. 12, no. 1, 2018.

14. W. Warner and J. Hirschberg, "Detecting hate speech on the world wide web," in *Second workshop on language in social media*, 2012.

15. Z. Waseem, "Are you a racist or am I seeing things? annotator influence on hate speech detection on twitter," in *Workshop on NLP and computational social science*, 2016, pp. 138–142. [Online]. Available: https://doi.org/10.18653/v1/w16-5618

16. A. Arango, J. Perez, and B. Poblete, "Hate speech detection is not as easy as you may think: A closer look at model validation," in SIGIR, 2019, pp. 45–54. [Online]. Available: https://doi.org/10.1016/j.is.2020.101584

17. P. Badjatiya, S. Gupta, M. Gupta, and V. Varma, "Deep learning for hate speech detection in tweets," in *International Conference on World Wide Web Companion*, 2017. [Online]. Available: https://doi.org/10.1145/3041021.3054223

18. B. Gamback and U. K. Sikdar, "Using convolutional neural networks to classify hate-speech," in *Workshop on abusive language online*, 2017, pp. 85–90. [Online]. Available: https://doi.org/10.18653/v1/w17-3013

19. G. Mou, P. Ye, and K. Lee, "Swe2: Subword enriched and significant word emphasized framework for hate speech detection," in *CIKM*, 2020, pp. 1145–1154. [Online]. Available: https://doi.org/10.1145/3340531.3411990

20. L. Sun, K. Hashimoto, W. Yin, A. Asai, J. Li, P. Yu, and C. Xiong, "Advbert: Bert is not robust on misspellings! generating nature adversarial samples on bert," arXiv preprint arXiv:2003.04985, 2020.

21. S. Garg and G. Ramakrishnan, "BAE: BERT-based adversarial examples for text classification," in *EMNLP*, 2020. [Online]. Available: https://doi.org/10.18653/v1/2020.emnlp-main.498

22. L. Li, R. Ma, Q. Guo, X. Xue, and X. Qiu, "Bert-attack: Adversarial attack against bert using bert," in *EMNLP*, 2020. [Online]. Available: https://doi.org/10.18653/v1/2020.emnlp-main.500

23. D. Li, Y. Zhang, H. Peng, L. Chen, C. Brockett, M.-T. Sun, and B. Dolan, "Contextualized perturbation for textual adversarial attack," arXiv preprint arXiv:2009.07502, 2020.

24. B. Mathew, P. Saha, H. Tharad, S. Rajgaria, P. Singhania, S. K. Maity, P. Goyal, and A. Mukherjee, "Thou shalt not hate: Countering online hate speech," in *ICWSM*, vol. 13, pp. 369–380, 2019.

25. Y.-L. Chung, E. Kuzmenko, S. S. Tekiroglu, and M. Guerini, "CONAN - COunter NArratives through nichesourcing: a multilingual dataset of responses to fight online hate speech," in *ACL*. Florence, Italy: Association for Computational Linguistics, Jul. 2019, pp. 2819–2829. [Online]. Available: https://www.aclweb.org/anthology/P19-1271

26. T. Tran, Y. Hu, C. Hu, K. Yen, F. Tan, K. Lee, and S. Park, "Habertor: An efficient and effective deep hatespeech detector," in *EMNLP*, 2020. [Online]. Available: https://doi.org/10.18653/v1/2020.emnlp-main.606

27. G. A. Miller, "Wordnet: a lexical database for English," *Communications of the ACM*, vol. 38, no. 11, pp. 39–41, 1995.

28. M. Alzantot, Y. Sharma, A. Elgohary, B.-J. Ho, M. Srivastava, and K.-W. Chang, "Generating natural language adversarial examples," in *EMNLP*, 2018. [Online]. Available: https://doi.org/10.18653/v1/d18-1316

29. M. T. Ribeiro, T. Wu, C. Guestrin, and S. Singh, "Beyond accuracy: Behavioral testing of NLP models with checklist," in *ACL*, 2020. [Online]. Available: https://doi.org/10.18653/v1/2020.acl-main.442

30. X. Jiao, Y. Yin, L. Shang, X. Jiang, X. Chen, L. Li, F. Wang, and Q. Liu, "Tinybert: Distilling BERT for natural language understanding," in *EMNLP*, T. Cohn, Y. He, and Y. Liu, Eds. Association for Computational Linguistics, 2020, pp. 4163–4174. [Online]. Available: https://doi.org/10.18653/v1/2020.findings-emnlp.372

31. X. Wu, S. Lv, L. Zang, J. Han, and S. Hu, "Conditional bert contextual augmentation," in *ICCS*. Springer, 2019, pp. 84–95.

32. Q. Xie, Z. Dai, E. H. Hovy, T. Luong, and Q. Le, "Unsupervised data augmentation for consistency training," in *NeurIPS*, H. Larochelle, M. Ranzato, R. Hadsell, M. Balcan, and H. Lin, Eds., 2020. [Online]. Available: https://proceedings.neurips.cc/paper/2020/hash/44feb0096faa8326192570788b38c1d1-Abstract.html

33. F. M. Luque, "Atalaya at TASS 2019: Data augmentation and robust embeddings for sentiment analysis," in Proceedings of the Iberian Languages Evaluation Forum co-located with 35th Conference of the Spanish Society for Natural Language Processing, IberLEF@SEPLN 2019, Bilbao, Spain, September 24th, 2019, ser. CEUR Workshop Proceedings, M. A. G. Cumbreras, J. Gonzalo, E. M. Camara, R. Martínez-Unanue, P. Rosso, J. Carrillo-de-Albornoz, S. Montalvo, L. Chiruzzo, S. Collovini, Y. Gutierrez, S. M. J. Zafra, M. Krallinger, M. Montes-y-Gomez, R. Ortega-Bueno, and A. Rosá, Eds., vol. 2421. CEUR-WS.org, 2019, pp. 561–570. [Online]. Available: http://ceur-ws.org/Vol-2421/TASS\paper\1.pdf

34. J. Li, S. Ji, T. Du, B. Li, and T. Wang, "Textbugger: Generating adversarial text against real-world applications," in *NDSS*, 2019. [Online]. Available: https://doi.org/10.14722/ndss.2019.23138

35. D. Pruthi, B. Dhingra, and Z. C. Lipton, "Combating adversarial misspellings with robust word recognition," in *ACL*, 2019. [Online]. Available: https://doi.org/10.18653/v1/p19-1561

36. D. Shen, M. Zheng, Y. Shen, Y. Qu, and W. Chen, "A simple but tough-to-beat data augmentation approach for natural language understanding and generation," arXiv preprint arXiv:2009.13818, 2020.

37. J. Wei and K. Zou, "EDA: Easy data augmentation techniques for boosting performance on text classification tasks," in *EMNLP-IJCNLP*. Hong Kong, China: Association for Computational Linguistics, Nov. 2019, pp. 6382–6388. [Online]. Available: https://www.aclweb.org/anthology/D19-1670

38. C. Coulombe, "Text data augmentation made simple by leveraging NLP cloud apis," *CoRR*, vol. abs/1812.04718, 2018. [Online]. Available: http://arxiv.org/abs/1812.04718

39. G. Rizos, K. Hemker, and B. Schuller, "Augment to prevent: short-text data augmentation in deep learning for hate-speech classification," in *CIKM*, 2019, pp. 991–1000. [Online]. Available: https://doi.org/10.1145/3357384.3358040

40. M. Yi, L. Hou, L. Shang, X. Jiang, Q. Liu, and Z.-M. Ma, "Reweighting augmented samples by minimizing the maximal expected loss," in *ICLR*, 2021. [Online]. Available: https://openreview.net/forum?id=9G5MIc-goqB

41. T. Wullach, A. Adler, and E. M. Minkov, "Towards hate speech detection at large via deep generative modeling," *IEEE Internet Computing*, pp. 1–1, 2020. [Online]. Available: https://doi.org/10.1109/mic.2020.3033161

42. A. Radford, J. Wu, R. Child, D. Luan, D. Amodei, and I. Sutskever, "Language models are unsupervised multitask learners," *OpenAI Blog*, vol. 1, no. 8, p. 9, 2019.

43. R. Cao and R. K.-W. Lee, "Hategan: Adversarial generative-based data augmentation for hate speech detection," in *COLING*, 2020, pp. 6327–6338. [Online]. Available: https://doi.org/10.18653/v1/2020.coling-main.557

44. A. Anaby-Tavor, B. Carmeli, E. Goldbraich, A. Kantor, G. Kour, S. Shlomov, N. Tepper, and N. Zwerdling, "Do not have enough data? deep learning to the rescue!" in *AAAI*, vol. 34, no. 05, 2020, pp. 7383–7390.

45. V. Kumar, A. Choudhary, and E. Cho, "Data augmentation using pretrained transformer models," arXiv preprint arXiv:2003.02245, 2020.

46. S. Frezal and L. Barry, "Fairness in uncertainty: Some limits and misinterpretations of actuarial fairness," *Journal of Business Ethics*, pp. 1–10, 2019. Available: https://doi.org/10.1007/s10551-019-04171-2

47. L. Wang and T. Joachims, "Fairness and diversity for rankings in twosided markets," arXiv preprint arXiv:2010.01470, 2020.

48. M. Nissim, R. van Noord, and R. van der Goot, "Fair is better than sensational: Man is to doctor as woman is to doctor," *Computational Linguistics*, 2020. Available: https://doi.org/10.1162/coli_a_00379

49. M. Hardt, E. Price, and N. Srebro, "Equality of opportunity in supervised learning," in *NeurIPS*, vol. 29, pp. 3315–3323, 2016.

50. J. Zhang and E. Bareinboim, "Equality of opportunity in classification: A causal approach," in *NeurIPS*, 2018, pp. 3671–3681.

51. A. Beutel, J. Chen, Z. Zhao, and E. H. Chi, "Data decisions and theoretical implications when adversarially learning fair representations," in *Workshop on Fairness, Accountability, and Transparency in Machine Learning (FAT/ML 2017)*, 2017.

52. B. H. Zhang, B. Lemoine, and M. Mitchell, "Mitigating unwanted biases with adversarial learning," in *AAAI/ACM Conference on AI, Ethics, and Society*, 2018, pp. 335–340. Available: https://doi.org/10.1145/3278721.3278779

53. L. E. Celis, L. Huang, V. Keswani, and N. K. Vishnoi, "Classification with fairness constraints: A meta-algorithm with provable guarantees," in *Conference on Fairness, Accountability, and Transparency*, 2019, pp. 319–328. Available: https://doi.org/10.1145/3287560.3287586

54. L. Dixon, J. Li, J. Sorensen, N. Thain, and L. Vasserman, "Measuring and mitigating unintended bias in text classification," in *AAAI/ACM Conference on AI, Ethics, and Society*, 2018, pp. 67–73. Available: https://doi.org/10.1145/3278721.3278729

55. B. Lakshminarayanan, A. Pritzel, and C. Blundell, "Simple and scalable predictive uncertainty estimation using deep ensembles," in *NeurIPS*, 2017, pp. 6402–6413.

56. Y. Gal and Z. Ghahramani, "Dropout as a Bayesian approximation: Representing model uncertainty in deep learning," in *ICML*, 2016, pp. 1050–1059.

57. A. Loquercio, M. Segu, and D. Scaramuzza, "A general framework for uncertainty estimation in deep learning," *IEEE Robotics and Automation Letters*, vol. 5, no. 2, pp. 3153–3160, 2020. Available: https://doi.org/10.1109/lra.2020.2974682

58. M. E. Borsuk, C. A. Stow, and K. H. Reckhow, "A Bayesian network of eutrophication models for synthesis, prediction, and uncertainty analysis," *Ecological Modelling*, vol. 173, no. 2-3, pp. 219–239, 2004. Available: https://doi.org/10.1016/j.ecolmodel.2003.08.020

59. J. Devlin, M.-W. Chang, K. Lee, & K. Toutanova, "BERT: Pre-training of deep bidirectional transformers for language understanding," 2018. arXiv preprint arXiv:1810.04805.
60. A. Vaswani, N. Shazeer, N. Parmar, J. Uszkoreit, L. Jones, A. N. Gomez, L. Kaiser, & I. Polosukhin, "Attention is all you need," 2017. arXiv preprint arXiv:1706.03762.
61. A. Radford, J. Wu, R. Child, D. Luan, D. Amodei, & I. Sutskever, "Language models are unsupervised multitask learners," 2019. https://openai.com/blog/better-language-models/

Chapter 20

Understanding Dark Web Protection against Cyber Attacks

Irfan Alam
Delhi Technological University, New Delhi, India

Shaikh Mohammed Faizan
Jamia Millia Islamia, New Delhi, India

20.1 Introduction

Advances in digitalization have led to an increase in cyberattacks. Since most people use the internet to fulfill their requirements, cybersecurity has become a critical problem. In the mid-to-late 1990s, the development of the internet began to change how things were done around the world, instant communication being the most significant shift. However, since privacy and anonymity were not considered when the internet was designed, everything can be traced. In the mid-1990s, a team of computer scientists and mathematicians at the Naval Research Laboratory (NRL), a division of the US Navy, started working on the groundbreaking technique of onion routing. When neither the source nor the destination is known to a third party, it enables anonymous two-way communication [1], using an overlay network, which is a network that is constructed on top of another network (see Figure 20.1). Any network that uses onion routing is referred to as a "darknet." The dark web began to exist when these darknets were all linked together. NRL staff members understood right away that everyone, not only the US government, needed to have access to the

DOI: 10.1201/9781003371380-20

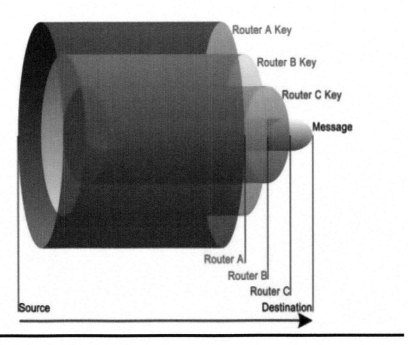

Figure 20.1 Overlay network.

network in order for it to maintain its anonymity. The NRL was compelled to make its onion routing technology, The Onion Router (TOR) [1], publicly available.

The three divisions of the world wide web are the surface web, deep web, and dark web, as shown in Figure 20.2. The public can use common web search engines to reach the surface web, also called the visible or indexed web. Surface web search engines only return 0.03% of the results. The deep web [2, 3], also known as the invisible or hidden web, is the complete antithesis of the surface web and is not accessible to the general public. According to estimations, the deep and dark web make up 96% of the internet. Most private correspondence takes place using it. Deep websites include things with a password or barrier, such as Netflix, online banking, Webmail, dynamic pages, and databases. The term "dark web" [3] refers to content on the internet that is not accessible using browsers that are typically used to access the surface web.

The dark web has thrived partly due to the US military, which used it to connect covertly with distant intelligence assets. Most unlawful and unpleasant activity occurs on the dark web, where covert services are stopped by the onion extension.

This study defines and discusses the various facets of the dark web. Section 20.2 covers its technology and protocols. The variety of crimes committed on the dark web is covered in Section 20.3. Defense mechanisms and cyberattacks are discussed in Section 20.4. Section 20.5 concludes the work.

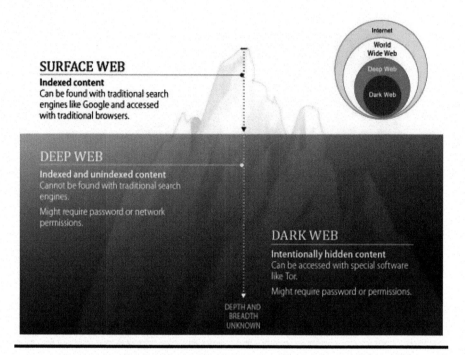

Figure 20.2   Layers of the internet.

20.2 Elements of the Dark Web

The dark web is made up of several essential elements, including browsers for accessing it, encryption methods for encrypting data, virtual private networks for transferring data, and routing algorithms [4]. Anonymity is essential when using the dark web. A good virtual private network (VPN) is needed in addition to the browser (VPN). There are two choices: Phantom VPN or Nord VPN.

Phantom VPN protects its users by preventing ISPs, internet snoopers, and advertisers from watching their online activity. NordVPN is a VPN service provider for individuals which offers iOS and Android desktop apps for macOS, Windows, and Linux.

The dark web relies heavily on encryption. By utilizing numerous degrees of cutting-edge encryption and random routing, the TOR browser safeguards users' identity. Encryption is performed using Pretty Good Privacy (PGP) [5], a dependable encryption technique that safeguards communications and data containing different kinds of sensitive information, and takes integrity, authentication, privacy, and non-repudiation into account. Asymmetric encryption is the basis of PGP, encrypting and decrypting data independently using private and public keys. A public key is visible to the general public, but the user is the only person who can decode and read a message encrypted with their public key. PGP makes use of both hashing

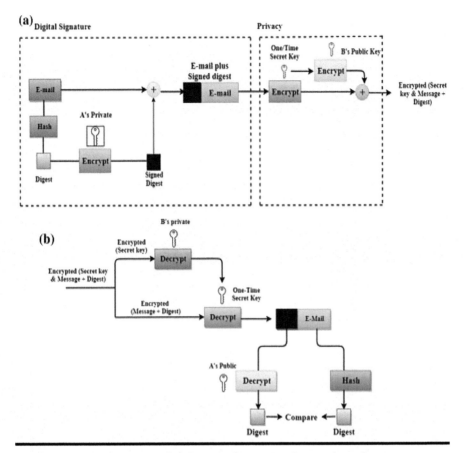

Figure 20.3   (a) PGP at sender site (A). (b) PGP at the receiver site (B).

and public-key encryption methods for authentication and to guarantee anonymity. Thus, as shown in Figure 20.3, two public-private key pairs, one hash function, and one secret key are needed for digital signatures. There are many benefits to using PGP encryption. To start, the data is never in danger of theft or unauthorized access because it is not accessible online. It is possible to exchange data or information online safely. It is impossible to recover deleted emails or other private information. The emails or SMS will not be able to spread any malware. This encryption technique validates the sender's information to ensure that a third party cannot intercept it. Security is provided by symmetric block encryption. Authentication is made available through digital signatures. Utilizing the radix-64 encoding method, it compresses data.

Of the numerous browsers that have been developed to visit the dark web, The Onion Routing browser (TOR) is the most popular. Its alpha version became accessible in September 2002 [6]. The user's data is initially encrypted in this system before being sent over the network's multiple relays (intermediate computers). As a result, a network with multiple layers of encryption is produced. More bandwidth is accessible, and the more relays there are, the more challenging it is to monitor specific users. Three relays are used by default by TOR to distribute connections [7, 8].

20.2.1 Guard and Middle Relays

The guard and middle relays are referred to as non-exit relays (Figure 20.4). The intermediate relay is a second node between the two nodes rather than a guard or exit relay. The guard relay requires little maintenance. It is initially possible to see the client's or user's actual IP address when they try to connect to the TOR circuit. The locations of the guard relays that are now operational are listed on some websites [8–10].

20.2.2 The Relay is Used to Exit the TOR Circuit

The device that transmits messages to their target location is called a relay. Instead of the customers' original IP addresses, the IP address of the exit relay will be displayed. Each node only keeps data on its ancestors and descendants (Figure 20.5) [11].

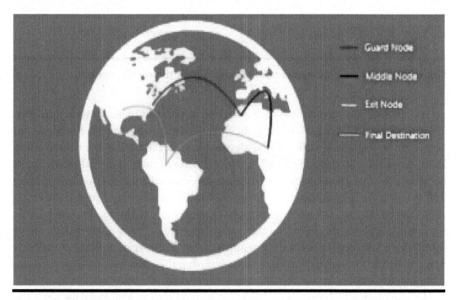

Figure 20.4   Relays used in dark web.

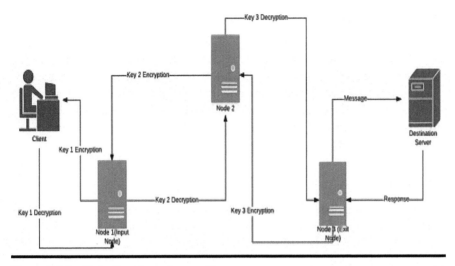

Figure 20.5   Data flow in onion routing.

20.2.3 Bridge

As previously stated, only relay IP addresses will be used by TOR users to communicate. By adding public TOR node IP addresses to a blacklist, governments and ISPs can still restrict users of TOR. The minimal amount of bandwidth needed for bridge operation makes them quite safe.

20.3 Criminal Activity

The dark web is a portal into the criminal underworld [12]. The following subsections describe some of the most well-known crimes committed on the dark web.

20.3.1 Trafficking

The dark web is a black market where dangerous and illegal goods are exchanged for cryptocurrencies like ripple, Ethereum, and bitcoin [13, 14].

20.3.2 Information Leakage

Numerous systems that provide anonymity, like TOR, are valuable tools for law enforcement, activists, and whistleblowers. The dark web is a platform that hackers utilize to share private data.

20.3.3 Proxying

The anonymity of users of services like TOR makes them more likely to be attacked. Such sites are secure because their URL lacks the typical HTTPS prefix. Users must bookmark the TOR page to ensure they are on the authentic site [15]. The user is fooled into believing they are on the original page when a fraudster uses website proxying, and the scammer then modifies the link to send the user to their scam URL. When a user utilizes cryptocurrencies to make a payment, the money is transferred to the fraudster.

20.3.4 Fraud

Card scams are the theft and sale of a user's personal information and credit card details. This is the most prevalent criminal activity on the dark web.

20.3.5 Onion Cloning

An approach similar to a proxy is onion cloning. In order to steal money from the user, the fraudster copies the original website or page and adjusts the links so that the user is taken to their false website [16].

20.4 Defense Mechanisms and Cyber Attacks

Several cyberattacks can be performed through the dark web, the anonymity of which gives attackers more freedom to attack their target easily [17–19].

20.4.1 Correlation Attacks

A correlation attack is passive from start to finish. By seizing control of the first and last routers in the TOR network, the attacker can break the network's anonymity by correlating the streams that pass through those routers using their timing and data properties. Several government agencies have successfully shattered many people's anonymity using correlation attacks. This attack uses a very sophisticated mathematical strategy, so there is no other way to stop it. Users, as well as software, are targets of this kind of attack. The use of a trustworthy VPN is the only practical security measure against this kind of attack.

20.4.2 Congestion Attacks

Congestion is a form of attack that keeps track of and develops a path between two nodes. It is sometimes referred to as clogging. The victim's connection speed should change if the attacker manages to block one of the nodes in the target path. This

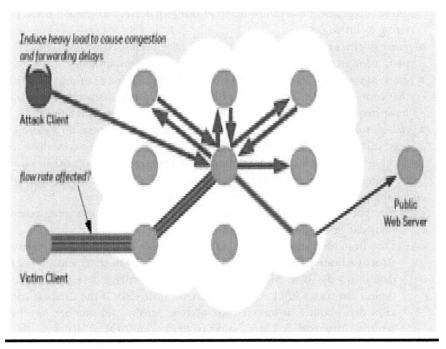

Figure 20.6   Congestion attack.

kind of attack may be avoided by avoiding the use of a fixed route length. End-to-end encryption is also a helpful option. Third, this kind of attack can be avoided by disabling JavaScript in clients and delaying connections (Figure 20.6) [20].

20.4.3 Distributed Denial of Service (DDoS) Attacks

The attacker bombards the target with many fictitious requests to delay or disable the victim's connection. Users are not identified as using it.

20.4.4 Phishing

Attackers frequently utilize phishing techniques or assume other identities when installing malware or accessing the user's sensitive information. This kind of attack can involve an attacker sending an email that appears to be from a reliable source. Clicking on the email's link or attachment will cause the virus to be installed. The following safety precautions should be adopted to prevent similar attacks:

■ *Malicious URLs in quarantine communications.* Messages in quarantine contain harmful URLs. Some attackers use graphics as part of their phishing messages. Given that the image contains text, some filters will ignore it.

These communications can be detected using character recognition-based filtering technologies.

■ *Filter suspicious attachments.* Because they have been used maliciously in the past, incoming attachments should be deleted and quarantined.

■ *Encourage responsible credential usage* by mandating the use of strong passwords that contain both letters and numbers as well as special characters. Passwords must frequently be refreshed. The use of two-step verification is advised.

■ *Attacks using cross-site scripting* (XSS). When an attacker focuses on a website's user, it is known as a cross-site scripting attack. The malicious code does not affect anything besides the user's browser. Such attacks damage the website's reputation by placing user information at risk without prior notice. The following precautions should be adopted to avoid such assaults:
   – Encrypt the output to stop browsers from loading and executing potentially dangerous user-provided data.
   – Data from users should only be utilized in moderation. An attack known as structured query language injection (SQLI) uses SQL statements to insert data into a database. Many servers use SQL to manage data, and they are typical targets of SQLI attacks. It may be quite risky if the database contains data about a customer's bank account, credit card number, or other sensitive information. Users should avoid dynamic SQL at all costs.
   – The security of stored procedures exceeds that of dynamic SQL.
   – Always utilize prepared statements and parameterized queries.

20.4.5 Malware

The most common types of malware are:

■ *Trojans that steal data.* These programs intercept keystrokes, stealthily copy passwords from the clipboard, bypass or turn off antivirus software, and transfer data to the attacker's email address.

■ *Ransomware.* It encrypts the user's data or system, seizing control of their computer and barring them from using it, and demands payment to decrypt it. An average virus costs $270 to acquire.

■ *Remote Access Trojans (RATs).* An attacker from far away can use RATs to track user activities, take pictures, execute files and commands, turn on the webcam and microphone, and download information from the internet.

■ *Botnet malware.* The infection can act as a keylogger, ransomware, or botnet. Virobot is an example. A machine infected by Virobot joins a spam botnet, which disperses the virus to new targets. The ransomware encrypts the victimized computer's data using RSA encryption [21].

■ *ATM malware.* Trojans like this are used to steal money from ATMs.

Malware attacks can be averted by implementing the preventive steps and processes outlined below:

- *User education.* This entails warning users not to download and run any unknown software on the system. Marketing and training should both be done to raise security awareness.
- *Use reliable software.* When installed on a system, appropriate antivirus software will detect and remove any already present malware and keep an eye on user activity. It is essential to keep the vendor's signature on it current.
- *Perform recurring website security audits.* It is crucial to check your company's website for vulnerabilities frequently because it can safeguard both the customers and the company from harm.
- *Create regular, verified backups.* In a virus or other attack, a regular backup will assist you in retrieving all your data or other materials.
- *Make sure your network is secure.* The use of intrusion prevention systems (IPS), intrusion detection systems (IDS), firewalls, and remote access over VPN can help to lessen the organization's vulnerability in the case of an attack.

20.5 Conclusion

The most significant advantage of the dark web is its anonymity. Not everyone who uses the dark web does so with evil intentions. Some are consumers worried about their privacy and security who want to remain anonymous about their online activity. The dark web is commonly used in nations with limited access to the clear internet (surface web). Many nations, including Russia and China, use the dark web more frequently.

The dark web is also used for crime and attacks that try to steal sensitive data. To avoid being a victim of these activities, one must be aware of and take the necessary safety precautions.

References

1. Chertoff, M. (2017). A public policy perspective of the Dark Web. *Journal Cyber Policy*, 2(1), 26–38.
2. Ciancaglini, V., Balduzzi, M., & Goncharov, M. [Online]. Retrieved December 20, 2019, from https://www.trendmicro.com/vinfo/pl/security/news/cybercrime-and-digitalthreats/deepweb-and-cybercrime-its-not-all-about-tor
3. Mirea, M., Wang, V., & Jung, J. (2018). The not so dark side of the darknet: A qualitative study. *Security Journal*, 32, 102–118.
4. Çalışkan, E., Minárik, T., & Osula, A.-M. (2015). *Technical and legal overview of the TOR anonymity network*. Tallinn: NATO Cooperative Cyber Defence Centre of Excellence.

5. PGP Encryption. [Online]. Retrieved December 16, 2019, from https://www.technadu. com/pgp-encryption-dark-web/57005/

6. Onion Routing. [Online]. Retrieved December 16, 2019, from https://www.geeksforgeeks. org/onion-routing/

7. Types of Relays. [Online]. Retrieved December 14, 2019, from https://community. torproject.org/relay/types-of-relays/

8. TOR Nodes List. [Online]. Retrieved December 20, 2019, from https://www.dan.me.uk/ tornodes

9. Welcome to the Tor Bulk Exit List exporting tool. [Online]. Retrieved December 20, 2019, from https://check.torproject.org/cgibin/TorBulkExitList.py

10. Relay Search. [Online]. Retrieved December 16, 2019, from https://metrics.torproject. org/rs.html

11. Rudesill, D. S., Caverlee, J., & Sui, D. (2015). The deep web and the darknet: A look inside the Internet's massive black box. Ohio State Public Law Working Paper No. 314.

12. Naseem, I., Kashyap, A. K., & Mandloi, D. (2016). Exploring anonymous depths of invisible web and the digi-underworld. *International Journal of Computer Applications, NCC, 3*, 21–25.

13. Van Hout, M. C., & Bingham, T. (2013). 'Silk Road', the virtual drug marketplace: A single case study of user experiences. *International Journal of Drug Policy*, 24(5), 385–391.

14. Foltz, R. (2013). Silk road and migration. In: *Encyclopedia of global human migration.* https://doi.org/10.1002/9781444351071.wbeghm484

15. Lacson, W., & Jones, B. (2016). The 21st century Dark Net market: Lessons from the fall of Silk Road. *International Journal of Cyber Criminology*, 10(1), 40–61.

16. Finklea, K. (2017) Dark web report published by Congressional Research Service.

17. Types of Attacks. [Online]. Retrieved December 16, 2019, from https://www.rapid7.com/ fundamentals/types-of-attacks/

18. Cambiaso, E., Vaccari, I., Patti, L., & Aiello, M. (2019). Darknet security: A categorization of attacks to the TOR network. In: *Italian Conference on Cyber Security.*

19. Evers, B., Hols, J., Kula, E., Schouten, J., den Toom, M., van der Laan, R. M., & Pouwelse, J. A. (2015). Thirteen years of TOR attacks. [Online]. https://github.com/Attacks-onTor/ Attacks-on-Tor. Accessed 18 November 2019.

20. Kaur, Shubhdeep, & Randhawa, Sukhchandan (2020). Dark web: A web of crimes, *Wireless Personal Communications.* https://doi.org/10.1007/s11277-020-07143-2

21. Beshiri, Arbër S., & Susuri, Arsim (2019). Dark web and its impact in online anonymity and privacy: A critical analysis and review, *Journal of Computer and Communications*, 7, 30.

Chapter 21

Various Elements of Analysis of Authentication Schemes for IoT devices: A Brief Overview

Irfan Alam and Manoj Kumar
Delhi Technological University, New Delhi, India

21.1 Introduction

The internet of things (IoT) is a new paradigm for communication that aims to connect the physical and digital worlds. The IoT vision has become a reality because of the decreased cost of IoT componentry, enhanced wireless services, longer battery life, and improved business models. Additionally, powerful technologies like internet protocol (IP), data analytics, cloud computing, nanotechnology, ubiquitous computing, IP-based networking, and other enabling technologies have accelerated the development of numerous IoT applications. As a result, concepts such as the "smart city," "smart grid," "smart house," and "smart health care," are no longer in the realm of science fiction.

Figure 21.1, illustrates the significance of IoT devices [1]. The significant aspects of conventional security to be concerned with are confidentiality, integrity, and availability (CIA). In contrast, IoT security protocols vary from application to

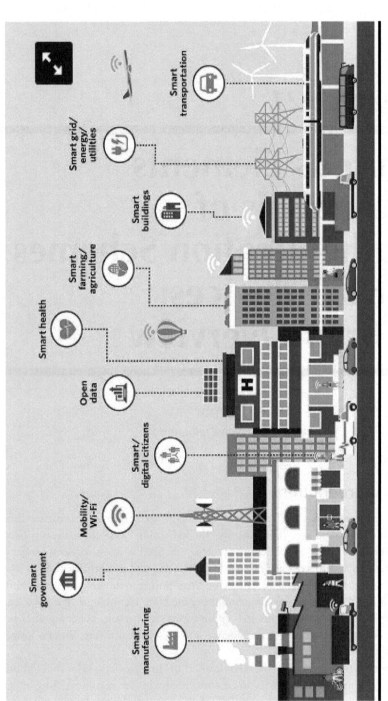

Figure 21.1 The IoT world.

application. Iqbal et al. [2] conducted a thorough assessment of IoT security requirements, difficulties, and solutions in 2020. Practically all applications connected to cloud-based IoT infrastructure must require authentication. Authentication is the process of verifying the identity of a user or information. Recent work on authentication for IoT devices can be found in ref. [3–7]. A particular authentication scheme must pass through a solid analysis before its implementation in any application. Cryptanalysis and performance analysis are the two main elements of analysis for IoT devices [8–10]. Cryptanalysis is the study of techniques for deciphering encrypted data without access to the confidential data generally needed. Knowing how the system operates and locating a secret key are typically required. Another name for cryptanalysis is code breaking or cracking the code.

When choosing or constructing schemes for IoT devices, performance analysis is one of the central factors to consider. In performance analysis, various factors are concentrated, such as computational cost, communication cost, and storage capacity. Various survey papers focus on IoT device security in different areas. Ashraf et al. focus on the maritime industry. [11] Yang et al. describe the physical security of IoT devices [12] but do not cover attacks. Similarly, Serror et al. focus on industrial IoT [13], although they do not describe the simulation tools for the security analysis of various schemes. Alam et al. describe a cloud-assisted IoT infrastructure [14]. Various informal and formal proofs of security and analysis are discussed in these manuscripts. Some extra features must be added to make it universally accepted. The aim of the present work is to provide information about all the necessary concepts in order to make analysis fruitful and effective. The work's principal contributions are:

- Detailed discussion of the importance of the security of IoT.
- Description of all types of attack and the associated simulation tools.
- Comparison of various authentication schemes to include all parameters of performance analysis.
- Assisting researchers to propose a solid and reliable application-oriented scheme for IoT infrastructures.

The paper is organized as follows. Section 21.2 explains the motivation behind our work. In Section 21.3, informal analysis and different possible attacks are discussed. Formal analysis is described in Section 21.4. Performance analysis is covered in Sections 21.5 and 21.6. Conclusions and future work are in Section 21.7.

21.2 Motivation

The IoT has the potential to enhance people's lives. Data exchange between machines not only makes information more accessible but also has the potential to improve safety, health, education, and other elements of daily life. IoT devices span almost all facets of human life, as shown in Figure 21.2 [15], making their security much

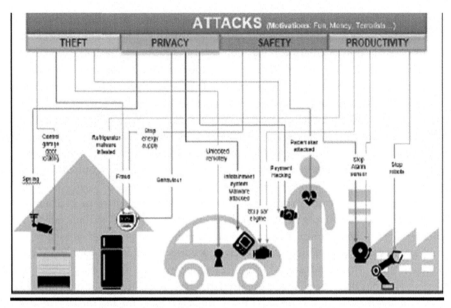

Figure 21.2   Importance of IoT devices.

more important than conventional network security. To ensure the appropriate level of security of the IoT infrastructure, users must perform a thorough analysis and implement appropriate safeguards. This study reviews pertinent papers from four major academic databases to understand better the cyber-security threats and vulnerabilities in the IoT ecosystem (IEEE Xplore, Web of Science, ACM digital library, and ScienceDirect).

21.3 Informal Analysis

In informal analysis, schemes are checked against all possible attacks. In this section, we shall first explore the limitations and capacities of adversaries. Later we study different attacks.

21.3.1 Adversary Model

In IoT architecture, adversaries are of two types: internal and external. Internal adversaries are legitimate users, and external adversaries are non-legitimate users. Dolev and Yao [16] proposed a popular basic and typical adversarial model in 1983. In this approach, adversaries can read, alter, and decrypt communications with the proper keys. No statistical or cryptanalytic attacks can be launched by adversaries. As Dolev and Yao's model shows, using a smart card power analysis, adversaries are likely to acquire critical information from lost or stolen smart cards [17]. Adversaries

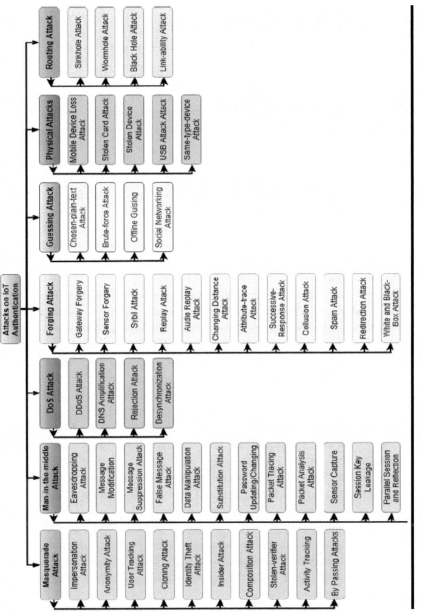

Figure 21.3 Attacks on IoT authentication.

can also use a network analyzer and contemporary AI techniques [18] to extract data from network flow.

21.3.2 Taxonomy of Attacks

The major categories of attacks to which IoT devices may be subject are:

Masquerade attack. In a masquerade attack, the adversary impersonates a real user on the network using a stolen identity, such as a user ID or password, or by observing user activity tracking. Impersonation attacks, anonymity attacks, user tracking attacks, insider attacks and activity tracking are some types of masquerade attack.

Man-in-the-middle attack. In a man-in-the-middle attack, an attacker breaks into a network and listens in on conversations between two parties who think they are speaking to one another directly. In this case, the attacker can forecast network and security patterns and drop, modify, and alter communication data. Additionally, they establish new communications within the system using legitimate user data. Eavesdropping, message modification attack, false message attack, and packet analysis attack are some variations of the man-in-the-middle attack.

DoS attack. A denial of service (DoS) attack prevents an authorized user from using a server or network by sending numerous requests to the server all at once. In a DoS attack, particularly prevalent in IoT-based networks, a malicious user floods the authentication server with requests, temporarily shutting down the function. DDoS attacks, DNS amplification attacks, rejection attacks and desynchronization attacks are some examples of DoS attacks.

Forging attack. An attacker can access private information through a forging attack, which lets them steal the authentication details of a legitimate network user and pass them off as that person's credentials. Gateway forgery, sensor forgery, sybil attack, replay attack, collision attack and white–black box attack are some major attacks in this category

Guessing attack. The IoT authentication server keeps the user and peripheral authentication data, including device ID, user ID, secret device key, and user password, for use in IoT networks. Intruders attempt to obtain those credentials to enter the system. If they have direct access to the server, they can extract credentials from it. Attackers try to guess passwords to establish their legitimacy as users; however, this is an attack based on speculation. Chosen plain text attack, brute force attack, offline and social networking attack are examples of guessing attacks.

Physical attack. Hundreds of IoT hardware devices are scattered across the network. These devices can be physically accessed if no physical security measures are in place. Physical attacks are carried out on mobile devices, which are more difficult to detect, and static devices, which can be easily traced. Mobile device loss attacks, stolen card attacks, USB attacks, and same-type-device attacks are examples of physical attacks.

Routing attack. A routing attack occurs when an untrusted node passes data packets to the wrong location. Examples include sinkhole attacks, wormhole attacks, black hole attacks, and likeability attacks. Nandy et al. [19] explain various types of attacks in IoT authentication (Figure 21.3).

21.4 Formal Analysis

In formal analya particular scheme is passed through verification techniques and simulation tools, which are briefly described in this section.

BAN logic. Burrows et al. [20] describe the accuracy, effectiveness, and applicability of an authentication mechanism known as BAN Logic.

Automated verification of internet security-relevant protocols and programs (AVISPA). A protocol designer uses this tool to express a security vulnerability. It uses the high-level protocol specification language (HLPSL) [21]. Some researchers also use Scyther and Proverif instead of AVISPA. In 2009, Cremers et al. compared these automated tools [22].

Random oracle. A random function known as a random oracle responds to each inquiry with an answer selected randomly and uniformly from its output domain. It is a mathematical function that, for each repeated unique query, always chooses the fixed random response from its output domain.

Real-or-random model (ROR). ROR is the protocol for two-party authentication key exchange. An adversary can pose Execute, Send, and Test questions in this model. The adversary may also send as many Test queries as required to differentiate between instances.

Other tools are used in various authentication schemes such as game theory, ROM model and SPI calculus. Some researchers prefer mathematical proof [23].

21.5 Performance Analysis

As demanding and novel authentication methods are protecting the IoT environment from many developing threats, evaluation of the efficiency of these proposed techniques is crucial. This section describes some performance analysis methods, their parameters, and supplementary equations.

Average response time. The time it takes the server or GWN to respond to a client's request is the response time. Several variables may impact this, including server configuration, user count, network bandwidth, volume, kind, and response time.

Handshake duration. The IoT network's hand-shaking process involves negotiating between two network parties. These parties may be nodes, servers, sensors, actuators, or users.

Computational cost. Computation in an IoT network also influences the protocols used. Most network devices have computing limitations. As a result, designers of protocols constantly strive to produce simple authentication methods for IoT networks. Many academics now use hash, XOR, and concatenation concepts to secure messages as they travel via networks. The IoT authentication technique also employs ECC, MOD, and fuzzy commitments.

Communication cost. Authentication communication in the IoT varies depending on the protocol. A process requires a minimum of four messages of varying sizes to create a secure authentication, and these messages are sent between the user, sensor, and gateway node or authentication server.

21.6 Simulator/Computation Analysis tools

Various tools, software and hardware for simulation or computational analysis exist. Hasan et al. [24] list several types of simulator and their uses in different applications. *NS3.* This well-known IoT simulator, widely used in real-time networks, uses Python and C++ programming languages. It determines whether the network infrastructure is strong enough to resist potential attacks and threat models. This simulator utilizes LTE, Zigbee, and 6LOWPAN protocols and includes three device types: gateways, blockchain nodes, and IoT nodes.

IoTIFY. This network simulator solves IoT network issues by simulating multiple IoT cloud endpoints.

MIMIC IoT simulator. Manages the different gateways, sensors, and more connected devices to create a true test lab to replicate the IoT networks in smart cities, manufacturing, agriculture, event-driven architecture, and Industry 4.0.

Cooja simulator for IoT. A Cooja is a standard network simulator explicitly designed for the WSN. It includes the most recent advances in its smart sensors, internet protocols, and communication technologies.

There are many other product-based simulators by different leading companies, such as MATLAB®, Bluemix by IBM, and Netsim.

21.7 Conclusion and Future Work

This study has highlighted the critical importance of IoT security. Different types of attacks are described and major techniques for formal and informal analysis are discussed. Performance analysis is also considered. We hope our study will educate readers on various IoT authentication threats and techniques. It will also assist incoming researchers in formulating their proposals for developing robust IoT authentication protocols to serve end users better.

Declarations

Authors also declare that no data has been used that may influence the proposed work.

Conflict of Interest

The authors declare that they have no known competing financial interests or personal relationships that could have appeared to influence the work reported in this paper.

References

1. "What is a Smart City? Definition from WhatIs.com. — techtarget.com," https://www.techtarget.com/iotagenda/definition/smart-city, [Accessed 24-Aug-2022].
2. W. Iqbal, H. Abbas, M. Daneshmand, B. Rauf, and Y. A. Bangash, "An in-depth analysis of IoT security requirements, challenges, and their countermeasures via software-defined security," *IEEE Internet of Things Journal*, vol. 7, no. 10, pp. 10250–10276, 2020.
3. A. Bedari, S. Wang, and J. Yang, "A two-stage feature transformation-based fingerprint authentication system for privacy protection in IoT," *IEEE Transactions on Industrial Informatics*, vol. 18, no. 4, pp. 2745–2752, 2022.
4. J. Zhang, C. Shen, H. Su, M. T. Arafin, and G. Qu, "Voltage over-scaling-based lightweight authentication for IoT security," *IEEE Transactions on Computers*, vol. 71, no. 2, pp. 323–336, 2022.
5. S. Velliangiri, R. Manoharn, S. Ramachandran, K. Venkatesan, V. Rajasekar, P. Karthikeyan, P. Kumar, A. Kumar, and S. S. Dhanabalan, "An efficient lightweight privacy-preserving mechanism for industry 4.0 based on elliptic curve cryptography," *IEEE Transactions on Industrial Informatics*, vol. 18, no. 9, pp. 6494–6502, 2022.
6. L. Wei, J. Cui, H. Zhong, Y. Xu, and L. Liu, "Proven secure tree-based authenticated key agreement for securing v2v and v2i communications in vanets," *IEEE Transactions on Mobile Computing*, vol. 21, no. 9, pp. 3280–3297, 2022.
7. I. Alam and M. Kumar, "A novel authentication scheme for group based communication for IoT oriented infrastructure in smart cities," 2022.
8. K. A. Siil, "An introduction to cryptanalysis," *ATT Technical Journal*, vol. 73, no. 5, pp. 24–29, 1994.
9. A. Sinkov and T. Feil, *Elementary cryptanalysis*. MAA, 2009, vol. 22.
10. L. Knudsen and D. Wagner, "Integral cryptanalysis," in *International Workshop on Fast Software Encryption*, Leuven, Belgium, February 4–6, 2002. Revised Papers 9. Springer, 2002, pp. 112–127.
11. I. Ashraf, Y. Park, S. Hur, S. W. Kim, R. Alroobaea, Y. B. Zikria, and S. Nosheen, "A survey on cyber security threats in IoT-enabled maritime industry," *IEEE Transactions on Intelligent Transportation Systems*, pp. 1–14, 2022.

12. X. Yang, L. Shu, Y. Liu, G. P. Hancke, M. A. Ferrag, and K. Huang, "Physical security and safety of IoT equipment: A survey of recent advances and opportunities," *IEEE Transactions on Industrial Informatics*, vol. 18, no. 7, pp. 4319–4330, 2022.

13. M. Serror, S. Hack, M. Henze, M. Schuba, and K. Wehrle, "Challenges and opportunities in securing the industrial internet of things," *IEEE Transactions on Industrial Informatics*, vol. 17, no. 5, pp. 2985–2996, 2021.

14. I. Alam and M. Kumar, "A novel protocol for efficient authentication in cloud-based IoT devices," *Multimedia Tools and Applications*, vol. 81, no. 10, pp. 823–843, 2022.

15. L. Miller and C. Johnson, *Iot security for dummies*, 2016.

16. D. Dolev and A. Yao, "On the security of public key protocols," *IEEE Transactions on Information Theory*, vol. 29, no. 2, pp. 198–208, 1983.

17. P. Kocher, J. Jaffe, and B. Jun, "Differential power analysis", *Proceedings of Advances in Cryptology*, pp. 388–397," 1999.

18. C. Do Xuan, M. H. Dao, and H. D. Nguyen, "Apt attack detection based on flow network analysis techniques using deep learning," *Journal of Intelligent & Fuzzy Systems*, vol. 39, no. 3, pp. 4785–4801, 2020.

19. T. Nandy, M. Y. I. B. Idris, R. M. Noor, L. M. Kiah, L. S. Lun, N. B. A. Juma'at, I. Ahmedy, N. A. Ghani, and S. Bhattacharyya, "Review on security of internet of things authentication mechanism," *IEEE Access*, vol. 7, pp. 151054–151089, 2019.

20. M. Burrows, M. Abadi, and R. Needham, "A logic of authentication," *ACM Transactions on Computer Systems (TOCS)*, vol. 8, no. 1, pp. 18– 36, 1990.

21. Team, A. (2006) HLPSL Tutorial, "A Beginner's Guide to Modelling and Analysing Internet Security Protocols Inf Technol Solut" 1–52.

22. C. J. Cremers, P. Lafourcade, and P. Nadeau, "Comparing state spaces in automatic security protocol analysis," in *Formal to practical security*: Papers Issued from the 2005–2008 French-Japanese Collaboration (2009): 7094. . Springer, 2009, pp. 70–94.

23. I. Alam and A. Basit, "An extended protected secret sharing scheme," in *2019 International Conference on Electrical, Electronics and Computer Engineering (UPCON)*. IEEE, 2019, pp. 1–4.

24. W. H. Hassan et al., "Current research on internet of things (IoT) security: A survey," *Computer Networks*, vol. 148, pp. 283–294, 201.

Chapter 22

A Study of Carbon Emissions in the Transport Sector

Aayesha Ashraf and Farheen Siddiqui

Jamia Hamdard (Deemed to be University), New Delhi, India

22.1 Introduction

Our carbon footprint is the amount of CO_2 equivalent that is released into the atmosphere as a result of our activities [17]. The main causes of greenhouse gas (GHG) emissions are human activities, as these are heavily dependent on fossil fuels, energy use and deforestation, all of which result in an increase of GHGs in the atmosphere. GHG is the mixture of carbon dioxide, methane, nitrous oxide and water vapor. The sources of GHGs are electricity, heat, agriculture, transportation, forestry, waste and manufacturing. Burning fossil fuels uses energy; during this process, all the stored carbon in fossil fuel is changed into CO_2 which is released into the atmosphere as a byproduct. The three major economic sectors using fossil fuels are electricity, transportation and industry (Figure 22.1).

Electricity. Three sectors – industrial, residential and commercial – are the primary consumers of electricity. Industrial sectors are heavy consumers in the production of chemicals, concrete, aluminum, steel, paper and pulp, etc. The residential and commercial sectors are heavily dependent on electricity especially for lighting, heating, cooling and other household appliances which run on electricity. Subcategories for electricity consumption include Delhi

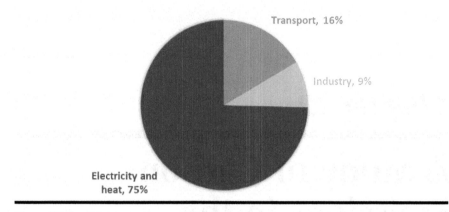

Figure 22.1 Primary sources of GHGs.

International Airport Limited (DIAL), Delhi Jal Board (DJB), Delhi Metro
Rail Corporation (DMRC), public lighting, railway infrastructure, agriculture
and hospitals.

Transportation. CO_2 emissions are produced while transporting goods and people
   around the world. CO_2 emissions are growing daily, with automobiles, trucks,
   and freight the main sources of emissions for the whole transport sector as
   they use petroleum-based fuels.

Industry. Manufacturing and industry combine to create a lot of each type of
   GHG in the atmosphere, and especially a lot of CO_2. They directly utilize
   fossil fuels to create heat and steam required in different stages of production.

Many problems arise due to rising carbon emissions, which lead to climate change
and global warming, which in turn is affecting changes in weather, supplies of food
and water, sea levels, etc. [2]. The major threat from increased CO_2 is the greenhouse
effect. An increase in CO_2 plays havoc with the Earth's environment by changing
atmospheric conditions. There are also effects on human health, including shivering,
pins and needles, trouble breathing, perspiring, sleepiness, raised pulse, increased
circulatory strain, unconsciousness, asphyxia, and spasms.

With the help of advanced technologies, we can reduce emissions. Electric vehicles (EVs) can reduce CO_2 and pollution in the transport sector. Solar panels help
us to reduce the amount of electricity produced by burning coal.

22.2 Literature Review

There are many authors working in the field of reducing carbon emissions and making policy recommendations. Some of their studies are discussed below.

The Intergovernmental Panel on Climate Change states that global warming is a
major threat to the world ecological system. [10]) derive the optimal order quantity

analytically and numerically examine the impacts of carbon trade. Transportation of foods is a major contributor to GHG emissions because food items frequently travel long distances to arrive at customers. [16]) review issues connected with transport and food from production to retail outlets. They recommend that home delivery is the best option and can reduce the transportation carbon footprint by almost half compared with consumers traveling independently to stores. Packaging is an important factor, and the use of plastics as opposed to glass will in general lower the carbon footprint. [7]) present an overview of different types of footprints: social, economic, combined and environmental footprint. Evaluation of carbon footprint calculator tools is also introduced. [8]) used a system dynamic approach to show and reproduce the most reasonable and functional strategies for reducing CO_2 emissions from public transportation in US urban areas. They concluded that such strategies could diminish or even eliminate the now expanding patterns of CO_2 emissions and energy use.

Many researchers have studied the impact of CO_2 outflows on climate change. [14]) proposed a block chain-based privacy-preserving scheme for multimedia data sharing in vehicular social networks to protect sensitive user and vehicle data and prevent attackers from fabricating multimedia data [12]) projected CO_2 emissions in Zambia till 2021 using the data mining WEKA technology. Continuous increments in the carbon footprint result from the population increase and the consequent increasing need for resources. [3]) found that their IoT-based model reduced building carbon footprint by more than 22%. In small cities CO_2 emissions are higher than in large and medium cities. [18]) proposed a smart carbon monitoring model to estimate real-time carbon emissions with the help of IoT technology. [1]) forecast carbon emissions in Turkey till 2030 using a time series forecasting algorithm and found a continuous increase in emissions. [6]) investigated public transport carbon footprints in Taiwan using a lifecycle assessment considering four types of fuel (diesel, electric, liquefied natural gas, and hydrogen) for buses. The hydrogen fuel cell bus showed the best reduction in GHGs over its lifecycle. A smart public transport framework is supposed to be a fundamental part of our lives to enhance our mobility and decrease the impact of our carbon footprint. [13]) proposed a methodology that combines block chain and deep learning methods to protect the smart public transport framework against cyberattacks such as distributed denial of service attempts that can impede the exchange of transport supply information across partners.

22.3 Data Collection, Analysis and Visualization

This section provides detailed information about the dataset, strategies, analysis and visualization used in our study. The dataset for India's CO_2 emissions is taken from https://ourworldindata.org/emissions-by-sector. Microsoft Excel is used for data filtering, analysis, calculations and visualization. We have used CO_2 emissions data for buildings, industry, transport, manufacturing, electricity and heat sectors in India for the period of 1990–2018; however, our analysis focuses only on the transport sector, a major source of CO_2 emissions.

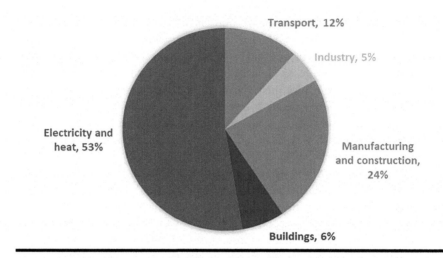

Figure 22.2   Major sources of CO$_2$ emissions in India.

We have analyzed the data and see that the percentage of CO$_2$ emissions are 6% for buildings, 5% for industry, 12% for transport, 24% for manufacturing and construction, and 53% for electricity and heat in India between 1990 and 2018 (Figure 22.2). To decrease emissions we have to know which areas contribute the most. As we can see in Figure 22.3, electricity and heat are the largest contributors of CO$_2$ emissions which are increasing year by year, followed by manufacturing and construction, transport, buildings and industry. There is no sign of a decline in emissions. Figure 22.4 shows the pattern of CO$_2$ emissions in the transport sector from 1990 to 2018, and we can see CO$_2$ emissions are increasing every year. Table 22.1 gives the percentage increase of CO$_2$ emissions in the transport sector every five years. If the present emissions rate continues, then by 2030 the situation is going to be worse.

Based on these results and data, there is an urgent need to rethink approaches to controlling carbon emissions in the transport sector. Governments should take steps to provide methodologies on reduction of emissions, guidelines, voluntary awareness programs, carbon footprint calculators and different kinds of assistance for states and neighborhoods to achieve their air quality and transportation goals. If we want to see a great impact in decreasing emissions we have to switch from non-renewables to renewables. For shorter trips cycling and walking are the best, are harmless to our ecosystem and at the same time they are good for our wellbeing. Documents can be shared online instead of being transported. We should follow the 3Rs (Reduce, Reuse and Recycle), whether for paper, electronic gadgets, bundling, or water, as everything has a carbon footprint. By reducing the amount of waste we generate and recycling the remainder, and reusing IT equipment, we can make a huge difference. Using alternative fuels, new vehicle technologies, systems to decrease the distances traveled and, most importantly, using public transport will

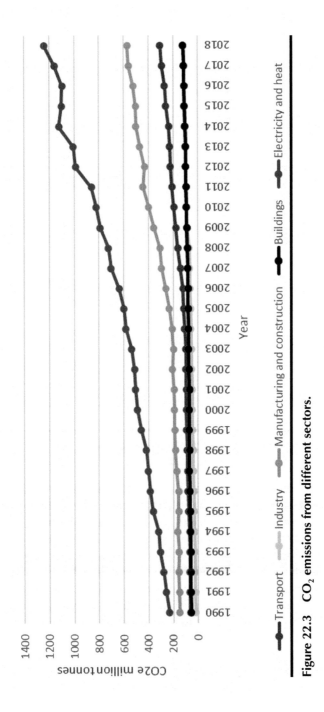

Figure 22.3   CO$_2$ emissions from different sectors.

Table 22.1 Percentage Increase of CO_2 Emissions in Transport Sector

Year	% Increase of CO_2 Emissions
1995–2000	25.76
2000–2005	16.31
2005–2010	49.64
2010–2015	47.01
2015–2020	32.65

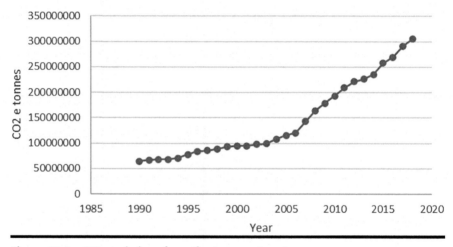

Figure 22.4 CO_2 emissions from the transport sector.

be a great contribution to reducing emissions [15]. We have to raise awareness of these issues; school projects and fundraising events can help educate students and their families about the significance of protecting the environment and can help people around us to reduce their carbon footprints. Planting trees also helps to stop environmental change by eliminating CO_2 from the air, storing carbon in the trees and soil during the carbon cycle and releasing oxygen into the atmosphere [5]. Trees mitigate the greenhouse effect by trapping heat, reducing ozone levels and releasing oxygen. Removing CO_2 from the atmosphere is a natural remedy for air pollution. Hence, instead of deforestation we have to work towards afforestation. The Paris Agreement set the goal of restricting global warming to below 2°C and intensifying efforts to restrict it to 1.5°C [11]. Governments should take steps to make public transport an attractive option. To lower the impact on the environment, we all have to switch to renewable energy, low-carbon fuels, biofuels, bio-methane etc. from non-renewables (Figure 22.5).

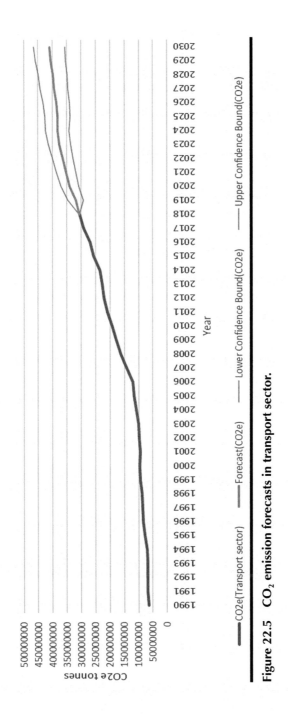

Figure 22.5 CO₂ emission forecasts in transport sector.

The next section discusses the vital role of technology in minimizing carbon footprint.

22.4 Technologies for Balancing Emissions

Technologies can play an important role in the transition to clean energy. They can neutralize or balance emissions that are currently technically challenging or prohibitively expensive to address. Carbon removal technologies are not an option to cut emissions, but they can be part of the portfolio of technologies and measures needed in a comprehensive response to environmental change. The technologies (Figure 22.6) that are helpful for minimizing carbon footprints include EVs, artificial intelligence, BECCS, machine learning, IoT, renewable energy, and direct air capture.

22.4.1 Artificial Intelligence (AI)

AI technology can reduce carbon emissions from transportation activities and revitalize the whole industry. With the help of AI, we can reduce traffic jams, collect information on parking availability and use advanced features to reduce travel time. An efficient route selection system helps us to travel the minimum distance.

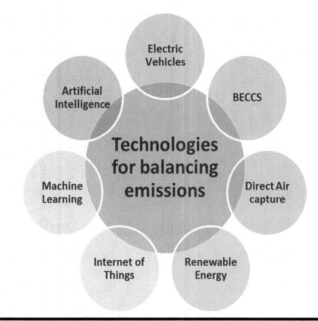

Figure 22.6 Technologies for balancing CO_2 emissions.

22.4.2 Machine Learning (ML)

Machine learning plays a very important role, and in the future, we will see driverless cars everywhere. ML technology uses supervised learning; machines that learn how to drive will drive smartly, reduce traffic jams and create a greener and cleaner environment, an essential step towards reducing carbon footprints.

22.4.3 Internet of Things (IoT)

IoT plays a vital role in enabling the transport sector to reduce its carbon footprint and minimize the negative effects on the environment. IoT can resolve issues in the transport sector like defective hardware, damaged engines, and poor route planning by using smart telematics gadgets, analytic sensors and accelerometers to accumulate data and alert fleet managers to damage or faults. The data can be utilized to restrict mileage and improve fuel consumption, contributing to decreasing emissions and limiting wastage by expanding the life expectancy of each vehicle.

22.4.4 Renewable Energy

Renewable energy is gathered from renewable sources: sunlight, wind, rain, tides and waves. Current innovations have empowered us to capture this energy and convert it into electricity through devices such as solar panels, wind and water turbines.

22.4.5 Electric Vehicles (EVs)

EVs show the positive impact of technology on the environment because they produce lower carbon emissions, and reduced impact on air pollution. Using EVs is less harmful to human health, to animals, plants, and water. De-carbonization of the transport sector is possible with EVs as a sustainable and efficient alternative to traditional diesel- and petrol-based vehicles [9].

22.4.6 Direct Air Capture (DAC)

DAC is the most common way of capturing CO_2 directly from the atmosphere and generating a concentrated stream of CO_2 for sequestration or utilization. The air is pushed through a filter by many large fans, where CO_2 is removed. It is suggested that this innovation can be utilized to manage emissions from distributed sources, for example, fumes exhaust from vehicles.

22.4.7 Bioenergy with Carbon Capture and Storage (BECCS)

BECCS is the process of capturing and storing the carbon and extracting bioenergy from biomass, in this way eliminating it from the air. BECCS enables carbon removal because biomass absorbs CO_2 as it grows, and this CO_2 is not re-released when it is burned. Instead, it is captured and injected into deep geological formations, eliminating it from the natural carbon cycle [4].

22.5 Conclusion and Future Scope

Climate change has been mainly impacted by CO_2 outflows. Most CO_2 emissions come from burning fossil fuel in the transport and industry sectors. In this study, future carbon emissions have been predicted using CO_2 emissions data from the transport sector in India for the period between 1990 and 2018. Analysis of our data forecasts until 2030 shows carbon emissions continuously increasing year by year. The transport sector plays a key role in the emission of carbon dioxide into the atmosphere. There is an urgent need to rethink approaches, policies and strategies for controlling CO_2 emissions in the transport sector. Demand for transport is expected to be high across the world in the coming decades as the population increases worldwide, salaries rise, and more individuals can afford vehicles, trains and flights. But major technological advancements can assist with balancing this rise in demand. As the world moves towards lower-carbon power sources, the ascent of EVs offers a feasible choice to decrease outflows from vehicles.

This work can be extended by breaking down emissions in different categories – buses, cars, trains, trucks, planes – to understand which transport category is responsible for high levels of CO_2 emissions. We can also explore the use of emerging technologies to reduce carbon footprints and contribute towards managing our climate change.

References

1. Akyol, M. and E. Ucar. 2021. Carbon footprint forecasting using time series data mining methods: The case of Turkey. *Environ. Sci. and Pollut. Res.*, 28:38552–38562.
2. Ali, K. A., M. I. Ahmed and Y. Yusup. 2020. Issues, impacts and mitigations of carbon dioxide emission in the building sector. *Sustainability*, 12:1–11.
3. Asopa, P., P. Purohit, R. R. Nadikattu and P. Whig. 2021. Reducing Carbon Footprint for Sustainable development of Smart Cities using IoT. In *2021 Third International Conference on Intelligent Communication Technologies and Virtual Mobile Networks (ICICV)*, 361–367, IEEE.
4. Azar, C., K. Lindgren, M. Obersteiner et al. 2010. The feasibility of low CO_2 concentration targets and the role of bio-energy with carbon capture and storage (BECCS). *Climate Change*, 100:195–202.
5. Booth, T. H., L. M. Broadhurst, E. Pinkard et al. 2015. Native forests and climate change: Lessons from eucalypts. *For. Ecol. Manag.*, 347:18–29.
6. Chang, C. and P. Huang. 2021. Carbon footprint of different fuels used in public transportation in Taiwan: A life cycle assessment. *Environ. Dev. Sustain.*, 24:5811–5825.

7. Cucek, L., J. J. Klemes and Z. A. Kravanja. 2012. A review of footprint analysis tools for monitoring impacts on sustainability. *J. Clean. Prod.*, 34:9–20.
8. Ercan, T., N. C. Onat and O. Tatari. 2016. Investigating carbon footprint reduction potential of public transportation in United States: A system dynamics approach. *J. Clean. Prod.*, 133:1260–1276.
9. Ghosh, A. 2020. Possibilities and challenges for the inclusion of the electric vehicle (EV) to reduce the carbon footprint in the transport sector: A review. *Energies*, 13:2602.
10. Hua, G., T. C. E. Cheng and S. Wang. 2011. Managing carbon footprints in inventory management. *Int. J. Prod. Econ.*, 132:178–185.
11. Hulme, M. 2016. 1.5°C and climate research after the Paris Agreement. *Nat. Clim. Change*, 6:222–224.
12. Kunda, D. and H. Phiri. 2017. An approach for predicting CO2 emissions using data mining techniques. *Int. J. Comput. Appl.*, 172:7–10.
13. Liu T., F. Sabrina, J. J. Jaccard, W. Xu and Y. Wei. 2021. Artificial intelligence-enabled DDoS detection for blockchain-based smart transport systems. *Sensors*, 22:1–22.
14. Shi, K., L. Zhu, C. Zhang, L. Xu and F. Gao. 2020. Blockchain-based multimedia sharing in vehicular social networks with privacy protection. *Multimed. Tools. Appl.*, 79:8085–8105.
15. Usman, M. and M. Radulescu. 2022. Examining the role of nuclear and renewable energy in reducing carbon footprint: Does the role of technological innovation really create some difference? *Sci. Total. Environ.*, 841:156662.
16. Wakeland, W., S. Cholette and K. Venkat. 2012. Food transportation issues and reducing carbon footprint. In *Green Technologies in Food Production and Processing*, ed. J. I. Boye, and Y. Arcand, 211–236, Springer, Boston, MA.
17. Wiedmann, T. and J. Minx. 2008. A definition of 'carbon footprint'. In *Ecological Economics Research Trends*, ed. C.C. Pertsova, 1–11, Nova Science Publishers.
18. Zhang, H., J. Zhang, R. Wang, Y. Huang, M. Zhang, X. Shang and C. Gao. 2021. Smart carbon monitoring platform under IoT-cloud architecture for small cities in B5G. *Wirel. Netw.*, 27:1–17.

Chapter 23

An Exploration of Blockchain Technology: Applicability, Limitations, and Opportunities

Amardeep Saha and Bam Bahadur Sinha

Indian Institute of Information Technology Ranchi, Ranchi, India

23.1 Introduction

The origin of the term blockchain can be traced back to 1991 when time stamping was first introduced by Stuart Haber and W. Scott Stornetta [1] but it rose to prominence in 2008 after Satoshi Nakamoto launched the first digital currency that could solve the problem of double-spend, a secured transaction with mathematically computed cryptographic hash in place of a third-party intervention [2]. But the use cases of blockchain extend beyond digital currency. Blockchain is now extensively used in various sections of society ranging from decentralized and tamper-free storage of supply-chain data to secure voting [3].

Blockchain can be understood as a transparent, distributed, digital record-keeping method providing a guarantee that data, once stored, cannot be changed in the future through new data, or modified versions of the old data can be added on top of the previous data. The immutability of the data is backed by its very essence, i.e., decentralization, which implies that no central body or person controls the blockchain network and the distributed nature, meaning that all the participants will have the same copy of the data. A blockchain system is a P2P (peer-to-peer)

DOI: 10.1201/9781003371380-23

network where each client is called a node, having a shared set of agreed-upon data. These nodes can be classified into two types:

i. *Regular nodes*: these are the nodes that input data or create transactions.
ii. *Validator nodes*: these nodes validate the transactions done by the other participating node before adding the transactions/data onto the blockchain and can also create transactions like any other nodes.

So, why the name "blockchain"? The data/transactions are grouped into a set called a block. These blocks are then linked (chained) together by linking the hash value of the previous block to the current block as the block header. Figure 23.1 shows what a blockchain instance looks like.

i. Tx Block header: It is the hash value of the previously validated block of the blockchain.
ii. Contents of the block data:
- *Timestamp:* When a block is being created. It is generally denoted as a UNIX timestamp (no. of seconds since January 01, 1970, UTC).
- *Transactions:* These are synonyms for the data that is being stored in the blockchain. In Bitcoin, the transactions are stored in the form of a Merkel tree root, as shown in Figure 23.2.
- *Security Value:* As many of the blockchain ecosystems are public, a security value is added to the contents of the block and the block header to obtain the desired hash with some definite characteristics to prevent tampering with data.

How can a blockchain be immutable and safe if it displays transparency? In the above-discussed model, we defined the term "security value," termed "nonce," which plays an important role here. The nonce is determined by burning computational

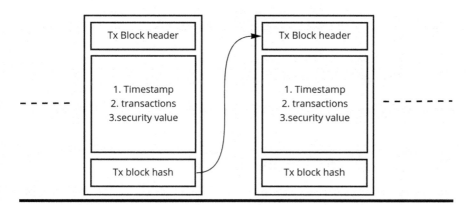

Figure 23.1 Instance of blockchain.

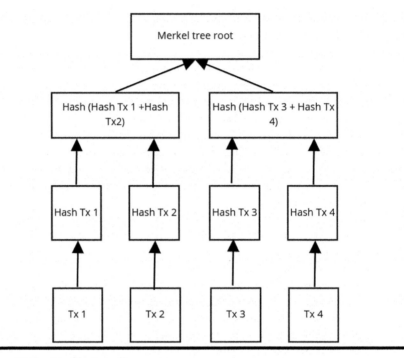

Figure 23.2 Merkle tree diagram.

energy to solve complex mathematical or scientific problems. In Bitcoin, this is done by solving a mathematical problem of finding a hash for the block with a certain degree of difficulty. If someone with malicious intent were to change the data of certain transactions in his/her favor, then the person has to first expend high computational resources to find a nonce for the data. And as we know that no two entities can have the same hash value, the person has to change the block header of all the next blocks while simultaneously finding a new nonce for each block of each node, which is practically impossible. Even if someone was able to pull this off, it would still be futile, as by that time many other blocks would have been added to the blockchain and the blockchain would be following the one with the longest chain, making it completely impossible. The next two sections discuss how blockchains are classified on the basis of permission, what the consensus mechanism is used for, and their various types.

23.2 Classification of Blockchain

Blockchain can be broadly divided into two categories, *permissioned* and *permission-less* blockchain, on the basis of their degree of anonymity and freedom.

23.2.1 *Permission-Less Blockchain*

These are the general types of blockchain that are seen being applied everywhere, also known as "public" blockchain. They are decentralized, which means no single person or a closed group of people can control the blockchain and all the participating members have an equal opportunity to define their own rules for certain transactions. They are open to anyone, which means anybody can join or leave the blockchain's ecosystem at any point in time without being required to inform anyone inside or outside the blockchain's ecosystem, thus maintaining their anonymity. Data transparency is also present as the transactions made are always present on the blockchain and are accessible by any participating node. Each and every node has the ability to validate any transaction by performing mathematical computations and broadcasting the "mined" block into the network. Other nodes agree upon the characteristics of the computation and add the newly mined block into their ledger. The disadvantage of permission-less blockchains is that they are susceptible to 51% attacks, whereby a pool of miners constituting 51% of the total computational power has the ability to alter the contents of the blockchain ledger. Though these kinds of attacks are very difficult to perform, they are not impossible. These blockchains can also be used to conduct illegal and fraudulent transactions. Examples of public blockchains are Bitcoin, Ethereum, and Solana.

23.2.2 *Permissioned Blockchain*

These types of blockchains are usually designed for organizations, companies, or closed user groups, and unlike permission-less blockchains, here the members are known to each other as not everybody can join these types of networks – hence the name "permissioned blockchain". These can further be divided into two categories based on their use cases.

i. *Private blockchain.* This type of blockchain is more or less centralized. They have a central authority at the top of the organization who sees which data to validate and which not to. The members of the blockchain are generally the members of the organizations where everybody's identity is known to everybody else. The advantage of these types of blockchain is that they are not susceptible to any sort of validation/consensus attacks but the disadvantage is that they are completely oriented towards the profit of the organization head. Examples of private blockchains are Ripple and Hyperledger.

ii. *Consortium blockchain.* This type of blockchain is midway between public and private blockchains. Generally, it is implemented in multiparty organizations which constitute many known parties bound by an agreement. The parties can have their own set of instructions defining their transactions. Unlike in public blockchains, the validation of the transactions is done by a pool of validators chosen by consensus by all the members. The advantage of this is that these kinds of blockchain are resilient to 51% attacks but also provide a sort of centralization to the blockchain ecosystem. The disadvantage is that if the validating pool consists of nefarious nodes, then the transactions will be stored in a distorted manner, thus defeating the purpose of security. Examples of consortium blockchains are Corda, Multichain, Ethermint, Tendermint, and Quorum.

23.3 Consensus Mechanism

In the blockchain ecosystem, as stated in ref. [4], there are basically two problems that need to be solved to maintain the data and transaction integrity: the double-spending problem (for digital currency transactions) and the Byzantine Generals Problem.

The double-spending problem means the attacker is able to reuse the money spent on one transaction again in a new transaction, i.e., by altering the contents of a block and upcoming blocks of the blockchain [5]. For Bitcoin-like chains, attackers can create a sub-chain from the current chain and mine new blocks in their favor, which may allow them to retrieve their currency. If the rate of block creation of the attacker's chain is behind the main blockchain then they will not be able to change the data; if the block creation rate is more than that of the main chain, according to the Bitcoin's chain selection property, the malicious longest chain would be selected, which would defy the immutability of transactions [6]. To cope with this the centralization method can be used, but since decentralization is the main essence here, other methods are used instead to secure the problem.

The Byzantine Generals Problem is a problem with a distributed system architecture which states that if the number of malicious elements (nodes in the case of blockchain ecosystem) is lower than a fraction of the total nodes then it will not prevent the honest nodes reaching a point of agreement. This can also be stated as: the presence of the malicious nodes is overlooked [7]. This is taken care of by implementing the Byzantine Fault Tolerance algorithm which ensures the safety of data provided that the number of malicious nodes is at most $(n - 1)/3$, where n is the total number of nodes [8].

The next section discusses in detail various available consensus mechanisms that are used to overcome the problems mentioned above. Table 23.1 provides an overall comparison of the consensus mechanisms [9–11].

23.3.1 Proof of Work (PoW)

This type of consensus algorithm is used in Bitcoin and Ethereum; it depends on the computational power of a node to secure a data of a block by finding a certain value for the contents of the block by doing complex calculations as proof that an appropriate number of computational resources have been spent to mine the block. This method is used because it is difficult to solve the problems but easy to

Table 23.1   Comparison of Consensus Mechanism

Consensus	Power Consumption	Robustness	Type of Blockchain Ecosystem
PoW	High	Low (51% attack)	Public
PoS	Low	Low (Risk to N@S)	Public
RPoS	Low	Greater than PoS	Public
DPoS	Low	Moderate	Public
DT-DPoS	Low	Moderate	Public
RPCA	Low	Depends on the #faulty nodes	Consortium
SCP	Low	Depends on the #faulty nodes	Consortium

verify them. This is done with the help of a nonce in Bitcoin. A nonce is a number appended to the contents of the block to give out a hash that satisfies the required difficulty. A sample algorithm to mine a data block is as follows:

```
function PoW( *block, difficulty, chain)
data -> block.data;
data.nonce -> randomInt;
while hash(data) not start with "difficulty"*'0':
data.nonce -> randomInt; block.data
-> data chain.append(block);
```

Verifying the nonce is very easy; one has to only pass the contents of the block (which contains the nonce as well) into a hash function and the difficulty can be verified. Various other methods that can be used as PoW are:

- *Micromint.* Collision hashes are required to be found for the set properties of coins having a set of hashes k h1, h2, h3, . , hn.
- *Data handling.* Using computational resources to store and retrieve data, maintaining its accountability. This is also the concept on which Proof of Retrievability [12] is based, which uses cloud storage to store the Merkle tree of the data and only stores the hash of the tree in the blockchain. When a challenge of PoR is requested, the cloud storage providers retrieve the Merkle tree and provide a PoR to the request with help of the blockchain.
- Solving scientific problems which include finding a prime number, DNA and RNA sequences, or protein-folding (cure coin) [13].

After validation of a block, the block is added to a chain in the form of a DAG (directed acyclic graph) where each block points to the previous one, which can be traced back to the genesis block using the block headers. The method of selecting a chain for the block to be added to is different for different blockchains. For example, Bitcoin uses the longest chain (it takes the cryptographic complexity into consideration) as the method to determine the main chain, whereas Ethereum uses the ghost protocol, i.e., selects the heaviest (greatest number of child nodes) subtree as the main chain [14].

All these cryptographic implementations make the problem of double spending low, as even mining a fake block would require huge computational resources, not to mention that by that time the size of the main chain would have been increased, making it infeasible for the attacker. Even so, there are various possible attacks that can be launched on a PoW consensus chain, some of which are 51% attacks, where 51% of the total mining pool comes under the control of a certain body or forms a body for their own benefit. This includes the block discarding and difficulty rising attacks. Other attacks include selfish mining attacks, network level attacks, DDoS attacks [13], fake identity attacks (Sybil attacks), P+epsilon attacks, and balance attacks [15].

Though no prevention can guarantee any sort of security against any new form of attack, a few future directions can be implemented in PoW protocol design to make it more secure, including creating awareness of the network condition, making large deposits rest with responsible parties (promotes centralization), introducing punishment rules, etc. [16].

23.3.2 Proof of Stake (PoS)

Proof-of-Stake consensus protocols work on the principle of the probability of selection. The leader for mining a block is selected on the basis of the index of the token that comes out as a result of passing the hash input of a previously validated block in the FTS (follow-the-satoshi) algorithm. The probability of being selected as the miner for a block increases with the stake [17]. The probability (Pi) of being selected is mathematically discussed via Equation (23.1).

$$P_i = \frac{S_i}{\sum_{j=1}^{n} S_j} \tag{23.1}$$

where S_i = stake of the ith node and $\sum_{j=1}^{n} S_j$ is the total pool of stake. Block generation in Proof of Stake is different from Proof of Work. Here computational resource is not significant as the miner is selected on the basis of probability stated in the above equation. The likelihood of getting the hash output depends on the coin age of the coin stake as shown in Equation (23.2) [18].

$$\text{hash}(s,c) <= N_{\text{coin}} \times T_{\text{coin}} \tag{23.2}$$

where s is the block contents, c is the challenge, N_{coin} is the number of coins and T_{coin} is the coin age. Therefore, the more coin age is consumed by the coin stack, the greater the chances of getting the target hash. The difference between this and PoW is that it has limited search space for computation, making it consume much less power [19].

Some of the variants of the PoS protocol are:

- *Robust Proof of Stake (RPoS)* [18] is used to avoid the accumulation of coin age and generation of dynamic coin age in the above equation to ensure that no person who has been accumulating coins for a long period of time is able to generate a hash for the same amount of coin and difficulty. The dynamic coin age is given by Equation (23.3).

$$\text{Age}_t = (D_t - D_{t-1}) \times N_{\text{coin}} + \text{Age}_{t-1} \tag{23.3}$$

where N_{coin} is number of coins, D_t is current block time, D_{t-1} is previous block time, Age_{t-1} is previous coinage. The mining process is done using Equation (23.4).

$$\text{hash}(s,c) < \text{Age}_t \times V_{\text{target}} \tag{23.4}$$

- *Delegated Proof of Stake (DPoS)* [20]. A set of delegates who are voted by the nodes participating in the network sign the block data. Every block being signed must have a block signed by a trusted delegate before it. This in turn reduces the number of verifications needed, reducing the time for the confirmation of the block. In DPoS a block is added every after 1–2 block confirmations.
- *Dynamic Trust Delegated Proof of Stake (DT-DPoS)* [10]. Here trust model and ring signature scheme are introduced on top of traditional DPoS which in turn improves the reliability of the delegate nodes, lessens the probability of collision attack and ensures the integrity and security of the ecosystem. The variations that DT-DPoS provides from DPoS are:
  i. Trust value is added on top of stake wise voting.
  ii. Security along with privacy is offered.

23.3.3 Practical Byzantine Fault Tolerance (PBFT)

This is a Byzantine Consensus algorithm and a general solution to the distributed-system Byzantine Generals Problem. It is a state machine that requires $3f + 1$ nodes to agree to get it into consensus, where f is the number of faulty nodes. In PBFT validating nodes (backup nodes) are selected by a voting process. The client sends a request to the leader node which in turn broadcasts the message to all other backup nodes. The backup nodes then process the message and send replies to the client node. If the client receives $3f + 1$ same replies from the nodes then the request will be processed and added to the ledger.

But PBFT has some shortcomings:

- PBFT uses C/S architecture and is unable to adapt to P2P networks.
- Nodes cannot be dynamically added to the network.
- Scalability of PBFT is very low.
- The primary nodes are selected randomly, which increases the probability of selecting a faulty node as a primary node.

PBFT is not generally used for consortium blockchains, but many other BFT consensuses are built upon on it that can be used for the same: egalitarian practical Byzantine Fault Tolerance (ePBFT) which optimizes the selection of master node; vBFT which works on the principle of division of work and roles among the nodes; ISODATA which solves the problem of poor scalability of the PBFT algorithm; and SHBFT which works on improving the scalability of nodes, promotes dynamic joining of nodes and makes selection of nodes efficient [21].

Protocols based upon PBFT include:

- *Ripple Protocol Consensus Algorithm (RPCA)* [22]. It divides the voting into rounds where in each round the collected transactions are broadcast to each node. If a certain fraction of nodes votes in favor of the transaction data, then it is passed onto the next round. In the final round 80% of the nodes should vote in favor of the transactions for it to be added into the ledger [23]. The correctness in RPCA is given by Equation (23.5).

$$f <= \frac{(n-1)}{5} \tag{23.5}$$

- *Stellar Consensus Protocol.* It follows the Federated Byzantine Fault Tolerance (FBFT). It works on the principle of quorum and its subset quorum slices. Initially, the nomination protocol is run where new candidate values are proposed for agreement to each node. After receiving the values the ballot protocol is deployed, where each node votes for a single value from which the selected values are used. This determines whether the values selected in the nomination protocol are committed or rejected. SCP flaunts its ability to manage the bottleneck in ballots where consensus cannot be reached in current voting by moving it up to higher valued ballot [24].

23.4 Use Cases of Blockchain Technology

23.4.1 Blockchain in the Supply Chain

Blockchain is implemented in supply chains because of its ability to securely transfer information to all or some of the nodes present in the network in real time depending upon the type of the blockchain network [25]. It also provides automated transfer of funds after verification of transactions with the help of smart contracts. These strong features contribute to blockchain being implemented in various directions, such as tracking product origin (tracing the origin, processing, and packaging of the product) and demand forecasting (making use of present data to predict future demand for a commodity). It is also used to reduce fraud risk.

23.4.2 Blockchain for Financial Applications

This is the most widespread use case of the blockchain, which has caused the definition of blockchain to shift from an immutable digital ledger to a cryptocurrency platform, especially since the introduction of the Nakamoto consensus protocol [2] which solved the double-spend problem – a problem for many other digital currency systems that preceded Bitcoin – with the help of the UTXO model. Other cryptocurrencies include Ether (Ethereum), Solana, Matic (Polygon), etc.

23.4.3 Blockchain for Non-financial Applications

There are various other applications of blockchain in the non-financial field. Blockchain can be used in the healthcare sector to make tests and prescriptions readily available to all the connected nodes, making the process of check-ups faster. Blockchain is also being used to conduct safe and secure voting in areas that are not yet developed to conduct free and fair elections. It can also be used to store information about property ownership.

23.5 Conclusion and Future Research Areas

Blockchain technology is still a relatively new area of interest in computer science and is currently mainly limited to cryptocurrencies, but the possibility of merging it with other fields like AI/ML and IoT is very likely. For example, blockchain technology can be used to store a tamper-free dataset for more accurate training of ML models for sensitive topics.

As blockchain relies on the methodology of consensus for keeping the data safe and immutable, it is important that consensus mechanisms should be viable. Current consensus mechanisms for public blockchains either require huge amounts of computational prowess (which causes excessive consumption of electricity) to reach consensus (like PoW) or major holding of stakes (like PoS), and current alternatives used to minimize it have resulted in partial centralization of blockchain ecosystems, defeating the decentralization property of the blockchains. One future research topic would be finding a way to reduce the use of computational power without defeating the intrinsic property of blockchain while maintaining or increasing data security. Similarly in consortium blockchain, PBFT consensus mechanisms and their derivatives have the problem of scalability. One such problem is addressed in ref. [21] but the node exit mechanism for inactive nodes is still not defined. We aim to solve this in our future research.

Being a new technology, blockchain is seeing a rise in its applications in various fields but its use is not monitored, as it is being used in areas where traditional database systems would be more than suitable to quickly conduct the tasks while maintaining security. This is resulting in the unnecessary utilization of computational resources to solve hard computational problems for consensus. A checking process is needed so that it is only used where necessary.

References

1. Haber, S., & Stornetta, W. S. (1990, August). How to time-stamp a digital document. In *Conference on the Theory and Application of Cryptography* (pp. 437–455). Springer, Berlin, Heidelberg.
2. Nakamoto, S. (2008). Bitcoin: A peer-to-peer electronic cash system. *Decentralized Business Review*, 21260.
3. Wüst, K., & Gervais, A. (2018, June). Do you need a blockchain? In *2018 Crypto Valley Conference on Blockchain Technology (CVCBT)* (pp. 45–54). IEEE.
4. Mingxiao, D., Xiaofeng, M., Zhe, Z., Xiangwei, W., & Qijun, C. (2017, October). A review on consensus algorithm of blockchain. In *2017 IEEE International Conference on Systems, Man, and Cybernetics (SMC)* (pp. 2567–2572). IEEE.
5. Karame, G. O., Androulaki, E., Roeschlin, M., Gervais, A., & Čapkun, S. (2015). Misbehavior in bitcoin: A study of double-spending and accountability. *ACM Transactions on Information and System Security (TISSEC)*, 18(1), 1–32.
6. Chohan, U. W. (2021). The double spending problem and cryptocurrencies. Available at SSRN 3090174.
7. Lamport, L., Shostak, R., & Pease, M. (2019). The Byzantine generals problem. In *Concurrency: The works of Leslie Lamport* (pp. 203–226) Association for Computing Machinery, New York, NY, USA. https://doi.org/10.1145/3335772.3335936
8. Castro, M., & Liskov, B. (2002). Practical Byzantine fault tolerance and proactive recovery. *ACM Transactions on Computer Systems (TOCS)*, 20(4), 398–461.
9. Bach, L. M., Mihaljevic, B., & Zagar, M. (2018, May). Comparative analysis of blockchain consensus algorithms. In *2018 41st International Convention on Information and Communication Technology, Electronics and Microelectronics (MIPRO)* (pp. 1545–1550). IEEE.
10. Sun, Y., Yan, B., Yao, Y., & Yu, J. (2021). DT-DPoS: A delegated proof of stake consensus algorithm with dynamic trust. *Procedia Computer Science*, 187, 371–376.

11. Lepore, C., Ceria, M., Visconti, A., Rao, U. P., Shah, K. A., & Zanolini, L. (2020). A survey on blockchain consensus with a performance comparison of PoW, PoS and pure PoS. *Mathematics*, 8(10), 1782.

12. Ren, Y., Guan, H., Zhao, Q., & Yi, Z. (2022). Blockchain-based proof of retrievability scheme. *Security and Communication Networks*, 2022, 3186112.

13. Meneghetti, A., Sala, M., & Taufer, D. (2020). A survey on pow-based consensus. *Annals of Emerging Technologies in Computing (AETiC)*, Print ISSN, 2516-0281.

14. Gramoli, V. (2020). From blockchain consensus back to Byzantine consensus. *Future Generation Computer Systems*, 107, 760–769.

15. Sayeed, S., & Marco-Gisbert, H. (2019). Assessing blockchain consensus and security mechanisms against the 51% attack. *Applied Sciences*, 9(9), 1788.

16. Zhang, R., & Preneel, B. (2019, May). Lay down the common metrics: Evaluating proof-of-work consensus protocols' security. In *2019 IEEE Symposium on Security and Privacy (SP)* (pp. 175–192). IEEE.

17. Nguyen, C. T., Hoang, D. T., Nguyen, D. N., Niyato, D., Nguyen, H. T., & Dutkiewicz, E. (2019). Proof-of-stake consensus mechanisms for future blockchain networks: fundamentals, applications and opportunities. *IEEE Access*, 7, 85727–85745.

18. Li, A., Wei, X., & He, Z. (2020). Robust proof of stake: A new consensus protocol for sustainable blockchain systems. *Sustainability*, 12(7), 2824.

19. King, S., & Nadal, S. (2012). Ppcoin: Peer-to-peer crypto-currency with proof-of-stake. Self-published paper, August, 19(1).

20. Schuh, F., & Larimer, D. (2017). Bitshares 2.0: General overview. Accessed June-2017. [Online]. Available: http://docs.bitshares.org/downloads/bitshares-general.pdf

21. Li, Y., Qiao, L., & Lv, Z. (2021). An optimized byzantine fault tolerance algorithm for consortium blockchain. *Peer-to-Peer Networking and Applications*, 14(5), 2826–2839.

22. Cole, R., & Cheng, L. (2018, July). Modeling the energy consumption of blockchain consensus algorithms. In *2018 IEEE International Conference on Internet of Things (iThings) and IEEE Green Computing and Communications (GreenCom) and IEEE Cyber, Physical and Social Computing (CP-SCom) and IEEE Smart Data (SmartData)* (pp. 1691–1696). IEEE.

23. Schwartz, D., Youngs, N., & Britto, A. (2014). The ripple protocol consensus algorithm. *Ripple Labs Inc White Paper*, 5(8), 151.

24. Sankar, L. S., Sindhu, M., & Sethumadhavan, M. (2017, January). Survey of consensus protocols on blockchain applications. In *2017 4th International Conference on Advanced Computing and Communication Systems (ICACCS)* (pp. 1–5). IEEE.

25. Kawa, A., & Maryniak, A. (Eds.). (2019). *SMART Supply Network*. Springer Cham.

Chapter 24

A Survey of Security Challenges and Existing Prevention Methods in FANET

Jatin Sharma and Pawan Singh Mehra
Delhi Technological University, New Delhi, India

24.1 Introduction

A drone is a small flying device that can be moved independently by remote control and can fly autonomously. Among the various applications of drones are disaster rescue, battlefield communication, photography, aerial delivery and device-to-device communication. The essential elements of drones are batteries, propellers and motors, flight controller, IMU and magnetometer. There are various type of drones such as quadrotor, multirotor drones, fixed wing UAS, fixed wing hybrid UAS (Figure 24.1).

The paper is organized as follows. Section 24.1 is an introduction to FANETs, Section 24.2 describes various FANET protocols, Section 24.3 explores various security attacks and Section 24.4 describes previous work. Section 24.5 provides a table of security solutions and conclusions are provided in Section 24.6.

DOI: 10.1201/9781003371380-24

Figure 24.1   A single UAV drone.

24.2 FANET and Communication Protocols

Flying adhoc networks are networks that build on the fly without infrastructure. Their various advantages are [1]:

1. *Expense.* The expense of smaller UAVs is lower than larger UAVs.
2. *Survivable.* The failure of one node in FANETs cannot affect the UAV system as other nodes can play the same role as the failed one in an emergency.
3. *Speed.* The speed of a multi-UAV system is much faster as the number of UAVs can accomplish the task in minimum time.
4. *Expandability.* The multi-UAV system has the power to expand in case of mission requirement.
5. *Extended antenna range.* The multi-UAV system has the capability to cover a large area in reconnaissance and rescue operations.

Various kinds of communications are possible in FANETs:

- Inter-plane communication
- Intra-plane communication
- Ground station communication
- Ground sensor communication
- FANET–VANET communication

Figure 24.2 represent the A2G (air-to-ground) and A2A (air-to-air) communication. The following sub-sections discuss various communication protocols.

24.2.1 Based on Physical Layer

- *FANET communication characterization.* Propagation model based on radio waves of FANET node-to-node links is identical to 2-ray ground schema.
- *Channel modeling.* The 2-state Markov model based on Rician fading is used to make the channel infrastructure-less among UAVs.

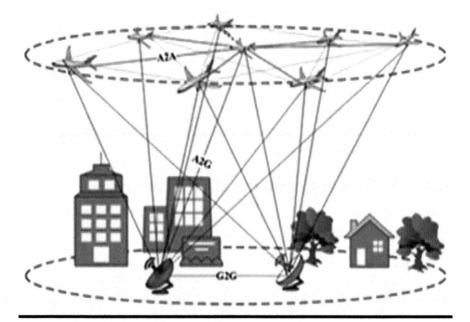

Figure 24.2 A2G and A2A communication.

- *Nakagami-based FANET radio propagation model.* In this model, the Nakagami-m fading channel was derived and a mathematical theorem evolved as output for link disconnection.
- *General link outage model.* In this model, the FANET node-to-node and UAV node-to-ground link disconnection over the defined fading channel was provided with the formula.
- *Many transmitters and receivers.* The packet transfer rate was improved in many receivers and transmitters for a longer time.

24.2.2 Based on MAC Layer

- *Adaptive MAC protocol approach for FANET nodes (AMUAV).* This approach delivers the controlling frames, i.e., CTS, RTS and ACK frames with its antennas propagating in every direction and DATA frame sent by antennas in a straightforward direction. This approach enhances E2E delay and error rate bit by bit in FANET UAVs.
- *Token-based MAC protocol.* This relies on the tokenization approach so as to modify link states and information on the link. The problem of code collision is resolved by the token-based approach. This approach enhances the number of bits per second using an MPR radio circuit and full duplex mode and also reduces latency.

24.2.3 Based on Network Layer/Routing Protocols

- *Proactive type.* For a limited time routing information is modified and kept in a 2D format such as DOLSR, in which the directed antenna concept is used so as to reduce latency and enhance packet delivery ratio.
- *Reactive type.* In this type of protocol, routing information is modified and kept only when the point or device finds a change in the network, such as on-demand routing based on a time slot which is used to eliminate collisions.
- *Hybrid Protocols.* In this type the functionality of two protocols – reactive and proactive – is joined together to achieve routing, for example, zone routing protocols.
- *Geographic type.* It predicts the movement of UAVs with the Gauss–Markov mobility model and uses this information to determine the next hop.
- *Position-based protocol.* This protocol determines the position of the particular UAV in the network. They are divided into two strategies, single path and multipath.
- *Swarm-based protocol.* This protocol is based on the behavior of animals.

24.3 Security Attacks and Issues

Attacks on the multi-UAV system can affect the whole network and, in such case, important information can be accessed by attackers while nodes are on the ground as well as on fly. There are two types of attacks.

24.3.1 Active Attacks

An active attack is used to modify data which affect operations or falsify statements. Active attacks include black hole and grey hole attacks [2], denial of service [3], and wormhole [4].

24.3.2 Passive Attacks

The purpose of a passive attack is to use the information without affecting resources, for example, monitoring UAV traffic and eavesdropping [5].

24.3.3 Other Types of Attack

- Spoofing attack based on GPS. The adversary sends a dummy GPS signal to the ground station which in turn forces navigation in a direction given by the adversary.
- Malware software installation attacks.

- Message alteration attacks.
- Distance-based attacks.
- Algorithmic-based attacks.
- Attacks based on integrity.
- Attacks based on confidentiality.
- Attacks based on privacy.
- Attacks based on availability.

The various security challenges are routing, UAV mobility and placement, scalability and reliability.

24.4 Literature Review and Related Works

Bekmezci et al. [1] cover various UAV design and protocol issues. They find security issues in omnidirectional antennas, location estimations and sharing of information, congestion avoidance, and flow control. The authors suggest various solutions but these are not relevant.

Cabuk et al. [6] describe SkyNet with manipulation of UAVs to collect information from individual nodes and desktops.

Khan et al. [7] describe threats between ground station and UAVs according to needs and types of assaults. and conclude that security is a significant issue.

Yaacoub et al. [8] examine information about a person's home, location, and behavior that can be found by aerial UAVs.

According to Youssef and Riham [6], there are risks when hackers use UAVs to make connection among internet of things (IoT) nodes. Adding FANET nodes to restricted areas in a no-fly-zone database is one way to protect yourself from these dangers.

Table 24.1 lists security requirements in the current scenario as represented by [1, 6, 8–12]. The security principles that are included, not included or partially included in these are labeled as covered, not covered and somewhat.

Existing security solutions proposed are the following.

In ref. [13], the OTP (one-time pad) technology was used to create secure communication between UAVs. In this approach, before encrypting the message, a replicated key is given and used with the message to obtain the cipher context with EX-OR operation, then to obtain the plain text, the cipher text and the replicated key were used with EX-OR. After successful decryption of the message the replicated keys were smashed. The performance was the best compared to AES-128.

In ref. [14], the enhanced frequency hopping technique was used to control UAVs. The authors of this paper have made the process complex by using passwords longer than 6 bytes.

In ref. [15], FANETs' systems are reviewed and their constraints analyzed. The authors present ECDSA digital signature algorithms based on elliptic curves and

Table 24.1   Requirements of Security

Ref.	Authentication	Authorization	Confiden.	Integrity	Availability	Non Repud.
[1]	Somewhat	Not covered	Somewhat	Not covered	Somewhat	Not covered
[6]	Covered	Somewhat	Covered	Covered	Covered	Somewhat
[8]	Covered	Covered	Covered	Covered	Covered	Covered
[9]	Not covered	Not covered	Not covered	Not covered	Not covered	Not covered
[10]	Covered	Covered	Covered	Covered	Covered	Covered
[11]	Not covered	Not covered	Not covered	Not covered	Somewhat	Not covered
[12]	Covered	Covered	Covered	Covered	Covered	Covered

RSA to protect the UAVs from adversaries. Both algorithms have two keys, a secret key to keep communication strong and a public key. This method ensures the integrity of messages from the ground station.

In ref. [16], blockchain technology to secure and maintain data privacy is described. The blockchain system developed is so strong that it provides danger alerts to prevent unauthorized and unreliable access.

In ref. [17], the author proposes a Caesar cipher technique to keep MAVs (micro aerial vehicles) secure. This technique enciphers the data between MAV and ground control station. It is best suited for authentication and system reliability.

In ref. [18], the author proposes MAVLink security in terms of MAV-Sec and discusses various vulnerabilities. The four advanced encryption standard algorithms described are AES-CBC, ChaCha20, RC4, and counter mode. For secure communication between UAVs and ground station, ChaCha20 is used.

In ref. [19], the authors describe an IoT-based solution using the naive Bayes algorithm. The data captured from sensors on UAVs help detect threats with an accuracy of 97%.

In ref. [20], the author describes an intelligent system preventing encroachment activity on UAVs.

Ref. [21] proposes an eCLSC-TKEM communication security protocol technique that produces a unique key between UAVs and intelligent device by preserving the schedule.

In ref. [22], the author introduces cipher techniques and authentication to encrypt useful data using ChaCha20 and HIGHT encryption algorithms.

In ref. [23], a Raspberry pi system for reverting to the previous state if any UAV is attacked is described. For this purpose AES public keys are introduced before the sending process and authenticated during sending, which in turn enables self-destruction of UAVs in case of encroachment.

In ref. [24], the authors propose a hash function scheme for encryption. The system is validated with the help of Automated Validation of Internet Security Protocols and Application (AVISPA). Various security solutions are proposed.

In ref. [25], an adaptive trust strategy is proposed in the form of a lightweight mutual identity authentication scheme (ATSLIA). The proposed 2-way system involves authentication and elliptic curve cryptography between the ground station on the road and UAVs.

In ref. [26], physically unclonable functions (PUFs) and programmable packet-processing data planes are described. Hardware-based PUFs are used to provide authentication between UAVs and the ground control station which in turn provides ultra-low latency. [27] describes software-defined networking-based solutions such as adaptive SDN-based routing, QoS-based multipath routing protocol, Fuzzy C-means and GAP.

24.5 Security Solutions in Tabular Format

We present the various preventive measures to overcome vulnerabilities in the current system in the form of a table (Table 24.2). The table describes various proposed solutions, the year in which they were put forward, and comments.

Table 24.2   Proposed Solution in Survey

S.No.	References	Duration	Proposed Solution	Remarks
1	[13]	2019	OTP technology	Better encryption scheme and takes two or three milliseconds.
2	[14]	2018	eFHSS	Less time taken to detect attack.
3	[15]	2019	ECDSA and RSA algorithm	Ensures integrity.
4	[16]	2020	Blockchain	Ensures security with digital signature.
5	[17]	2015	Caesar cipher	This technique is best suited for authentication and system reliability.

(Continued)

Table 24.2 (Continued)

S.No.	References	Duration	Proposed Solution	Remarks
6	[18]	2019	MAVSec	For secure communication between UAVs and ground station, ChaCha20 algorithm is used.
7	[19]	2021	Naive Bayes algorithm	The data captured from sensors on UAVs helps in detection of threats with accuracy of 97%.
8	[20]	2020	K-nearest neighbor algorithm	Intelligent system to prevent intrusion and various attacks on UAVs.
9	[21]	2015	eCLSC-TKEM	Saves time needed to produce a key between UAV and intelligent device.
10	[22]	2021	ChaCha20 and HIGHT encryption	Proper UAV communication with fast execution of cipher technique.
11	[23]	2017	AES, Raspberry pi	To get back to the previous state if any UAV is attacked by any using Raspberry pi.
12	[24]		Hash function	Encryption scheme based on one-way hash functionality. AVISPA technique provides verification in this context.

(Continued)

Table 24.2 (Continued)

S.No.	References	Duration	Proposed Solution	Remarks
13	[25]	2022	ATS-LIA	Two-way system with authentication and elliptic curve cryptography approach between ground station on the road and UAVs.
14	[26]	2022	PUF-based UAV authentication	Provide authentication between UAVs and ground control station which in turn provides ultra-low latency.
15	[27]	2022	SDN-FANET	Software-defined networking-based solutions such as adaptive SDN-based routing, QoS-based multipath routing protocol, Fuzzy C-means and GAP

24.6 Conclusion

This chapter has described various vulnerabilities in the current system and discussed security solutions. Various FANET communication protocols and attacks have been defined. This paper can help researchers to identify techniques and solution to obtain secure communication between UAVs.

References

1. I. Bekmezci, O. K. Sahingoz, and Ş. Temel, "Flying ad-hoc networks (FANETs): A survey," *Ad Hoc Networks*, vol. 11, no. 3, pp. 1254–1270, May 2013, doi: 10.1016/J. ADHOC.2012.12.004.

2. J. Cai, J. Chen, and Z. Wang, "An adaptive approach to detecting black and gray hole attacks in ad hoc network," *2010 24th IEEE Int. Conf. Adv. Inf. Netw. Appl.*, 2010, doi: 10.1109/AINA.2010.143.

3. J. P. Condomines, R. Zhang, and N. Larrieu, "Network intrusion detection system for UAV ad-hoc communication: From methodology design to real test validation," *Ad Hoc Networks*, vol. 90, p. 101759, Jul. 2019, doi: 10.1016/J.ADHOC.2018.09.004.

4. E. E. Tatar and M. Dener, "Wormhole attacks in IoT based networks," *Proc. - 6th Int. Conf. Comput. Sci. Eng. UBMK 2021*, pp. 478–482, 2021, doi: 10.1109/UBMK52708.2021.9558996.

5. X. Zhong, C. Fan, and S. Zhou, "Eavesdropping area for evaluating the security of wireless communications," *China Commun.*, vol. 19, no. 3, pp. 145–157, Mar. 2022, doi: 10.23919/JCC.2022.03.010.

6. R. Altawy and A. M. Youssef, "Security, privacy, and safety aspects of civilian drones," *ACM Trans. Cyber-Physical Syst.*, vol. 1, no. 2, Nov. 2016, doi: 10.1145/3001836.

7. N. A. Khan, S. N. Brohi, and N. Jhanjhi, "UAV's applications, architecture, security issues and attack scenarios: A survey," pp. 753–760, 2020, doi: 10.1007/978-981-15-3284-9_81.

8. J. P. Yaacoub, H. Noura, O. Salman, and A. Chehab, "Security analysis of drones systems: Attacks, limitations, and recommendations," *Internet of Things*, vol. 11, p. 100218, Sep. 2020, doi: 10.1016/J.IOT.2020.100218.

9. A. Chriki, H. Touati, H. Snoussi, and F. Kamoun, "FANET: Communication, mobility models and security issues," *Comput. Networks*, vol. 163, p. 106877, Nov. 2019, doi: 10.1016/J.COMNET.2019.106877.

10. "Scopus - Document details - Security issues in flying ad-hoc networks (FANETS) | Signed in." https://www.scopus.com/record/display.uri?eid=2-s2.0-85044241946&origin=inward (accessed Sep. 14, 2022).

11. A. Bujari, C. E. Palazzi, and D. Ronzani, "FANET application scenarios and mobility models", *Proceedings of the 3rd Workshop on Micro Aerial Vehicle Networks, Systems, and Applications*, doi: 10.1145/3086439.3086440.

12. S. Rezwan and W. Choi, "A survey on applications of reinforcement learning in flying ad-hoc networks," *Electron*, vol. 10, no. 4, p. 449, Feb. 2021, doi: 10.3390/ELECTRONICS10040449.

13. S. Atoev, O.-J. Kwon, C.-Y. Kim, S.-H. Lee, Y.-R. Choi, and K.-R. Kwon, "The secure UAV communication link based on OTP encryption technique; the secure UAV communication link based on OTP encryption technique," *2019 Elev. Int. Conf. Ubiquitous Futur. Networks*, 2019, Accessed: Sep. 14, 2022. [Online]. Available: https://mavlink.io/en/protocol/overview.html

14. C. Bunse and S. Plotz, "Security analysis of drone communication protocols," *Lect. Notes Comput. Sci. (including Subser. Lect. Notes Artif. Intell. Lect. Notes Bioinformatics)*, vol. 10953 LNCS, pp. 96–107, 2018, doi: 10.1007/978-3-319-94496-8_7.

15. M. J. Fernandez, P. J. Sanchez-Cuevas, G. Heredia, and A. Ollero, "Securing UAV communications using ROS with custom ECIES-based method," *2019 Workshop on Research, Education and Development of Unmanned Aerial Systems (RED UAS)*, 2019. doi: 10.0/Linux-x86_64.

16. R. Ch, G. Srivastava, T. Reddy Gadekallu, P. K. R. Maddikunta, and S. Bhattacharya, "Security and privacy of UAV data using blockchain technology," *J. Inf. Secur. Appl.*, vol. 55, p. 102670, Dec. 2020, doi: 10.1016/j.jisa.2020.102670.

17. B. S. Rajatha, C. M. Ananda, and S. Nagaraj, "Authentication of MAV communication using Caesar Cipher cryptography," *2015 Int. Conf. Smart Technol. Manag. Comput. Commun. Control. Energy Mater. ICSTM 2015 - Proc.*, pp. 58–63, Aug. 2015, doi: 10.1109/ICSTM.2015.7225390.

18. A. Allouch, O. Cheikhrouhou, A. Koubaa, M. Khalgui, and T. Abbes, "MAVSec: Securing the MAVLink protocol for Ardupilot/PX4 unmanned aerial systems," *2019 15th Int. Wirel. Commun. Mob. Comput. Conf. IWCMC 2019*, pp. 621–628, Jun. 2019, doi: 10.1109/IWCMC.2019.8766667.

19. R. Majeed, N. A. Abdullah, and M. F. Mushtaq, "IoT-based cyber-security of drones using the Naïve Bayes algorithm," *Int. J. Adv. Comput. Sci. Appl.*, vol. 12, no. 7, pp. 422–427, Sep. 2021, doi: 10.14569/IJACSA.2021.0120748.

20. S. M. Al-Abrez, K. M. A. Alheeti, and A. K. A. N. Alaloosy, "A hybrid security system for unmanned aerial vehicles," *J. Southwest Jiaotong Univ.*, vol. 55, no. 2, 2020, doi: 10.35741/ISSN.0258-2724.55.2.1.

21. J. Won, S. H. Seo, and E. Bertino, "A secure communication protocol for drones and smart objects," *ASIACCS 2015 - Proc. 10th ACM Symp. Information, Comput. Commun. Secur.*, pp. 249–260, Apr. 2015, doi: 10.1145/2714576.2714616.

22. H. M. Ismael, Z. Tariq Mustafa Al-Ta, and A. Emails Mordasshani, "Authentication and encryption drone communication by using HIGHT Lightweight algorithm," *Turkish J. Comput. Math. Educ.*, vol. 12, no. 11, pp. 5891–5908, May 2021, Accessed: Sep. 14, 2022. [Online]. Available: https://turcomat.org/index.php/turkbilmat/article/view/6875

23. K. Yoon, D. Park, Y. Yim, K. Kim, S. K. Yang, and M. Robinson, "Security authentication system using encrypted channel on UAV network," *2017 First IEEE Int. Conf. Robot. Comput.*, 2017, doi: 10.1109/IRC.2017.56.

24. M. Wazid, A. K. Das, N. Kumar, A. V. Vasilakos, and J. J. P. C. Rodrigues, "Design and analysis of secure lightweight remote user authentication and key agreement scheme in internet of drones deployment," *IEEE Internet Things J.*, vol. 6, no. 2, pp. 3572–3584, Apr. 2019, doi: 10.1109/JIOT.2018.2888821.

25. X. Du, Y. Li, S. Zhou, and Y. Zhou, "ATS-LIA: A lightweight mutual authentication based on adaptive trust strategy in flying ad-hoc networks," *Peer-to-Peer Netw. Appl.*, vol. 15, no. 4, pp. 1979–1993, 2022, doi: 10.1007/s12083-022-01330-7.

26. D. Pathak, P. Tammana, A. A. Franklin, and T. Alladi, "Accelerating PUF-based UAV authentication protocols using programmable switch," *2022 14th Int. Conf. Commun. Syst. NETworkS*, 2022, doi: 10.1109/COMSNETS53615.2022.9668481.

27. M. Abdelhafidh, N. Charef, A. Ben Mnaouer, and L. C. Fourati, "Software-defined networking for flying ad-hoc network security: A survey; software-defined networking for flying ad-hoc network security: A survey," *2022 2nd Int. Conf. Smart Syst. Emerg. Technol.*, 2022, doi: 10.1109/SMARTTECH54121.2022.00057.

Chapter 25

MENA Sukuk Price Prediction Modeling using Prophet Algorithm

Taufeeque Ahmad Siddiqui, Mohd Raagib Shakeel, and Shahzad Alam

Jamia Millia, Islamia, New Delhi, India

25.1 Introduction

Unlike several other Islamic finance products, the sukuk capital market has expanded to the point that it is now a viable option for investors. Sukuk are certificates of investment that reflect securities of equivalent worth that represent equal interests in property ownership, usufruct, and services, as stated by the Accounting and Auditing Organization for Islamic Financial Institutions (AAOIFI). They are granted in the context of a contract that follows Shariah guidelines and is based on the idea of profit and loss sharing. A sukuk is based on the idea that the bearer has an equal interest in an asset and is eligible to receive the asset's return. Sukuks are used to raise funds for an organization. In exchange for taking on the risk of lending, sukuk investors get a return based on the rent of the asset [1–3].[1]

Sukuk issued in US dollars in the Middle East and Africa are listed in the Standard and Poor's (S&P) Dow Jones indices as the Standard and Poor's (S&P) MENA Sukuk index to give worldwide exposure, whereas GCC Sukuk are issued in US dollars by Gulf Cooperation Council countries and are featured in the Standard and Poor's (S&P) Dow Jones indices as the Standard and Poor's (S&P) GCC Sukuk index. In this study, we are using the Prophet model to forecast the MENA Sukuk price for 1, 3, and 6 days ahead of the prediction horizon. We want to examine the accuracy for several short-term horizon periods, although the numbers 1, 3, and 6 were selected at random. We use the GCC Sukuk price as a regressor in the model to increase its accuracy. We use the evaluation metrics RMSE, MAPE, and R^2 to assess the model's performance. This research will be crucial for everyone, especially finance professionals, seeking to optimize their portfolio allocation and increase their profits, as well as for academics seeking to develop more precise and reliable sukuk prediction models.

This study is divided into the following sections. Section 25.2 presents a review of prior or similar research that is relevant to our study. Section 25.3 contains the methodology, namely the Prophet model and its design. Section 25.4 describes the datasets and their sources that we use for training and testing the models in our study. In Section 25.5, experimental analysis of the methodology is presented, along with its findings. In the last part of the paper, Section 25.6, there is a short discussion and some suggestions for future research.

25.2 Literature Review

Over the years, numerous statistical techniques have been utilized to analyze topics in the realm of Shariah indices and sukuk, and now the notion of predictive modeling has also been included. Few studies are available on the forecasting of sukuk prices, and none on predicting MENA Sukuk prices. Table 25.1 summarizes the studies pertinent to assessing the concepts of Islamic finance and predictive modeling.

Table 25.1 Literature Review

S.no	References	Data, Research Methodology and Findings
1	[4]	The authors used an artificial neural network model to anticipate Turkish sovereign sukuk prices and to discover the drivers of sukuk price forecasting. The study's sample period was 10 years. The sovereign sukuk prices were predicted using evaluation criteria such as RMSE, MAE, MAPE, and R^2. The result showed 99.98 percent fitness value of R^2.
2	[5]	To predict the Islamic KMI-30 index, the authors employed artificial neural networks. The research study was conducted from 2009 to 2019. The outcome of the feature selection revealed that indicators such as the Aroon Oscillator, Bollinger Bands, Directional Movement, Forecast Oscillator, and Williams Accumulation Distribution played a critical role in affecting the stock index.

(Continued)

Table 25.1 (Continued)

S.no	References	Data, Research Methodology and Findings
3	[6]	The researchers analyzed the returns of several indices, such as the Standard and Poor's (S&P) MENA Sukuk index and the Dow Jones MENA stock index for the period 2013–2017, in order to solve the asset pricing problem. The GMM estimation approach was utilized. The indices were not found to be cointegrated, however the MENA Sukuk index had a considerable influence on MENA bonds indices and vice versa.
4	[7]	The authors analyzed the association between sukuk and Shariah-compliant stock indexes in the Gulf Cooperation Council area using bivariate and multivariate wavelet methods. The degree of connection between sukuk bonds and Shariah stock indexes was discovered to be substantial, albeit the degree of correlation varied over time and scale.
5	[8]	The factors that impact bond and sukuk ratings traded on the Indonesia stock market for the period 2013–2017 were studied using an ordinal logit model. It was discovered that for corporate bonds, criteria like leverage ratio, security structure, and so on are important, but profitability and liquidity ratio are not. Sukuk ratings, on the other hand, were the polar opposite.
6	[9]	The authors looked at whether Shariah-compliant stocks in the MENA may aid investors during a crisis for the period 2007–2015. This was accomplished by contrasting Islamic and non-Islamic portfolios. The study was conducted using the Sharpe ratio and the multi-factor model. The results were determined to be unfavorable for investors.
7	[10]	To assess the risk–return of the Indian Shariah index and benchmark indexes such as the Sensex and Nifty, the researchers used a variety of statistical approaches such as the t-test, Beta, correlation, and CAGR. The research took place between 2010 and 2012. The results revealed that the returns of the Shariah index and the benchmark indices were not significantly different

(Continued)

Table 25.1 (Continued)

S.no	References	Data, Research Methodology and Findings
8	[11]	The authors utilized a binomial decision tree approach to forecast the sovereign sukuk returns that the government provided to support R&D activities in Indonesia. The results showed that the risk–return balance was consistent, and that in a full-continuity event, the prediction values that were closest to existing project-based sukuk returns were found.
9	[12]	The authors created a hybrid model to anticipate the sukuk price by using the statistical parameter of the moving average as an input layer to the artificial neural network model. The hybrid moving average ANN proved to be more accurate in predicting the sukuk than the usual statistical model.
10	[13]	IILM sukuk model was presented not only in its structural form, but also in its formulae, with the goal of diversifying Indonesia's existing Islamic monetary tools and eventually providing liquidity allocation benefits.
11	[14]	Using the multivariate GARCH model, authors investigated the volatility connection and conditional relationship between sukuk and conventional bond markets in countries such as Europe and the United States. Both bonds were discovered to have a reduced response to conditional fluctuation. Furthermore, there was a positive conditional association between sukuk return and traditional bond markets. A considerable behavioral alteration in the sukuk–bond interaction was also discovered.
12	[15]	The researchers looked into the relationships between bond indexes and volatility in nations including India, China, Malaysia, and South Korea, etc. with the Malaysian sukuk index. The investigations were conducted using wavelet coherence and a multivariate GARCH model. The study found that portfolio diversification is not practicable for localized investors, although it is possible for global investors.

(Continued)

Table 25.1   (Continued)

S.no	References	Data, Research Methodology and Findings
13	[16]	Using the K-nearest neighbor method, authors anticipated Vakif asset management sukuk prices. Forecasting was done for 1, 3, and 5 days ahead, with success rates of 98, 96, and 94 percent, respectively.
14	[17]	The authors used KPSS, LM, and other tests to investigate Shariah indices for the period of 5 years and 6 months in Middle Eastern nations. Despite being linked, these indexes were shown to be inefficient.
15	[18]	The authors intended to see if the rise of the sukuk market in sukuk-issuing nations may contribute to economic growth. For this, the system GMM model was employed. Even after controlling for major economic development determinants, a favorable link between the two was discovered.
16	[19]	Researchers predicted conventional and Shariah indices based on a number of macroeconomic variables using neural a network approach. For Saudi Arabia, Oman, UAE, BRIC, and GCC countries, macroeconomic indicators such as Brent crude oil and the corresponding country currency rates were shown to be more accurate in forecasting stock prices.
17	[20]	The authors attempted to determine the impact of macroeconomic factors on Indian Islamic stock indexes. The analysis was carried out using the traditional OLS approach. Macroeconomic variables including interest rates and currency rates have been proven to have a major influence on Shariah stock indexes.
18	[21]	On the Dow Jones Islamic market outcomes, author looked at the influence of traditional financial markets, investor mood tempo, and major macroeconomic factors. Although stock market returns were significant for all quantiles, the influence of oil prices and the investor mood measure was only significant for the lower quantiles.

(Continued)

Table 25.1 (Continued)

S.no	References	Data, Research Methodology and Findings
19	[22]	To predict sukuk ratings, the authors employed neural networks, MLR, and DT methods. The authors studied Malaysian corporate sukuk and discovered that neural networks outperformed the other two techniques.
20	[23]	The authors used machine learning techniques such as neural networks and multinomial logistic to construct a sukuk rating prediction model. The neural network was shown to be more effective than the other. Furthermore, key determinants are share price and sukuk structure.
21	[24]	The association between GCC Sukuk and Shariah stocks was investigated by the researchers. For all time scales, they were discovered to have a negative relationship in the long run. For the study, the wavelet squared coherence approach was applied. The study found that co-movement varies with time and frequency. Furthermore, co-movement has a varied effect on VaR levels.
22	[25]	Using cointegration and the VDC test, the author evaluated the causative association between five ASEAN Shariah indices: MSPHISL, MSTHFIL, MvSSNGIL, FTSEMY, and JAKSEIS. All of the indices were found to be cointegrated, with the Malaysian stock index topping the others in terms of leadership.

25.3 Research Methodology

25.3.1 Prophet Model

The present study makes use of the Prophet model. It is a general additive model for forecasting time series data. This model incorporates non-linear patterns, such as yearly, weekly, and daily seasonality, as well as holiday effects. This model is particularly resilient in the handling of missing data, and it works fairly well with outliers and changing trends. Prophet makes use of a disintegrated time series framework with three main components: trend, holidays, and seasonality [26].

$$Z_t = T_t + S_t + H_t + e_t$$

where,

T_t – Trend function handles the irregular changes.

S_t – reflects periodic changes(seasonality).

H_t – denotes the implications of holidays, which may occur on one or more days with irregular schedules.

e_t – denotes any peculiar changes that the model does not account for.

Trend Function (T). The trend function represents the data's general trend. The growth trend is present or may be adjusted at all data points in the Prophet model, which are referred to as changepoints. Changepoints, in other words, are points in time when the data changes direction. The trend function encompasses all potential kinds, including linear, logistic, and flat.

Seasonality Function(S). The seasonality function is a Fourier series that is time dependent. The Fourier series may be used to create a smooth seasonal impact.

$$F(t) = \sum_{n=1}^{N} \left(an \cos\left(\frac{2\pi nt}{T} \right) + bn \sin\left(\frac{2\pi nt}{T} \right) \right)$$

where,

T – Expected regular period of the time series

a_n, b_n – *Coefficients*

Holiday Function(H). When a holiday or important event takes place, this function modifies the forecasts. This function lists all such dates, both built in and user defined, and then adds or subtracts the number from the growth or seasonality estimate [26].

25.4 Data Representation

Daily data for the Standard and Poor's (S&P) MENA and GCC Sukuk price indices is obtained from the Standard and Poor's (S&P) Dow Jones indices website (https://www.spglobal.com/spdji/en/index-family/fixed-income/sukuk/#indices) for the period January 1, 2017 to December 31, 2021. The data has been imputed for missing values using the predictive mean matching (PMM) method. In our study, we are using 80percent of the data to train the models and 20 percent of the data to assess their performance. A quick overview of the data and its characteristics can be found in Table 25.2.

Table 25.2 Data Description

Sukuk Index	Data Period	Total Number of Initial Samples	Total number of Samples After Data Pre-processing	Number of Training Samples	Number of Testing Samples
MENA Sukuk	01-01-2017 to 31-12-2021	1299	1296	1044	252
GCC Sukuk (Regressor)	01-01-2017 to 31-12-2021	1298	1296	1044	252

25.5 Experimental Results and Analyses

The evaluation measures that were used, as well as the experimental findings and analyses, are discussed in this section.

25.5.1 Evaluation Metrics

To evaluate and analyze prediction accuracy, MAPE (mean absolute percentage error), RMSE (root mean squared error), and R^2 score (coefficient of determination) are employed.

25.5.2 Result and Analyses

The model is tested with test data once the parameters of the model have been defined in the training phase. The regression line for actual and expected MENA Sukuk prices is shown in Figure 25.1. It reveals a minimal difference between the actual and anticipated values, indicating that our model adequately explains the extremely high variability observed. In other words, the regressor (GCC Sukuk price) explained a substantial part of the variation in MENA Sukuk prices. The graph clearly shows the best fit line with R^2 scores of 0.9999, 0.9999, and 0.9998 over a prediction horizon of 1, 3, and 6 days, respectively. Table 25.3 demonstrates the Prophet model's performance for 1, 3, and 6 days forward predictions using evaluation metrics. For a forecast horizon of one day, the result exhibits the lowest RMSE and MAPE values of 0.0191 and 0.0001, respectively, as well as the highest R^2 score of 0.9999. The values are similarly low for other anticipated horizons. For forecast horizons of three days and six days, the RMSE values are 0.0455

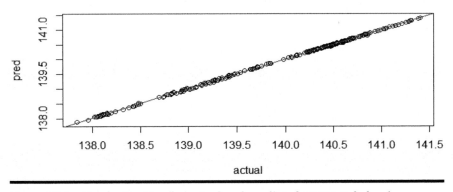

Figure 25.1   Regression Line for actual and predicted MENA Sukuk prices.

Table 25.3 Comparison of RMSE, MAPE and R^2 for Different Forecast Horizon

		Forecast Horizon (in days)		
Model	*Evaluation Metrics*	*1*	*3*	*6*
Prophet	RMSE	0.01911633	0.04558336	0.09120269
	MAPE	0.000147389	0.000324483	0.000606266
	R^2	0.9999	0.9999	0.9998

and 0.0912, respectively. For the same horizons, the MAPE values are 0.0003 and 0.0006, respectively. In other words, the MAPE values are 0.14 and 0.32 per thousand, with a success rate of 99.99 percent for a prediction horizon of 1 day and 3 days, respectively. The success percentage for a 6-day forecast horizon with a MAPE value of 0.60 per thousand is 99.98 percent. Our model's error assessment measures outperform those of Cetin and Metlek, [4].

Figure 25.2 depicts the various plot components of the forecast, such as trend, weekly, and yearly components. The forecast's trend component showed almost a flat trend. The weekly component displays the MENA Sukuk's sharp and continuous price increase from Monday through Friday. The yearly component displays the highest price increases in January, February, November, and December. The prediction is enhanced due to the addition of a regressor, the GCC Sukuk. Figure 25.3 depicts the final graph for actual values as well as in-sample and out-of-sample predicted values of the MENA Sukuk prices. The actual values are shown in dark black, while the anticipated values are shown in light black. The closeness between predicted and actual values is evident from the graph.

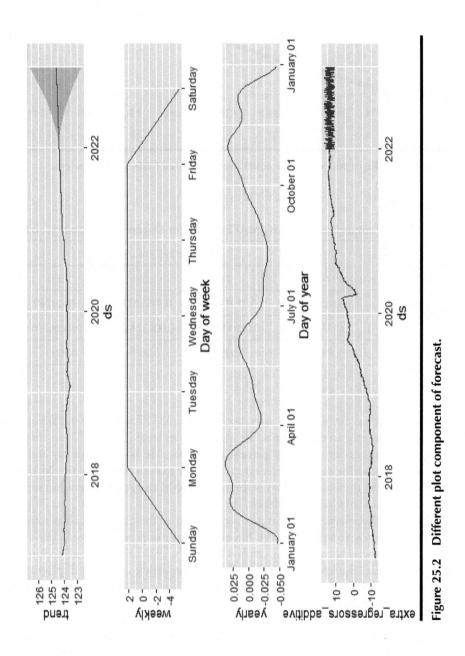

Figure 25.2 Different plot component of forecast.

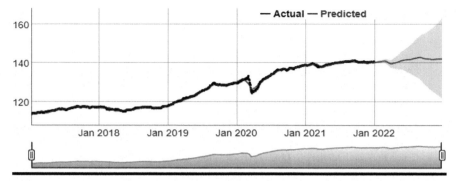

Figure 25.3 Graph of actual and predicted values of MENA Sukuk prices.

25.6 Conclusion and Implications

Sukuk are Shariah-compliant investment certificates based on profit and loss sharing. The holder of a sukuk has equal ownership of an asset and is entitled to its return. Due to its structure, sukuk has become one of the most lucrative Shariah investment vehicles. In this study, we are using the Prophet model to forecast the MENA Sukuk price for 1, 3, and 6 days ahead of the prediction horizon. The results of the study show a significantly higher R^2 score for all prediction horizons and substantially lower error values. The MAPE values are 0.14 and 0.32 per thousand, respectively, with a 99.99 percent success rate for 1 day and 3 days of prediction horizon. The success rate for 6 days of forecast horizon is 99.98 percent, with an MAPE value of 0.60 per thousand. The results also illustrate the trend in the dataset, as well as the yearly and weekly seasonality, giving us a clear picture of the model's accurate prediction ability. Our work clearly outperforms a recent study by ref. [4], who, while using a different dataset (Turkish Sovereign Sukuk price), had a MAPE value of 2.8 per thousand and an R^2 score of 99.98 percent. Furthermore, our study outperforms previous research such as ref. [16], which had an R^2 score of 94 percent, and ref. [11], which had an R^2 score of 80 percent.

This research will be of importance for everyone, especially finance professionals seeking to optimize their portfolio allocation and increase their profits, as well as academics seeking to develop more precise and reliable sukuk prediction models. In the future, different determinants with a strong correlation with sukuk prices might be employed to make more precise predictions. Furthermore, various machine learning or ensemble approaches can be employed to boost prediction accuracy.

Note

1 AAOIFI, Sharia's Standards (No:17 Investment Sukuk), available at http://aaoifi.com/ss-17-investment-sukuk/?lang=en (accessed 02 April 2022).

References

1. Alam, S. et al. (2020), "A novel hybrid watermarking scheme with image authentication based on frequency domain, 2-level SVD using chaotic map", *EAI Endorsed Transactions on Energy Web*. https://doi.org/10.4108/eai.13-7-2018.165512

2. Alam, S. et al. (2021), "Dual secure robust watermaking scheme based on hybrid optimization algorithm for image security", *Personal and Ubiquitous Computing*, pp. 1–13. https://doi.org/10.1007/s00779-021-01597-2

3. Amrani, M.B., Hamza, F. and Mostapha, E.H. (2017), "Sukuk: Literature review", *Journal of Social and Administrative Sciences*, Vol. 4 No. 1. https://doi.org/10.1453/jsas.v4i1.1241

4. Cetin, D.T. and Metlek, S. (2021), "Forecasting of Turkish sovereign sukuk prices using artificial neural network model", *Acta Infologica*, Vol. 5 No. 2, pp. 241–254. https://doi.org/10.26650/acin.907990

5. Aslam, F., Mughal, K. S., Ali, A. and Mohmand, Y.T. (2021), "Forecasting Islamic securities index using artificial neural networks: performance evaluation of technical indicators", *Journal of Economic and Administrative Sciences*, Vol. 37 No. 2, pp. 253–271. https://doi.org/10.1108/jeas-04-2020-0038

6. Seth, N., Singhania, M. and Siddiqui, S. (2021), "Modeling returns of Sukuk and related indices with system GMM: evidence from the MENA region", *International Journal of Islamic and Middle Eastern Finance and Management*, Vol. ahead-of-print. https://doi.org/10.1108/IMEFM-07-2018-0222

7. Nasreen, S., Naqvi, S. A. A., Tiwari, A. K., Hammoudeh, S. and Shah, S. A. R. (2020), "A wavelet-based analysis of the co-movement between Sukuk bonds and Shariah stock indices in the GCC region: Implications for risk diversification", *Journal of Risk and Financial Management*, Vol. 13 No. 4, p. 63. https://doi.org/10.3390/jrfm13040063

8. Ni'mah, A., Laila, N., Rusmita, S.A. and Cahyono, E.F. (2020), "Determinants of corporate bond and Sukuk ratings in Indonesia", *Journal of Islamic Monetary Economics and Finance*, Vol. 6 No. 3, pp. 689–712.

9. Abadi, R.T. and Silva, F. (2020), "Do Islamic fundamental weighted indices outperform their conventional counterparts? An empirical investigation during the crises in the MENA region", *Eurasian Economic Review*, online first, available at: https://link.springer.com/article/10.1007/s40822-020-00158-x

10. Irfan, M. (2020), "Performance of Sharia index in India: An Empirical study of Risk and Return behavior", *National Conference on Paradigm for Sustainable Business: People, Planet and Profit*, pp. 1–9.

11. Wardani, L., Viverita, V., Husodo, Z.A. and Sunaryo, S. (2019), "Contingent claim approach for pricing of sovereign Sukuk for R&D financing in Indonesia", *Emerging Markets Finance and Trade*, Vol. 56 No. 2, pp. 338–350. https://doi.org/10.1080/1540496X.2019.1658067

12. Hila, N.Z., Muhamad Safiih, L. and Mohamed, N.A. (2019), "Empirical study of sukuk investment forecasting using artificial neural network base algorithm", *International Journal of innovations in Engineering and Technology*, Vol. 13 No. 3, pp. 124–127. https://doi.org/10.21172/ijiet.133.19

13. Ismal, R. (2019), "Sukuk model for Islamic monetary instrument in Indonesia", *Journal of Economic Cooperation and Development*, Vol. 40 No. 4, pp. 119–138.

14. Hassan, M. K. et al., (2018), "The determinants of co-movement dynamics between Sukuk and conventional bonds", *Quarterly Review of Economics and Finance*, Vol. 68(C), pp. 73–84.

15. Bhuiyan, R. A., Rahman, M. P., Saiti, B. and Mat Ghani, G. (2018), "Financial integration between sukuk and bond indices of emerging markets: Insights from wavelet coherence and multivariate GARCH analysis", *Borsa Istanbul Review*, Vol. 18 No. 3, pp. 218–230. https://doi.org/10.1016/j.bir.2017.11.006

16. Yigiter, S.Y., Sari, S.S., Karabulut, T. and Basakin, E.E. (2018), "Estimation of lease certificate price evaluation through machine learning method", *International Journal of Islamic Economics and Finance Studies*, Vol. 4 No. 3, pp. 74–82. https://doi.org/10.25272/ijisef.412760

17. Ashraf, S. and Ellili, N. (2017), "Revisiting informational efficiency and market integration: evidence from Gulf Cooperation Council (GCC) Shariah equity market", *Arabian Journal of Business and Management Review*, Vol. 7 No. 2, pp. 1–6.

18. Smaoui, H. and Nechi, S. (2017), "Does Sukuk market development spur economic growth?", *Research in International Business and Finance*, Vol. 41(C), pp. 136–147. https://doi.org/10.1016/j.ribaf.2017.04.018

19. Siddiqui, T.A. and Abdullah, Y. (2017), "Testing for predictive ability of conventional and shariah indices of selected Gulf countries and economic regions using neural network modelling", *Journal of Islamic Economics, Banking and Finance*, Vol. 13 No. 1, pp. 171–186. https://doi.org/10.12816/0051161

20. Habib, M. and Islam, K.U. (2017), "Impact of macroeconomic variables on Islamic stock market returns: evidence from nifty 50 Shariah index", *Journal of Commerce and Accounting Research*, Vol. 6 No. 1, pp. 37–44.

21. Naifar, N. (2016), "Do global risk factors and macroeconomic conditions affect global Islamic index dynamics? A quantile regression approach", *Quarterly Review of Economics and Finance*. Vol. 61, pp. 29–39. https://doi.org/10.1016/j.qref.2015.10.004

22. Arundina, T., Kartiwi, M. and Omar, M.A. (2016), "Artificial intelligence for islamic sukuk rating predictions", *Artificial Intelligence in Financial Markets*, pp. 211–241. https://doi.org/10.1057/978-1-137-48880-0_8

23. Arundina, T., Azmi Omar, M. and Kartiwi, M. (2015), "The predictive accuracy of sukuk ratings; multinomial logistic and neural network inferences", *Pacific-Basin Finance Journal*, Vol. 34 No. 34, pp. 273–292. https://doi.org/10.1016/j.pacfin.2015.03.002

24. Aloui, C., Hammoudeh, S. and Hamida, H. Ben. (2015), "Co-movement between sharia stocks and sukuk in the GCC markets: A time-frequency analysis", *Journal of International Financial Markets, Institutions and Money*, Vol. 34(C), pp. 69–79. https://doi.org/10.1016/j.intfin.2014.11.003

25. Saiti, B. (2015), "Cointegration of Islamic stock indices: evidence from five ASEAN countries", *International Journal of Scientific and Engineering Research*, Vol. 6 No. 7, pp. 1392–1405.

26. Taylor, S.J. and Letham, B. (2017), "Forecasting at scale", *PeerJ Preprints*, Vol. 5, p. e3190v2. https://doi.org/10.7287/peerj.preprints.3190v2

Chapter 26

Cancer Biomarkers Identification from Transcriptomic Data Using Supervised Machine Learning Approaches

Rubi, Farhan Jalees Ahmad, Bhavya Alankar, and Harleen Kaur
Jamia Hamdard, New Delhi, India

26.1 Introduction

Cancer is one of the major causes of mortality globally and the fourth major cause of death for women in South-East Asia [1]. In the year 2020, out of total global cancer patients, 49.3% were found to be in Asia, amounting to an incidence of 169.1 per 100,000 of the population [2]. Countries with a high human development index (HDI) show higher rates of cancer incidence and mortality for most types of cancer. Countries with lower HDI show half (76.7–78.0 per 100,000) the number of deaths of higher HDI countries (122.9–141.1 per 100,000) [3]. In the year 2017, in the USA, 35% of total cancer patients detected died [4]. In 2016,

DOI: 10.1201/9781003371380-26

in Germany, 25% of men and 20% of women died of cancer [5]. The high rate of cancer death is because cancer is proliferative, metastatic, and invasive [6–8]. Timely intervention by medical practitioners and oncologists is crucial to control the high mortality rate, and this is only possible when cancer is detected and diagnosed in its initial stages or even prior to its occurrence. Biochemical methods like different types of radiation-based methods are very time-consuming, requiring a lot of human effort and resources. Correctly interpreting images obtained through different medical tests is challenging for clinicians and researchers because of human bias and mistakes, so computer-aided diagnosis has been going on for cancer since the early 1980s [9]. Fast and efficient machine learning-based methods, bioinformatics tools and software are therefore needed.

In recent years, many computation algorithms and models for statistical analysis have been developed to do variable selection, which can be further applied to identify the biomarkers in clustering, regression, and classification problems [10]. The survival time for metastatic cancer patients has been predicted on the basis of clinical data available from the year 2008 to 2017 [11]. Several machine learning approaches have been used to identify biomarkers or feature selection for diagnosis and prognosis of different types of cancer, including support vector machines, ensemble methods, genetic algorithms, binary decision trees [12]. The correlation between some gene expression levels like the P53 gene with cancer can be analyzed to find certain patterns associated with different types of cancer, while the remaining genes are irrelevant to classification and diagnosis of many tissue types [13]. The objectives of supervised machine learning approaches are expanding from identifying cancer biomarkers to identifying drug targets to identifying driver genes involved in cancer. In this chapter, we discuss supervised machine learning methods applied to cancer biomarker detection on transcriptomic data.

26.2 Microarrays in Cancer

Microarray technology is a recent advance for both clinical laboratories and traditional disease diagnostic methods, as it suggests disease-specific biomarkers, leading to improvement in the accuracy of diagnosis, classification, and prognosis. There are many publicly available resources for cancer microarrays and RNASeq data, such as GEO (Gene Expression Omnibus) available at NCBI (National Center for Biotechnology Information), TCGA (The Cancer Genome Atlas- https:// cancergenome.nih.gov/), TARGET (Therapeutically Applicable Research to Generate Effective Treatments- https://ocg.cancer.gov/programs/target). Resource data are also available at the GDC (Genomic Data Commons) website [14, 15]. The GDC helps centralize both storage and processing of transcriptomic data [16]. There is a browser named UCSC Xena (https://xenabrowser.net/) for publicly accessing the TCGA and GDC data of both genomic and phenotypic type. One further resource for gene expression data for cancer is ArrayExpress, available at the EMBL-EBI (European Bioinformatics Institute) website [17].

Different methods are being applied by researchers and scientists to identify cancer type, aggressiveness, and chances of occurrence even before onset of any symptoms; and outcome of the treatment preferred is very interesting to the doctors and medical professionals [18]. One of the biggest challenges is how to gain knowledge from the enormous amount of microarray raw data present and being generated. This knowledge will help improve understanding of carcinogenesis and cellular events involved in the progression of cancer as well as metastasis. This improved insight will help in development of targeted therapy for different types of cancer for cellular events that take place during the pathogenesis of cancer – and hence of personalized medicines [19]. Machine learning methods are becoming well known among scientists because of their potential to identify hidden patterns and their relationships with other patterns, and their capability of accurate prediction from complex datasets like high-throughput transcriptomic data. Previous studies and literature available indicate that machine learning methods and publicly available transcriptomic data collectively have the strength and potential to fulfill the target of accurate and timely cancer diagnosis and classification.

26.3 Supervised Machine Learning in Cancer Biomarkers Detection

There are two main kinds of machine learning, supervised and unsupervised. Supervised machine learning techniques use labeled data, whereas unsupervised machine learning does not need labeled data. Both types of machine learning have various subtypes. Some of these are already being applied to survival prediction, prognosis, and biomarker identification [20]. Other types of machine learning are not yet used at large scale. This study discusses supervised machine learning techniques and the corresponding identification of functional class and prediction of patterns.

In recent years, many algorithms for computation and models for statistical analysis have been developed to do variable selection, and these can be further applied to identify the biomarkers in clustering, regression, and classification problems [10]. In a study, survival time for metastatic cancer patients was predicted on the basis of clinical data available from the year 2008 to 2017 [11]. Several machine learning approaches have been used to identify biomarkers or feature selection for diagnosis and prognosis of different types of cancer, including support vector machines, ensemble methods, genetic algorithms and binary decision trees [12]. The correlation between some gene expression levels like the P53 gene with cancer can be analyzed to find certain patterns associated with different types of cancer, while the rest of the genes are irrelevant to classification and diagnosis of many tissue types [13].

Gene expression data and PPI (protein–protein interaction) data were integrated to find biomarkers using an integrated approach called netSVM, which gave better performance than individual network methods and individual SVM (support vector machine)-based methods. This method was successively applied on breast cancer data sets to identify prognostic signatures in 2011 [21]. An app was developed in 2017, based on a netSVM method named CyNetSVM which is integrated with Cytoscape [22]. In 2019 another ensemble method was used that combined SVM, KNN (k-nearest neighbor), naïve Bayes and decision tree (C4.5) algorithms as classifier for leukemia gene expression data. The classification accuracy and performance of this method were better than other individual classifiers, leading to the conclusion that this method can be used for diagnosis of cancer and other diseases [23]. Self-organizing map (SOM), support vector machine (SVM) and k-nearest neighbor have been applied to various cancer data to identify significant key genes. In one study, a Fisher criterion score was used, in which Fisher's linear discriminant was used prior to training the machine for classification and validation of gene expression data using SVMs [24–26].

There are many gene expression data analysis-based cancer biomarker identification-related bioinformatics tools. One of these, recently developed, is CAncer bioMarker Prediction Pipeline (CAMPP). CAMPP is an R (programming language)-based open-source tool that performs many data analysis tasks like k-means clustering, differential expression analysis, survival analysis using mclust, limma, and Cox proportional hazard regression, respectively. This tool also generates protein-protein/miRNA–gene interaction networks retrieved from STRING, miRTarBase and TargetScan, and does correlation and co-expression analysis. The result is given in the form of tabular files and graphical representations by CAMPP [27–29]. Table 26.1 summarizes research done on cancer biomarkers identification using transcriptomic data.

26.4   Conclusion

Efficient machine learning techniques and algorithms are needed to overcome the limitations of high redundancy and dependency of transcriptomic data in cancer biomarkers identification research. This paper discusses supervised machine learning methods and their uses in cancer biomarkers identification work in recent years. We have chosen those papers discussing SVM, ensembled SVM, GeneRank, kNN, naïve Bayes etc. There is no doubt that an abundance of work has been done using supervised machine learning techniques but there remain many opportunities to acquire the information needed to speed up cancer drug research, and unexplored carcinogenesis-related heterogenous molecular mechanisms, like higher accuracy.

Table 26.1 Supervised Gene Selection Techniques Applied for Cancer Biomarkers Identification

S. No.	Ideology	Feature Selection Algorithm	Classifier	Dataset	Performance Evaluation Metrics	Reference
1.	An efficient classification algorithm solving the sparse logistic regression problem of multicategory classification was proposed which is based on the Gauss–Seidel method	Gauss–Seidel method	Gauss–Seidel method based	Colon cancer Breast cancer	Average validation error	[30]
2.	A hybrid approach between genetic algorithm and SVM is used to identify key feature genes. Genetic algorithm was used as the search engine.	Genetic algorithm	SVM	Diffuse large B cell lymphoma	Accuracy	[31]

| 3. | Gene expression difference was compared using MRMR method, then DEGs were ranked. Optimal biomarkers were then selected. Finally, an SVM classifier based on the optimal biomarkers was constructed and evaluated. | Incremental feature selection | SVM | Non-small cell lung cancer | LOOCV | [32] |
| 4. | Identification of the functional alteration signatures was done using SVM. Identification of alteration features was done by Monte Carlo feature selection (MCFS) method, followed by the | MCFS, IFS | SVM | Breast cancer, colorectal adenocarcinoma, head and neck squamous cell carcinoma, kidney renal clear cell carcinoma, ovarian cancer | Accuracy | [33] |

(Continued)

Table 26.1 (Continued)

S. No.	Ideology	Feature Selection Algorithm	Classifier	Dataset	Performance Evaluation Metrics	Reference
	incremental feature selection (IFS) method, then these features were used to build the SVM-based classifier					
5.	Pathway-based weighted method called GeneRank was used to calculate rank of genes and LASSO method was used to select genes significant in subtype segmentation that are linked with overall survival upon weighted gene expression values.	GeneRank method	LASSO	Lung adenocarcinoma, squamous cell carcinoma	For classification, error rate and GBS For prognosis Log-rank p-values and C- index	[34]

Acknowledgment

The present study was supported by the University Grant Commission, Ministry of Social Justice & Empowerment (Grant No. F1-17.1/2015-16/ RGNF-2015-17-SC-HAR-20221).

References

1. Torre, L. A., Islami, F., Siegel, R. L., Ward, E. M., & Jemal, A. (2017). Global cancer in women: Burden and trends. *Cancer Epidemiology Biomarkers & Prevention, 26*(4), 444–457. https://doi.org/10.1158/1055-9965.EPI-16-0858

2. Huang, J., Ngai, C. H., Deng, Y., Tin, M. S., Lok, V., Zhang, L., Yuan, J., Xu, W., Zheng, Z.-J., & Wong, M. C. S. (2022). Cancer incidence and mortality in Asian countries: A trend analysis. *Cancer Control, 29*, 107327482210959. https://doi.org/10.1177/10732748221095955

3. Sung, H., Ferlay, J., Siegel, R. L., Laversanne, M., Soerjomataram, I., Jemal, A., & Bray, F. (2021). Global cancer statistics 2020: GLOBOCAN estimates of incidence and mortality worldwide for 36 cancers in 185 countries. *CA: A Cancer Journal for Clinicians, 71*(3), 209–249. https://doi.org/10.3322/caac.21660

4. Siegel, R. L., Miller, K. D., & Jemal, A. (2017). Cancer statistics, 2017. *CA: A Cancer Journal for Clinicians, 67*(1), 7–30.

5. Quante, A. S., Ming, C., Rottmann, M., Engel, J., Boeck, S., Heinemann, V., Westphalen, C. B., & Strauch, K. (2016). Projections of cancer incidence and cancer-related deaths in Germany by 2020 and 2030. *Cancer Medicine, 5*(9), 2649–2656.

6. Kobayashi, A., Okuda, H., Xing, F., Pandey, P. R., Watabe, M., Hirota, S., Pai, S. K., Liu, W., Fukuda, K., Chambers, C., Wilber, A., & Watabe, K. (2011). Bone morphogenetic protein 7 in dormancy and metastasis of prostate cancer stem-like cells in bone. *Journal of Experimental Medicine, 208*(13), 2641–2655. https://doi.org/10.1084/jem.20110840

7. Li, M., Mukasa, A., del-Mar Inda, M., Zhang, J., Chin, L., Cavenee, W., & Furnari, F. (2011). Guanylate binding protein 1 is a novel effector of EGFR-driven invasion in glioblastoma. *The Journal of Experimental Medicine, 208*(13), 2657–2673. https://doi.org/10.1084/jem.20111102

8. Yang, W., Xia, Y., Ji, H., Zheng, Y., Liang, J., Huang, W., Gao, X., Aldape, K., & Lu, Z. (2011). Nuclear PKM2 regulates β-catenin transactivation upon EGFR activation. *Nature, 480*(7375), 118–122. https://doi.org/10.1038/nature10598

9. Wang, C., Elazab, A., Wu, J., & Hu, Q. (2017). Lung nodule classification using deep feature fusion in chest radiography. *Computerized Medical Imaging and Graphics, 57*, 10–18. https://doi.org/10.1016/j.compmedimag.2016.11.004

10. Chen, L., & Huang, J. Z. (2012). Sparse reduced-rank regression for simultaneous dimension reduction and variable selection. *Journal of the American Statistical Association, 107*(500), 1533–1545. https://doi.org/10.1080/01621459.2012.734178

11. Gensheimer, M. F., Henry, A. S., Wood, D. J., Hastie, T. J., Aggarwal, S., Dudley, S. A., Pradhan, P., Banerjee, I., Cho, E., Ramchandran, K., & others. (2019). Automated survival prediction in metastatic cancer patients using high-dimensional electronic medical record data. *JNCI: Journal of the National Cancer Institute, 111*(6), 568–574.

12. Akay, M. F. (2009). Support vector machines combined with feature selection for breast cancer diagnosis. *Expert Systems with Applications, 36*(2), 3240–3247.

13. Chen, X., Cheung, S. T., So, S., Fan, S. T., Barry, C., Higgins, J., Lai, K.-M., Ji, J., Dudoit, S., Ng, I. O., & others. (2002). Gene expression patterns in human liver cancers. *Molecular Biology of the Cell, 13*(6), 1929–1939.

14. Clough, E., & Barrett, T. (2016). The gene expression omnibus database. In E. Mathé & S. Davis (Eds), *Statistical Genomics* (Vol. 1418, pp. 93–110). New York: Springer. https://doi.org/10.1007/978-1-4939-3578-9_5

15. Wang, Z., Jensen, M. A., & Zenklusen, J. C. (2016). A practical guide to the cancer genome atlas (TCGA). In E. Mathé & S. Davis (Eds.), *Statistical Genomics* (Vol. 1418, pp. 111–141). New York: Springer. https://doi.org/10.1007/978-1-4939-3578-9_6

16. Zhang, Z., Hernandez, K., Savage, J., Li, S., Miller, D., Agrawal, S., Ortuno, F., Staudt, L. M., Heath, A., & Grossman, R. L. (2021). Uniform genomic data analysis in the NCI Genomic Data Commons. *Nature Communications, 12*(1), 1226. https://doi.org/10.1038/s41467-021-21254-9

17. Parkinson, H., Kapushesky, M., Shojatalab, M., Abeygunawardena, N., Coulson, R., Farne, A., Holloway, E., Kolesnykov, N., Lilja, P., Lukk, M., Mani, R., Rayner, T., Sharma, A., William, E., Sarkans, U., & Brazma, A. (2007). ArrayExpress—A public database of microarray experiments and gene expression profiles. *Nucleic Acids Research, 35*(Database issue), D747–D750. https://doi.org/10.1093/nar/gkl995

18. Schena, M., Shalon, D., Davis, R. W., & Brown, P. O. (1995). Quantitative monitoring of gene expression patterns with a complementary DNA microarray. *Science, 270*(5235), 467–470. https://doi.org/10.1126/science.270.5235.467

19. Kamel, H. F. M., & Al-Amodi, H. S. A. B. (2017). Exploitation of gene expression and cancer biomarkers in paving the path to era of personalized medicine. *Genomics, Proteomics & Bioinformatics, 15*(4), 220–235. https://doi.org/10.1016/j.gpb.2016.11.005

20. Liu, H., Motoda, H., Setiono, R., & Zhao, Z. (2010). Feature selection: An ever evolving frontier in data mining. *Feature Selection in Data Mining,* 10, 4–13.

21. Chen, L., Xuan, J., Riggins, R. B., Clarke, R., & Wang, Y. (2011). Identifying cancer biomarkers by network-constrained support vector machines. *BMC Systems Biology, 5,* 161. https://doi.org/10.1186/1752-0509-5-161

22. Shi, X., Banerjee, S., Chen, L., Hilakivi-Clarke, L., Clarke, R., & Xuan, J. (2017). CyNetSVM: A cytoscape app for cancer biomarker identification using network constrained support vector machines. *PloS One, 12*(1), e0170482. https://doi.org/10.1371/journal.pone.0170482

23. Nashat, Alrefai. (2019). Ensemble machine learning for leukemia cancer diagnosis based on microarray datasets. *Journal of Applied Engineering Research, 14*(21), 4077–4084.

24. Furey, T. S., Cristianini, N., Duffy, N., Bednarski, D. W., Schummer, M., & Haussler, D. (2000). Support vector machine classification and validation of cancer tissue samples using microarray expression data. *Bioinformatics, 16*(10), 906–914. https://doi.org/10.1093/bioinformatics/16.10.906

25. Golub, T. R., Slonim, D. K., Tamayo, P., Huard, C., Gaasenbeek, M., Mesirov, J. P., Coller, H., Loh, M. L., Downing, J. R., Caligiuri, M. A., Bloomfield, C. D., & Lander, E. S. (1999). Molecular classification of cancer: Class discovery and class prediction by gene expression monitoring. *Science, 286*(5439), 531–537. https://doi.org/10.1126/science.286.5439.531

26. Li, L., Darden, T. A., Weinberg, C. R., Levine, A. J., & Pedersen, L. G. (2001). Gene assessment and sample classification for gene expression data using a genetic algorithm/k-nearest neighbor method. *Combinatorial Chemistry & High Throughput Screening, 4*(8), 727–739. https://doi.org/10.2174/1386207013330733

27. Hsu, S.-D., Lin, F.-M., Wu, W.-Y., Liang, C., Huang, W.-C., Chan, W.-L., Tsai, W.-T., Chen, G.-Z., Lee, C.-J., Chiu, C.-M., Chien, C.-H., Wu, M.-C., Huang, C.-Y., Tsou, A.-P., & Huang, H.-D. (2011). miRTarBase: A database curates experimentally validated microRNA–target interactions. *Nucleic Acids Research*, *39*(suppl_1), D163–D169. https://doi.org/10.1093/nar/gkq1107

28. Mering, C. V. (2003). STRING: A database of predicted functional associations between proteins. *Nucleic Acids Research*, *31*(1), 258–261. https://doi.org/10.1093/nar/gkg034

29. Terkelsen, T., Krogh, A., & Papaleo, E. (2020). CAncer bioMarker prediction pipeline (CAMPP)-A standardized framework for the analysis of quantitative biological data. *PLoS Computational Biology*, *16*(3), e1007665. https://doi.org/10.1371/journal.pcbi.1007665

30. Shevade, S. K., & Keerthi, S. S. (2003). A simple and efficient algorithm for gene selection using sparse logistic regression. *Bioinformatics*, *19*(17), 2246–2253. https://doi.org/10.1093/bioinformatics/btg308

31. Li, L., Jiang, W., Li, X., Moser, K. L., Guo, Z., Du, L., Wang, Q., Topol, E. J., Wang, Q., & Rao, S. (2005). A robust hybrid between genetic algorithm and support vector machine for extracting an optimal feature gene subset. *Genomics*, *85*(1), 16–23. https://doi.org/10.1016/j.ygeno.2004.09.007

32. Sheng, M., Dong, Z., & Xie, Y. (2018). Identification of tumor-educated platelet biomarkers of non-small-cell lung cancer. *OncoTargets and Therapy*, *11*, 8143.

33. Wang, S., & Cai, Y. (2018). Identification of the functional alteration signatures across different cancer types with support vector machine and feature analysis. *Biochimica et Biophysica Acta (BBA) - Molecular Basis of Disease*, *1864*(6), 2218–2227. https://doi.org/10.1016/j.bbadis.2017.12.026

34. Wu, X., Wang, L., Feng, F., & Tian, S. (2020). Weighted gene expression profiles identify diagnostic and prognostic genes for lung adenocarcinoma and squamous cell carcinoma. *Journal of International Medical Research*, *48*(3), 030006051989383. https://doi.org/10.1177/0300060519893837

Chapter 27

Development of a Secured and Interoperable Multi-Tenant Software-as-a-Service Electronic Health Record System

Aderonke J. Ikuomola and Kehinde S. Owoputi

Olusegun Agagu University of Science and Technology, Okitipupa, Nigeria.

27.1 Introduction

Patient health records are mostly collected, stored and managed manually by healthcare providers, especially in less developed countries. The inefficiencies of paper-based health record have led many healthcare providers, mostly in developed countries, to develop an electronic health record (EHR) system for collecting, managing and storing their patient health data. With EHR, information on health can be created and managed by authorized providers and shared with other providers in the healthcare organization.

Due to the cost involved in developing and maintaining a full-fledged EHR system, the time taken to recruit software engineers and train staff on how to use the software, many healthcare providers are still using paper-based methods. The

DOI: 10.1201/9781003371380-27

available EHRs cannot be easily upgraded and can only be accessed on the system in which the software is installed.

Many organizations that want to remain in business today are now seeking computing technologies that offer the following features: pay-as-use model, low-cost provisioning, rapid elasticity, security, resource pooling and measured service [1]. The services provided by cloud technologies are infrastructure as a service (IaaS), platform as a service (PaaS), software as a service (SaaS), and data as a service (DaaS) [2]. Cloud computing involves sharing resources to achieve the best utility over a network [3, 4]. EHR sharing among personnel is known to be an important application in cloud computing.

SaaS is a software application delivered over the internet on demand. It is done mostly on a subscription basis and the end user does not need to download, install or store the software and its components on their devices. With the SaaS offering, there is no need to think about how the services are maintained or how the underlying infrastructure is managed. The main focus will be on how to use the software [5].

Most SaaS solutions are built on a multi-tenant architecture. Multi-tenancy is an architectural pattern in which many tenants share resources at different layers of an application but each tenant only has access to functions/components and data that belong to their business entity [1]. With this model, an application with a single configuration is used for all the tenants [6], although a typical multi-tenant application is customized to meet the needs of the tenant. In addition to the cost saving of implementing an EHR system, as tenants pay for what they use on a subscription basis, other core benefits that come with using multi-tenant SaaS include automatic upgrades and protection from data loss [7], resources being shared among multiple tenants, ease of maintenance, and improved clinical workflow.

Multi-tenancy architecture has many advantages over multiple-instance architecture because the updates are faster, it is scalable and cheaper to run since computing resources are being shared. Nonetheless, the challenges of running software for many tenants include security and capacity optimization [6, 8].

With the basic understanding of cloud computing, an electronic health record SaaS will be a prime solution to various problems besetting the health sector, especially in less or mid-developed countries. In this work, a secured and interoperable multi-tenant software-as-a-service electronic health record system was developed to solve the problems/challenges mitigating against the existing EHR system. This system can serve multiple tenants at a time and has strong security measures. The patient's health record can be shared among various healthcare providers, tenants' data can be backed up in case of data loss, the system ensures strong isolation of data as each tenant has their own separate databases, and monitoring and logging features in the system can be used for auditing.

The work is organized as follows. A brief literature review is given in Section 27.2. Section 27.3 provides a design methodology for a secured and interoperable multi-tenant software-as-a-service electronic health record system. The implementation is shown in Section 27.4. Section 27.5 concludes the research work.

27.1.1 Problem Statement

The issues that arise with paper-based health record-keeping include: slow retrieval of patient data or information when needed; inconsistencies in data format; difficulty in analyzing patient data; poor handwriting of some health practitioners leading to problems with reading/processing patient information; patients lacking access to their information; difficulty backing up health records; and inability to share patient information with other healthcare providers. One of the reasons for the low adoption of EHRs in the past has been the cost of building a private data center and maintaining the system.

27.2 Literature Review

The authors of Abayomi-Alli et al. [9] developed an electronic health record system which leverages on cloud computing. The system is designed to efficiently store and retrieve patient records on a local database or cloud database. The cloud database contains data and resources pooled from various healthcare providers (i.e., collaborating hospitals) to facilitate ease of record sharing. Although the system can easily be accessed on demand via an e-health web portal without the need for any setup or installation, data privacy, integrity and availability can easily be compromised since administrators in one hospital can have access to data from a collaborating hospital. If a hospital EHR has been hijacked by a hacker, the collaborating hospital also risks losing data.

A secured and reliable cloud computing-based electronic health record system was proposed with the aim of reducing the medical errors which occurred as a result of mismanagement of patients' information [10]. The cloud computing technology platform used reduces the cost of storing data and provides security for the information stored. The proposed system does not make use of a multiple-tenant application.

The article [11] focuses on clinical decisions, functional and mobile services as a cloud service. In designing the architecture of the cloud-based HSP, the authors also took international standards into consideration. A shared database with separate schema model was used, allowing for resource sharing and data isolation, and a clinical decision service was incorporated into the system, allowing for faster generation of reports and decision making for medical practitioners. The following challenges were not addressed by the authors: performance, interoperability, usability, semantics and security.

A digital solution that will help refugees to have easy access to health services was designed by ref. [12]. Records are made available to authorized external providers on demand. Various security mechanisms including AES encryption, PIN and captcha check were used in the system to mitigate against vulnerabilities and threat. The cost of implementation is relatively high because the system does not employ the multi-tenant SaaS.

A security framework for an EHR system was proposed in ref. [13]. The STRIDE modeling tool was used to model the threats posed to the system while DREAD was used to calculate the amount of risk. Various security mechanisms, including AES encryption, digital signature and hashing, Single Sign-On (SSO), and attribute-based access control, were used in the system to mitigates against various threats.

Authors of Kavitha et al. [14] designed a cloud-based EHR system for Indian healthcare needs. Data are stored in the cloud using the iweb cloud server, and the system was based on the Windows platform. The main challenge is that centralized data storage was used for all healthcare providers, meaning that data storage downtime can affect all providers.

Various issues that come with multi-tenancy and customization were highlighted and various frameworks proposed that enable their uses in the development of e-health SaaS [15]. Centralized data storage was used for all healthcare providers, which means downtime will affect all providers.

SaaS with a multi-tenant architecture was proposed in ref. [16]. The system is efficient, scalable and has easy access to patient data on demand at high speed and reduced cost. The challenge is that multi-tenant data was managed using a single database which, if not configured properly, can lead to data leakage between tenants. The tenant data backup requires more work than separate databases per tenant.

As a results of the challenges with the existing electronic health record system, a secured and interoperable multi-tenant software-as-a-service electronic health record system was developed. This system can serve multiple tenants at a time and has strong authentication and authorization modules. Patient health records can be shared among various healthcare providers, and tenants' data backed up in case of data loss. The system ensures strong isolation of data as each tenant has their own separate database, and the monitoring and logging feature in the system can be used for auditing. Table 27.1 compares systems described in this section.

Table 27.1 Comparison of EHR systems

Author(s)	Interoperable	Secured	Performance	Multi-tenant
[11]	No	Yes	High	No
[12]	No	Yes	High	No
[13]	No	Yes	Not Addressed	No
[15]	No	Yes	Medium	Yes
[10]	No	Yes	High	No
[9]	Yes	Yes	Medium	Yes
[14]	No	Not Addressed	Medium	Yes
[16]	Yes	Yes	Medium	Yes

27.3 Design Methodology

27.3.1 Architecture of a Secured and Interoperable Multi-tenant SaaS Electronic Health Record System

The architecture of a secured and interoperable multi-tenant software-as-a-service is shown in Figure 27.1. The system comprises multiple tenants, a software application which is hosted in the cloud, a database and external application. The software application consists of the tenant identifier, security layer, customization/extension point, business layer and service layer.

During the process of on-boarding a new tenant (hospital), the hospital administrators visit the application via a customized web user interface, enter the hospital credentials and details, then proceed to select the payment plan that will work best for the organization. A request is then made to the back-end (business and service) layer of the application where this information is processed and validated before being stored to the catalog (master database), and a new dedicated database is automatically created for the new tenant following a defined schema which makes this system a complete multi-tenant application. Once this processing is done, tenants can have access to their customized and configured electronic health record platform via a unique subdomain. The hospital administration (with an administrative role and permissions) can therefore manage the overall application. A role-based access control (RBAC) system is used for authorization in the proposed system. The proposed system supports interoperability with other existing and new technology/solutions via a standard interface exposed using standard network protocols (i.e., Restful HTTP).

27.3.2 Components of the Architectural Design

1) *Multiple tenants.* A group of users sharing a common access with specific privileges to the software instance is referred to as a tenant. In this system, tenants simply refer to the healthcare providers using platforms such as hospitals, teaching hospital or healthcare centers.
2) *Software application.* This is made up of the tenant identifier, security layer, customization/extension point, business layer and service layer.
   a) *Tenant identifier.* This is a module or package for identifying which tenant is accessing the application and which data are to be displayed to the users. This module is responsible for strict isolation in the application.
   b) *Security layer.* It is used for ensuring strict security policy in the system to ensure data confidentiality and integrity.
   c) *Customization/extension point.* This is a modification of a software feature that requires custom coding.
   d) *Business layer.* The user requests from the browser are accepted and then processed in this layer.

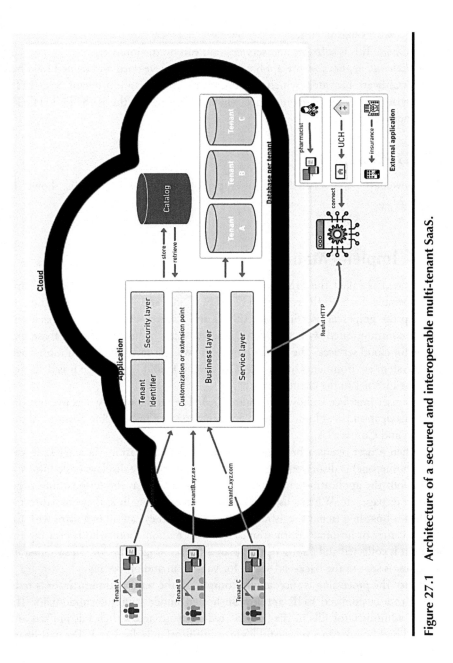

Figure 27.1 Architecture of a secured and interoperable multi-tenant SaaS.

e) *Service layer.* It is a gateway that allows other software to have access to your business logic and resources without interacting with those resources directly. In this layer, messages are passed through a separate interface. It works like an API.

3) *Cloud.* This is software and services that run on the internet.

4) *External applications* are applications/software developed and owned by other healthcare providers which communicate with the multi-tenant SaaS-EHR system via a standard interface which makes use of the RESTFUL HTTP network protocol.

27.3.3 Flowchart

The flowchart of a secured and interoperable multi-tenant SaaS is shown in Figure 27.2.

27.4 Implementation

The system is called the SIM-SaaS-EHR system, which stands for "Secured and interoperable SaaS EHR system". HTMLS, CSS3 and Javascript were used to develop the graphical user interface (GUI) and Laravel was used as the back end which communicated with the MySQL server used in hosting the database and Azure for cloud services. The system portability was designed to work in most operating system environments including Windows, iOS and Linux since it is delivered over the internet to the client browser.

The user interface is shown in Figure 27.3. The Home window has five buttons at the navigation bar: Home Session, Sign-in Session, On-boarding Session, About Session and Contact Us.

When a user opens a browser and accesses the application via a URL, a web page (homepage) is displayed (Figure 27.3). This homepage displays basic information about the application and links to other pages such as the on-boarding page, contact us page, etc. When a user clicks on the on-boarding link, they are redirected to the on-boarding (tenant registration) page, where they can fill in a form with the health center or hospital information. Here information about who is creating the account is collected and a subscription plan is chosen (Figure 27.4). On submission, a request is sent to the back-end server for validation and processing.

Once the processing is successfully completed, the tenant administrator is redirected to a customized EHR application hosted under a unique subdomain. The tenant administrator fills in their login credentials to access their customized and secured dashboard. On a successful login, a notification is displayed. The dashboard of the tenant administrators who oversee the customized EHR application is shown in Figure 27.5. As shown on the dashboard, there are various modules listed on the side navigation bar.

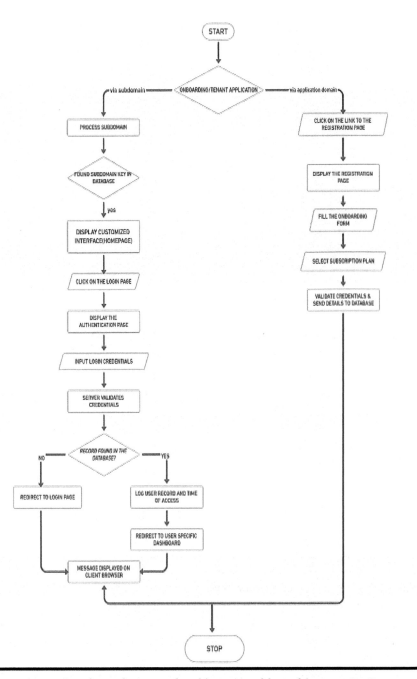

Figure 27.2 Flowchart of a secured and interoperable multi-tenant SaaS.

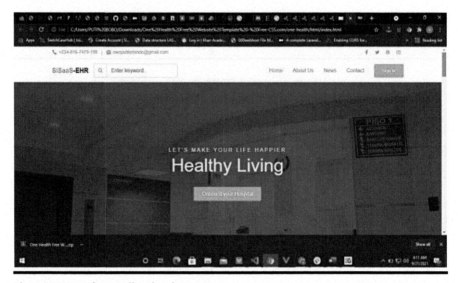

Figure 27.3 The application homepage.

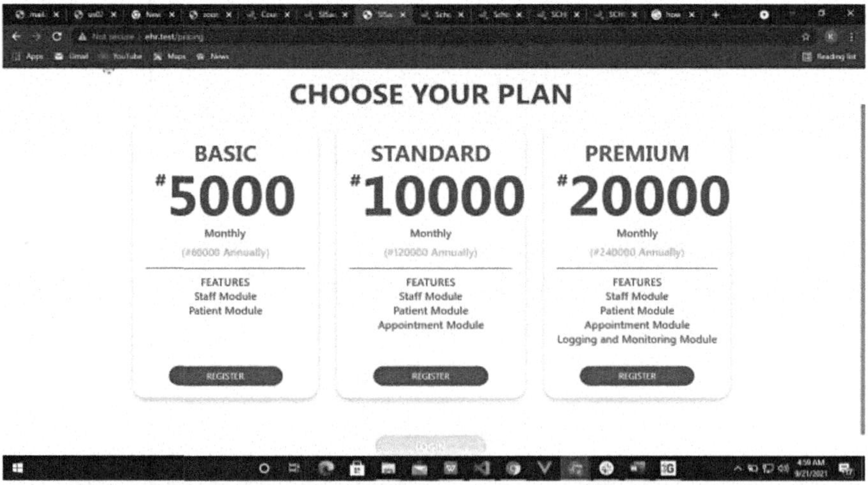

Figure 27.4 Subscription plan pricing.

When a user clicks on the patient module, a drop-down navigation link is displayed (Figure 27.6). The 'add new patient' navigation link will redirect a user to a page where they can register new patient (data) coming to the healthcare center (hospital) for the first time and receive their health card number which will be used to identify them in subsequent visits or appointments. Existing patient information can also be modified and deleted by the tenant (hospital) administrator or user with the necessary access rights and permissions. Figure 27.7 shows the appointment

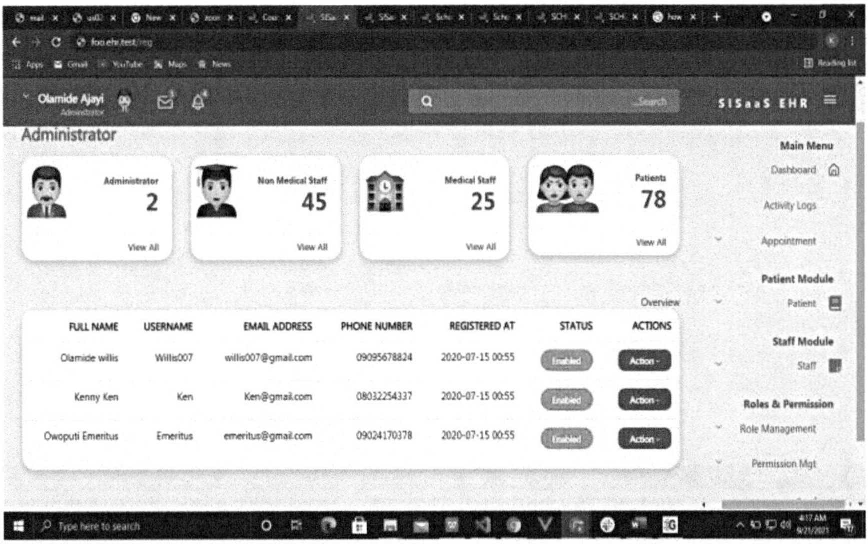

Figure 27.5   The dashboard page.

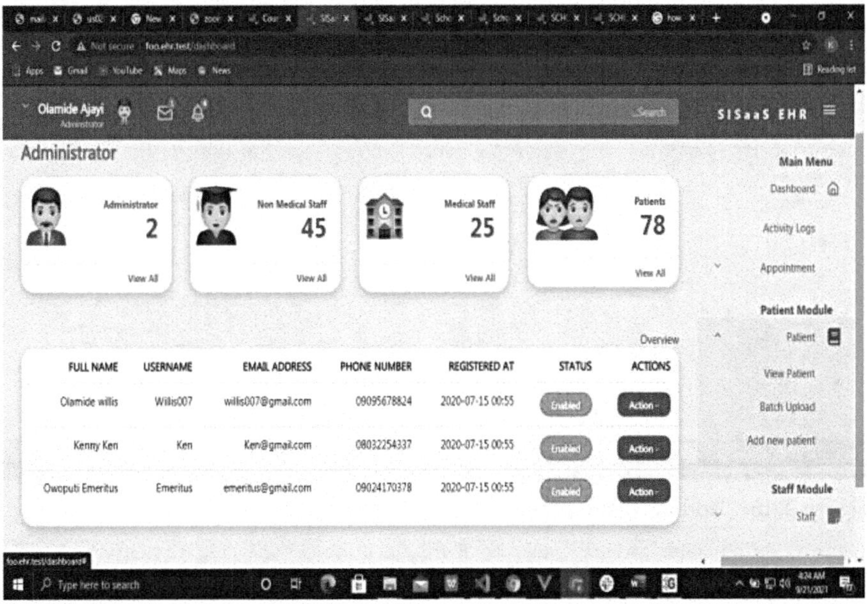

Figure 27.6   Patient module drop-down.

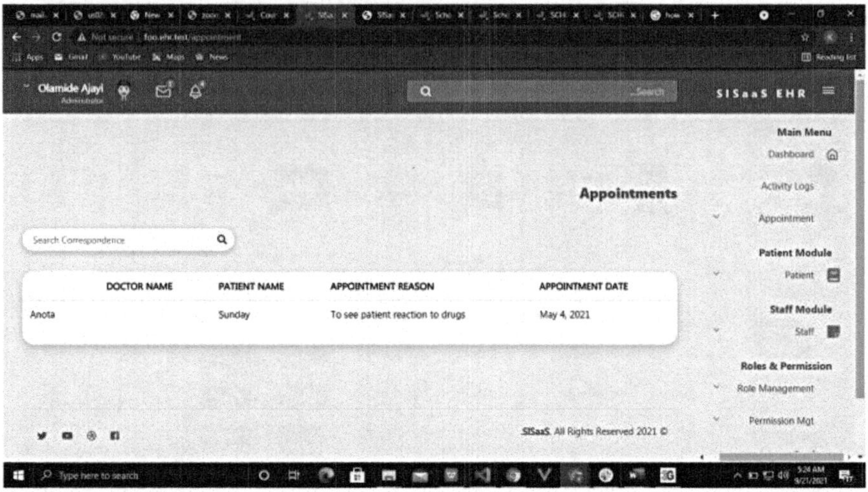

Figure 27.7 Appointment list page.

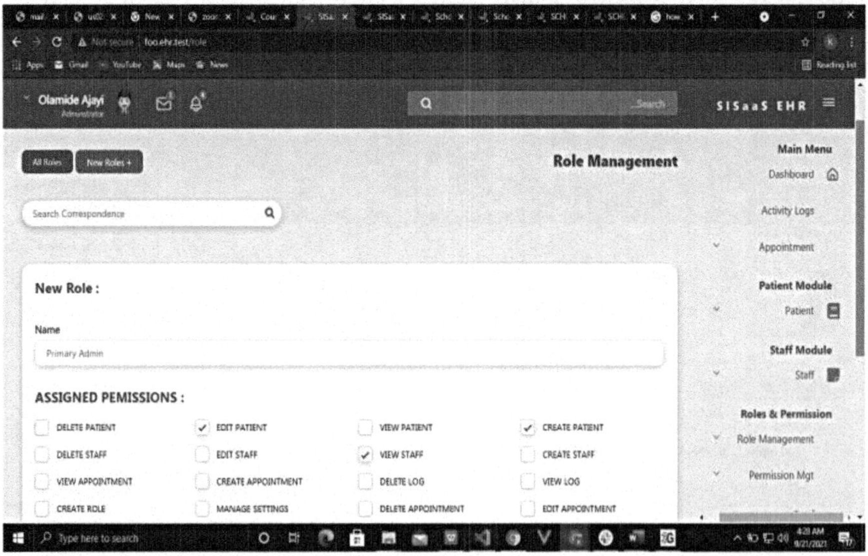

Figure 27.8 Add new role page.

module where administrators can see all pending appointments scheduled by a doctor with their patient. Other functionalities to be managed by the tenant administrator include healthcare center subscription plan, adding new staff records, viewing/updating/deleting existing staff records, managing roles and permissions, assigning new roles and permissions to staff/users, and scheduling a regular backup of their database which can either be daily, weekly or monthly. Figures 27.8 to 27.11 show

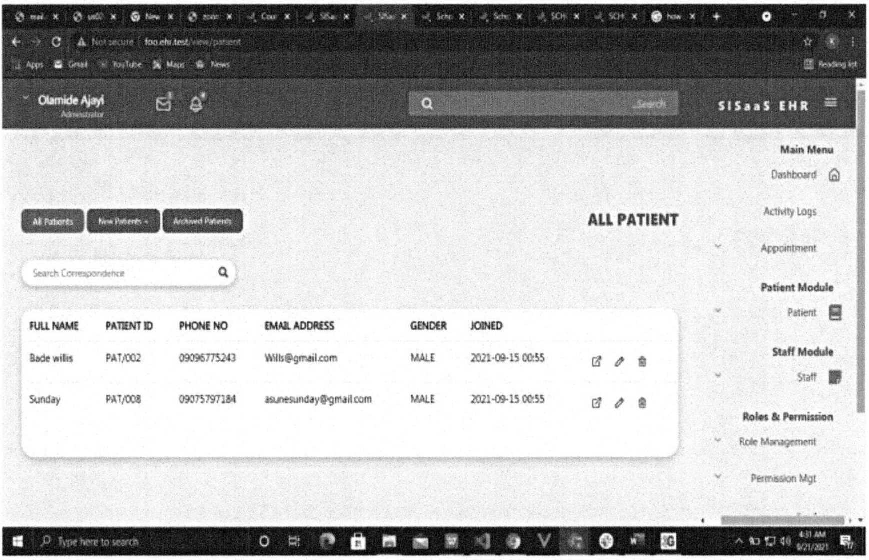

Figure 27.9 Patient list page.

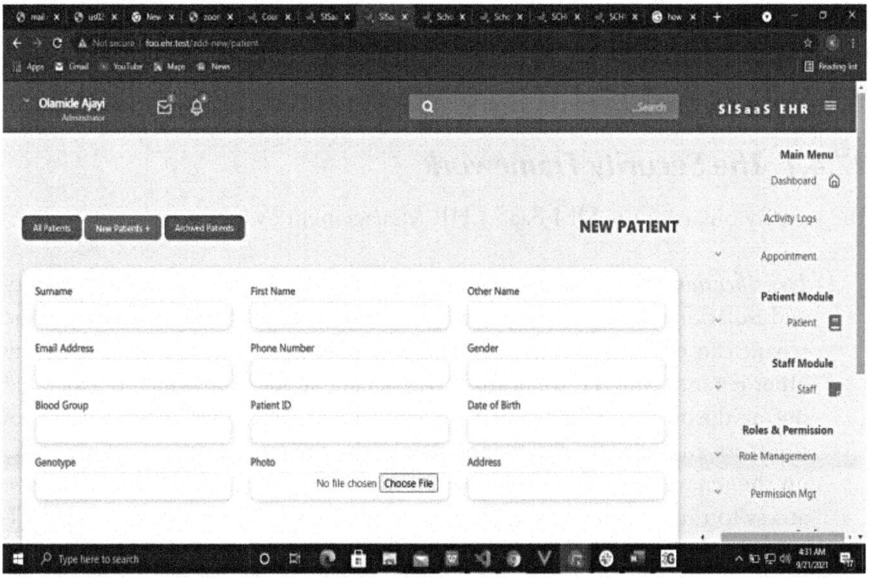

Figure 27.10 Add new patient page.

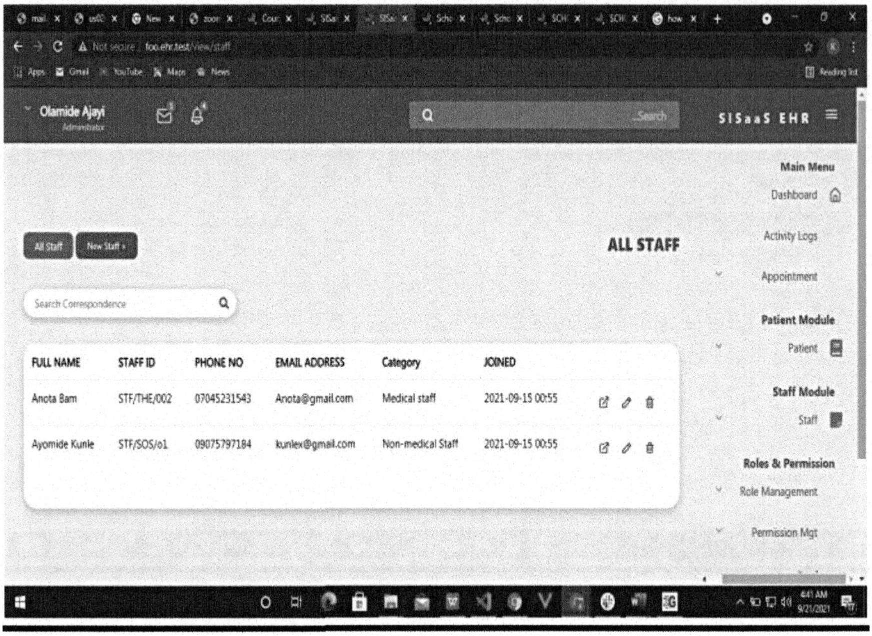

Figure 27.11   Staff list page.

the Add new role page, Patient list page, Add new patient page and Staff list page, respectively.

27.4.1 The Security Framework

The security pillars of the SIM-SaaS-EHR Management System are:

1) *Identification.* This is a very important step for ensuring data confidentiality and isolation among multiple tenants. This is needed to ensure that a specific tenant can only have access to their own data without interfering with any other tenant using the application. The tenant subdomain which is generated during the on-boarding process is used as a tenant identifier. When a user tries to access an instance of the application, the tenant identifier module looks up the tenant identifier ID in the database. If it is found, the user can have access to their customized applications, otherwise a '404-Not found' HTTP response is displayed.

2) *Authentication.* For tenants and application users to have access to dashboard or confidential information. Users are required to log into the application with their staff ID/email and password. To further strengthen system security, as sign-in with username and password is not enough, the user can enable two-factor authentication from their dashboard.

3) *Authorization.* A Role-Based Access Control (RBAC) system is built into this application to ensure that only users with specific roles and permission can have access to protected resources or data.

4) *Logging and Monitoring.* Logging was built into the system to ensure that all errors or exceptions thrown during the use of the application are stored to enable the administrator to keep track of what is working and not working in the system. This application includes a monitoring feature which ensures that all actions carried out on the application and who was responsible for the action are logged into the database. This is done to ensure easy traceability in case of misconduct or falsification of data.

5) *Database backup and recovery.* To ensure accessibility and continuity of information, data are backed up either daily, weekly, or monthly. So, in case of data loss or when the server is down, tenant data can easily be recovered and restored.

6) *Rate Limiter.* This module is used to ensure that no tenant is consuming the cloud resource by sending many requests to the server. The rate limiter module was configured to ensure that, at any point, a user of the system can only send 60 HTTP requests per second.

7) *Encryption.* Sensitive and highly confidential data such as user passwords are not stored in plain text in the database but are encrypted with powerful algorithms.

27.5 Conclusion

The amount of data produced by healthcare providers is growing so fast that it is becoming inefficient to continue storing paper patient health records, but the cost of developing EHRs is very high. Hence only tertiary healthcare providers can afford to invest resources in building such systems. It also takes time, sometimes longer than expected, to develop a full-fledged EHR system. Leveraging the cloud multi-tenancy concept can help provide a large pool of storage and the computing resources needed to run multiple instances of software so that multiple users can use them on a pay-as-you-go or subscription model. Healthcare providers can acquire a fully functioning EHR in a matter of days and focus on how to use the software rather than how to build it. Information can be shared between various healthcare providers, enabling seamless interoperability.

This work shows how to present a separate database-per-tenant storage system, helping to achieve strict data isolation. In future, the secured and interoperable multi-tenant software-as-a-service electronic health record system can be extended to have artificial intelligence (AI) capabilities. In some cases this could reduce the time spent by doctors on drug administration and making appointments. An intelligent system built into the EHR could help suggest appropriate medication after each appointment as well as health and lifestyle advice based on the patient's existing health record.

References

1. A.O. Abdul, J. Bass, H. Ghavimi, N. Macrae and P. Adam (2018). Multi-tenancy design patterns in SaaS applications: A performance evaluation case study. *International Journal of Digital Society (IJDS)*, *9*(1), 1367–1375.
2. R.J. Victor and M. Singh (2018). Security analysis in multi-tenant cloud computing healthcare system. *International Journal of Mechanical Engineering and Technology (IJMET)*, *9*(3), 71–78.
3. A.J. Ikuomola and O. Arowolo (2014). Securing patient privacy in e-health cloud using homomorphic encryption and access control. *International Journal of Computer Networks and Communications Security*, *2*(1), 15–21.
4. A.J. Ikuomola (2015). A secured cloud-based electronic health record system using finger-print biometric and attribute-based encryption. *African Journal of Computing and ICTs*, *8*(2), 171–182.
5. M.B. Alotaibi (2016). Antecedents of software-as-a-service (SaaS) adoption: A structural equation model. *International Journal of Advanced Computer Research*, *6*(25), 114–129. [Online]. Available at https://doi.org/10.19101/ijacr.2016.626019
6. S. Kanade and R. Manza (2019). A comprehensive study on multi tenancy in SAAS applications. *International Journal of Computer Applications*, *181*(44), 25–27. [Online]. Available at https://doi.org/10.5120/ijca2019918531
7. I. Odunayo, M. Sanjay, A. Abayomi-Alli and O. Ajayi (2017). *Cloud Multi-Tenancy: Issues and Developments*. In: UCIoT 2017 Workshop Presentation, Association for Computing Machinery, 209–214. [Online]. Available at https://doi.org/10.1145/3147234.3148095
8. C. Mukundha, M. Kavya, O.S. Reddy and R. Tejaswini (2017). A comprehensive study on multi-tenancy techniques in cloud computing models. *International Journal of Engineering Research and Development*, *13*(9), 59–64.
9. A.A. Abayomi-Alli, A.J. Ikuomola, I.S. Robert and O.O. Abayomi-Alli (2014). An enterprise cloud-based electronic health records system. *Journal of Computer Science and Information Technology*, *2*(2), 21–36.
10. S. Ashwini, A.C. Kumar and S. Bhargavi (2019). Cloud computing based EHR, *International Journal of Recent Technology and Engineering (IJRTE)*, *8*(1C), 202–206.
11. S. Oh, J. Cha, M. Ji, H. Kang, S. Kim, E. Heo, J.S. Han, H. Kan, H. Chae and H. Hwang (2015). Architecture design of healthcare software-as-a-service platform for cloud-based clinical decision support service. *Healthcare Informatics Research*, *21*(2), 102–110.
12. S. Saleh, N. El-Arnaout, L. Abdouni, Z. Jammoul, N. Hachach and A. Dasgupta (2020). Sijilli: A scalable model of cloud-based electronic health records for migrating populations in low-resource settings. *Journal of Medical Internet Research*, *22*(8). [Online]. Available at https://doi.org/10.2196/18183
13. R. Ganiga, R.M. Pai and R.K. Sinha (2020). Security framework for cloud based electronic health record (EHR) system. *International Journal of Electrical and Computer Engineering*, *10*(1), 455–466. [Online]. Available at https://doi.org/10.11591/ijece.v10i1

14. R. Kavitha, E. Kannan and S. Koteeswaran (2016). Implementation of cloud based electronic health record (EHR) for Indian healthcare needs. *Indian Journal of Science and Technology*, *9*(3), 1–5. [Online]. Available at https://doi.org/10.17485/ijst/2016/v9i3/86391

15. R.P. Trivedi and D.S. Vishwavidyalaya (2015). *Multi Tenancy and Customizations Issues in e-Health SaaS Applications*, *4*(November), 266–271.

16. D. Sena, I. Nicholas and A.Y.O. Charles (2011). E-health cloud for Nigerian teaching hospitals. *E-Health Cloud for Nigerian Teaching Hospitals*, *17*(2), 175–178.

Chapter 28

Investigating Classification with Quantum Computing

Muhammad Hamid and Bashir Alam
Jamia Millia Islamia University, New Delhi, India

Om Pal
MeitY, Government of India, New Delhi, India

Shamimul Qamar
King Khalid University, Abha, K.S.A.

28.1 Introduction

It is more than three decades since Richard Feynman simulated computation using quantum properties [1]. Today quantum computers can perform fast computation, whereas classical computers require an extensive amount of time. The potential applications of quantum computers include cryptography, communications, optimization such as route optimization and optimization problems in chemistry, artificial intelligence, and finance. Quantum algorithms such as Shor's algorithm [2] and Grover's algorithm have shown speed-up for factorization for large numbers and searching in unstructured databases, respectively. Quantum computing uses quantum phenomena like supposition, entanglement, and interference to work on information. The smallest unit in quantum computation is qubits, whereas the smallest unit for classical computing is a bit. A bit can be either in 0 or 1 state whereas the

DOI: 10.1201/9781003371380-28

qubit can be in 0 states, 1 state, or in a superposition of 0 and 1 state. Qubits can be represented in Hilbert space as a unit vector. To represent qubits states we use Bra and Ket notation. Let us consider a two-dimensional system with basis states of $|0\rangle$ and $|1\rangle$. State $|0\rangle$ is represented by column matrix $\begin{bmatrix} 1 \\ 0 \end{bmatrix}$ and $|1\rangle$ is represented using $\begin{bmatrix} 0 \\ 1 \end{bmatrix}$. A qubit is the superposition of these two states.

$$|\psi\rangle = \alpha\,|0\rangle + \beta\,|1\rangle \tag{28.1}$$

where α, β are probability amplitudes where $|\alpha|^2 + |\beta|^2 = 1$, if we measure the qubit at any time, we will get either $|0\rangle$ or $|1\rangle$ with the probability of $|\alpha|^2$ and $|\beta|^2$ respectively. In a quantum scenario the qubits can be in combination of all the possible states simultaneously, that is

$$|0\rangle + |1\rangle \tag{28.2}$$

For a two-qubit system, there will be 2^2 possible states

$$|00\rangle + |01\rangle + |10\rangle + |11\rangle \tag{28.3}$$

For n qubit system there will be 2^n possible states

There are many challenges for which quantum computation is the only solution that is useful compared to classical computation. A theory may be present in relation to a certain problem, but due to lack of space and computation speed it is nearly impossible to implement. Therefore, there is a need for a large-scale quantum processor with more reliable quantum devices, the best quantum algorithms, and error-correcting code for fault-tolerant near-term computation. In the last three years, we have witnessed massive growth in the field of quantum computing. Companies like IBM, Google, Microsoft, Amazon, and many more are working on new developments in this discipline. Countries like the USA, Australia, and many European countries are investing a huge amount in research with the intention that it will give a major advantage in technology. The best example of this race is the US National Quantum Initiative Act, which enables a $1.2 billion investment for the next 5 years [3].

28.2 Quantum Computation Background

In classical computing, we operate on bits and use gates to change and manipulate the bits to execute instructions. Similarly, in quantum computing, we do have several single and multiple quantum gates to manipulate the quantum states. Here we are discussing all the important gates for single qubits and multiple qubits (Table 28.1).

Table 28.1 An Overview of Quantum Gates and Their Specifications

Gates	Notation	Matrix	No. of Qubits	Operation
		One Qubit Quantum Gates		
X Gate		$\begin{bmatrix} 0 & 1 \\ 1 & 0 \end{bmatrix}$	1	It "flips" between $\lvert 0 \rangle$ and $\lvert 1 \rangle$
Z Gate	Z	$\begin{bmatrix} 1 & 0 \\ 0 & -1 \end{bmatrix}$	1	It swaps $\lvert + \rangle$ and $\lvert - \rangle$ as well as $\lvert i \rangle$ and $\lvert -i \rangle$. It leaves $\lvert 0 \rangle$ and $\lvert 1 \rangle$ alone
Y Gate	Y	$i\begin{bmatrix} 0 & -1 \\ 1 & 0 \end{bmatrix}$	1	It swaps $\lvert 0 \rangle$ and $\lvert 1 \rangle$ and so is a bit flip. It also swaps $\lvert + \rangle$ and $\lvert - \rangle$ but leaves $\lvert i \rangle$ and $\lvert -i \rangle$ alone.
ID Gate	I	$\begin{bmatrix} 1 & 1 \\ 1 & 1 \end{bmatrix}$	1	**ID** gate does nothing
H Gate	H	$\dfrac{1}{\sqrt{2}}\begin{bmatrix} 1 & 1 \\ 1 & -1 \end{bmatrix}$	1	Hadamard gate puts qubit in superposition states
		Multi Qubits Quantum Gates		
H⊗n Gate	H H	$\dfrac{\sqrt{2}}{2}\begin{bmatrix} 1 & 1 \\ 1 & -1 \end{bmatrix}$	2	It creates superposition

Gate	Symbol	Matrix	Qubits	Description
SWAP Gate		$\begin{bmatrix} 1 & 0 & 0 & 0 \\ 0 & 0 & 1 & 0 \\ 0 & 1 & 0 & 0 \\ 0 & 0 & 0 & 1 \end{bmatrix}$	2	It swaps two qubits states
CNOT/CX Gate		$\begin{bmatrix} 1 & 0 & 0 & 0 \\ 0 & 1 & 0 & 0 \\ 0 & 0 & 0 & 1 \\ 0 & 0 & 1 & 0 \end{bmatrix}$	2	It is used to create entangled qubits
Toffoli CCNOT Gate		$\begin{bmatrix} 1 & 0 & 0 & 0 & 0 & 0 & 0 & 0 \\ 0 & 1 & 0 & 0 & 0 & 0 & 0 & 0 \\ 0 & 0 & 1 & 0 & 0 & 0 & 0 & 0 \\ 0 & 0 & 0 & 1 & 0 & 0 & 0 & 0 \\ 0 & 0 & 0 & 0 & 1 & 0 & 0 & 0 \\ 0 & 0 & 0 & 0 & 0 & 1 & 0 & 0 \\ 0 & 0 & 0 & 0 & 0 & 0 & 0 & 1 \\ 0 & 0 & 0 & 0 & 0 & 0 & 1 & 0 \end{bmatrix}$	3	CCNOT flip target quantum bits if both control qubits are one

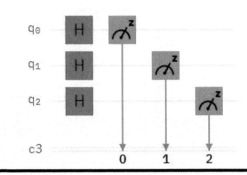

Figure 28.1   Quantum circuit for random bits generator.

28.2.1 Circuits and Measurements

Figure 28.1 represents a typical quantum circuit where some gates are applied to qubits and their results are measured to get the values. In this circuit, we have three qubits and Hadamard gates applied to it. This gate puts qubits in superposition states which means now qubits can have values 0 and 1 simultaneously; after measurements the qubits collapse to either 0 or 1. We can see results in classical register c. If we measure the basis state of $|0\rangle$ we obtain binary value 0 and if we measure the basis state $|1\rangle$ we obtain binary value 1.

28.3 Quantum Machine Learning

The combination of quantum information theory and machine learning generates a new discipline known as quantum machine learning (QML). Lloyd et al. [4] first introduced the term quantum machine learning. This field is very promising in achieving an improved performance speed over classical machine learning. Since then, an enormous increment can be seen in the number of scientific publications from the research community. QML algorithms can be studied in several groups.

The first one is classical-classical (CC), in which the quantum-like data is being processed and the algorithm executed on classical computers [5]. The second approach is classical-quantum (CQ). It is the most explored method so far for implementing machine learning. In this approach, we translate the machine learning process into quantum computation. Wittek [6], Schuld [7], Schuld, and Petruccione [8] argue that two different approaches are used in QML: 1) translation of machine learning algorithm into a quantum algorithm; and 2) application of quantum algorithms to machine learning problems. This method requires preprocessing of data, i.e., encoding of data into quantum data. There are several ways of encoding: basis encoding, amplitude encoding, product encoding, angle encoding, encoding with quantum feature map, Hamiltonian encoding. Other techniques include dynamic encoding, phase encoding, qsample encoding, squeezing encoding, and displacement encoding [9]. The performance of the encoding technique depends on the chosen dataset. In the CQ approach we analyze the quantum system using classical machine learning methods. The final approach, quantum-quantum, uses quantum algorithms to analyze quantum data. The data need not be encoded.

28.3.1 Quantum Encoding

In general, implementing a quantum algorithm requires three major steps: (i) encoding the data, (ii) a quantum computation that uses a quantum circuit and (iii) the decoding of quantum results into classical data. Classical data needs encoding into a quantum state before working with it. There are various ways of doing this, basis and amplitude encoding being the most common techniques [4–6].

1) *Basis Encoding.* In this encoding technique, the same binary string is encoded into a quantum computational basis state. Let's say we have binary string 101, which becomes encoded as quantum state $|\psi\rangle = |101\rangle$. This practice is a little bit costly because we require n qubits to encode n bit information. The mathematical representation of basis encoding is as follows.

$$D\rangle = \frac{1}{\sqrt{M}} \sum_{m=1}^{M} |X^m\rangle \tag{28.4}$$

where D is an element of data set in binary forms.

2) *Amplitude Encoding.* This is quite different from other encoding methods. In this method, a normalized input vector is encoded with the amplitude of quantum states. For example, we have a two-dimensional vector $\begin{bmatrix} 0.3 \\ 0.5 \end{bmatrix}$ which can be represented in the quantum state as $\psi\rangle = 0.3|0\rangle + 0.5|1\rangle$. Using n qubits 2^n bit of information can represented. In general, it is the most commonly used encoding technique among researchers. To represent classical data into quantum amplitude we must convert the data vector into a normalized data vector.

$$X = \begin{bmatrix} x_1 \\ x_2 \\ . \\ . \\ x_{2^n} \end{bmatrix} \tag{28.5}$$

Here, X is a normalized data vector and x are in complex number. And quantum amplitude can be encoded in the following way.

$$|\psi_x\rangle = \sum_{i=1}^{2^n-1} x_i \, |i\rangle \qquad (28.6)$$

where $|\psi\rangle$ is Hilbert space and $\sum_i |x_i|^2 = 1$

28.4 Literature Review

In recent years many different approaches and algorithms have been developed in quantum-enhanced machine learning to overcome the failures of classical machine learning. The quantum version of support vector machine [10] shows logarithmic speed-up over its classical counterpart. Sergioli et al. [11] achieved speed-up using the binary quantum classifier. Havlicek et al. [12] used a variational quantum circuit to design a hybrid classifier. Nowadays there are many models in quantum neural networks (QNNs) like quantum neurons [13], gate model quantum neural networks [14], quantum multi-perceptron NN [15], QCNN [16], and QDNN [17, 18].

Mostly the kernel method is used for classification with QNN. Changpeng Shao et al. proposed a kernel method to design QNN [19]. Lloyd and Weedbrook worked with a quantum generative adversarial network [20]. Havlicek et al. [12] use the quantum variational classifier for classification problems. Schuld et al. [21] used a nonlinear feature map for mapping quantum feature space with the data and proposed two models for classification. In their paper Montanaro et al. [22] present an overview of quantum algorithms and discussed applications. Jeswal et al. [23] discussed QNNs and their application for machine learning, showing that the quantum version of a neural network is more powerful and advanced than a classical neural network. Benedetti et al. [14] presented a review of a parametrized quantum circuit, a hybrid-quantum classical machine learning model for supervised and unsupervised learning.

This paper also gives information about circuits used in the encoder and variational quantum circuit. Riccardo Mengoni et al. [24] discussed the kernel method of machine learning for NISQ (noisy intermediate-scale quantum) devices. Giuseppe Sergioli [5] summarizes the differences and advantages between QML and quantum-inspired machine learning. Its shows that the recent version of QiML is more robust and easier to implement on a classical computer. On the other hand, QML is preferable to NQiML in terms of computation complexity. Viraj Kulkarni et al. [25] presented a study of the quantum version of KNN and support vector machine. Frank Phillipson [26] discusses the benefits and practical uses of QML in terms of improvement in capacity, improvement in learning, and improvement in runtime. For the improvement in runtime, he advocates for a quantum hybrid Helmholtz machine, quantum Hopfield neural network, and quantum variational circuit for capacity and learning improvement respectively. Michael Broughton et al. [27] proposed an open-source library for a hybrid-quantum-classical model which supports quantum simulation and facilitates the design and training of models. Table 28.2 illustrates recent research for classification.

Table 28.2 An Illustration of An Experiment Carried Out Using Quantum Machine Learning

Research	Algorithm	Learning	Data Set	Task
Vojtech Havlicek et al. [12]	VQC and quantum kernel	Supervised	Artificial data	Classification
Iordanis Kerenidis et al. [16]	Quantum CNN	Supervised	MNIST	Classification
Junhua Liu et al. [28]	Hybrid QCCNN	Supervised	TETRIS	Classification
Ji Guan et al. [29]	Quantum CNN	Supervised	MNIST	Classification
Teppei Suzuki et al. [30]	VQC	Supervised	221 PHENOLS	Classification
Song Cheng et al. [31]	Tree tensor network	Supervised	MNIST	Classification
D. Lazarev et al. [32]	Self-organizing feature map	Unsupervised	MNIST	Clustering
Sebastien Piat et al. [33]	Quantum-RBM	Supervised	MNIST, X-ray	Classification
Yijie Dang et al. [34]	Quantum KNN	Supervised	Caltech-101	Classification
Sheir Yarkoni et al. [35]	QUBO	Semi-Supervised	Time Serie	Classification
Soumik Adhikary et al. [36]	VQC, quantum feature space	Supervised	CANCER	Classification
Jiaying Yang et al. [37]	Quantum SVM	Supervised	OCR, IRIS	Classification
Asel Sagingalieva, et.al [38]	Hybrid QNN	Supervised	CAR	Classification
Guangxi Li et. al. [39]	QSANN	Supervised	IMDb, Amazon	Classification
Oleksandr et al. [40]	OC-SVM	Unsupervised	Credit card	Classification

QDNN = quantum deep neural network, QCNN = quantum convolutional neural network, QCCNN = quantum-classical convolutional neural network, QKNN = quantum K-nearest-neighbor, QUBO = quadratic unconstrained binary optimization, QSVM = quantum support vector machine.

QSANN = quantum self-attention neural network, OC-SVM = one-class support vector machine.

28.5 Quantum Machine Learning Algorithms

In general, machine learning algorithms work on a training set that consists of instances with the labels in supervised learning. The algorithms draw a model and learn from the patterns of a dataset, then this model can be used to process unseen data and predict their label. Quantum support vector machine and quantum K-nearest neighbor take O (log (MN)) whereas a classical algorithm requires O(MN). Quantum neural network uses linear algebra heavily and the randomness property of quantum mechanics can be used in the training process to make the model more robust. Some of them are introduced to solve different task that include supervised, unsupervised, and reinforcement learning. There are two disciplines in QML: quantum-enhanced machine learning which deals with techniques and methods to train quantum computers using classical data; and the training of quantum computers using quantum data. Currently, researchers are working on both fronts. Here we are talking about only quantum-enhanced machine learning. For work on quantum generalizations, readers are directed to ref. [41–44]. Quantum computing principles have opened doors for classical randomized algorithms which have exponential speed-up in comparison with traditional algorithms [14]. Another method of solving the QML problem is the use of parametrized or variation quantum circuits [36, 45, 46]. In this approach, several optimized quantum gates with parameters are used. Commonly these gates consist of a combination of rotation gates: R_x, R_y, R_z, and CNOT gates. This quantum circuit can be used to find the cost function of the model. For a good machine learning model, it should be minimal. We use a classical computer for parameter tuning. The optimized circuit is used for classification (Figure 28.2).

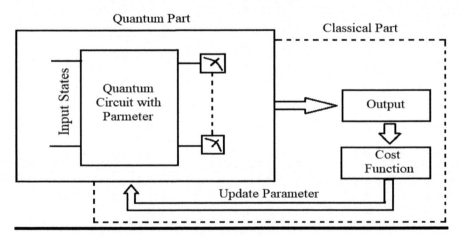

Figure 28.2 Schematic illustration of variational quantum circuit.

Generally, VQC can be written as:

$$U(\theta)|\psi\rangle = \prod_{i=1}^{n} U_i |\psi\rangle$$

where $U(\theta)$ is universal gates with θ as a parameter, n is the number of total gates, and $|\psi\rangle$ is input quantum states. By changing parameters θ, the operation of U can be modified. The stochastic gradient descent approach is used to optimize parameters; it also helps avoid barren plateaus. Farhi et al. [47] proposed a VQC for binary classification which includes a series of unitary gate operations. Meinhardt et al. [48] present this framework with more details.

28.6 Challenges and Future Scope

The number of qubits is growing rapidly but at present we face a huge challenge to build a quantum computer with greater volume and many qubits. For now, the number of qubits is restricted to a small amount of data. We need more robust encoding techniques to work with machine learning processes. Nonlinear feature maps which map data to quantum data are also required. Compression of an image then encoding can reduce the effort of encoding quantum data, which requires a smaller amount of qubits to encode images and other techniques to improve robustness.

More advanced theoretical and new applied machine learning algorithms are able to work with a smaller number of qubits. NQiML, quantum-enhanced machine learning, quantum neural networks and quantum deep learning models are examples of such disciplines. Quantum parametric circuits are nowadays more popular for classification which sometimes requires larger quantum circuits, reducing the depth of quantum circuits is a new field of research. QML can be used in solving optimization problems. QML is superior to classical ML in the classification of big data, spam filtering series forecasting, and medical imaging. Besides image classification, QML is useful in recommendation systems, natural language processing (NLP), speech recognition, drug design, and discovery. QML can also be used in signal processing and electronic calculations, and a hybrid classical-quantum model is useful for job scheduling.

28.7 Conclusion

This chapter presents a survey of the most recent research for classification problems using quantum machine learning. The preference for selecting QML over traditional ML is its performance and speed-up. Near-term intermediate quantum systems require robust quantum algorithms to work with a small number of qubits. As the depth of circuit increases, so too does the noise in the result. Shorter quantum circuits and better quantum encoding techniques can improve the performance of quantum algorithms. The hybrid quantum-classical model is used widely for classification tasks. This study shows that quantum versions of existing classical machine learning algorithms are being developed. QSVM, Q KNN, Q K-means and quantum-restricted Boltzmann machine are the best examples of such algorithms. These quantum algorithms can be used to classify real data from healthcare, transport, finance, and manufacturing industry.

References

1. Feynman, Richard P. "Quantum mechanical computers." *Optics News* 11, no. 2 (1985): 11–20.
2. Shor, Peter W. "Polynomial-time algorithms for prime factorization and discrete logarithms on a quantum computer." *SIAM Review* 41, no. 2 (1999): 303–332.
3. Smith, L. (2018) H.R.6227–115th congress (2017–2018): National Quantum Initiative Act. Dec 21, 2018. https://www.congress.gov/bill/115th-congress/housebill/6227
4. Lloyd, Seth, Masoud Mohseni, and Patrick Rebentrost. "Quantum algorithms for supervised and unsupervised machine learning." *arXiv preprint arXiv:1307.0411* (2013).
5. Sergioli, Giuseppe. "Quantum and quantum-like machine learning: A note on differences and similarities." *Soft Computing* 24, no. 14 (2020): 10247–10255.
6. Wittek, Peter. *Quantum machine learning: What quantum computing means to data mining.* Academic Press, 2014.
7. Schuld, Maria, Alex Bocharov, Krysta M. Svore, and Nathan Wiebe. "Circuit-centric quantum classifiers." *Physical Review A* 101, no. 3 (2020): 032308.
8. Schuld, Maria, Ilya Sinayskiy, and Francesco Petruccione. "An introduction to quantum machine learning." *Contemporary Physics* 56, no. 2 (2015): 172–185.
9. Schuld, Maria, and Francesco Petruccione. *Supervised learning with quantum computers.* Vol. 17. Berlin: Springer, 2018.
10. Rebentrost, Patrick, Masoud Mohseni, and Seth Lloyd. "Quantum support vector machine for big data classification." *Physical Review Letters* 113, no. 13 (2014): 130503.
11. Sergioli, Giuseppe, Roberto Giuntini, and Hector Freytes. "A new quantum approach to binary classification." *PloS One* 14, no. 5 (2019): e0216224.
12. Havlíček, Vojtěch, Antonio D. Córcoles, Kristan Temme, Aram W. Harrow, Abhinav Kandala, Jerry M. Chow, and Jay M. Gambetta. "Supervised learning with quantum-enhanced feature spaces." *Nature* 567, no. 7747 (2019): 209–212.
13. Sagheer, Alaa, Mohammed Zidan, and Mohammed M. Abdelsamea. "A novel autonomous perceptron model for pattern classification applications." *Entropy* 21, no. 8 (2019): 763.
14. Benedetti, Marcello, Erika Lloyd, Stefan Sack, and Mattia Fiorentini. "Parameterized quantum circuits as machine learning models." *Quantum Science and Technology* 4, no. 4 (2019): 04300.
15. Pronin, Cesar Borisovich, and Andrey Vladimirovich Ostroukh. "Development of quantum circuits for perceptron neural network training, based on the principles of Grover's algorithm." *arXiv preprint arXiv:2110.09891* (2021).

16. Kerenidis, Iordanis, Jonas Landman, and Anupam Prakash. "Quantum algorithms for deep convolutional neural networks." *arXiv preprint arXiv:1911.01117* (2019).

17. Li, YaoChong, Ri-Gui Zhou, RuQing Xu, Jia Luo, and WenWen Hu. "A quantum deep convolutional neural network for image recognition." *Quantum Science and Technology* 5, no. 4 (2020): 044003.

18. Zhao, Chen, and Xiao-Shan Gao. "QDNN: DNN with quantum neural network layers." *arXiv preprint arXiv:1912.12660* (2019).

19. Shao, Changpeng. "A simple approach to design quantum neural networks and its applications to Kernel-learning methods." *arXiv preprint arXiv:1910.08798* (2019).

20. Lloyd, Seth, and Christian Weedbrook. "Quantum generative adversarial learning." *Physical Review Letters* 121, no. 4 (2018): 040502.

21. Schuld, Maria, and Nathan Killoran. "Quantum machine learning in feature Hilbert spaces." *Physical Review Letters* 122, no. 4 (2019): 040504.

22. Montanaro, Ashley. "Quantum algorithms: An overview." *npj Quantum Information* 2, no. 1 (2016): 1–8.

23. Jeswal, S. K., and S. Chakraverty. "Recent developments and applications in quantum neural network: A review." *Archives of Computational Methods in Engineering* 26, no. 4 (2019): 793–807.

24. Mengoni, Riccardo, and Alessandra Di Pierro. "Kernel methods in quantum machine learning." *Quantum Machine Intelligence* 1, no. 3 (2019): 65–71.

25. Kulkarni, Viraj, Milind Kulkarni, and Aniruddha Pant. "Quantum computing methods for supervised learning." *Quantum Machine Intelligence* 3, no. 2 (2021): 1–14.

26. Phillipson, Frank. "Quantum machine learning: Benefits and practical examples." In *QANSWER*, pp. 51–56, 2020.

27. Broughton, Michael, Guillaume Verdon, Trevor McCourt, Antonio J. Martinez, Jae Hyeon Yoo, Sergei V. Isakov, Philip Massey et al." Tensorflow quantum: A software framework for quantum machine learning." *arXiv preprint arXiv:2003.02989* (2020).

28. Liu, Junhua, Kwan Hui Lim, Kristin L. Wood, Wei Huang, Chu Guo, and He-Liang Huang. "Hybrid quantum-classical convolutional neural networks." *Science China Physics, Mechanics & Astronomy* 64, no. 9 (2021): 1–8.

29. Guan, Ji, Wang Fang, and Mingsheng Ying. "Robustness verification of quantum classifiers." In *International Conference on Computer Aided Verification*, pp. 151–174. Springer, Cham, 2021.

30. Suzuki, Teppei, and Michio Katouda. "Predicting toxicity by quantum machine learning." *Journal of Physics Communications* 4, no. 12 (2020): 125012.

31. Cheng, Song, Lei Wang, Tao Xiang, and Pan Zhang. "Tree tensor networks for generative modeling." *Physical Review B* 99, no. 15 (2019): 155131.

32. Lazarev, Ilia D., Marek Narozniak, Tim Byrnes, and Alexey N. Pyrkov. "Hybrid quantum-classical unsupervised data clustering based on the Self-Organizing Feature Map." *arXiv preprint arXiv:2009.09246* (2020).

33. Piat, Sebastien, Nairi Usher, Simone Severini, Mark Herbster, Tommaso Mansi, and Peter Mountney. "Image classification with quantum pre-training and auto-encoders." *International Journal of Quantum Information* 16, no. 08 (2018): 1840009.

34. Dang, Yijie, Nan Jiang, Hao Hu, Zhuoxiao Ji, and Wenyin Zhang. "Image classification based on quantum K-Nearest-Neighbor algorithm." *Quantum Information Processing* 17, no. 9 (2018): 1–18.

35. Yarkoni, Sheir, Andrii Kleshchonok, Yury Dzerin, Florian Neukart, and Marc Hilbert. "Semi-supervised time series classification method for quantum computing." *Quantum Machine Intelligence* 3, no. 1 (2021): 1–11.

36. Adhikary, Soumik, Siddharth Dangwal, and Debanjan Bhowmik. "Supervised learning with a quantum classifier using multi-level systems." *Quantum Information Processing* 19, no. 3 (2020): 1–12.

37. Yang, Jiaying, Ahsan Javed Awan, and Gemma Vall-Llosera. "Support vector machines on noisy intermediate scale quantum computers." *arXiv preprint arXiv:1909.11988* (2019).

38. Sagingalieva, Asel, Andrii Kurkin, Artem Melnikov, Daniil Kuhmistrov, Michael Perelshtein, Alexey Melnikov, Andrea Skolik, and David Von Dollen. "Hyperparameter optimization of hybrid quantum neural networks for car classification." *arXiv preprint arXiv:2205.04878* (2022).

39. Li, Guangxi, Xuanqiang Zhao, and Xin Wang. "Quantum self attention neural networks for text classification." *arXiv preprint arXiv:2205.05625* (2022).

40. Kyriienko, Oleksandr, and Einar B. Magnusson. "Unsupervised quantum machine learning for fraud detection." *arXiv preprint arXiv:2208.01203* (2022).

41. Rebentrost, Patrick, Thomas R. Bromley, Christian Weedbrook, and Seth Lloyd. "Quantum Hopfield neural network." *Physical Review A* 98, no. 4 (2018): 042308.

42. Preskill, John. "Quantum computing in the NISQ era and beyond." *Quantum* 2 (2018): 79.

43. Behrman, Elizabeth C., L. R. Nash, James Edward Steck, V. G. Chandrashekar, and Steven R. Skinner. "Simulations of quantum neural networks." *Information Sciences* 128, no. 3–4 (2000): 257–269.

44. Biamonte, Jacob, Peter Wittek, Nicola Pancotti, Patrick Rebentrost, Nathan Wiebe, and Seth Lloyd. "Quantum machine learning." *Nature* 549, no. 7671 (2017): 195–202.

45. Paquet, Eric, and Farzan Soleymani. "QuantumLeap: Hybrid quantum neural network for financial predictions." *Expert Systems with Applications* 195 (2022): 116583.

46. Cappelletti, William, Rebecca Erbanni, and Joaquín Keller. "Polyadic quantum classifier." In *2020 IEEE International Conference on Quantum Computing and Engineering (QCE)*, pp. 22–29. IEEE, 2020.

47. Farhi, Edward, and Hartmut Neven. "Classification with quantum neural networks on near term processors." *arXiv preprint arXiv:1802.06002* (2018).

48. Meinhardt, Nicholas, Bastiaan Dekker, Niels MP Neumann, and Frank Phillipson. "Implementation of a variational quantum circuit for machine learning with compact data representation." *Digitale Welt* 4, no. 1 (2020): 95–101.

Chapter 29

A Comprehensive Analysis of Techniques Offering Dynamic Group Management in a Cloud Computing Environment

Pranav Shrivastava, Bashir Alam, and Mansaf Alam

JMI, New Delhi India

29.1 Introduction

The computing industry has been significantly changed by the latest enhancements in cloud computing technology, which have provided companies with the capability to procure desired computing assets from a cloud service provider (CSP) [1, 2]. For example, Amazon EC2 is exploiting the innovative technology as an alternative to establishing and handling their own individual computing environment, which is generally uneconomical compared to equivalent cloud services [3, 4]. This expenditure saving may enable investment to enhance organizations' primary productivity and competitiveness [5, 6]. Several organizations and businesses have recently adopted the cloud computing paradigm owing to these benefits.

In the cloud computing concept, a concurrent collection of systems, amalgamated in public or private networks, provides an expendable and dynamic framework for applications, filing and storing data. Cloud computing considerably reduces the expenses of computing, application hosting, data storage and delivery. It is an uncomplicated and exceptionally straightforward way of reusing IT resources. Cloud computing is able to extend its potential across the boundaries of an organization, in contrast to conventional perceptions of "grid computing", "autonomic computing", "utility computing", or "distributed computing".

Forrester [58] characterizes cloud computing as resembling: "A pool of abstracted, highly scalable, and managed compute infrastructure capable of hosting end-customer applications and billed by consumption."

For an organization, conversion from a personal computing setup to a cloud computing environment provides massive financial benefits. At the same time, it introduces a critical security concern: that entire organization's data including confidential information is available to another organization [7]. Stored information might be exposed during an attack on the cloud server [8]. Another significant issue is data leakage and confidentiality violation by CSPs [9]. To facilitate adoption of the cloud computing model for an extensive assortment of applications, it is therefore essential for cloud systems to ensure and warrant that they can safeguard information secrecy.

Buyya et al. [27] summarize the numerous security challenges related to interconnected cloud environments. They emphasize the following as the main parameters of security in relation to cloud computing; trust, identity management and authorization, semantic interoperability, and federated policy. While research has been done previously in the area of dynamic group management for efficient user revocation and secure data sharing, there is an absence of research on systems with minimal user overheads and efficient user revocation. This study aims to examine the model efficiently in the following terms:

a) Systems management overheads should be minimal during data sharing.
b) There should be protected data sharing in the cloud computing setup.
c) When group membership changes, the minimum encryption keys should be affected.

29.2 Existing Solutions Based on Encryption Mechanisms

Blaze et al. (BBS) [10] recommended atomic proxy re-encryption in 1998. In this method a partially reliable proxy translates an encrypted message for Alice into an encrypted message for Bob without comprehending the original plaintext. The considerable security risks associated with BBS have hindered its widespread adoption. Proxy re-encryption (PRE) was pioneered for managing issues associated with secure group information sharing in a cloud setup [10, 11].

Hohenberger et al. [12] developed PRE schemes intended to secure distributed storage. The data creator uses symmetric data keys to encrypt data, and re-encrypts with a master public key. If any other users require data, PRE is exercised by the server to precisely encrypt the appropriate data key to the user's public key from the master public key. However, there is a critical side effect. In the case of Alice creating a re-encryption key in favor of Bob, every message encoded using Alice's private key incorporating formerly produced and upcoming cipher text could be re-encoded by the re-encoding key, known as abuse of re-encoding key. Collusion attacks can also occur in this scheme, that is, with the help of a semi-faithful server, a revoked malevolent abuser can ascertain the decryption keys of the entire encoded blocks.

For handling issues faced earlier, CPRE (conditional proxy re-encryption) was presented [13, 14]. In this, User A fabricates re-encoding keys (single key in favor of every group member) over and above encoded messages, comprising a specific conditional value *w* (in favor of the entire group). Then, User A utilizes *w* and his private key for encoding the messages. Simultaneously, User A generates a re-encoding key in favor of every member, utilizing *w* and member's public key. Subsequently, similarly to PRE method, the encoded message, *w*, and re-encoding keys are communicated to the cloud storage for re-encoding and distribution of messages. In case of amendments to membership, User A chooses another novel condition value w_0 and replicates the procedure for all existing messages in cloud storage in addition to the new messages. In this way, every revoked member is unable to retrieve the latest messages, and new members are unable to comprehend old messages.

Son et al. [15] argued that in a large group and with the frequent changes in membership, CPRE can experience a critical efficiency drawback, for the reason that on every occasion of change in membership, the data originator generates a new re-encoding key in favor of every group member and messages stored in the cloud need to be encoded once more by means of the fresh condition value. They suggested an E-CPRE (efficient CPRE) to reduce operational costs. In this new method they proposed that in case of a change in group membership, the user intending to upload new data is required to choose a fresh condition value and communicate it to the cloud server, mitigating the obligation of creating and uploading the re-encoding keys in favor of existing members. As the extra work for the user to generate new encoding keys and to store them in the cloud is mitigated, the ECPRE mechanism is more efficient than the existing CPRE. However, they both necessitate encrypting messages stored in the cloud by exercising the fresh condition value and storing them again. Therefore, both are incompetent and uneconomical for securing big data in a cloud setup.

Son et al. [16] developed a novel CPRE identified as an O-CPRE (outsourcing CPRE) procedure, which significantly moderates user overhead. In O-CPRE the only originator requirement is to decide on a fresh condition value and store that on the cloud, in case of a change in group membership. Accordingly, O-CPRE is ideally suited to securing a cloud setup for big data, compared with existing methods.

But this system suffers from traffic bottlenecks which may occur at the outsourcing server [23].

In ref. [17] Zheng et al proposed an identity-based encryption (IBE) procedure in which a single user performs data encryption, and then the user realizes a receiver identity, so they may communicate the encoded information to the receiver. This IBE procedure does not function in practical applications where the sender is not acquainted with the exact identity of a user.

Sahai et al. [18] proposed attribute-based encryption (ABE) which utilizes an attribute like an encryption feature which permits an individual user in possession of a confidential key to an attribute to decode a ciphertext. Here, for each user, Alice designates an attribute value, designs an attribute policy and produces cipher text which emulates the policy. This procedure encompasses a benefit that helps Alice to categorize sharing objects centered on attribute values. However, it cannot exploit the cloud's operational potential, so system performance is not improved. Additionally, attribute policy needs to be renewed as membership modifies.

Lu et al. [20] designed a safe provenance method that depends on group signatures and ciphertext policy attribute-based encryption (CP-ABE). The group is created by means of a sole attribute and post-registration every client acquires a set of keys: an attribute key and a group signature key. As a result, every client is enabled to encode information by means of ABE and other group members may decode information with the attribute keys. In the interim, clients re-encrypt encoded data using the group signature key in support of upholding traceability and privacy.

Yu et al. [19] designed an extensible and fine-grained information access control procedure based on key policy attribute-based encryption (KP-ABE). The data creator utilizes an arbitrary key to encrypt information, then an attributes suite using KP-ABE is exercised to encode the arbitrary key. Subsequently, the manager of the group delegates an access policy and corresponding undisclosed key to validated users, to facilitate decryption of ciphertext as long as the data attributes comply with the access policy. ABE also suffers from the open problem of user revocation; it is also inappropriate for cloud computing as it inflicts more computational overheads on the client who is then unable to profit from cloud resources.

Zheng et al. [20] proposed an identity-based encryption (IBE) scheme that facilitates an individual user to encode information, and then the user asserts the receiver's identity so he may communicate the encoded information to the receiver. Liang et al. [21] designed IB-PRE (identity-based PRE) which suffers from the same problem as IBE. Gujar et al. [22] proposed an RBAC-based scheme for multiple cloud environments. Banu et al. [23] proposed AFS for untrusted cloud storage using data deduplication. Salagar et al. [24] utilized accessible techniques for retrieving fine-grain data access control of key policy attribute that establishes "encryption, proxy re-encryption and lazy re-encryption" and further employs ECC for mitigating the key size used. Pabitha et al. [25] exploited the concept of genetic programming to propose a technique based on PRE.

Jiang et al. [29] designed an auditing procedure centered on scheme vector commitment, group signatures with member revocation and asymmetric group key agreement (AGKA). This amalgamation of primitives facilitates the designed procedure for outsourcing ciphertext database to remote cloud and assists the securing of user revocations for sharing dynamic data. Examination of the security of this procedure demonstrated that group users' data confidentiality was provided for, and it was, moreover, secure against collusion attacks. The procedure was also more efficient than other relevant schemes in different phases of the performance analysis.

Hwang et al. [28] established that in services offered by cloud storage, a crucial concern is data integrity of remote verification. The idea of public audit is capable of solving remote verification of data integrity and extending to verification of shared data. They list and analyze the four representative approaches to public auditing and state that in future research they will focus on the following:

1. *Efficiency* as users demand elevated performance; the system should satisfy an impressive procedure for reducing computing resources, which should additionally support dynamic data, user revocation, and public audit.
2. *Security* because the public auditing must also take into account confidentiality of data along with data integrity.
3. *Data recovery*, as the client stores information on the cloud server before the user deletes data, resulting in a reduction in the user's storage space.

29.3 Kerberos-Based Solutions

Kaffel et al. [30] conducted an extensive survey on the latest developments in access control systems [35–45]. They identified four categories – token-based, role-based, encryption-based, and trust-based access control – and categorized the access models, which demonstrated that the majority of the systems were developed keeping in mind their explicit application domain focusing on either data or resources. After analyzing the various models they anticipated a single sign-on (SSO) system established on Kerberos for access control in favor of the cloud environment.

They identified the following requirements for access control systems based on cloud models:

1. *Scalability.* An increasing number of users must be supported without affecting access control and policy evaluation mechanisms [37].
2. *Authentication and trust.* Strong and reliable user authentication mechanisms are needed in cloud-based access control models [38]. CSPs and users must establish mutual trust relationships, containing well-defined behavioral trust policies [39].

3. *Heterogeneity and interoperability.* The diversity of procedures and technologies employed for delivering services by CSPs is defined as heterogeneity in cloud computing [40]. When clients/users change providers, interoperability and cooperation involving specific providers is mandatory [41].

4. *Fine-grained admittance.* It must be possible for data owners to define and enforce meaningful access mechanisms for every user. Additionally, every secured asset or provision must have well-defined, safe and rational allocation and description of access permissions and policies [42].

5. *Quality of service.* In cloud computing systems, access control systems are presumed to encompass significant users for authenticating and admittance. Access decisions must be granted in a reasonable time as per the requirements of enterprises. For every access control system, the processing complexity of admittance regulations continues to be a strict undertaking [43]. As it can hinder decision processes, it may affect QOS and efficiency.

6. *Entrustment of competence.* In the cloud environment, users/clients cooperate with each other to accomplish wide-ranging responsibilities. Delegation of permissions and roles is required for ensuring flexibility and dynamic resource management [44].

For execution of admittance policy without replay, the planned elucidation relied on ACLs, Kerberos, and authorization tickets. Several other [31–34] models were proposed using Kerberos as the authentication mechanism for providing cloud access. None of the proposed models were able to clearly identify the issues involved in managing user revocation and data sharing in the cloud computing environment. An innovative model should diminish client overheads in a given set of circumstances as soon as a modification occurs in group membership. The novel proposal for this scheme with reduced overheads at the diverse setup stages will be further appropriate for safe and sound data sharing in the cloud environment.

29.4 Access Control-Based Solutions

Sumathy et al. [46] performed an extensive survey among the access mechanisms available and divided them as follows:

i) **Discretionary Access Control (DAC)**
   The disparity between computer program and human user is not properly differentiated by DAC mechanisms [47]. By and large, the owner of the object (file or directory) regulates it. DAC is adaptable for policy identification. Conventional multiple-user platforms such as Novell, UNIX, etc. in general determine access control [48]. The issue of data leakage in information sharing has moved the security concern from industry solutions to CSPs.

ii) **Mandatory Access Control (MAC)**

The central management of clandestine security policy factors provides protection. The network configuration decides the policy [49]. MAC models establish control access, establishing an understanding of objects and subjects. This agreement is in addition acknowledged as multilevel security replication and lattice-based admittance policy. In multilevel scenarios such as government and military systems, the DAC arrangement problems can be rectified by exercising MAC arrangement [50]. Greater security is provided as only a system manager can access control mechanisms.

iii) **Attribute-Based Access Control (ABAC)**

ABAC comprises resources which measure automated contact with attributes through policy agreements. ABAC utilizes attributes, with their rules and requirements, as part of the logical language [51]. Each attribute has a pair of key values, such as "Role= Supervisor". ABAC's core components are: "Protocol Store, Protocol Editor, Protocol Information Point and Protocol Enforcement Point". Extensible access is one of the standard application functionalities and the regulation-dependent ability to use power. In ABAC [52], a request to access data is accepted depending on the attributes of the application, anywhere that files or data are assigned with descriptive attributes.

iv) **Role-Based Access Control (RBAC)**

Another access control technique for using computer or network facilities depends upon roles of individual customers within an activity. Under these circumstances, access policies permit users to perform a definite job, such as analyzing, modifying, or creating any file [53]. Roles are described within the activity according to job competency, esteem and authority. Many management practices rely on admittance policies on "the roles that independent users take on as part of management" [54]. Three outstanding safety frameworks bear RBAC perception. They are data abstraction, separation of duties and least privilege.

v) **Identity Access Management (IAM)**

Identity management (IdM) systems dynamically cooperate in cloud environments to exchange data and resources [55]. It is the management and development process of infrastructure which supports these processes, involving an admittance policy based on individual identities [56]. Federated identity management systems (FIdMs) [57] facilitate sharing resources among partners for online services in public, private, and hybrid cloud [57].

29.5 Conclusion

None of the above-mentioned methods were able to efficiently manage all the security aspects associated with a dynamic group in the cloud computing environment [26]. All these schemes, techniques, models, and methodologies are therefore unacceptable and inappropriate for secure data sharing amongst affiliates of a group in a cloud environment. Since numerous applications are vulnerable to assault in several ways, security policies require advances in security techniques.

The procedures involving DAC and MAC were found not to support current security requirements, while RBAC and ABAC are capable of meeting them. IAM is the most recent and admired research domain which possesses potential for additional improvements.

Computational efficiency is the sole requirement in the design of the Efficient Data Sharing and User Revocation scheme. The Data Sharing and Dynamic Group affiliation scheme operations include:

1. Effective encryption and decryption of user data.
2. Effective user revocation without giving additional overheads to the cloud server or the system administrator.

The two major requirements for an efficient user revocation scheme are:

i. *Backward security.* The latest cipher texts cannot be decoded by the revoked user.
ii. *Forward security.* Recently joined members can also decode previously published cipher texts encoded with previous keys.

Various techniques for handling dynamic groups in the cloud computing setting have been suggested, but these approaches do not provide a complete solution to the dynamic groups management problems and requirements. Therefore a novel method needs to be devised that can incorporate all these requirements and handle all the problems.

References

1. Joshi Bansidhar, Vijayan A. Santhana, and Joshi Bineet Kumar, "Securing Cloud Computing Environment against DDoS Attacks", *2012 International Conference on Computer Communication and Informatics*, IEEE, 2011, pp. 1–5.
2. Lv Haoyong and Yin Hu, "Analysis and Research about Cloud Computing Security Protect Policy", *2011 International Conference on Intelligence Science and Information Engineering*, IEEE, 2011, pp. 214–216.
3. Bakshi Aman and Yogesh B. Dujodwala, "Securing Cloud from DDOS Attacks using Intrusion Detection System in VM", *2010 Second International Conference on Communication Software and Networks*, IEEE, 2010, pp. 260–264.
4. Ramgovind, S., Eloff, M.M., and Smith, E., "The Management of Security in Cloud Computing", *2010 Information Security for South Africa*, IEEE, 2010.
5. Minqi, Z., Rong, Z., Wei, X., Weining, Q., and Aoying, Z., "Security and Privacy in Cloud Computing: A Survey", *Sixth international conference on Semantics Knowledge and Grid (SKG)*, pp. 105, 1–3 Nov. 2010.

6. Khan, K.M. and Malluhi, Q., "Establishing Trust in Cloud Computing", *IT Professional* 12, 5, 20–27, 2010.
7. Takabi, H., Joshi, J., and Ahn, G., "Security and Privacy Challenges in Cloud Computing Environments", *IEEE Security & Privacy* 8, 6, 24–31, 2010.
8. Kaufman, L.M., "Data Security in the World of Cloud Computing", *IEEE Security & Privacy* 7, 4, 61–64, 2009.
9. Ren, K., Wang, C., and Wang, Q., "Security Challenges for the Public Cloud", *IEEE Internet Computing bibemph* 16, 1, 59–73, 2012.
10. Blaze, M., Beumer, G., and Strauss, M., "Divertible Protocols and Atomic Proxy Cryptography", *Proceeding of International Conference on the Theory and Application of Crypto-graphic Techniques (Eurocrypt)*, pp. 127–144, 1998.
11. Mambo, M. and Okamoto, E., "Proxy Cryptosystems: Delegation of the Power to Decrypt Ciphertext," *IEICE Transactions on Fundamentals of Electronics, Communications and Computer Sciences (TFECCS)*, 1997.
12. Hohenberger, S., Fu, K., Green, M., and Ateniese, G. Improved Proxy Re-encryption Schemes with Applications to Secure Distributed Storage. *ACM Transactions on Information and System Security (TISSEC)* 9, 1, 1–30, 2006.
13. Weng, J., Yang, Y., Tang, Q., Deng, R.H., and Bao, F., "Efficient Conditional Proxy Re-encryption with Chosen-Ciphertext Security", *Proceedings of the 12th Information Security Conference (ISC)*, 151–166, 2009.
14. Chu, C.K., Weng, J., Chow, S.S.M., Zhou J., and Deng, R.H., "Conditional Proxy Broadcast Re-Encryption", *Proceedings of the 14th Australasian Conference on Information Security and Privacy (ACISP)*, 327–342, 2009.
15. Son, J., Kim, H., Kim, D., and Oh, H., "On Secure Data Sharing in Cloud Environment," *Proceedings of International Conference on Ubiquitous Information Management and Communication (IMCOM)*, 2014.
16. Son, J., Kim, D., Hussain, R. and Oh, H., "Conditional Proxy Re-Encryption for Secure Big Data Group Sharing in CloudEnvironment," *2014 IEEE Conference on Computer Communications Workshops (INFOCOM WKSHPS)*, IEEE, May-June 2014.
17. Zheng, Qingji and Shouhuai, Xu, "Identity-based Encryption from the Wei Pairing", *CRYPTO, LNCS2139*, Springer-Verlag, pp. 213–229, 2001.
18. Goyal, Vipul, Pandey, Omkant, Sahai, Amit, and Waters, Brent, "Attribute Based Encryption for Fine-Grained Access Control of Encrypted Data", *ACM Conference on Computer and Communications Security*, pp. 99–112, 2006.
19. Ostrovsky, Rafail, Sahai, Amit, and Waters, Brent, "Attribute-Based Encryption with Non-Monotonic Access Structures", *14th ACM Conference on Computer and Communications Security*, pp. 195–203, 2007.
20. Bethencourt, John, Sahai, Amit, and Waters, Brent, "Ciphertext-policy Attribute Based Encryption", *IEEE Symposium on Security & Privacy*, pp. 321–334. 2007.
21. An Efficient Cloud-based Revocable Identity-based Proxy Re-encryption Scheme for Public Clouds Data Sharing Kaitai Liang, Joseph K. Liu, Duncan S. Wong, Willy Susilo, 2014.
22. Bhosale, Smita and Gujar, Anil, "Secure Key Distribution and Data Sharing for Dynamic Groups in Multiple Clouds", *Procedia International Journal on Emerging Trends in Technology (IJETT) (cPGCON 2017)*, 2017.
23. Kavitha, G., Latchoumy, P., and Afreen Banu, H., "A Secure Anti-Collusion File Sharing System for Untrusted Cloud Storage", *IJSRST* 3, 6, 2017.
24. Soudagar, Mahejuba and Salagar, Rajashekhar D., "An Efficient Scheme For Data Sharing Among Dynamic Cloud Members", *International Research Journal of Engineering and Technology (IRJET)*, 4, 7, July 2017.

25. Pabitha, C., Jayapreetha, K., Bharathi, P., and Jayanthi, J., "Minimum Replication of User Data Integrating Anti-Collusion Scheme in Cloud Groups", *IJRTI*, 2, 4, 2017.
26. Agarwal, Prerna, Singh, Satya Prakash, and Shrivastava, Pranav, "Review of Dynamic Group Membership Preferred By Cryptographic Systems In Cloud Computing Environment", *Proceedings of the 12thINDIACom; INDIACom-2018*, 2018.
27. Toosi, Adel Nadjaran, Calheiros, Rodrigo N., and Buyya, Rajkumar, "Interconnected Cloud Computing Environments Challenges Taxonomy and Survey", *ACM Computing Surveys* 47, 1, Article 7, Publication date: April 2014.
28. Liu, Chi-Wei, Hsien, Wei-Fu, Yang, Chou-Chen, and Hwang, Min-Shiang, "A Survey of Public Auditing for Shared Data Storage with User Revocation in Cloud Computing", *International Journal of Network Security* 18, 4, 650–666, July 2016.
29. Jiang, Tao, Chen, Xiaofeng, and Ma, Jianfeng, "Public Integrity Auditing for Shared Dynamic Cloud Data with Group User Revocation" *IEEE Transactions on Computers* 65, 8, 99, 2015.
30. Kaffel-Ben Ayed, H. and Zaghdoudi, B., "A Generic Kerberos-based Access Control System for the Cloud", *Annals of Telecommunications* 71, 555, 2016. https://doi.org/10.1007/s12243-016-0534-7
31. Agrawal, Arpit and Verma, Shubhangi, "A Tpa-Authentication Scheme for Public Cloud Using Kerberos Protocol", *OJCST* 10, 2, 460–466, June 2017. ISSN: 0974-6471.
32. Shashikumar, Prasanna B., "Cloud Security Using Kerberos Protocol ", *IJTRE* 4, 10, June-2017.
33. Jain, Sweta and Richhariya, Vineet, "Kerberos based Enhanced Authentication Protocol for Cloud Computing Environment", *International Journal of Theoretical & Applied Sciences*, 9, 2, 25–30, 2017.
34. Kim, Young-Soo and Lee, Byoung Yup, "Kerberos System Based Security Model Using Two Factor Authentication for Cloud Computing", *IJET* 7, 4.39, 531–534, 2018.
35. Younis, Y.A., Kifayat, K., and Merabti, M., "An Access Control Model for Cloud Computing. *Journal of Information Security and Applications* 19, 1, 45–60, 2014.
36. Yao, X., Han, X., and Du, X., "A Lightweight Access Control Mechanism for Mobile Cloud Computing", *Computer Communications Workshops (INFOCOM WKSHPS)*, pp. 380–385, 2014.
37. Keromytis, A.D. and Smith, J.M. (2007) Requirements for Scalable Access Control and Security Management Architectures. *ACM Trans Internet Technol (TOIT)* 7, 2, 8.
38. Choudhury, A.J., Kumar, P., Sain, M., Lim, H., Jae-Lee, H. (2011) A strong user authentication framework for Cloud computing. In: *Services Computing Conference (APSCC)*, I.E. AsiaPacific, IEEE, pp. 110–115, 2011.
39. Wang, W., Han, J., Song, M., Wang, X., "The Design of a Trust and Role Based Access Control Model in Cloud Computing", *Pervasive Computing and Applications (ICPCA), 2011 6th International Conference on*, IEEE, pp. 330–334, 2011.
40. Crago, S., Dunn, K., Eads, P., Hochstein, L., Kang, D.-I., Kang, M., Modium, D., Singh, K., Suh, J., and Walters, J.P., "Heterogeneous Cloud Computing", *IEEE International Conference on Cluster Computing (CLUSTER)*, pp 378–385, 2011.
41. Patil, V., Mei, A., and Mancini, L.V., "Addressing Interoperability Issues in Access Control Models", *Proceedings of the 2nd ACM Symposium on Information, Computer and Communications Security*, ACM, pp. 389–391, 2007.
42. Lin, G., Bie, Y., and Lei, M., Trust based Access Control Policy in Multi-domain of Cloud Computing. *Journal of Computers* 8, 5, 1357–1365, 2013.

43. Hu, V.C., Kuhn, D.R., and Ferraiolo, D.F., "The Computational Complexity of Enforceability Validation for Generic Access Control Rules", *IEEE International Conference on Sensor Networks, Ubiquitous, and Trustworthy Computing*, IEEE, p. 7, 2006.

44. Hasebe, K., Mabuchi, M., and Matsushita, A., "Capability-based Delegation Model in RBAC", *Proceedings of the15th ACM Symposium on Access Control Models and Technologies*, ACM, pp. 109–118, 2010.

45. Nurmi, D., Wolski, R., Grzegorczyk, C., Obertelli, G., Soman, S., Youseff, L., and Zagorodnov, D., "The Eucalyptus Open-source Cloud-computing System", *9th IEEE/ ACM International Symposium on Cluster Computing and the Grid*. CCGRID'09, pp. 124–131, 2009.

46. Anilkumar, Chunduru and Sumathy, S., "Security Strategies for Cloud Identity Management - A Study", *International Journal of Engineering & Technology*, 7(2), 732–741, 2018. DOI: 10.14419/ijet.v7i2.10410

47. Wang, Q. and Jin, H., "Data Leakage Mitigation for Discretionary Access Control in Collaboration Clouds," *Proceedings of the 16th ACM Symposium on Access Control Models and Technologies, SACMAT'11*, p. 103, 2011. https://doi.org/10.1145/1998441.1998457

48. Li, N. and Tripunitara, M.V., "On Safety in Discretionary Access Control", *Proceedings of IEEE Symposium on Security and Privacy*, pp. 96–109, 2005.

49. Hu, V.C., Kuhn, D.R., Xie, T., and Hwang, J., "Model Checking for Verification of Mandatory Access Control Models and Properties", *International Journal of Software Engineering and Knowledge Engineering* 21(1), 103–127, 2011. https://doi.org/10.1142/ S021819401100513X

50. Zhang, X., Covington, M.J., Chen, S., and Sandhu, R., "SecureBus: Towards Application-Transparent Trusted Computing with Mandatory Access Control", *ACM Symposium on Information, Computer and Communications Security*, pp. 117–126, 2007.

51. Yuen, T.H., Liu, J.K., Au, M.H., Huang, X., Susilo, W., and Zhou, J., "*k-times Attribute-Based Anonymous Access Control for Cloud Computing*", vol. 9340, no. c, pp. 1–13, 2014.

52. Yu, S., Wang, C., Ren, K., and Lou, W., "Achieving Secure, Scalable and Fine-grained Data Access Control in Cloud Computing", *Infocom, 2010 Proceedings IEEE* IEEE, pp. 1–9, 2010, March.

53. Workflows, A. et al., "Security Constraints in Temporal RoleBased", *Codaspy*, 207–218, 2016.

54. Li, J., Liao, Z., Zhang, C., and Shi, Y., "A 4D-Role Based Access Control Model for Multitenancy Cloud Platform", vol. 2016, 2016.

55. Goulding, J.T., "Identity and Access Management for the Cloud: CA Technologies Strategy and Vision", no. April, p. 18, 2011.

56. Jansen, W., and Grance, T. Guidelines on security and privacy in public Cloud computing, 2012.

57. Ghazizadeh, E., Zamani, M., Ab Manan, J.L., and Pashang, A., "A Survey on Security Issues of Federated Identity in the Cloud Computing", *CloudCom 2012 - Proc. 2012 4th IEEE Int. Conf. Cloud Comput. Technol. Sci.*, pp. 562–565, 2012. https://doi.org/10.1109/ CloudCom.2012.6427513

58. Wilson, S. AppEngine Outage. CIO Weblog, June 2008. Available from: http://www.cio-weblog.com/50226711/appengine_outage.php

Chapter 30

Improved YOLOv5 with Attention Mechanism for Real-Time Weed Detection in the Paddy Field: A Deep Learning Approach

Bhuvaneswari Swaminathan, Prabu Selvam,
Joseph Abraham Sundar K., and Subramaniyaswamy
Vairavasundaram
SASTRA Deemed University, Thanjavur, India

30.1 Introduction

Rice is one of the world's most important crops, and its quality and yield are negatively impacted by weeds. Rice yields are reduced when weeds compete with rice for nutrients from soil and water, as well as sunlight and growing space [1]. As well as providing habitat for pests, weeds can also become a host for plant diseases which may affect paddy crops. Early detection is key to preventing and controlling rice weeds [2]. Manual inspection methods in the field require a lot of labor [3, 4], and

DOI: 10.1201/9781003371380-30

are also subjective, so that weeds may not be detected in time [5]. Precision agriculture or digital agriculture strategies can mitigate this issue through an automated weed control system providing farmers with economic and environmental benefits.

It has become increasingly common to detect objects with the help of computer vision and deep learning. Some of the most popular methods and networks for detecting objects are the Fast R-CNN, Faster R-CNN, and the Mask R-CNN represent two-stage object detection methods. These detection methods make it possible to detect objects based on region proposals extracted from selective search algorithms or region proposal networks (RPNs). Even though detection accuracy is better than with traditional object detection methods, these methods are more complex, time-consuming, and may not be suitable for real-time applications. Additionally, there are also one-stage object detection methods and their representative networks, such as SSD detection methods, YOLO detection methods, and RetinaNet. The speed of detection of objects by these methods is greater than that of two-stage methods.

Using deep learning for weed detection based on field images has received substantial attention among researchers [6]. YOLO is an excellent object detection algorithm for real-time applications that utilizes convolutional neural networks [7] as a backbone network. A weed detection and identification algorithm based on the YOLOv3-tiny was developed by [8]. According to [9], YOLOv3-tiny was used to detect weeds in sugarbeet fields. The author developed a weed detection system based on the YOLO model [10]. The YOLOv5 model delivers the fastest inference speed, is perfect for detecting small and distant objects, and has higher detection accuracy than all other models at the forefront of technology. This study performs in-field, real-time online detection of rice weed using an improved YOLOv5 algorithm for early-stage identification. The following features are included:

- An enhanced feature fusion layer is employed to automatically detect smaller weed objects on agricultural land.
- An improvised deep learning detection algorithm is proposed based on the YOLOv5 technique.
- The proposed technique is validated on the publicly available paddy field weed image dataset.

This chapter is structured as follows. Section 30.1 discusses the importance of weed detection in the paddy field, along with an overview of other object detection methods. Section 30.2 discusses relevant existing works. Section 30.3 describes working procedure of the classical YOLOv5 algorithm and the significance of the improved YOLOv5 algorithm, and Section 30.4 discusses the implementation details. Section 30.5 explain the performance analysis of the proposed system, and Section 30.6 provide some conclusions.

30.2 Related Works

Traditional machine learning methodologies require substantial domain expertise to extract features from raw data, whereas representation deep learning methods allow machines to learn discriminative features from raw data. Many scholars have investigated deep learning for weed detection. Authors [11] used 101-dimensional features to identify weeds in rice fields by analyzing their colors, shapes, and textures. A deep belief network with fusion features enabled them to achieve a recognition rate of 91.13%. A UAV image captured from rice fields was classified using fully convolutional neural networks (FCN) at the pixel level [12], and these authors achieved an accuracy of 91.96% and a mean intersection over union (mean IoU) of 84.73%. An analysis of Inception-ResNet-v2's ability to detect crop plants and weeds by [13] found that it scored 72.7% (IoU all) and 96.9% (IoU0.5). To solve the unbalanced categories problem, [14] used SegNet to classify pixels in images into rice seedlings, weeds, and backgrounds. This was suggested for detection of weeds in paddy fields [15], but inaccuracy and instability were present. Detecting weed species was made possible by deep convolutional neural networks (DCNNs), according to [16]. According to the authors [17], tiny YOLO-v3 in real-time applications could detect goosegrass 82% of the time and with 82% accuracy. With pre-training, Faster R-CNNs detected late-season weeds in the field in 0.21 seconds, with a recall of 60%, precision of 65% and F1 score of 6% [18]. Compared to other models, Faster R-CNN produced better accuracy and inference time. UAV imagery was post-processed using FCNs and CRFs for weed mapping [19], and an inference speed of 326.8 milliseconds was obtained, resulting in an accuracy of 80.2%. A fully convolutional neural network resulted in an accuracy of 93.5% in detecting the weeds, and it outperformed the CNN [20]. A fully convolutional encoder-decoder network was proposed by [21], achieving accuracy of 92.6% over other models such as U-Net, FCN8, DeepLab-v3, Faster R-CNN, and EDNet. In [22], grass and broad-leaved weeds were detected using the proposed system with an accuracy of 96.5%.

30.3 Proposed System

In this section, we introduce a technique for detecting weeds in rice crop images. We describe our improvements on the YOLOv5 algorithm. Figure 30.1 shows the overall trajectory of the improved YOLOv5 algorithm.

30.3.1 Improved YOLOv5 Algorithm

In this paper, we modify the architecture of the YOLOv5 object detection algorithm to identify weeds from rice crop images. The YOLOv5 architecture has been adjusted in three places (see Figure 30.2): (i) a new feature fusion layer (denoted by

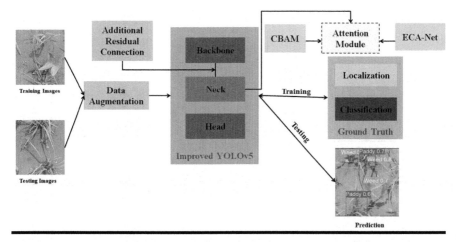

Figure 30.1   Overview of the workflow system using improved YOLOv5.

orange background) is added in the neck module to capture more shallow feature information of tiny weeds; (ii) an attention block (represented by a purple color block) is added in the feature fusion layer to pay attention to the information that helps the smaller weed detection; and (iii) features extracted from the backbone network are sent to the feature fusion layers (illustrated by the red dotted lines) to minimize smaller weed feature information loss. The conventional YOLOv5 algorithm has three feature fusion layers [23]. In contrast, the improved YOLOv5 algorithm has four feature fusion layers (shown in Figure 30.1). The addition of the feature fusion layer to the neck module produces a larger feature map of scale 152×152; it enhances the performance of the YOLOv5 algorithm in localizing smaller weed objects. Based on the conventional network, fused feature maps are upsampled again and concatenated at a scale of 152×152 from the backbone network to obtain new fused feature maps. CSP and CBL are also employed for this task.

The main advantage of adding an attention module in the feature fusion layers is that it can accurately amplify information on smaller weed objects.

The attention module is built by combining ECA-Net and CBAM networks. The spatial and channel attention are selected from CBAM and ECA-Net, respectively. The ECA-Net module performs two steps to generate a new feature map. First, it sends the features directly to the Global Average Pooling (GAP) layer, which performs 1D convolution on the features. Second, updated weights are multiplied with the input feature map. The newly generated feature map is given as input to the spatial attention component of CBAM. The spatial attention component generates a spatial attention feature map, which can be added to the actual feature map to develop the residual block layout. Finally, the Relu activation function is applied to the summed feature map to generate the final feature map (Figure 30.3).

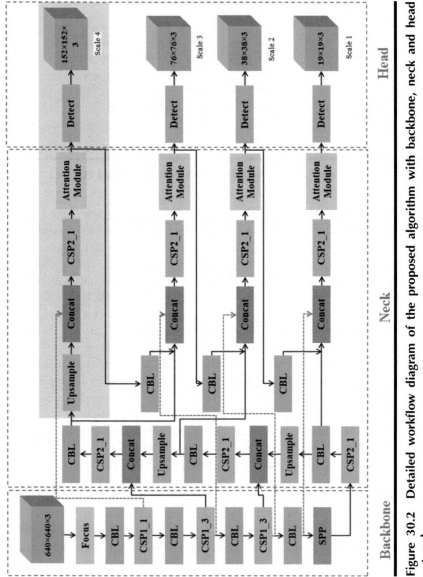

Figure 30.2 Detailed workflow diagram of the proposed algorithm with backbone, neck and head network.

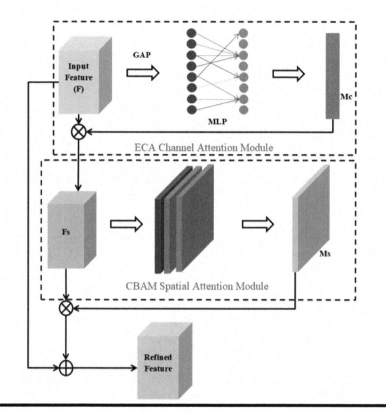

Figure 30.3   Attention mechanism with channel and spatial attention module.

Four residual connections denoted by the red dotted lines bring the feature information from the backbone network to the feature fusion layers in the neck module. These four residual connections can improve the backpropagation of gradients, minimize feature information loss and avoid gradient fading.

30.3.2 Attention Mechanism

The attention mechanism is used to acquire the essential weed and rice crop information by concentrating on the critical regions of the input weed plant image. Various attention mechanisms are used in multiple applications; however, they all have distinct implementations. CBAM is a simple and commonly used attention mechanism that concatenates channel and spatial attention modules. In addition, ECA-Net is an attention mechanism widely used to capture information about cross-channel interactions.

30.3.3 CBAM

The CBAM mechanism combines both channel attention (CA) and spatial attention (SA). Initially, channel attention learns the weights of various channels and then multiplies these weights with different channels to improve the focus on the key channel domain. The generated feature map is represented using Equation (30.1).

$$F = \mathbb{R}^{H \times W \times C} \tag{30.1}$$

where H and W denote the height and width of the feature map, and C represents the number of channels. The weights of each channel ($W_c \in \mathbb{R}^{1 \times 1 \times C}$) are calculated using Equation (30.2).

$$W_c(F) = \sigma\left(W_1\left(W_2\left(F_{avg}^C\right)\right)\right) + \sigma\left(W_1\left(W_2\left(F_{max}^C\right)\right)\right) \tag{30.2}$$

where W_1 and W_2 represent weights of MLP, F_{avg}^C and F_{max}^C represent feature map obtained after performing average pooling and max pooling, respectively. σ denotes the sigmoid activation function. The channel attention feature map is generated after performing element-wise multiplication between ($W_c \in \mathbb{R}^{1 \times 1 \times C}$) and the original feature map. The feature map of the channel attention module ($F_c \in \mathbb{R}^{H \times W \times C}$) is given as input to the SA module. This module concentrates more on weed position information and accumulates specific spatial features of each space using the weighted sum of spatial features (see Equation (30.3)). Initially, the SA mechanism takes the CA feature map as input, and max and average pooling are performed on it. Next, the SA weight map ($W_s \in \mathbb{R}^{H \times W \times 1}$) is generated using 7×7 convolution (see Equation (30.4)).

$$F_s = \frac{1}{c}\sum_{i \in c} F_c(i) + \max_{i \in c} F_c(i) \tag{30.3}$$

$$M_s = \sigma\left(f^{(7 \times 7)}(F_s)\right) \tag{30.4}$$

Finally, the final attention feature map is obtained by performing an element-wise multiplication between the SA weight map and the CA feature map.

30.3.4 ECA-Net

The CA module in CBAM has the dimensionality reduction property that manages the model complexity and captures the cross-channel interactions by applying average and max pooling on the feature map. Meanwhile, dimensionality reduction has side effects that introduce additional complexity to dependency computation tasks. This work uses the ECA-Net mechanism to overcome the side effects during CA and SA computation. It introduces a few parameters that capture cross-channel interaction information, avoid dimensionality reduction and enhance performance. ECA-Net considers each channel and its K neighbors to capture information about local cross-channel interaction. K contains the number of neighbors involved in the attention calculation at the particular iteration. K can be determined using Equation (30.5).

$$K = \partial(C) = \left| \frac{\log_2(c)}{r} + \frac{d}{r} \right|_{odd} \tag{30.5}$$

where C, $|t|_{odd}$ represent channel dimension and the nearest odd number of t. The constants d and r are set to 1 and 2, respectively.

30.4 Experiments

30.4.1 Implementation Details

We implemented improved YOLOv5 on PyTorch 1.8.1. All the experiments were performed on a DELL Precision Tower 7810 workstation having 4 GPU of NVIDIA graphics cards. We utilize a chunk of the pre-trained model from YOLOv5x during the training phase because improved YOLOv5 and conventional YOLOv5 share most of the backbone and head sections; using these weights, we can significantly reduce the training time. The learning rate is set to 0.01 with a batch size of 64. We adopted an Adam optimizer, whereas the conventional YOLOv5 algorithm uses stochastic gradient descent. We divided the dataset into 80:10:10 for training, validation and testing. The proposed model is trained for 200 epochs.

30.4.2 Evaluation Metrics

Performances can be evaluated over the training and validation dataset by obtaining a precision, recall, F1-score and precision–recall curve. Models used for object detection can predict a positive or negative class, and they can be true or false. Three significant accuracy metrics are considered for the proposed performance analysis, described briefly using Equations (30.6)–(30.8). Precision is expressed as the ratio of true positives over the total number of correct predictions; recall metric refers to the number of true positives divided by the total number of actual objects. F1-score metric refers to the harmonic mean of precision and recall.

$$\text{Precision} = \frac{TP}{TP + FP} \tag{30.6}$$

$$\text{Recall} = \frac{TP}{TP + FN} \tag{30.7}$$

$$\text{F1} - \text{Score} = 2 \times \frac{\text{Precison} \times \text{Recall}}{\text{Precison} + \text{Recall}} \tag{3.8}$$

where TP, FP and FN denote true positive, false positive and false negative, respectively.

30.4.3 Training

The whole training dataset has been processed using an improved YOLOv5 object detection algorithm, and the pixel-wise classified training images are shown below in Figure 30.4. The image's red bounding boxes indicate the object correctly detected as a crop or weed from the agricultural land. During annotation, the paddy crop is set as class 0 and the weed is set as class 1. The figure clearly shows that the red bounding boxes with value 0 denote the paddy crop, whereas the bounding boxes with value 1 indicate weeds present near the paddy crop.

The visual representation of the weed detection results has been extracted to evaluate the model performance. Figure 30.5 represents the batches of validation input data with the output results. The validated results separately contain output labels and the red bounding boxes for paddy crops and weeds.

30.4.4 Ablation Studies

The proposed weed detection work begins with collecting the paddy field image dataset. This study was conducted using a publicly available paddy-weed dataset. Before classification, each image was pre-processed. Labels for each image were annotated, and a binary classification was conducted to detect paddy and weed. The performance analysis of improved YOLOv5 is explained through three loss functions: box loss, object loss, and class loss. Based on the above illustration, it is clear that the network converges very quickly; recall and precision all show a trend of rapid growth within 200 epochs. Upon training 200 epochs, the network stabilized in all evaluation metrics, with final precision and recall stabilizing at 0.96 and 0.90,

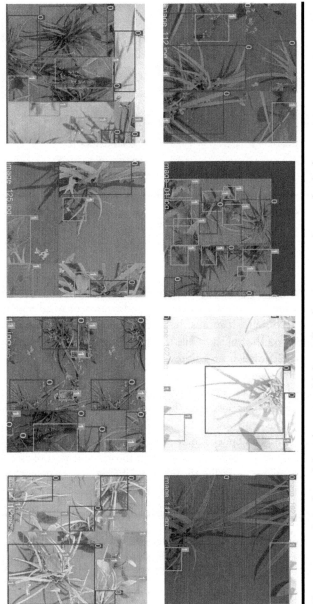

Figure 30.4 Sample training dataset with bounding boxes annotating each pixel.

Figure 30.5 Validation dataset with classification label outputs in black bounding box.

respectively. Based on the proposed technique, the box loss represents the regression loss of the bounding box to differentiate the paddy crop or weed region as a result of the proposed technique. It means that the learning constantly increases in terms of bounding boxes on the objects while the iterations grow. The mean squared error values have been recorded from the training and validation phrases. The training box loss value is less than 0.4, whereas the validation box loss lies at 0.02. Improved YOLOv5 losses and metrics are summarized in Figure 30.6.

In the same way, object loss represents the confidence level of the object present in the binary cross entropy of the detection result. It was observed during the training period that when epochs increased, the training loss of detecting the present object as an object reduces constantly. But, in the validation phase, the reduced validation mean squared loss slightly increases during the very small epoch. Still, it reaches less than 0.2 loss when epochs increase above 150. Likewise, the next class loss denotes the classification accuracy of the training and validation phases using the paddy-weed dataset. It is worth noting that the classification accuracy is constantly reduced during the weed detection algorithm's training and testing phases. After the first three graphs, the other two graphs reveal the performance analysis through performance metrics. The highest precision value reaches 95% with a 0.5 MAP value, and the highest recall value reaches 94% with a 0.95 MAP value, denoting that the improved YOLOv5 algorithm performs better in the case of weed detection with high accuracy.

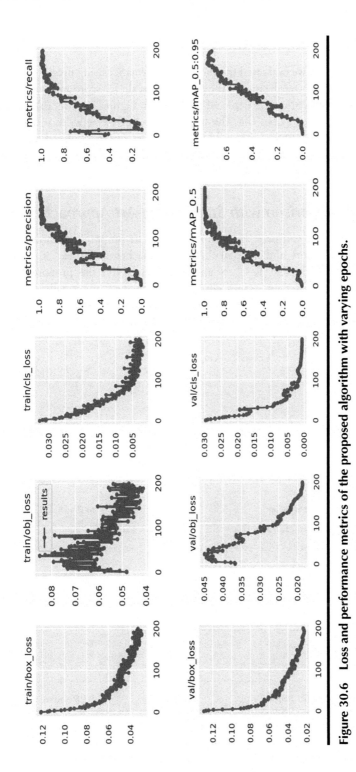

Figure 30.6 **Loss and performance metrics of the proposed algorithm with varying epochs.**

30.5 Performance Analysis

After the training, we evaluated the model's performance using precision, recall, F1-score and precision–recall curves. The precision, recall, F1-score and precision–recall curve for each validation are depicted as graphs in Figures 30.7(a), (b), (c) and (d), respectively. It can be seen that the improved YOLOv5 network provides a high precision value of 0.99 for both paddy and weed classification. Based on the results, the performance metrics value confirms that our proposed method is capable of predicting weeds correctly in a variety of environments.

30.5.1 Comparison with State-of-the-Art Approaches

In this section, we compare the performance of the proposed method with object detection algorithms and state-of-the-art approaches in Tables 30.1 and 30.2. Compared to SSD, Fast R-CNN and Faster R-CNN, the proposed improved YOLOv5 trains faster and more efficiently when detecting smaller objects. The improved YOLOv5 can handle 240 frames per second which is more than are

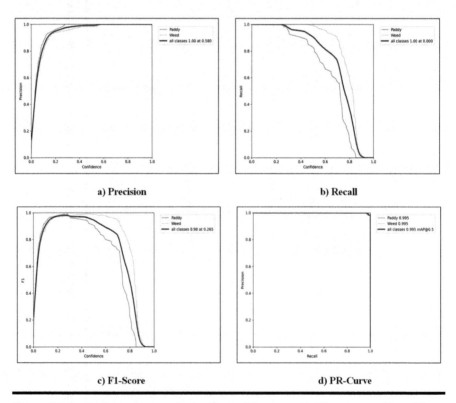

a) Precision   b) Recall

c) F1-Score   d) PR-Curve

Figure 30.7   Performance analysis of precision, recall, F1-score and precision–recall curve for the proposed method.

Table 30.1 Comparison of the Proposed Method with Object Detection Algorithms

Methods	Precision	Recall	F1-Score
SSD	68.4	66.3	67.33
Fast R-CNN	79.2	68.8	73.63
Faster R-CNN	82.5	76.0	79.12
YOLOv5	85.9	92.4	89.03
YOLOv5 + CBAM	91.4	88.6	89.98
YOLOv5 + ECA-Net	93.7	94.6	94.15
Improved YOLOv5	**99.0**	**96.0**	**97.5**

Table 30.2 Comparison of the Proposed Method with State-of-the-Art Approaches

Methods	Precision	Recall	F1-Score
Razfar et al. [4]	86.1	71.2	77.9
Deng et al. [11]	82.3	80.6	81.4
Ma et al. [14]	79.2	71.3	75.0
Yu et al. [16]	83.3	77.4	80.2
Li et al. [3]	80.5	83.0	81.7
Zhang et al. [8]	88.3	85.4	86.8
Jabir et al. [10]	92.4	95.4	93.9
Proposed Method	**99.0**	**96.0**	**97.5**

handled by YOLOv5. We also conducted a series of experiments by adding and removing attention blocks such as CBAM and ECA-Net. However, the combined attention mechanisms help the model to detect and recognize small, medium and large paddy and rice plants. It also eliminates the overlapping bounding boxes around the paddy and rice fields.

The approaches of Razfar et al. [4] and Li et al. [3] are not efficient for real-time weed detection, because they are based on manual inspection. These approaches fail miserably in weed detection in a large paddy field and also require large human resources. Deng et al. [11] use shape, color and texture features for weed detection;

however, these features can be utilized efficiently only if the background and object are distinguishable. In this problem, both paddy and weed look similar in shape, color and texture; hence this approach is not recommended. Our proposed method outperforms that of Deng et al. [11] by a large margin.

The approaches of Zhang et al. [8], Jabir et al. [10], Ma et al. [14] and Yu et al. [16] achieve state-of-the-art performance. On the other hand, the proposed algorithm outperforms these approaches comfortably. The attention mechanism in the improved YOLOv5 algorithm assists the proposed method in focusing more on the weed plant, hence it can differentiate weed and paddy accurately.

30.6 Conclusion

In this work, an attention-based improved YOLOv5 real-time weed detection algorithm is developed for paddy-weed identification. A feature fusion layer is first added to the neck module to improve detection performance on small weed images among the paddy crops. Then the employment of spatial and channel attention using CBAM and ECA-Net amplifies the smaller weed objects present on the land for precise detection results. Afterwards, the residual connection is made from the backbone network to the neck module for transferring extracting feature maps. This residual connection improves the backpropagation of gradients, minimizes feature information loss, and avoids gradient fading. The experiments to analyze the performance of the improved YOLOv5 technique were conducted using a publicly available paddy-weed real-time dataset. In terms of early detection of paddy crops and weeds, the results showed that the precision and recall values reach 0.99. In future research, issues related to the real-time camera capturing images must be solved to develop an enhanced weed detection support system for farmers.

References

1. N. Iqbal, S. Manalil, B. S. Chauhan, and S. W. Adkins, "Investigation of alternate herbicides for effective weed management in glyphosate-tolerant cotton," *Arch. Agron. Soil Sci.*, vol. 65, no. 13, pp. 1885–1899, 2019.
2. J. K. Reaser, S. W. Burgiel, J. Kirkey, K. A. Brantley, S. D. Veatch, and J. Burgos-Rodríguez, "The early detection of and rapid response (EDRR) to invasive species: A conceptual framework and federal capacities assessment," *Biol. Invasions*, vol. 22, no. 1, pp. 1–19, 2020.
3. Y. Li, Z. Guo, F. Shuang, M. Zhang, and X. Li, "Key technologies of machine vision for weeding robots: A review and benchmark," *Comput. Electron. Agric.*, vol. 196, p. 106880, 2022.
4. N. Razfar, J. True, R. Bassiouny, V. Venkatesh, and R. Kashef, "Weed detection in soybean crops using custom lightweight deep learning models," *J. Agric. Food Res.*, vol. 8, p. 100308, 2022.
5. A. Wang, W. Zhang, and X. Wei, "A review on weed detection using ground-based machine vision and image processing techniques," *Comput. Electron. Agric.*, vol. 158, pp. 226–240, 2019.

6. A. S. M. M. Hasan, F. Sohel, D. Diepeveen, H. Laga, and M. G. K. Jones, "A survey of deep learning techniques for weed detection from images," *Comput. Electron. Agric.*, vol. 184, p. 106067, 2021.

7. J. Redmon, S. Divvala, R. Girshick, and A. Farhadi, "You only look once: Unified, real-time object detection," In *Proceedings of the IEEE conference on computer vision and pattern recognition*, pp. 779–788, 2016.

8. R. Zhang, C. Wang, X. Hu, Y. Liu, S. Chen et al., "Weed location and recognition based on UAV imaging and deep learning," *Int. J. Precis. Agric. Aviat.*, vol. 3, no. 1, 2020.

9. J. Gao, A. P. French, M. P. Pound, Y. He, T. P. Pridmore, and J. G. Pieters, "Deep convolutional neural networks for image-based Convolvulus sepium detection in sugar beet fields," *Plant Methods*, vol. 16, no. 1, pp. 1–12, 2020.

10. B. Jabir and N. Falih, "Deep learning-based decision support system for weeds detection in wheat fields," *Int. J. Electr. Comput. Eng.*, vol. 12, no. 1, p. 816, 2022.

11. X. Deng et al., "Recognition of weeds at seedling stage in paddy fields using multi-feature fusion and deep belief networks.," *Trans. Chinese Soc. Agric. Eng.*, vol. 34, no. 14, pp. 165–172, 2018.

12. H. Huang et al., "Accurate weed mapping and prescription map generation based on fully convolutional networks using UAV imagery," *Sensors*, vol. 18, no. 10, p. 3299, 2018.

13. Y. Jiang, C. Li, A. H. Paterson, and J. S. Robertson, "DeepSeedling: Deep convolutional network and Kalman filter for plant seedling detection and counting in the field," *Plant Methods*, vol. 15, no. 1, pp. 1–19, 2019.

14. X. Ma et al., "Fully convolutional network for rice seedling and weed image segmentation at the seedling stage in paddy fields," *PLoS One*, vol. 14, no. 4, p. e0215676, 2019.

15. Z. Wu, Y. Chen, B. Zhao, X. Kang, and Y. Ding, "Review of weed detection methods based on computer vision," *Sensors*, vol. 21, no. 11, p. 3647, 2021.

16. J. Yu, S. M. Sharpe, A. W. Schumann, and N. S. Boyd, "Deep learning for image-based weed detection in turfgrass," *Eur. J. Agron.*, vol. 104, pp. 78–84, 2019.

17. S. M. Sharpe, A. W. Schumann, and N. S. Boyd, "Goosegrass detection in strawberry and tomato using a convolutional neural network," *Sci. Rep.*, vol. 10, no. 1, pp. 1–8, 2020.

18. A. N. Veeranampalayam Sivakumar et al., "Comparison of object detection and patch-based classification deep learning models on mid-to late-season weed detection in UAV imagery," *Remote Sens.*, vol. 12, no. 13, p. 2136, 2020.

19. H. Huang, Y. Lan, A. Yang, Y. Zhang, S. Wen, and J. Deng, "Deep learning versus object-based image analysis (OBIA) in weed mapping of UAV imagery," *Int. J. Remote Sens.*, vol. 41, no. 9, pp. 3446–3479, 2020.

20. H. Huang, J. Deng, Y. Lan, A. Yang, X. Deng, and L. Zhang, "A fully convolutional network for weed mapping of unmanned aerial vehicle (UAV) imagery," *PLoS One*, 13, pp. 1–19, 2018.

21. Z. Qu, L.Y. Gao, S.Y. Wang, H.N. Yin and T.M. Yi, "An improved YOLOv5 method for large objects detection with multi-scale feature cross-layer fusion network," *Image Vis. Comput.*, vol. 125, p. 104518, 2022.

22. D. Stroppiana, P. Villa, G. Sona, G. Ronchetti, G. Candiani, M. Pepe, L. Busetto, M. Migliazzi, and M. Boschetti, "Early season weed mapping in rice crops using multi-spectral UAV data," *Int. J. Remote Sens.*, 39, pp. 5432–5452, 2018.

23. P. Selvam and J.A.S. Koilraj, "A deep learning framework for grocery product detection and recognition," *Food Anal. Methods*, vol. 15, pp. 3498–3522, 2022.

Index

Pages in *italics* refer to figures and pages in **bold** refer to tables.